Caring for Veterans With Deployment-Related Stress Disorders

IRAQ, AFGHANISTAN, and BEYOND

Caring for Veterans With Deployment-Related Stress Disorders

IRAQ, AFGHANISTAN, and BEYOND

EDITED BY
Josef I. Ruzek
Paula P. Schnurr
Jennifer J. Vasterling
Matthew J. Friedman

AMERICAN PSYCHOLOGICAL ASSOCIATION
WASHINGTON, DC

Published by
American Psychological Association
750 First Street, NE
Washington, DC 20002
www.apa.org

To order
APA Order Department
P.O. Box 92984
Washington, DC 20090-2984
Tel: (800) 374-2721; Direct: (202) 336-5510
Fax: (202) 336-5502; TDD/TTY: (202) 336-6123
Online: www.apa.org/pubs/books
E-mail: order@apa.org

In the U.K., Europe, Africa, and the Middle East, copies may be ordered from
American Psychological Association
3 Henrietta Street
Covent Garden, London
WC2E 8LU England

Typeset in Goudy by Circle Graphics, Inc., Columbia, MD

Printer: Edwards Brothers, Ann Arbor, MI
Cover Designer: Berg Design, Albany, NY

Library of Congress Cataloging-in-Publication Data

Caring for veterans with deployment-related stress disorders : Iraq, Afghanistan, and beyond / edited by Josef I. Ruzek . . . [et al.]. — 1st ed.
    p. cm.
  Includes bibliographical references and index.
  ISBN-13: 978-1-4338-0925-5
  ISBN-10: 1-4338-0925-7
 1. Psychology, Military. 2. Soldiers—Mental health services—United States. 3. Soldiers—Mental health—United States. 4. Veterans—Mental health services—United States.
5. Veterans—Mental health—United States. 6. Post-traumatic stress disorder.
7. War—Psychological aspects. 8. Combat—Pyschological aspects. I. Ruzek, Josef I.

  U22.3.C375 2011
  616.85'24200973—dc22

                          2010031424

British Library Cataloguing-in-Publication Data

A CIP record is available from the British Library.

Printed in the United States of America
First Edition

doi: 10.1037/12323-000

CONTENTS

CONTRIBUTORS

Sonja V. Batten, PhD, Office of Mental Health Services, VA Central Office, Washington, DC

Margret E. Bell, PhD, National Center for PTSD, Women's Health Sciences Division, VA Boston Healthcare System, Boston, MA

Bekh Bradley, PhD, Trauma Recovery Program, Atlanta VA Medical Center, Decatur, GA

David L. Butler, PhD, Mental Illness Research, Education, and Clinical Centers, W.G. Hefner VA Medical Center, Salisbury, NC

Cynthia A. Claassen, PhD, Department of Psychiatry, University of North Texas Health Science Center, Fort Worth

Stephen J. Cozza, MD, Center for the Study of Traumatic Stress, Department of Psychiatry, Uniformed Services University of the Health Sciences, Bethesda, MD

Erin S. Daly, PhD, Psychology Service and National Center for PTSD, VA Boston Healthcare System, Boston, MA; and Department of Psychiatry, Boston University School of Medicine, Boston, MA

Lissa Dutra, PhD, Department of Psychology, Clinical Psychology Program, University of Massachusetts, Boston

John Fortney, PhD, VA South Central Mental Illness, Research, Education and Clinical Center; VA HSR&D Center for Mental Healthcare and Outcomes Research; and Department of Psychiatry, University of Arkansas for Medical Sciences, Little Rock

Steffany J. Fredman, PhD, National Center for PTSD, Women's Health Sciences Division, Boston University School of Medicine, VA Boston Healthcare System, Boston, MA

Matthew J. Friedman, MD, PhD, National Center for PTSD, Executive Division, VA Medical Center, White River Junction, VT; and Departments of Psychiatry and Pharmacology, Dartmouth Medical School, Hanover, NH

Maryrose Gerardi, PhD, Trauma and Anxiety Recovery Program, Emory University School of Medicine, Atlanta, GA

Robin A. Hurley, MD, Mental Illness Research, Education, and Clinical Centers, W. G. Hefner VA Medical Center, Salisbury, NC

Lisa H. Jaycox, PhD, RAND Corporation, Arlington, VA

Rachel Kimerling, PhD, National Center for PTSD, Dissemination and Training Division, VA Palo Alto Healthcare System, Menlo Park, CA

Kerry L. Knox, PhD, VISN 2 Center of Excellence for Suicide Prevention, Canandaigua, NY; and Department of Psychiatry, University of Rochester School of Medicine, Rochester, NY

Lillian Krantz, BA, National Center for PTSD, Behavioral Science Division, VA Boston Healthcare System, Boston, MA

Brett Litz, PhD, National Center for PTSD, Behavioral Science Division, VA Boston Healthcare System, Boston, MA

Mark W. Miller, PhD, National Center for PTSD, Behavioral Science Division, VA Boston Healthcare System; and Division of Psychiatry, Boston University School of Medicine, Boston, MA

Candice M. Monson, PhD, Department of Psychology, Ryerson University, Toronto, ON; and National Center for PTSD, Women's Health Sciences Division, Boston, MA

William P. Nash, MD, VA San Diego Center of Excellence for Stress and Mental Health, University of California at San Diego

Joanne Pavao, MPH, National Center for PTSD, Dissemination and Training Division, VA Palo Alto Healthcare System, Menlo Park, CA

Rajeev Ramchand, PhD, RAND Corporation, Arlington, VA

Annemarie Reardon, PhD, National Center for PTSD, Behavioral Science Division, VA Boston Healthcare System, Boston, MA

Barbara O. Rothbaum, PhD, Trauma and Anxiety Recovery Program, Emory University School of Medicine, Atlanta, GA

Josef I. Ruzek, PhD, National Center for PTSD, Dissemination and Training Division, VA Palo Alto Healthcare System, Menlo Park, CA

Terry L. Schell, PhD, RAND Corporation, Santa Monica, CA

Paula P. Schnurr, PhD, National Center for PTSD, Executive Division, VA Medical Center, White River Junction, VT; and Department of Psychiatry, Dartmouth Medical School, Hanover, NH

Tracy Stecker, PhD, Department of Community and Family Medicine, Dartmouth Medical School, Hanover, NH

Nathan Stein, PhD, National Center for PTSD, Behavioral Science Division, VA Boston Healthcare System, Boston, MA

Amy E. Street, PhD, National Center for PTSD, Women's Health Sciences Division, VA Boston Healthcare System, Boston, MA

Katherine H. Taber, PhD, Mental Illness Research, Education, and Clinical Centers, W. G. Hefner VA Medical Center, Salisbury, NC

Casey T. Taft, PhD, National Center for PTSD, Behavioral Science Division, Boston University School of Medicine, VA Boston Healthcare System, Boston, MA

Terri Tanielian, MA, RAND Corporation, Arlington, VA

Jennifer J. Vasterling, PhD, Psychology Service and National Center for PTSD, Behavioral Science Division, VA Boston Healthcare System, Boston, MA; Department of Psychiatry, Boston University School of Medicine, Boston, MA

Dawne S. Vogt, PhD, Psychology Service and National Center for PTSD, Women's Health Sciences Division, VA Boston Healthcare System; and Division of Psychiatry, Boston University School of Medicine, Boston, MA

Richard J. Westphal, MD, Bureau of Medicine and Surgery, U.S. Navy, Washington, DC

Rebecca Zisserson, PhD, Department of Psychology, Boston University, Boston, MA

Caring for Veterans With Deployment-Related Stress Disorders

IRAQ, AFGHANISTAN, and BEYOND

INTRODUCTION: ADDRESSING THE MENTAL HEALTH NEEDS OF ACTIVE-DUTY PERSONNEL AND VETERANS

JOSEF I. RUZEK, PAULA P. SCHNURR, JENNIFER J. VASTERLING, AND MATTHEW J. FRIEDMAN

15% exp PTSD

Approximately 15% of the military personnel who have returned from the wars in Iraq and Afghanistan will experience significant posttraumatic stress symptoms following deployment (Ramchand et al., 2010). At least one quarter of veterans from these wars who access Department of Veterans Affairs health care services have received a diagnosis of posttraumatic stress disorder (PTSD; Office of Public Health and Environmental Hazards, Veterans Health Administration, 2010). The distress and impairments in family, work, and social functioning associated with these symptoms will often persist for long periods of time.

We must all broaden our skills to help these men and women. As practitioners, researchers, program administrators, policy makers, or students, we are called to go beyond our current understanding of the mental health consequences of deployment to master emerging knowledge. We must also effectively tackle the sometimes unfamiliar problems presented by those back from the wars, and treat their partners and children, to increase the likelihood of early recovery and prevent the development of long-term distress and disability. Our challenge is to provide the best possible support for the more than 2 million members of America's all-volunteer military force who have served in Operation Enduring Freedom (OEF) in Afghanistan and Operation Iraqi Freedom (OIF).

These post-9/11 conflicts infuse the war zone with the pervasive element of terror—the "asymmetrical" nature of organized military forces doing battle against a diffuse enemy subjects the former to a high level of perceived threat in a harsh and malevolent environment. Missions have shifted rapidly between humanitarian assistance and the delivery of lethal force; in such a mercurial operational zone, it is rarely certain who is friend or foe. Improvised explosive devices (IEDs) have become the enemy's main weapon of choice. That this particular weapon has become so popular and widespread among "the enemy" in these post-9/11 conflicts should come as no surprise: The tragic encounters of armored personnel vehicles with IEDs destroy not only the vehicles but also the soldiers inside. Such encounters are recurrent settings for much carnage and death—and intense trauma for the survivors. Better battlefield medical care has translated into more survivability of combat trauma among U.S. forces in OEF and OIF. It has also translated into higher rates of morbidity among the veterans of these military operations. Because of better protective equipment and the unprecedented efficiency and effectiveness of the medical evacuation response on the battlefield, many who would have died from such combat trauma in previous wars have been able to return from these recent military operations, often with physical injuries that affect their mental health and functioning. The powerful impact of IEDs has meant that more warriors are surviving their wounds with serious injuries, including high rates of traumatic brain injury.

A cursory look at the complex issues examined in this book makes clear that the mental health needs of those who have served in Iraq and Afghanistan are varied and interrelated: the course of posttraumatic stress reactions and associated problems, contemporary assessment and treatment methods, specific stressors associated with these particular wars, and public health issues regarding the facilitation of help-seeking and the integration of health care sectors. Our goal is to assist the large community of professionals and volunteers representing diverse disciplines and perspectives whose collective efforts are required for an effective mental health response to a burgeoning array of war-related mental health needs.

In the pursuit of that goal, we face new challenges with these post-9/11 military engagements: A large number of servicewomen have been exposed to combat (and serious injury), as have many older military personnel. Large numbers of Reserve and National Guard troops who have seen action, often for several tours, must transition quickly from a civilian to a military way of life (and then back again). In some respects, the challenges of reintegration for reserve component troops are much more complicated and difficult than for active-duty personnel. Relative to previous wars, more servicemen and servicewomen are embedded in families, as spouses and parents. While in the war zone, they have had unprecedented access to their loved ones at home via e-mail, cell phones, video streams, and Internet blogs. Also, there has never been so much media attention to, and public and institutional awareness of, the mental health needs of warriors.

As with the experience and environment of troops during deployment, the environment of support for those affected by postdeployment and post-traumatic stress reactions has also changed. Knowledge about the mental health consequences of war-zone exposure has expanded dramatically since the United States went to war in the Persian Gulf in 1991. Much more is now understood about the treatment of PTSD and other posttraumatic stress–related problems. We are better positioned than ever to prepare military personnel, newly inducted civilians, and military reservists for the psychological rigors of war. We know much more about how to treat PTSD and other problems stemming from deployment. Programs have been established to facilitate reintegration after homecoming. Routine PTSD screening procedures are in place in both the Departments of Defense and Veterans Affairs. Mental health care is being integrated into primary care medicine. Major training initiatives are underway to enable widespread delivery of effective evidence-based treatments. Research is being undertaken that will significantly advance management of the well-being of those who have served.

The large number of individuals affected by postdeployment problems, together with the unique aspects of these conflicts and the accelerating rate of change in the mental health support mission, will challenge all of us to move toward continually learning better ways to serve those who return from these wars. Health care providers, members of the clergy, and other helping professionals, everywhere, in all systems of care, can expect to encounter individuals who are continuing to cope with the consequences of their deployment experiences. Many will be suffering from combat-related PTSD and other problems that may emerge after difficult deployments. Families, too, will be forced to adapt to the stresses associated with reintegration, which include, but are not limited to, the challenge of reunification with their loved ones who are troubled by the symptoms of PTSD. Indeed, family members themselves may often experience distress, diminished mental health functioning and well-being, and sometimes frank depression or some other psychological disorder.

Consider but a few of the challenges facing providers. It is widely accepted that the traumatic stress experiences of those deployed take place in a unique occupational context; exposure to potentially traumatic events is, after all, an expected and necessary element of deployment to a war zone. However, many providers understandably lack familiarity with military cultures and therefore have one less tool with which to provide mental health services to war-zone veterans. Much treatment is being provided in the context of possible redeployment, which can significantly complicate the helping process. With greater and greater frequency, practitioners are being asked to learn and deliver evidence-based treatments with which most have been unfamiliar. Internet education and support (e.g., afterdeployment.org) is increasingly part of the fabric of care. There is increasing awareness that we must assist not only the combatants but their families as well. More research regarding psychological treatment must be translated into practical approaches to service delivery. In short, these wars present a unique challenge to society, government, the health care system, and practitioners of all kinds. Yet these wars also provide us with a historic opportunity: Through prevention and treatment programs, we can minimize the development of chronic and pervasive mental health problems.

ABOUT THIS BOOK

The chapters in this book summarize current scientific and clinical knowledge about psychological trauma, PTSD, and related posttraumatic stress reactions among military veterans and civilians deployed to OEF and OIF. Although the content is focused on individuals serving in Iraq and Afghanistan, the book also offers a framework to help those not only in the United States but elsewhere around the world who will be directly affected by future wars. This book is designed to support clinical practice by providing clinicians with solid, evidence-based information. To that end, the chapters include clinical case illustrations intended to help practitioners integrate the material with real-world scenarios. The book should also stimulate research by providing a comprehensive summary of the existing literature. We anticipate that it may function as a practical tool for clinicians interested in trauma work and as a textbook for use in instructional settings.

A comprehensive approach to the management of posttraumatic stress reactions must encompass both prevention and treatment. It must also incorporate both clinical and public health perspectives. Problems experienced by individuals affect the larger community, so care at the individual level should be offered within the context of a larger system of services. Thus, this book comprises five major parts: epidemiology and course of problems; assessment of trauma, PTSD, related mental health outcomes (including the context of co-occurring traumatic brain injury), and suicidal states; specific noncombat stressors and problems and their ramifications; prevention and treatment of

PTSD; and public health challenges related to barriers to care and integration of service delivery systems.

The first two chapters address the epidemiology and course of posttraumatic stress reactions and provide the context for the remainder of the book by describing the spectrum of trauma-related psychological problems that can arise from serving in a war zone and addressing the phenomenology and scope of stress-related disorders from the perspective of affected individuals. In Chapter 1, Ramchand, Schell, Jaycox, and Tanielian review current knowledge about rates of exposure to traumatic events in the OEF and OIF war zones and the prevalence of PTSD and associated disorders among those deployed. In fact, most deployed service members have experienced some type of potentially traumatic event (e.g., receiving incoming hostile fire or seeing human remains) that could lead to immediate or eventual psychological consequences. Almost half have had an IED or other type of explosive detonate near them, and half have known someone seriously wounded or killed. In Chapter 2, Vasterling, Daly, and Friedman describe different ways in which posttraumatic stress reactions may unfold over time, starting with initial stress reactions in the war zone, proceeding to homecoming and the transition to the home front, and then addressing potential longer-term outcomes. They remind us that posttraumatic stress symptoms are dynamic, often change over time, and may vary from one individual to the next. Better understanding of the possible courses of posttraumatic reactions can help clinicians deliver assistance that fits the clinical stage of the stress reaction, distinguish transient from chronic psychopathology, and recognize how such chronic stress reactions may affect entire families.

The second section of the book covers assessment of more persistent clinical presentations. Faced with an individual needing help, practitioners must first seek to understand the person in front of them. Assessment is crucial to the determination of a well-constructed, comprehensive treatment plan. In Chapter 3, Vogt, Dutra, Reardon, Zisserson, and Miller describe state-of-the-art methods for the assessment of trauma exposure, PTSD, and functional impairment in OEF and OIF veterans, reviewing ways to identify the traumatic event, establish a diagnosis through structured interviews, and use self-report measures. Vogt et al. argue for the importance of a comprehensive assessment of psychological functioning, emphasizing that the assessment process offers an opportunity to establish rapport and build trust, as well as to offer the kind of patient education that can help strengthen commitment to treatment.

Reflecting the complexity of the clinical contexts that clinicians now face, two chapters address the assessment (and treatment) of subpopulations warranting special attention. Most of us now understand that the wars in Iraq and Afghanistan have produced many individuals who have suffered "polytrauma." In Chapter 4, Butler, Hurley, and Taber focus specifically on patients who present with both PTSD and physical injuries, including traumatic brain injury. They discuss the assessment and psychosocial and psychopharmacological treatment of these individuals, exploring how clinical care can be modified and treatment methods adapted to this complex constellation of problems.

Practitioners helping previously deployed military personnel and veterans must never lose sight of their unusually high risk for suicide. Suicide is a leading cause of death among those who have served, and there is a growing concern about military suicide rates. Fortunately, as Claassen and Knox point out in Chapter 5, most suicidal crises are time limited, and much can be done to intervene with these patients. These authors provide guidance as to the timely identification, assessment, and management of suicide risk that can enable mental health practitioners to prevent suicide more effectively.

The third part of this volume addresses several specific stressor events and problems that characterize both current and past wars. Many of the problems experienced by those returning from these wars stem from exposure to explosions, firefights, and the death and dying that occur during combat. Yet an all-too-common traumatic stressor largely responsible for the problems of both male and female service members is sexual harassment and assault. Given that experiences of sexual trauma during military service can have a significant negative impact on postdeployment mental health and well-being, it is crucial that every practitioner knows how to assess and treat the aftereffects of these experiences. In Chapter 6, Street, Kimerling, Bell, and Pavao describe the problems associated with military sexual trauma and summarize what is known about the prevalence of these experiences and their mental health consequences. Street et al. review the specific trauma of those who have been sexually assaulted in a war zone and suggest strategies for assessment and diagnosis. They also make us aware that many sexual trauma survivors have the mistaken belief that their traumatic experiences and resulting mental health difficulties are not as "legitimate" as those who have experienced combat trauma. This is why screening is so crucial for this group, because they are unlikely to disclose these experiences unless asked directly.

There has been high public visibility of major traumatic events in recent years (e.g., the World Trade Center attacks, Hurricane Katrina, and the Indian Ocean tsunami), and the potential for traumatic exposure to be associated with the onset of PTSD is now more widely recognized by both health care professionals and members of the general public. What is still underappreciated is that the trauma of war also takes a tremendous toll on those left behind—the families of servicemen and servicewomen. More than half of the active-duty and reserve force are married. Although having a loved one deployed to a war zone is itself stressful, the experience of living with someone with PTSD and other mental health concerns is also difficult; it can break apart an already strained family dynamic and heavily tax the resources of individual family members. In Chapter 7, Monson, Fredman, and Taft review existing research on family adjustment and deployment, offer an overview of current couples-focused interventions for military veterans and their partners, and identify important clinical considerations in the assessment and treatment of families. In Chapter 8, Cozza examines the experience of the children in these families, whose needs too often go unrecognized and unaddressed. He points out that although children of deployed parents experience more emotional and behavioral difficulties than children in the general population, mental health clinicians are less aware of the needs of children in the unique circumstances that accompany combat-related deployment. Practitioners, many of whom are unfamiliar with treatments for couples, families, and children, are challenged to learn how to better sustain families during deployment, to treat children who are affected by living with a parent with mental health problems or a severe combat-related injury, and to help families trying to deal with the war-related death of a spouse or parent.

The next two chapters summarize current thinking and evidence about prevention and treatment of PTSD. Currently we have a window of opportunity to try to prevent development of PTSD and other clinical disorders in returning veterans. In Chapter 9, Nash, Krantz, Stein, Westphal, and Litz review the conceptual evolution of military mental health prevention services and outline past and present challenges of implementing prevention programs in the military environment. Nash et al. also examine two current approaches to accomplishing prevention of mental health problems in the active-duty setting: the Army's Battlemind initiative and the Navy–Marine Corps Stress Continuum Model.

Fortunately, more is known about psychological and pharmacological treatment of PTSD than ever before. Carefully considered clinical practice guidelines have been developed in recent years, and evidence-based treatments are available. In Chapter 10, Rothbaum, Gerardi, Bradley, and Friedman describe current treatment approaches, review what is known about the effectiveness of both psychotherapy and pharmacotherapy for PTSD, discuss key issues related to the combined use of psychosocial and pharmacotherapeutic interventions, and identify treatment issues to consider when working with OEF and OIF service members.

The last part of the book presents an applied public health perspective to focus on identification and practical remediation of barriers to care and a systems perspective on our support for returning service personnel and veterans. For treatment to commence, individuals with PTSD or other problems must present themselves for care. However, many of those who might benefit most are reluctant to seek mental health treatment. Clinicians must engage the hesitant individual and find ways to offer assistance that is both personally acceptable and respectful of the service member's strengths and dignity. In Chapter 11, Stecker and Fortney describe the logistical, institutional–cultural, and attitudinal barriers to help-seeking and suggest ways to overcome these obstacles. In Chapter 12, Ruzek and Batten guide readers through a sometimes confusing system of care that includes the Department of Veterans Affairs, Department of Defense, and community-based practitioners and agencies. The efforts of many individuals representing a range of helping disciplines are required to meet the often extensive needs of those returning from service in Afghanistan and Iraq. Ruzek and Batten discuss the interacting sectors of care from the perspectives of both the individual practitioner and the managers responsible for design and operation of segments of the larger system. They also identify cross-system challenges in service improvement, draw attention to ways in which individual practitioners can learn about continuing developments, and suggest means to improve systems to support the practitioner.

In the concluding chapter, we highlight the take-home issues of this volume that must be considered when working to improve care for those who have served. We summarize what is known about caring for military personnel and civilians returning from contemporary war zones, discuss opportunities to draw from current knowledge regarding PTSD care in civilian contexts, and outline the public health and research agenda necessary to move forward in optimizing care of all those affected psychologically by war.

Our collective task, and our collective opportunity, is to provide the best possible care and support for those deployed to Iraq and Afghanistan, and, if necessary, to future wars. We hope that this book will help readers stay on top of emerging knowledge and thereby better ensure that our clinical decisions, the design of our prevention and treatment services, and our health care policies are all informed by the best available research evidence and expert clinical consensus.

REFERENCES

Ramchand, R., Schell, T. L., Karney, B. R., Osilla, K. C., Burns, R. M., & Caldarone, L. B. (2010). Disparate prevalence estimates of PTSD among service members who served in Iraq and Afghanistan: Possible explanations. *Journal of Traumatic Stress, 23,* 59–68. doi:10.1002/jts.20486

Office of Public Health and Environmental Hazards, Veterans Health Administration. (2010). *Analysis of VA health care utilization among Operation Enduring Freedom (OEF) and Operation Iraqi Freedom (OIF) veterans.* Washington, DC: Author.

I
EPIDEMIOLOGY AND COURSE

1

EPIDEMIOLOGY OF TRAUMA EVENTS AND MENTAL HEALTH OUTCOMES AMONG SERVICE MEMBERS DEPLOYED TO IRAQ AND AFGHANISTAN

RAJEEV RAMCHAND, TERRY L. SCHELL, LISA H. JAYCOX, AND TERRI TANIELIAN

Since 2001, more than 1.7 million members of the United States' all-volunteer military force have been called on to serve in the official military operations in Afghanistan (in support of Operation Enduring Freedom [OEF]) and Iraq (in support of Operation Iraqi Freedom [OIF]; Sollinger, Fisher, & Metscher, 2008). In this chapter, we draw from the existing literature to present the prevalence of various types of trauma exposures and other war-zone stressors experienced by service members serving or who have served in OEF or OIF. We then turn to posttraumatic stress disorder (PTSD) and present prevalence estimates of PTSD from existing studies of those deployed to OEF and OIF, along with observable patterns that emerge from these studies. Finally, we discuss other mental conditions that service members may experience in conjunction with or independent of PTSD.

TRAUMA EVENTS ASSOCIATED WITH DEPLOYMENT TO IRAQ AND AFGHANISTAN

Prior work based on the experiences of Vietnam veterans found that potentially traumatic or stressful war-zone experiences could be generally categorized into four indices: traditional combat events, atrocities or episodes of extraordinarily abusive violence, subjective or perceived threat, and general milieu of a harsh or malevolent environment (D. W. King, King, Gudanowski, & Vreven, 1995). These categories were later expanded on the basis of the experiences of veterans from later combat operations (e.g., Persian Gulf War) into 10 deployment or war-zone factors that could lead to health problems: preparedness, difficult living and working environment, concerns about life and family disruptions, deployment social support, sexual harassment, general harassment, perceived threat, combat experiences, aftermath of battle, and exposure to nuclear, biological, and chemical agents (L. A. King, King, Vogt, Knight, & Samper, 2006; Vogt, Proctor, King, King, & Vasterling, 2008). We describe in this section OEF and OIF service members' reports of experiences across six of these domains.

Traditional Combat Events

Traditional combat events are those that have historically characterized combat-related experiences. They include being injured or wounded in combat; killing, injuring, or wounding someone else; and handling or smelling dead and decomposing bodies. Killgore et al. (2008) further classified these events into six categories: violent combat exposure, human trauma exposure, survived close call, buddy killed or injured, killed enemy, and killed friendly or nonhostiles. Approximately 75% of select military units surveyed in theater reported that they received incoming artillery, rocket, or mortar fire; approximately 60% received small-arms fire; nearly 50% reported being in threatening situations in which they were unable to respond; and more than 50% reported having an improvised explosive device or booby trap detonate near them. Approximately 15% reported being directly responsible for the death of enemy combatants (U.S. Department of the Army, Office of the Surgeon General, 2004, 2005, 2006a, 2006b). Postdeployment screenings yield similar estimates: approximately 50% reported witnessing someone wounded or killed, and between 15% and 25% reported having discharged their weapon (Hoge, Auchterlonie, & Milliken, 2006; Milliken, Auchterlonie, & Hoge, 2007).[1] Surveys conducted postdeployment similarly indicate that almost all Army soldiers and Marines from select units reported seeing dead bodies or human remains, and more than half reported handling or uncovering human remains (Hoge et al., 2004). In a sample designed to be representative of all of those who have served in Afghanistan or Iraq between 2001 and 2008,

---

[1]Actual estimates vary based on who is being assessed (i.e., Marine or Army units), the time at which they were assessed, and whether they served in Iraq or Afghanistan.

close to 50% reported seeing dead or seriously injured noncombatants, and more than one third reported having smelled decomposing bodies (Schell & Marshall, 2008).

Atrocities or Episodes of Extraordinarily Abusive Violence

Events that fall into this domain are those that are generally thought to surpass what are considered "normal" warfare experiences. There are documented accounts of U.S. service members participating in what most would consider atrocities or abusive violence, such as the abuse of detainees in Abu Ghraib (Danner, 2004; Greenberg & Dratel, 2005), but few reports present the extent of exposure to these events to date. One exception is the study by the RAND Corporation in which 5% of respondents reported witnessing brutality toward detainees or prisoners (Schell & Marshall, 2008). A survey conducted in theater in 2006 revealed that 4% of soldiers and 7% of Marines reported hitting or kicking a noncombatant when it was not necessary, and just under 10% reported that their unit modified or ignored Rules of Engagement to accomplish the mission (U.S. Department of the Army, Office of the Surgeon General, 2006b).

Subjective or Perceived Threat

Experiences categorized as *subjective* or *perceived threat* are defined according to individual assessments of events as being harmful or threatening. Analyses of postdeployment screening data indicate that approximately half of Army soldiers who served in Iraq felt in danger of being killed during their deployment (Hoge et al., 2006; Milliken et al., 2007). In a survey of medical personnel who served in OEF or OIF (or both), 38% reported that they frequently perceived themselves to be in personal danger, and almost one quarter reported being frequently concerned about dying (Kolkow, Spira, Morse, & Grieger, 2007). In one Army brigade of 202 soldiers who experienced a traumatic event, 21% reported responding to traumatic events with intense fear, helplessness, or terror (Adler, Wright, Bliese, Eckford, & Hoge, 2008). Also falling within this category is the experience of knowing of or witnessing someone killed or injured. In theater, close to three quarters of service members reported knowing someone seriously injured or killed and the same proportion reported having a member of their own unit become a casualty; approximately half reported seeing dead or seriously injured Americans (U.S. Department of the Army, 2004, 2005, 2006a, 2006b). In interviews conducted after their return home, approximately 50% of service members reported having a friend who was seriously injured or killed, and 45% reported witnessing an accident resulting in serious injury or death (Schell & Marshall, 2008).

General Milieu of a Harsh or Malevolent Environment

In the war zone, some experiences represent common irritations, annoyances, and grievances. In theater, 39% of soldiers surveyed in Iraq in 2007 reported lack of privacy or personal space to be a "major issue," and approximately one third reported boring or repetitive work to be a "main deployment concern" (U.S. Department of the Army, 2006b). Epidemiologic studies focused on non-combat-related ailments (disease nonbattle injuries) provide another source of information about the environmental conditions to which deployed service members are exposed. Concerns about food and air quality, for example, are reflected by the most commonly reported illnesses among U.S. service members: diarrhea and respiratory illnesses (Aronson, Sanders, & Moran, 2006; Sanders et al., 2005). Flies and insects also may be an issue because there is concern over leishmaniasis, a parasitic cutaneous infection caused by a sand fly endemic to both Afghanistan and Iraq (Sanders et al., 2005; Vickery et al., 2008), and other insect-borne diseases (Aronson et al., 2006). Validation of these malevolent environmental conditions is found in a retrospective chart review of 56 service members seeking care at a Department of Veterans Affairs (VA) facility: Clinicians expressed concerns over environmentally based issues for approximately 50% of these patients, most of which were attributable to poor air quality due to burning trash and feces, smoke from oil-well fires, or sand and dust; 9% due to contaminated food and water; and 7% related to insects (Helmer et al., 2007).

Sexual Harassment

We identified no published study estimating the prevalence of sexual harassment events among active-duty service members in theater. However, a survey conducted among U.S. veterans who had served in prior conflicts seeking VA disability benefits for PTSD indicated that 71% of women and 4% men experienced an in-service sexual assault (Murdoch et al., 2003; Murdoch, Polusny, Hodges, & O'Brien, 2004). In a 2008 study, 3.7% of active duty military personnel reported unwanted sexual contact since joining the services: 2.3% of male service members reported such contact versus 12.3% of female service members (Bray, 2009). We refer readers to Chapter 6 of this volume for information on this topic.

Exposure to Chemical, Biological, or Nuclear Agents

Chemical and biological weapons represent a relatively new class of war-related traumas to which deployed service members may be exposed; fear of such exposures has also emerged as a significant subjective or perceived threat.

There have been few reports of exposure to toxic chemical agents in OEF and OIF. Clinicians expressed concern about chemical weapons exposure for 9% and about depleted uranium exposure for 32% of a sample of 56 patients who had served in OEF or OIF (Helmer et al., 2007).[2] Among a sample of previously deployed health professionals, 18% reported frequent concern regarding chemical or biological weapons (Kolkow et al., 2007).

Summary

U.S. service members report a variety of experiences during deployments in support of OEF and OIF that could lead to immediate or eventual physical or psychological consequences. The most prevalent are traditional combat events, particularly witnessing somebody being injured or killed or seeing or handling dead bodies. Many of those deployed also report being concerned that they, too, will die, a fear possibly borne out of having friends and colleagues killed or injured. Poor environmental conditions are also common in the war zone. There is less information about exposure to other stressors: The extent to which service members may be involved in perpetrating abusive violence, be exposed to chemical, biologic, and nuclear agents, or have been sexual assaulted, has not yet been determined.

MENTAL HEALTH OUTCOMES ASSOCIATED WITH DEPLOYMENT IN THE GLOBAL WAR ON TERROR

Posttraumatic Stress Disorder

PTSD is an anxiety disorder that may develop among people exposed to a traumatic event or events. Because deployment to war zones often entails exposure to traumatic events and experiences, and because PTSD is predicated on such exposures, it is the most discussed and studied mental health outcome during and after deployment (see Chapter 2 for a more complete discussion of PTSD symptoms and diagnosis).

Measuring PTSD

The Department of Defense requires that returning service members complete the Post-Deployment Health Assessment (PDHA) immediately after returning from deployment and Post-Deployment Health Reassessment

---

[2]"Depleted uranium" is uranium that has been processed to have most of the highly radioactive isotopes removed. The resulting heavy metal is toxic if ingested; it is slightly radioactive and extremely dense. It is used by the U.S. military in ammunition and armor (Harley et al., 1999).

(PDHRA) 3 to 6 months later. Both the PDHA and PDHRA use a scale consisting of four yes–no items, the Primary Care PTSD Screen (PC-PTSD; Prins et al., 2004), to identify those who are more likely to meet diagnostic PTSD criteria among all service members previously deployed. Answering yes to three questions is the criterion often used to identify those who warrant further clinical questioning about PTSD symptoms (Prins et al., 2004) and is the threshold used in mandatory screenings in VA primary care clinics (U.S. Veterans Health Administration, 2005). Some studies have defined a positive screen as answering yes to only two questions on the PC-PTSD, which correctly identifies more of those with the disorder but also causes more false positives (i.e., people who screen positive but who do not have the disorder). In short, this brief screening instrument is designed to identify individuals who would benefit from additional evaluation, but the percentage who screen positive for a referral is likely to exceed the number of cases that meet diagnostic criteria for the disorder.

Research studies designed to estimate the diagnostic prevalence of PTSD commonly use the PTSD Checklist (PCL; Weathers, Litz, Herman, Huska, & Keane, 1993) to identify probable PTSD cases. The PCL asks respondents how bothered they are by each of 17 symptoms associated with PTSD. Among the studies conducted of U.S. service members who served in OEF or OIF, different scoring algorithms have been used to identify probably PTSD cases: Responses have been mapped onto diagnostic criteria (e.g., Schell & Marshall, 2008), a threshold has been set based on the total score on the scale (e.g., Erbes, Westermeyer, Engdahl, & Johnsen, 2007), or a combination thereof (e.g., Hoge et al., 2004). Each method represents a different trade-off between specificity (correctly identifying who does not have PTSD) and sensitivity (correctly identifying who has the disease). Thus, when comparing estimates across studies, it is important that one consider the method used to define PTSD and whether, for example, a more specific technique contributes to lower prevalence estimates, as has been seen in studies that have used more than one scoring criteria on the same sample (e.g., Hoge et al., 2004, 2006; Milliken et al., 2007; Smith, Ryan, Wingard, et al., 2008).

Prevalence Estimates of PTSD Among Service Members in Iraq and Afghanistan

Although studies have generally estimated prevalence of PTSD at one or more postdeployment intervals, only two studies have examined the increased risk of PTSD among those service members who deployed relative to those who have not. One study found that PTSD was higher among Army soldiers who had already deployed than among those about to deploy (Hoge et al., 2004), and in one study, new-onset PTSD developed in 8.7% of those who deployed and experienced combat exposures relative to 2.1% among those who deployed but did not experience combat exposures, and 3.0% among those who did not deploy (Smith, Ryan, Wingard, et al., 2008).

The U.S. Army Surgeon General has chartered Mental Health Advisory Teams (MHAT) six times since 2003 to produce reports on mental health issues related to deployment, all of which have produced prevalence estimates of PTSD symptoms among U.S. service members in theater (U.S. Department of the Army, 2004, 2005, 2006a, 2006b, 2008, 2009). Published MHAT studies to date have consistently estimated that approximately 15% of Army soldiers or Marines met criteria that mapped onto PTSD diagnostic criteria and also had a total score of greater or equal to 50 on the PCL. The exception was in 2004, when 10% of soldiers surveyed met these criteria (U.S. Department of the Army, 2004, 2005, 2006a, 2006b) and may reflect reductions in traumatic exposures during that time (Sollinger et al., 2008).[3]

We provide an overview of studies that produced prevalence estimates of PTSD among U.S. service members at some point postdeployment in nonclinical settings in Table 1.1; among non–U.S. service members who had served in Iraq, Afghanistan, or both in Table 1.2; and among samples of U.S. service members drawn from clinical settings in Table 1.3. We refer readers to other publications (Ramchand, Karney, Osilla, Burns, & Calderone, 2008; Ramchand, Schell, Karney, Osilla, Burns, & Caldarone, 2010; Sundin, Fear, Iversen, Rona, & Wessely, 2010) for a more complete review of these studies.

Most studies, including those that have published results from the PDHA and PDHRA screening assessments, present prevalence estimates that range from between 5% and 20%, although non–U.S. service members who previously deployed to the region tend to have lower estimates, whereas U.S. service members in treatment have, on average, higher estimates. In our own prior work, we estimated PTSD among a sample designed to be representative of all U.S. service members who had served in OEF or OIF and estimated that 14% reported symptoms on the PCL that corresponded with a diagnosis of PTSD (Schell & Marshall, 2008). This compares with 4% of a sample of previously deployed soldiers from the United Kingdom (Hotopf et al., 2006) as well as surveys of OEF and OIF veterans accessing care at select VA facilities, where as many as 50% screened positive (i.e., reported three or more symptoms) on the PC-PTSD (Seal et al., 2008), although only 13% to 23% of OEF and OIF veterans seeking VA treatment had a diagnosis of PTSD on their medical records (Seal, Bertenthal, Miner, Sen, & Marmar, 2007; U.S. Veterans Health Administration, 2008).

---

[3]Because these surveys cannot establish whether symptoms persisted for 30 days, they are termed *acute stress reactions* (U.S. Department of the Army, 2004, 2005, 2006a, 2006b).

TABLE 1.1

Estimated Prevalence of PTSD Among Service Members Previously Deployed to Iraq, Afghanistan, or Both

Reference	Sample	Time since deployment	Year	N	Case definition[a]	%
Hoge et al., 2004	Army unit (Iraq)	3–4 months	2003	881	PCL-DSM	18.0
					PCL-DSM-50	12.9
	Army unit (Afghanistan)	3–4 months	2003	811	PCL-DSM	11.5
					PCL-DSM-50	6.2
	Marine unit (Iraq)	3–4 months	2003	1,956	PCL-DSM	19.9
					PCL-DSM-50	12.2
Hoge et al., 2006	Army and marine (Iraq)	PDHA (2 weeks)	2003–2004	222,620	PC-PTSD-2	9.8
					PC-PTSD-3	4.8
	Army and marine (Afghanistan)	PDHA (2 weeks)	2003–2004	16,318	PC-PTSD-2	4.7
					PC-PTSD-3	2.1
Vasterling et al., 2006	Army units (Iraq)	4–7 months	2005	1,028	PCL-DSM-50	11.6
Abt Associates Inc., 2006	All services, active component	6–12 months	2003–2004	1,382	PCL-DSM	7.3
Hoge et al., 2007	Army units (Iraq)	1 year	2001–2005	2,815	PCL-DSM-50	16.6
Kolkow et al., 2007	Military health care providers (Iraq/ Afghanistan)	Wide range (0–months to >2 years)	2004	102	PCL-DSM-50	9.0
Martin, 2007	All services (Iraq)	PDHA (2 weeks)	2005	222,183	PC-PTSD-2	10.5
Milliken et al., 2007	Active duty army (Iraq)	PDHA (2 weeks)	2005–2006	56,350	PC-PTSD-2	11.8
					PC-PTSD-3	6.2
	Army reservists (Iraq)	PDHRA (3–6 months)	2005–2006	56,350	PC-PTSD-2	16.7
					PC-PTSD-3	9.1
		PDHA (2 weeks)	2005–2006	31,885	PC-PTSD-2	12.7
					PC-PTSD-3	6.6
		PDHRA (3–6 months)	2005–2006	31,885	PC-PTSD-2	24.5
					PC-PTSD-3	14.3
				1,810		

Study	Population	Time frame	Year	N	Measure	%
Lapierre, Schwegler, & Labauve, 2007	Army (Afghanistan)	5–8 weeks	2005	2,266	SPTSS	30.0
	Army (Iraq)	5–8 weeks	2005		SPTSS	31.0
Stecker, Fortney, Hamilton, & Ajzen, 2007	Army National Guard unit (Iraq)	N/A	2006	20	MINI	60.0
Bliese et al., 2007	Army unit (Iraq)	7 days	2004	503	PCL ≥50	1.39
			2004	503	PCL ≥44	2.98
		120 days	2004	499	PCL ≥50	4.81
			2004	499	PCL ≥44	8.42
Smith, Ryan, Wingard, et al., 2008	All services, without PTSD before deployment, who experienced combat exposure (Iraq/Afghanistan)	Wide range (0–months to > 2 years)	2001–2006	5,382	PCL-DSM or self-reported diagnosis in previous 3 years	7.6
				5,299	PCL-DSM-50 or self-reported diagnosis in previous 3 years	8.7
	All services, without PTSD before deployment who did not experience combat exposure (Iraq/Afghanistan)	Wide range (0–months to > 2 years)	2001–2006	6,357	PCL-DSM or self-reported diagnosis in previous 3 years	1.4
				6,095	PCL-DSM-50 or self-reported diagnosis in previous 3 years	2.1
	All services, with PTSD before deployment who experienced combat exposure (Iraq/Afghanistan)	Wide range (0–months to > 2 years)	2001–2006	64	PCL-DSM or self-reported diagnosis in previous 3 years	43.5
				134	PCL-DSM-50 or self-reported diagnosis in previous 3 years	47.9

(continues)

TABLE 1.1

Estimated Prevalence of PTSD Among Service Members Previously Deployed to Iraq, Afghanistan, or Both (Continued)

Reference	Sample	Time since deployment	Year	N	Case definition[a]	%
	All services, with PTSD before deployment who did not experience combat exposure (Iraq/Afghanistan)	Wide range (0 months to > 2 years)	2001–2006	108	PCL-DSM or self-reported diagnosis in previous 3 years	26.2
				186	PCL-DSM-50 or self-reported diagnosis in previous 3 years	22.4
Schell & Marshall, 2008	All services	Wide range (0 months to > 2 years)	2007–2008	1,965	PCL-DSM	13.8
Ouimette et al., 2008	Army National Guard unit (Iraq)	M = 14.9 months	—	31	CAPS	41.9
Schneiderman et al., 2008	All services living in a select geographic area (Iraq/Afghanistan)	≤ 6 months	2005	2,235	PCL≥50	11
Hoge et al., 2008	Army unit (Iraq)	3–4 months	2006	2,517	PCL-DSM-50	13.9
Larson et al., 2008	Marines—active component (Iraq/Afghanistan)	Wide range (0 months to > 2 years)	2001–2005	41,561	ICD-9 CM	1.6

Note. CAPS = Clinician-Administered PTSD Scale; DSM = *Diagnostic and Statistical Manual of Mental Disorders,* 4th ed.—text revision (American Psychiatric Association, 2000); ICD-9 = *International Classification of Disease,* 9th ed.; ICD-9 CM = *ICD-9* clinical modification); MINI=Mini International Neuropsychiatric Interview; PC-PTSD = Primary Care PTSD Screen; PCL = PTSD Checklist; PTSD = posttraumatic stress disorder; SPTSS = Screen for Posttraumatic Stress Symptoms.
[a]PCL-DSM = reporting at least one intrusion symptom, three avoidance symptoms, and two hyperarousal symptoms on the PCL; PCL ≥ 50 (44) = total score of at least 50 (or 44) on the PCL; PCL-DSM-50 = PCL-DSM + a total score of at least 50 on the PCL; PC-PTSD-2(3) = reporting two (or three) or more of four items on the PC-PTSD; SPTSS = an average total score of 4 or more on the SPTSS.

TABLE 1.2
Estimated Prevalence of PTSD Among Non–U.S. Service Members Previously Deployed to Iraq, Afghanistan, or Both

Reference	Sample	Time since deployment	Year	N	Case definition[a]	%
Hotopf et al., 2006	U.K. armed forces personnel	≥1 year	2003	4,613	PCL ≥ 50	4
	SFIR 3	5 months	2005–2006	170	PSS	21
				148	SCID	12
Engelhard et al., 2007	SFIR 4	5 months	2005–2006	140	PSS	4
				129	SCID	3
	SFIR 5	5 months	2005–2006	72	PSS	6
				62	SCID	3

Note. PCL = PTSD checklist; PSS = PTSD Symptom Scale; PTSD = posttraumatic stress disorder; SCID = Structured Clinical Interview for *DSM* Disorders; SFIR = Stabilisation Force Iraq (Royal Netherlands Army).
[a]PCL ≥50 = total score of at least 50 on the PCL; PSS = total score of 14 on the PSS.

TABLE 1.3
Estimated Prevalence of PTSD Among Treatment-Seeking Service Members Previously Deployed to Iraq, Afghanistan, or Both

Reference	Sample	Time since deployment	Year	N	Case definition[a]	%
Helmer et al., 2007	VA—regional	0 months to >2 years	2004–2006	56	Chart review	45.0
Seal et al., 2007	VA—national (Iraq/Afghanistan)	0 months to >2 years)	2001–2005	103,788	ICD-9-CM	13.0
Grieger et al., 2006	Army—wounded (Iraq/Afghanistan)	1 month	2003–2004	613	PCL-DSM-50	4.2
		4 months	2003–2004	395	PCL-DSM-50	12.2
		7 months	2003–2004	301	PCL-DSM-50	12.0
Erbes, Westermeyer, Engdahl, & Johnsen, 2007	VA—regional (Iraq/Afghanistan)	0 months to > 2 years	2005–2007	120	PCL ≥ 50	12.0
Gaylord et al., 2008	U.S. AISR—burn victims (Iraq/Afghanistan)	N/A	2005–2006	76	PCL ≥ 44	32.0
Seal et al., 2008	VA—regional	0 months to > 2 years	2001–2006	338	PC-PTSD-3	50.0
Sayer et al., 2008	VA polytrauma rehabilitation centers	0 months to >2 years	2001–2006	188	Chart review	35.0
Rundell, 2006	Medical evacuations for psychiatric reasons (Iraq/Afghanistan)	0 months to > 2 years	2001–2004	1,264	Psychiatric evaluations	4.4
McGhee, Maani, Garza, Gaylord, & Black, 2008	U.S. AISR—burn victims (Iraq/Afghanistan)	0 months to > 2 years	2002–2007	147	PCL ≥ 44	30.6
Jakupcak, Luterek, Hunt, Conybeare, & McFall, 2008	VA—regional (Iraq and Afghanistan)	0 months to > 2 years	2004–2005	108	PCL-DSM-50	37.8

Note. PTSD = posttraumatic stress disorder; U.S. AISR = U.S. Army Institute of Surgical Research; VA = U.S. Department of Veterans Affairs.
[a]ICD-9-CM = diagnostic code of PTSD from medical records. PCL-DSM = reporting at least one intrusion symptom, three avoidance symptoms, and two hyperarousal symptoms on the PCL; PCL ≥ 50 (44) = total score of at least 50 (or 44) on the PCL; PCL-DSM-50 = PCL-DSM + a total score of at least 50 on the PCL; PC-PTSD-2(3) = reporting two (or three) or more of four items on the PC-PTSD.

Viewed as a whole, there has been a lack of uniform definitions of cases of PTSD across studies, and only a handful of studies estimate prevalence in a representative sample, although even these are not fully representative of the entire deployed population. Discounting estimates from studies that may not be representative of U.S. service members' deployment experiences (e.g., Hotopf et al., 2006) or those from select military units for which generalizability is uncertain (e.g., Hoge et al., 2004), the best available evidence suggests that the overall prevalence of PTSD among previously deployed service members is between 10% and 15%. Likewise, discounting smaller studies (e.g., Helmer et al., 2007), evidence from across VA health care services indicates that at least one quarter of OEF and OIF veterans accessing treatment receive a diagnosis of PTSD. When interpreting these latter estimates, however, one must keep in mind that studies requiring documentation of a diagnosis in the medical record are likely to produce underestimates of prevalence among the entire deployed force, because many of those with PTSD never seek treatment (Dohrenwend, Sloan, Marx, Kaloupek, & Keane, 2008; Hoge, 2008; Hoge et al., 2004; Schell & Marshall, 2008; Smith, Ryan, Smith et al., 2008; Wang et al., 2005).

Correlates of PTSD and Comparisons Across Relevant Subgroups

Across studies, combat exposure was consistently associated with an increased likelihood of meeting criteria for PTSD (Grieger et al., 2006; Hoge et al., 2004, 2006; Kolkow et al., 2007; Schell & Marshall, 2008; Smith, Ryan, Wingard, et al., 2008; U.S. Department of the Army, 2006b). It is probable that many of the studies that have found differences in PTSD across groups are reflecting differences in exposure to combat. For example, differential exposure to combat has been offered as a potential explanation as to why U.K. service members have lower PTSD prevalence than U.S. service members (Hoge & Castro, 2006) and may also explain why those deployed to Iraq tend to have higher prevalence estimates of PTSD than those deployed to Afghanistan (Abt Associates Inc., 2006; Hoge et al., 2004, 2006; Lapierre et al., 2007; U.S. Department of the Army, 2005), a trend that may shift as trauma exposures among U.S. service members in Afghanistan increase (Mazzetti, 2008). Being injured or wounded is also often correlated with PTSD (Grieger et al., 2006; Hoge et al., 2004, 2006; Hoge, Terhakopian, Castro, Messer, & Engel, 2007; Schell & Marshall, 2008) but is likely to be experienced differentially on the basis of service members' exposure to combat.

There are no other characteristics that are associated with PTSD across all of the studies reviewed, although there are some noteworthy findings. In multivariable regression analyses that controlled for trauma exposure as well as demographic and military services characteristics, Schell and Marshall

(2008) found that previously deployed female and Hispanic service members were more likely than their counterparts to report PTSD symptoms.[4] Although Hispanic service members had a higher prevalence of PTSD than any other racial or ethnic group in both bivariate and multivariate models, women had unadjusted prevalence estimates comparable to their male counterparts. This is consistent with a view that female service members are not at increased total risk of PTSD (and may actually be at decreased risk; e.g., Kulka et al., 1990), in part due to explicit military policies that are designed to reduce their risk of exposure to combat. When comparing male and female service members who have been exposed to similar levels of trauma (in this study, measured as number of deployment-related traumas), however, female service members appear more likely to develop PTSD symptoms. This finding is similar to results from epidemiologic studies among civilians who have been exposed to trauma that also show higher rates of PTSD symptoms among women and Hispanics (e.g., Adams & Boscarino, 2006; Galea et al., 2002; Kessler, Chiu, Demler, Merikangas, & Walters, 2005; Kulka et al., 1990; Pole et al., 2001). There is no consistent relationship between age, rank, or component (i.e., reservists vs. active) and reporting PTSD symptoms across the studies reviewed (see Ramchand, Schell, et al., 2010).

Depression, Substance Use Disorders, and Other Comorbidities

Depression is the second most commonly studied mental health condition among service members, but thus far no studies have been able to specify whether service members were depressed before deployment or whether their depressive symptoms emerged in theater or upon returning home. However, Schell and Marshall (2008) did find that combat trauma was the best predictor of depression among individuals previously deployed. Depressive symptoms may emerge independent of or co-occur with PTSD. In the RAND study, the estimated prevalence of depression was 13.7%: Of these individuals, 34% met only criteria for depression, whereas 66% were comorbid for PTSD and depression (Schell & Marshall, 2008). In theater, between 5% and 9% of troops meet criteria for probable major depression (U.S. Department of the Army, 2004, 2005, 2006a, 2006b); studies using the PDHA generally indicate that approximately 5% report affirmatively to one of two depression screening items (Hoge et al., 2006; Milliken et al., 2007), although in longitudinal studies, the estimated prevalence of depression generally tends to increase

---

[4]The RAND multivariable model controlled for branch (Army, Navy, Air Force, Marine Corps), current duty status (Active/Reserve, Guard, Discharged/Retired), rank (Enlisted, Officer/Warrant Officer), gender (male, female), race (White, Black, Hispanic, Other), current marital status (married, not married), age, months since last return, length of last deployment, number of traumas, and seriously injured.

to approximately 10% as the time from returning from deployment increases (Grieger et al., 2006; Milliken et al., 2007). Hoge and colleagues' (2004) surveys of postdeployment service units indicated that 15% met criteria for depression, which was higher than the estimated prevalence of 10% reported among the comparison group, an Army unit assessed 1 week before deployment. Two other studies found the prevalence of depression to be much higher, estimated at 25% (Vasterling et al., 2006) and up to 38% (Lapierre et al., 2007).

The other commonly studied mental health outcome among service members postdeployment to OEF and OIF is alcohol misuse or abuse. In analyses using the PDHRA, 12% of more than 50,000 deployed Army soldiers from the active component and 15% of more than 31,000 deployed Army soldiers from the Reserves or National Guard reported either using more alcohol than they intended to use, wanting or needing to cut down on their drinking, or both (Milliken et al., 2007). Hoge and colleagues (2004) found that 25% of soldiers across two Army units and 35% of Marines from a unit, all assessed 3-months postdeployment, had significantly higher rates of alcohol problems than of soldiers in an Army unit about to deploy, among which 17% reported this outcome. Finally, one cohort study that assessed service members both before and after being deployed indicated that members of the active component who were deployed and experienced combat exposures were significantly more likely to start binge drinking than those who did not deploy over the same time period (27% vs. 19%). Deployed reservists and National Guard members with combat exposures were more likely than their counterparts who did not deploy to start heavy weekly drinking (9% vs. 5%), binge drinking (26% vs. 17%), and to develop alcohol-related problems (7% vs. 4%; Jacobson et al., 2008).

When they return from service, deployed service members may experience many other problems that, like alcohol use disorders, may occur independently or in conjunction with other disorders. Karney and colleagues (2008) examined the existing literature to identify the immediate and long-term consequences of PTSD and depression. Deployed service members who develop PTSD or depression may be at risk of other anxiety disorders; declines in physical functioning and other physical morbidity; adverse education, employment, and relationship (e.g., interpersonal, marital) outcomes; homelessness; and an increased mortality risk, including a higher risk of dying by suicide. The extent to which these outcomes are experienced among those who served in Iraq and Afghanistan, and how these outcomes present in relation to PTSD and other mental health outcomes, remains an area for future inquiry and investigation.

In summary, little research to date has gone beyond PTSD in estimating the impact of deployment to OEF and OIF on mental and behavioral outcomes. Although some data exist on depression and alcohol use, much more data are needed to understand the array of problems experienced and to determine the interrelationship among them.

SUMMARY

Studies concerning the experiences and mental health of service members deployed to OEF and OIF have been conducted before deployment, in theater, and upon returning from duty. Although these studies have certain limitations, they collectively suggest that most service members experience some type of trauma while deployed. PTSD, an anxiety disorder predicated on being exposed to trauma, appears to affect between 5% and 20% of previously deployed service members. Other mental health conditions may also emerge in conjunction with or independent of PTSD; of these, depression and alcohol misuse have been the best studied.

Understanding the nature of the experiences U.S. service members face during their support of military operations remains an important area of study. Current efforts to screen service members upon redeployment to identify those at risk of PTSD or depression represent important steps in facilitating care for these individuals but also in conducting population-level surveillance. Research studies that have surveyed this population using measures such as the PCL have also informed our understanding of the population-level prevalence of these conditions among returning troops. These estimates are vital to the nation's ability to plan appropriately for and deliver care to returning veterans.

REFERENCES

Abt Associates Inc. (2006). *2003–2004 Active Duty Health Study: Final report.* Falls Church, VA: TRICARE Management Activity, Health Program Analysis and Evaluation Directorate.

Adams, R. E., & Boscarino, J. A. (2006). Predictors of PTSD and delayed PTSD after disaster: The impact of exposure and psychosocial resources. *Journal of Nervous and Mental Disease, 194,* 485–493. doi:10.1097/01.nmd.0000228503.95503.e9

Adler, A. B., Wright, K. M., Bliese, P. D., Eckford, R., & Hoge, C. W. (2008). A2 diagnostic criterion for combat-related posttraumatic stress disorder. *Journal of Traumatic Stress, 21,* 301–308. doi:10.1002/jts.20336

Aronson, N. E., Sanders, J. W., & Moran, K. A. (2006). In harm's way: Infections in deployed American military forces. *Clinical Infectious Diseases, 43,* 1045–1051. doi:10.1086/507539

Bliese, P. D., Wright, K. M., Adler, A. B., Thomas, J. L., & Hoge, C. W. (2007). Timing of postcombat mental health assessments. *Psychological Services, 4,* 141–148. doi:10.1037/1541-1559.4.3.141

Bray, R. M., Pemberton, M. R., Hourani, L. L., Witt, M., Olmsted, K. L. R., & Brown, J. M. (2009). *Department of Defense survey of health related behaviors among active duty military personnel.* Research Triangle Park, NC: RTI International.

Danner, M. (2004). *Torture and truth: America, Abu Ghraib, and the war on terror.* New York, NY: New York Review Books.

Dohrenwend, B. P., Sloan, D. M., Marx, B. P., Kaloupek, D., & Keane, T. M. (2008). Re: Psychiatric diagnoses in historic and contemporary military cohorts: Combat deployment and the healthy warrior effect. *American Journal of Epidemiology, 168,* 1093–1094; author reply 1096–1098. doi:10.1093/aje/kwn275

Engelhard, I. M., van den Hout, M. A., Weerts, J., Arntz, A., Hox, J. J., & McNally, R. J. (2007). Deployment-related stress and trauma in Dutch soldiers returning from Iraq. Prospective study. *The British Journal of Psychiatry, 191,* 140–145. doi:10.1192/bjp.bp.106.034884

Erbes, C., Westermeyer, J., Engdahl, B., & Johnsen, E. (2007). Post-traumatic stress disorder and service utilization in a sample of service members from Iraq and Afghanistan. *Military Medicine, 172,* 359–363.

Galea, S., Ahern, J., Resnick, H., Kilpatrick, D., Bucuvalas, M., Gold, J., & Vlahov, D. (2002). Psychological sequelae of the September 11 terrorist attacks in New York City. *The New England Journal of Medicine, 346,* 982–987. doi:10.1056/NEJMsa013404

Gaylord, K. M., Cooper, D. B., Mercado, J. M., Kennedy, J. E., Yoder, L. H., & Holcomb, J. B. (2008). Incidence of posttraumatic stress disorder and mild traumatic brain injury in burned service members: Preliminary report. *Journal of Trauma: Injury, Infection, and Critical Care, 64,* S200–205; discussion S205–206.

Greenberg, K. J., & Dratel, J. L. (2005). *The torture papers: The road to Abu Ghraib.* New York, NY: Cambridge University Press.

Grieger, T. A., Cozza, S. J., Ursano, R. J., Hoge, C., Martinez, P. E., Engel, C. C., & Wain, H. J. (2006). Posttraumatic stress disorder and depression in battle-injured soldiers. *The American Journal of Psychiatry, 163,* 1777–1783. doi:10.1176/appi.ajp.163.10.1777

Harley, N. H., Foulkes, E. C., Hilborne, L. H., Hudson, A., Anthony, C. R., & RAND National Defense Research Institute. (1999). *A review of the scientific literature as it pertains to Gulf War Illnesses. Volume 7: Depleted uranium.* Santa Monica, CA: RAND.

Helmer, D. A., Rossignol, M., Blatt, M., Agarwal, R., Teichman, R., & Lange, G. (2007). Health and exposure concerns of veterans deployed to Iraq and Afghanistan. *Journal of Occupational and Environmental Medicine, 49,* 475–480. doi:10.1097/JOM.0b013e318042d682

Hoge, C. W. (2008). Re: Psychiatric diagnoses in historic and contemporary military cohorts: Combat deployment and the healthy warrior effect. *American Journal of Epidemiology, 168,* 1095–1096; author reply 1096–1098. doi:10.1093/aje/kwn261

Hoge, C. W., Auchterlonie, J. L., & Milliken, C. S. (2006). Mental health problems, use of mental health services, and attrition from military service after returning from deployment to Iraq or Afghanistan. *JAMA, 295*, 1023–1032. doi:10.1001/jama.295.9.1023

Hoge, C. W., & Castro, C. A. (2006). Post-traumatic stress disorder in UK and US forces deployed to Iraq. *Lancet, 368*, 837. doi:10.1016/S0140-6736(06)69315-X

Hoge, C. W., Castro, C. A., Messer, S. C., McGurk, D., Cotting, D. I., & Koffman, R. L. (2004). Combat duty in Iraq and Afghanistan, mental health problems, and barriers to care. *The New England Journal of Medicine, 351*, 13–22. doi:10.1056/NEJMoa040603

Hoge, C. W., McGurk, D., Thomas, J. L., Cox, A. L., Engel, C. C., & Castro, C. A. (2008). Mild traumatic brain injury in U.S. Soldiers returning from Iraq. *The New England Journal of Medicine, 358*, 453–463. doi:10.1056/NEJMoa072972

Hoge, C. W., Terhakopian, A., Castro, C. A., Messer, S. C., & Engel, C. C. (2007). Association of posttraumatic stress disorder with somatic symptoms, health care visits, and absenteeism among Iraq war veterans. *The American Journal of Psychiatry, 164*, 150–153. doi:10.1176/appi.ajp.164.1.150

Hotopf, M., Hull, L., Fear, N. T., Browne, T., Horn, O., Iversen, A., . . . Wessely, S. (2006). The health of UK military personnel who deployed to the 2003 Iraq war: A cohort study. *The Lancet, 367*, 1731–1741. doi:10.1016/S0140-6736(06)68662-5

Jacobson, I. G., Ryan, M. A., Hooper, T. I., Smith, T. C., Amoroso, P. J., Boyko, E. J., . . . Bell, N. S. (2008). Alcohol use and alcohol-related problems before and after military combat deployment. *JAMA, 300*, 663–675. doi:10.1001/jama.300.6.663

Jakupcak, M., Luterek, J., Hunt, S., Conybeare, D., & McFall, M. (2008). Post-traumatic stress and its relationship to physical health functioning in a sample of Iraq and Afghanistan War veterans seeking postdeployment VA health care. *Journal of Nervous and Mental Disease, 196*, 425–428. doi:10.1097/NMD.0b013e31817108ed

Karney, B. R., Ramchand, R., Osilla, K. C., Calderone, L. B., & Burns, R. M. (2008). Predicting the immediate and long-term consequences of post-traumatic stress disorder, depression, and traumatic brain injury in veterans of Operation Enduring Freedom and Operation Iraqi Freedom. In T. L. Tanielian, L. Jaycox, & Rand Corporation (Eds.), *Invisible wounds of war: Psychological and cognitive injuries, their consequences, and services to assist recovery* (pp. 119–166). Santa Monica, CA: RAND.

Kessler, R. C., Chiu, W. T., Demler, O., Merikangas, K. R., & Walters, E. E. (2005). Prevalence, severity, and comorbidity of 12-month *DSM-IV* disorders in the National Comorbidity Survey Replication. *Archives of General Psychiatry, 62*, 617–627. doi:10.1001/archpsyc.62.6.617

Killgore, W. D. S., Cotting, D. I., Thomas, J. L., Cox, A. L., McGurk, D., Vo, A. G., . . . Hoge, C. W. (2008). Post-combat invincibility: Violent combat experiences are associated with increased risk-taking propensity following deployment. *Journal of Psychiatric Research, 42,* 1112–1121. doi:10.1016/j.jpsychires.2008.01.001

King, D. W., King, L. A., Gudanowski, D. M., & Vreven, D. L. (1995). Alternative representations of war zone stressors: Relationships to posttraumatic stress disorder in male and female Vietnam veterans. *Journal of Abnormal Psychology, 104,* 184–196. doi:10.1037/0021-843X.104.1.184

King, L. A., King, D. W., Vogt, D. S., Knight, J., & Samper, R. E. (2006). Deployment Risk and Resilience Inventory: A collection of measures for studying deployment-related experiences of military personnel and veterans. *Military Psychology, 18,* 89–120. doi:10.1207/s15327876mp1802_1

Kolkow, T. T., Spira, J. L., Morse, J. S., & Grieger, T. A. (2007). Post-traumatic stress disorder and depression in health care providers returning from deployment to Iraq and Afghanistan. *Military Medicine, 172,* 451–455.

Kulka, R. A., Schlenger, W. E., Fairbank, J. A., Jordan, B. K., Weiss, D., & Cranston, A. (1990). *The National Vietnam Veterans Readjustment Study: Table of findings and appendices.* New York, NY: Bruner/Mazel.

Lapierre, C. B., Schwegler, A. F., & Labauve, B. J. (2007). Posttraumatic stress and depression symptoms in soldiers returning from combat operations in Iraq and Afghanistan. *Journal of Traumatic Stress, 20,* 933–943. doi:10.1002/jts.20278

Larson, G. E., Highfill-McRoy, R. M., & Booth-Kewley, S. (2008). Psychiatric diagnoses in historic and contemporary military cohorts: Combat deployment and the healthy warrior effect. *American Journal of Epidemiology, 167,* 1269–1276. doi:10.1093/aje/kwn084

Martin, C. B. (2007). Routine screening and referrals for PTSD after returning from Operation Iraqi Freedom in 2005, U.S. Armed Forces. *Medical Surveillance Monthly Report, 14,* 2–7.

Mazzetti, M. (2008, July 2). Military death toll rises in Afghanistan. *The New York Times,* p. A6.

McGhee, L. L., Maani, C. V., Garza, T. H., Gaylord, K. M., & Black, I. H. (2008). The correlation between ketamine and posttraumatic stress disorder in burned service members. *Journal of Trauma: Injury, Infection, and Critical Care, 64,* S195–198; discussion S197–198.

Milliken, C. S., Auchterlonie, J. L., & Hoge, C. W. (2007). Longitudinal assessment of mental health problems among active and reserve component soldiers returning from the Iraq war. *JAMA, 298,* 2141–2148. doi:10.1001/jama.298.18.2141

Murdoch, M., Hodges, J., Hunt, C., Cowper, D., Kressin, N., & O'Brien, N. (2003). Gender differences in service connection for PTSD. *Medical Care, 41,* 950–961. doi:10.1097/00005650-200308000-00008

Murdoch, M., Polusny, M. A., Hodges, J., & O'Brien, N. (2004). Prevalence of in-service and post-service sexual assault among combat and noncombat veterans applying for Department of Veterans Affairs posttraumatic stress disorder disability benefits. *Military Medicine, 169,* 392–395.

Ouimette, P., Coolhart, D., Sugarman, D., Funderburk, J. S., Zelman, R. H., & Dornau, C. (2008). A pilot study of posttraumatic stress and associated functioning of Army National Guard following exposure to Iraq warzone trauma. *Traumatology*, *14*, 51–56. doi:10.1177/1534765608320330

Pole, N., Best, S. R., Weiss, D. S., Metzler, T., Liberman, A. M., Fagan, J., & Marmar, C. R. (2001). Effects of gender and ethnicity on duty-related posttraumatic stress symptoms among urban police officers. *Journal of Nervous and Mental Disease*, *189*, 442–448. doi:10.1097/00005053-200107000-00005

Prins, A., Ouimette, P., Kimerling, R., Camerond, R. P., Hugelshofer, D. S., Shaw-Hegwer, J., . . . Sheikh, J. I. (2003). The primary care PTSD screen (PC-PTSD): Development and operating characteristics. *Primary Care Psychiatry*, *9*, 9–14. doi:10.1185/135525703125002360

Ramchand, R., Karney, B. R., Osilla, K. C., Burns, R. M., & Calderone, L. B. (2008). Prevalence of PTSD, depression, and TBI among returning servicemembers. In T. L. Tanielian, L. Jaycox, & RAND Corporation (Eds.), *Invisible wounds of war: Psychological and cognitive injuries, their consequences, and services to assist recovery* (pp. 35–85). Santa Monica, CA: RAND.

Ramchand, R., Schell, T. L., Karney, B. R., Osilla, K. C., Burns, R. M., & Calderone, L. B. (2010). Disparate prevalence estimates of PTSD among service members who served in Iraq and Afghanistan: Possible explanations. *Journal of Traumatic Stress*, *23*, 59–68.

Rundell, J. R. (2006). Demographics of and diagnoses in Operation Enduring Freedom and Operation Iraqi Freedom personnel who were psychiatrically evacuated from the theater of operations. *General Hospital Psychiatry*, *28*, 352–356. doi:10.1016/j.genhosppsych.2006.04.006

Sanders, J. W., Putnam, S. D., Frankart, C., Frenck, R. W., Monteville, M. R., Riddle, M. S., . . . Tribble, D. R. (2005). Impact of illness and non-combat injury during Operations Iraqi Freedom and Enduring Freedom (Afghanistan). *The American Journal of Tropical Medicine and Hygiene*, *73*, 713–719.

Sayer, N. A., Chiros, C. E., Sigford, B., Scott, S., Clothier, B., Pickett, T., & Lew, H. L. (2008). Characteristics and rehabilitation outcomes among patients with blast and other injuries sustained during the Global War on Terror. *Archives of Physical Medicine and Rehabilitation*, *89*, 163–170. doi:10.1016/j.apmr.2007.05.025

Schell, T. L., & Marshall, G. N. (2008). Survey of individuals previously deployed for OEF/OIF. In T. L. Tanielian, L. Jaycox, & RAND Corporation (Eds.), *Invisible wounds of war: Psychological and cognitive injuries, their consequences, and services to assist recovery* (pp. 87–115). Santa Monica, CA: RAND.

Schneiderman, A. I., Braver, E. R., & Kang, H. K. (2008). Understanding sequelae of injury mechanisms and mild traumatic brain injury incurred during the conflicts in Iraq and Afghanistan: Persistent postconcussive symptoms and posttraumatic stress disorder. *American Journal of Epidemiology*, *167*, 1446–1452. doi:10.1093/aje/kwn068

Seal, K. H., Bertenthal, D., Maguen, S., Gima, K., Chu, A., & Marmar, C. R. (2008). Getting beyond "Don't ask; don't tell": An evaluation of U.S. Veterans Administration postdeployment mental health screening of veterans returning from Iraq and Afghanistan. *American Journal of Public Health, 98,* 714–720. doi:10.2105/AJPH.2007.115519

Seal, K. H., Bertenthal, D., Miner, C. R., Sen, S., & Marmar, C. (2007). Bringing the war back home: Mental health disorders among 103,788 U.S. veterans returning from Iraq and Afghanistan seen at Department of Veterans Affairs facilities. *Archives of Internal Medicine, 167,* 476–482. doi:10.1001/archinte.167.5.476

Smith, T. C., Ryan, M. A., Smith, B., Gackstetter, G. D., Wells, T. S., Amoroso, P. J., . . . Millennium Cohort Study Team. (2008). Re: Psychiatric diagnoses in historic and contemporary military cohorts: Combat deployment and the healthy warrior effect. *American Journal of Epidemiology, 168,* 1094–1095; author reply 1096–1098. doi:10.1093/aje/kwn262

Smith, T. C., Ryan, M. A., Wingard, D. L., Slymen, D. J., Sallis, J. F., & Kritz-Silverstein, D. (2008). New onset and persistent symptoms of post-traumatic stress disorder self reported after deployment and combat exposures: Prospective population based U.S. military cohort study. *British Medical Journal, 336,* 366–371. doi:10.1136/bmj.39430.638241.AE

Sollinger, J. M., Fisher, G., & Metscher, K. N. (2008). The wars in Afghanistan and Iraq—An overview. In T. L. Tanielian, L. Jaycox, & Rand Corporation (Eds.), *Invisible wounds of war: Psychological and cognitive injuries, their consequences, and services to assist recovery* (pp. 19–31). Santa Monica, CA: RAND.

Sundin, J., Fear, N. T., Iversen, A., Rona, R. J., & Wessely, S. (2010). PTSD after deployment to Iraq: Conflicting rates, conflicting claims. *Psychological Medicine, 40,* 367–382. doi:10.1017/S0033291709990791

U.S. Department of the Army, Office of the Surgeon General. (2004). *Operation Iraqi Freedom (OIF–II) Mental Health Advisory Team (MHAT) report.* Washington, DC: U.S. Army Surgeon General.

U.S. Department of the Army, Office of the Surgeon General. (2005). *Operation Iraqi Freedom (OIF–II) Mental Health Advisory Team (MHAT–II) report.* Washington, DC: U.S. Army Surgeon General.

U.S. Department of the Army, Office of the Surgeon General. (2006a). *Mental Health Advisory Team (MHAT–III) Operation Iraqi Freedom 04-06 report.* Washington, DC: Office of the Surgeon, Multinational Force-Iraq, and Office of the Surgeon General, U.S. Army Medical Command.

U.S. Department of the Army, Office of the Surgeon General. (2006b). *Mental Health Advisory Team (MHAT–IV) Operation Iraqi Freedom 05-07 report: Final report.* Washington, DC: Office of the Surgeon, Multinational Force-Iraq, and Office of the Surgeon General, U.S. Army Medical Command.

U.S. Department of the Army, Office of the Surgeon General. (2008). *Mental Health Advisory Team (MHAT–V) Operation Iraqi Freedom 06-08 report: Final report.* Washington, DC: Office of the Surgeon, Multinational Force-Iraq, and Office of the Surgeon General, U.S. Army Medical Command.

U.S. Department of the Army Office of the Surgeon General. (2009). *Mental Health Advisory Team (MHAT–VI) Operation Iraqi Freedom 07-09 report: Final report.* Washington, DC: Office of the Surgeon, Multi-National Force-Iraq, and Office of the Surgeon General, U.S. Army Medical Command.

U.S. Veterans Health Administration. (2005). Implementation of the National Clinical Reminder for Afghan and Iraq Post-deployment Screening (VHA Directive No. 2005-055). Washington, DC: Jonathan B. Perlin. Retrieved from http://www1.va.gov/vhapublications/ViewPublication.asp?pub_ID=1346

U.S. Veterans Health Administration, Office of Public Health and Environmental Hazards. (2008). *Analysis of VA health care utilization among US Global War on Terrorism (GWOT) Veterans. Unpublished quarterly report (cumulative through 3rd quarter FY2008).* Washington, DC: Author. Vasterling, J. J., Proctor, S. P., Amoroso, P., Kane, R., Heeren, T., & White, R. F. (2006). Neuropsychological outcomes of Army personnel following deployment to the Iraq war. *JAMA, 296,* 519–529. doi:10.1001/jama.296.5.519

Vickery, J. P., Tribble, D. R., Putnam, S. D., McGraw, T., Sanders, J. W., Armstrong, A. W., & Riddle, M. S. (2008). Factors associated with the use of protective measures against vector-borne diseases among troops deployed to Iraq and Afghanistan. *Military Medicine, 173,* 1060–1067.

Vogt, D. S., Proctor, S. P., King, D. W., King, L. A., & Vasterling, J. J. (2008). Validation of scales from the Deployment Risk and Resilience Inventory in a sample of Operation Iraqi Freedom veterans. *Assessment, 15,* 391–403. doi:10.1177/1073191108316030

Wang, P. S., Lane, M., Olfson, M., Pincus, H. A., Wells, K. B., & Kessler, R. C. (2005). Twelve-month use of mental health services in the United States: Results from the National Comorbidity Survey Replication. *Archives of General Psychiatry, 62,* 629–640. doi:10.1001/archpsyc.62.6.629

Weathers, F., Litz, B., Herman, D., Huska, H., & Keane, T. (1993, October). *The PTSD Checklist: Description, use, and psychometric properties.* Paper presented at the annual meeting of the International Society for Traumatic Stress Studies, San Antonio, TX.

2

POSTTRAUMATIC STRESS REACTIONS OVER TIME: THE BATTLEFIELD, HOMECOMING, AND LONG-TERM COURSE

JENNIFER J. VASTERLING, ERIN S. DALY, AND MATTHEW J. FRIEDMAN

Military operational deployments often involve exposure to extremely stressful events. Each service member, however, may react differently over time to deployment stressors. Posttraumatic stress disorder (PTSD), as a diagnostic entity, captures a subset of reactions to stress exposures (American Psychiatric Association, 1994), but war-zone veterans may also experience a host of other emotional and behavioral responses. Some reactions may be negative (e.g., anxiety, depressed mood, anger, guilt, irritability, increased alcohol consumption, social withdrawal; see Chapter 1, this volume), whereas others may be positive (e.g., greater appreciation for life, sense of mastery; Aldwin, Levenson, & Spiro, 1994; Maguen, Vogt, King, King, & Litz, 2006; Schnurr, Rosenberg, & Friedman, 1993). Not all negative reactions constitute clinical disorders, with some returning veterans experiencing lower intensity or lower frequency distress that may nonetheless result in functional impairment (Grubaugh et al., 2005). Psychological reactions to the battlefield may

This chapter was coauthored by an employee of the United States government as part of official duty and is considered to be in the public domain. Any views expressed herein do not necessarily represent the views of the United States government, and the author's participation in the work is not meant to serve as an official endorsement.

also change over time, with different reactions potentially following different longitudinal trajectories.

This chapter focuses on how posttraumatic stress reactions, in particular, may manifest at different times following contemporary war-zone service. Reflecting the predominant focus of longitudinal studies on the course of distress symptoms, the chapter necessarily emphasizes the potential courses of adverse reactions to war-zone participation. No single trajectory accurately characterizes the progression of posttraumatic stress reactions following exposure to extreme stress. Bonanno (2004) posited that interpersonal loss or exposure to traumatic events can result in at least four longitudinal patterns of functioning: (a) *resilience* in which immediate postexposure stress reactions are absent or very mild and quickly return to baseline; (b) *recovery* in which immediate postexposure stress reactions are at least moderately elevated but return to baseline over time; (c) *chronicity* in which reactions to trauma are severe from the outset and remain so over time; and (d) *delayed* onset in which mild to moderate postexposure reactions increase to severe, clinically significant levels over time or partially subside only to become reactivated later. Thus, as we illustrate through case examples, we suggest that the progression of posttraumatic reactions also varies among war-zone veterans.

The evidence base regarding the longitudinal trajectories of posttraumatic reactions in war-zone veterans is not yet strongly developed, however. Most of what we know about the course of posttraumatic reactions has been inferred from cross-sectional research, longitudinal studies that present aggregated data at each time point, or retrospective accounts of individual trajectories. Cross-sectional and aggregated approaches have contributed significantly to our understanding of phasic trends relevant to the longitudinal course of posttraumatic stress reactions but do not permit direct examination of how reactions change within individuals (King, King, Salgado, & Shalev, 2003). Retrospective accounts have provided critical information regarding the course of stress reactions but are potentially vulnerable to recall biases. Fewer studies model prospectively how reactions change within individuals.

From a clinical perspective, understanding how posttraumatic stress reactions unfold in returning veterans may help shape interventions appropriate to the developmental stage of the stress reaction. From a public health perspective, veterans and their families may benefit from education that helps them distinguish reactions that are more concerning from reactions at higher probability of resolving with time. Public awareness regarding potential recovery patterns could additionally help to depathologize normal and transient reactions to stress, yet aid recognition of the significant negative societal impacts of chronic stress reactions.

Each section in this chapter depicts a different time period in relation to war-zone deployment. In keeping with much of the existing literature, we provide primarily cross-sectional snapshots of possible psychological responses but, when possible, integrate data pertaining to longitudinal trajectories. Each section additionally addresses interpersonal and social contexts relevant to that chronological period and presents case illustrations.

THE WAR ZONE: EXPOSURES AND RESPONSES TO STRESS

While deployed, service members may concurrently face stressors inherent to their military mission (e.g., combat stressors) as well as home-related stressors such as separation from loved ones and learning of difficulties that their friends and families may be confronted with in their absence. Likewise, families must adjust to the service member's absence while he or she is deployed. In this section, we describe the types of stressors that service members and their families may confront during the deployment period, focusing on the many forms that stress responses may take during deployment.

Initial Stress Responses

War zones hold considerable dangers that are often recurrent, unpredictable, and ambiguous. Humans and other animal species typically react to dangers in ways that promote survival, with the specific nature of the responses differing across individuals. Collectively, these reactions constitute the *fight or flight response,* which involves biological changes that help prepare a person in danger to take action. In this regard, the stress responses many service members experience while in the theater of operations reflect a desirable adaptation to a dangerous environment. Concurrent with biological survival responses, a person in danger often becomes more alert to potential threats in the environment. At an emotional level, fear regions of the brain, together with a person's individual perceptions, translate potential danger to a range of emotional responses, including fear, alarm, anxiety, horror, helplessness, and disgust, or, conversely, emotional detachment (Hathaway, Boals, & Banks, 2009).

The battlefield differs from many other life-threatening contexts. Dangers often persist for days or months at a time, potentially leading to prolonged stress responses. Such unremitting stress is thought to take an increased emotional and physiological toll because there are limited opportunities to recover (McEwen, 1998). While deployed, service members may also experience other, non-life-threatening, stressors that complicate their initial (and longer term) stress responses. For example, both home-front concerns and the more generically "malevolent" environment of many war zones contribute to poor psychological outcomes following deployment (Bartone, Adler, & Viatkus, 1998; King, King, Gudanowski, & Vreven, 1995; Vasterling et al., 2010). Service members may also grieve as they confront the deaths of fellow service members (Pivar & Field, 2004) or experience guilt that they survived when others did not (Hendin & Haas, 1991; Kubany, 1994). Finally, service members may face moral dilemmas that stem from tensions between typical peacetime values and broader military mission goals (e.g., taking actions necessary for survival that result in death and destruction; Grossman, 1996).

A study of combat-prepared soldiers revealed that soldiers exposed to combat-related trauma reported a range of responses to the traumatic event, including those encompassed by PTSD Criterion A2 (i.e., reacted to the trauma with fear, helplessness, or horror), as well as non-A2 reactions such as occupationally relevant statements (e.g., "I did what I was trained to do") and anger (Adler, Wright, Bliese, Eckford, & Hoge, 2008). Thus, as suggested by Adler et al. (2008) and as depicted in the case illustrations that follow, even at an early stage, individuals may react differently to the same stressor. Of particular relevance to the subsequent longitudinal progression of posttraumatic distress, Adler et al.'s findings further indicate that soldiers responding with training-related statements and other non-A2 responses were as likely to report clinically significant PTSD symptoms as those reporting A2 responses, suggesting that a variety of initial responses, including those seemingly devoid of emotional content, may precede clinically significant outcomes.

Interpersonal and Social Context

While deployed, service members may feel a loss of social support due to separation from family and nondeployed friends. Deployed women may confront uncomfortable social situations reflective of being embedded in a predominantly male military context. However, the focus in the war zone on shared missions, dangers, and positive diversions and the vital necessity of working as a team lead some servicemen and servicewomen to bond closely with other members in their military units while deployed (Hosek, Kavanagh, & Miller, 2006). Unit support (i.e., the extent to which service members feel supported by their leaders and other unit members) and cohesion (i.e., the sense of overall organizational cohesiveness and camaraderie within the unit) have proven important in protecting military personnel against stress (e.g., Iversen et al. 2008; Oliver, Harman, Hoover, Hayes, & Pandhi, 1999; Rona et al., 2009).

The U.S. Army Morale, Welfare, and Recreation Command documented the stressors family members confront while service members are deployed

(Booth, Segal, & Bell, 2007). Partners of deployed service members often assume all household responsibilities with little time to prepare, including caring for children or elderly family members. Loved ones may also be confronted with loneliness and worry over the safety of the deployed service member. Children may have particular trouble understanding and adjusting to a lengthy parental absence, potentially leading to trouble in school and social interactions. Finances may also be stretched during this time. Not surprisingly, those left at home may feel lonely, anxious, frustrated, and overwhelmed (Eaton et al., 2008; McFarlane, 2009; Slone & Friedman, 2008).

In contrast to many past military conflicts, deployed service members and their families can now often communicate via e-mail, cell phone, video streams, and Web blogs on a fairly regular and immediate basis. The ultimate impact of such immediate communication on service members and their family and friends, however, is unknown. Immediate communication potentially offers enhanced reassurances of well-being and social support for both deployed service members and their loved ones at home. However, bad news, or the possibility of bad news, may reach home prematurely and without warning. Similarly, it may distract mission-focused deployed service members to learn of financial, health, and other problems confronting those at home. Immediate communication within the context of unstable or dysfunctional relationships may create additional stress.

Case Illustrations: Exposures and Initial Responses

Chris and Carla, both in their early 20s, deploy to Iraq from the same regular active-duty Army brigade combat team. Sam is activated at age 34 from the National Guard and stationed at the same forward operating base as Chris and Carla. The base receives almost daily incoming artillery fire. When sent to complete missions in the city, Chris, Carla, and Sam confront the constant possibility of armed insurgents dressed as civilians and improvised explosive devices (IEDs) on the road. They never let their guard down. During one trip in which the three travel together, a Humvee ahead rolls over an IED. The IED detonates on contact. As first on the scene, Chris, Carla, and Sam conduct the initial rescue of survivors. They find only one survivor, who is severely injured. Chris is horrified. Carla is oddly detached and feels a stunned disbelief, tinged with anger at the enemy. Sam has lost two of his friends and is immediately overwhelmed by profound sadness.

These cases depict how, even at this early-stage stress response, individual reactions to the same stressor vary. Although the IED explosion is a particularly vivid event, the cases also illustrate the unremitting nature of other war-zone stressors (e.g., daily incoming fire, uncertainty of danger) that can lead to constant vigilance and other prolonged responses.

HOMECOMING: ACUTE RESPONSES AND IMMEDIATE CONSEQUENCES OF DEPLOYMENT

Service members returning from war may be filled with joyful anticipation of reunions with family and friends, relief at being out of harm's way, and excitement to return to a treasured way of life. However, transitioning from life in a combat zone to the expectations and experiences of the civilian world can be complicated. This section focuses on the homecoming period.

Common Early Reactions

At best, the transition from the war zone to the home front can present unique challenges (e.g., dividing up household responsibilities, reestablishing intimacy); at worst, transitional demands may feel insurmountable (e.g., inability to engage with anyone who did not serve). Returning veterans may also continue to exhibit emotional, behavioral, and physiological reactions first expressed while deployed. Because war-zone demands may have prevented service members from attending to their reactions during deployment, for some returning veterans, homecoming may be the first time they notice their own stress responses. For others, psychological distress may only begin to emerge during this period. Therefore, mixed with the positive feelings that often accompany returning home, service members may experience undesirable stress-related reactions, such as irritability, nervousness, sleep disturbance, and difficulty concentrating. In a sample of Army volunteers surveyed during a reintegration training program after returning from Iraq or Afghanistan, nearly half reported clinically significant levels of depressive symptoms, posttraumatic stress symptoms, or both (Lapierre, Schwegler, & LaBauve, 2007). Another study noted that 19% of Iraq war veterans and 11% of Afghanistan war veterans reported clinically significant mental health difficulties immediately post-deployment (Hoge, Auchterlonie, & Milliken, 2006). As in the more general veteran population receiving Department of Veterans Affairs (VA) health care (Grubaugh et al., 2005), we have observed a significant subset of recently returned veterans who experience adjustment problems that do not reach the threshold for a clinical diagnosis.

To appreciate the challenges returnees face as they transition from the battlefield to the home front, it is important to understand the demands of a war zone. All service members must learn skills that are essential, but specific, to survival in a combat environment; these same skills, if not sufficiently adapted, can lead to significant problems upon returning home. This notion is captured by the U.S. Army "Battlemind" concept, which emphasizes, for example, that the targeted aggression required in a war zone is not the same as inappropriate aggression toward others in the civilian world and that the emotional control and mental toughness required to function effectively in combat can be problematic if applied to family and interpersonal relationships (see Chapter 9, this volume, for descriptions of programs across service branches). Thus, especially in the initial weeks and months following deployment, a service member's seemingly concerning or unexpected postdeployment behaviors may not signal a pathological reaction to deployment but instead reflect the persistent and inappropriate application of effective battlefield survival skills to a civilian context.

The interpretation of posttraumatic reactions by the veteran and others in the veteran's community during this transitional period may be particularly important. Immediate postreturn reactions to war-zone trauma, such as occasional intrusive thoughts, a tendency to avoid talking about traumatic events, and feeling hyperalert, are not unusual and in our experience often dissipate with time (consistent with Bonanno's resilience or recovery courses, depending on the extent of immediate postreturn distress). At the same time, however, veterans and families must be aware that if symptoms are severe, persist, or cause functional impairment, they may be warning signs of a more problematic posttraumatic course in need of intervention.

Coping strategies, social support, and other individual and environmental resources available during this transitional phase may influence future outcomes (Hobfoll et al., 1991). Research examining early symptom predictors of subsequent psychological outcomes indicates that veterans who have clinical presentations predominated by high arousal may be at particular risk of further development of PTSD and other psychological symptoms (e.g., Schell, Marshall, & Jaycox, 2004; Solomon, Horesh, & Ein-Dor, 2009; Thompson et al., 2004). Thus, homecoming represents a window of opportunity to help returning veterans and their families understand the veteran's experience and manage their reactions, as well as address signs of distress, such as arousal, that may forecast subsequent difficulties.

Interpersonal and Social Context

The return of a deployed service member may significantly affect the family, interpersonal network, and community to which he or she returns. As shown in the cases of Carla and Sam, families and friends must readjust to their loved one's presence, reestablish routines, and, at the same time, cope with possible emotional and behavioral changes displayed by the returning veteran. Families and friends may also place unrealistic demands on the returning veteran, increasing his or her stress.

The current wars in Iraq and Afghanistan have led to deployments of large numbers of Reserve and National Guard troops. The National Military Family Association has referred to these families as the "suddenly military," reflecting the challenges reservists may face when transitioning quickly from a civilian to a military way of life and back again (National Military Family Association, 2006). Compared with regular active-duty families, Reserve and National Guard families may remain in relative isolation from others who understand the military context and the effects of deployment and homecoming. The return home can also be complicated for reservists by an immediate return to the civilian workforce. Although a veteran may be guaranteed a job upon return, the specific position may be different, presenting additional challenges for reintegration. Highlighting the negative impact of homecoming stressors on reservists, a study of U.K. reservists deployed to Iraq found that homecoming stressors affected posttraumatic distress more strongly than did war-zone stressors (Browne et al., 2007). Our own longitudinal work indicated that stressful life events experienced during the homecoming period were more strongly associated with increases in posttraumatic distress from pre- to postdeployment among National Guard, compared with regular active-duty, soldiers (Vasterling et al., 2010), suggesting that activated reservists may be particularly vulnerable to homecoming stress.

Societal reactions to returning veterans during the homecoming period may also affect the veteran's long-term adjustment. For example, the retrospective report of "homecoming stress," including shame, was correlated with current PTSD symptoms in Vietnam veterans (Fontana & Rosenheck, 1994; Johnson et al., 1997). Since the Vietnam War, our society has made great progress in its attitude toward returning war-zone veterans, but political debates about the country's ongoing involvement in war may still lead to actual or perceived rejection of the combat veteran (Fontana & Rosenheck, 1994; Johnson et al., 1997). In addition, when community members lack knowledge about a veteran's experiences and reactions, establishing an appropriate platform for constructive discourse may be problematic (Slone & Friedman, 2008).

Case Illustrations: Transitioning Home

Chris and Carla return from Iraq together. After 2 weeks at their military installation, they are allowed extended leave. Chris uses his vacation to visit family. When he returns, his parents and older brother, Joe, excitedly welcome him back. Chris spends much of his time sharing deployment stories with Joe, who was deployed during the 1991 Gulf War. However, Chris is now uncomfortable in contexts he once enjoyed. He feels overwhelmed by crowds and makes excuses during a baseball game to leave his seat to stand in an open concourse. Chris feels frustrated that he is unable to sleep and sometimes awakens with his heart racing. He thinks about the IED attack at times, especially when he hears a sudden noise. He cannot believe that two soldiers died in the attack, but he is relieved that he and his buddies saved Jim, the third soldier in the

Humvee. When Chris calls Jim, he learns that he is in rehabilitation but doing a lot better. Chris feels awkward talking with anyone about what he is experiencing but mentions it to Joe and to Carla when she calls.

Carla's boyfriend lives in town, and she stays with him often. Carla, an only child, was never close to her parents. She has had nightly dreams about the IED attack, and the face of one of the dead soldiers she helped to remove from the Humvee, John, keeps popping into her mind unexpectedly. She did not know John well, but she knows John had a wife and child. Every time she sees a family, she tears up and wonders about John's family. Carla starts making excuses not to spend as many nights with her boyfriend. She is embarrassed that she screams at night. Before she deployed, Carla had thought she and her boyfriend would get married, but she no longer feels close to him. She calls Chris and feels like he is the only person who understands.

After a brief demobilization process, Sam returns home to his wife, Jane, and their two young children. He has looked forward to seeing his family, especially his children, who have changed so much since he deployed a year ago. Jane is excited to see him and finally have a partner to help with the many chores she managed alone for so long. Their 5-year-old son has been more aggressive and defiant since Sam deployed, and Jane hopes that Sam can take over disciplining him because she is exhausted from working and caring for the children by herself. Sam, however, feels extremely angry and irritable most of the time. He avoids his children because he fears his own anger. He starts going to a local bar by himself. Sam cannot shake the memory of the IED explosion. He was initially assigned to the first vehicle that day, but he switched vehicles at the last minute. He tells himself, "It should have been me" and feels intense guilt and shame that he survived and his two buddies died.

In each case, homecoming is accompanied by posttraumatic stress reactions, some continued from the war-zone and some new. Although the reactions continue to take different forms among the three (e.g., loss of pleasure in certain activities, reexperiencing symptoms, sleep disturbance, anger dyscontrol, guilt, emotional detachment, social withdrawal), Chris, Carla, and Sam are all affected to varying degrees by the stress of the deployment and their reintegration back home. We can also begin to see the different contexts to which people return, and how these contexts may facilitate—or, conversely—complicate recovery. Likewise, different coping strategies (e.g., seeking social support, avoidance, alcohol use) begin to emerge among the three returnees. Although troubling, the reactions at this stage do not necessarily forecast chronic problems. For Chris, his mild reactions may stay mild or diminish further (Bonanno's resilience trajectory), or they may increase (Bonanno's delayed onset trajectory). Likewise, Carla and Sam's more significant early reactions may also evolve differently over time, with the potential to recover (Bonanno's recovery trajectory) or persist or worsen (Bonanno's chronicity trajectory). In the next section, we review the varied ways in which the subsequent course of posttraumatic reactions may evolve.

CONTINUED BATTLE ON THE HOME FRONT: PROLONGED AND RECURRENT STRESS RESPONSES

Long-Term Trajectories

If findings generated by studies of mental health outcomes of prior wars (e.g., Kulka et al. 1990; Toomey et al., 2007) hold for the wars in Iraq and Afghanistan, only a subset of veterans will experience clinically significant stress-related problems in the long term. For the majority of returning veterans, difficulties experienced during homecoming and the initial readjustment period will be transient and resolve with the use of existing support networks and effective coping strategies. However, for many returning veterans, difficulties will persist, increase, or recur after a period of resolution.

Given the relative recency of the wars in Iraq and Afghanistan, longitudinal studies of longer term psychological outcomes in this population are not yet available. However, two short-term longitudinal studies provide information relevant to the timing of postdeployment assessments. In the first, Bliese et al. (2007) assessed 509 Army soldiers within the 7-day reintegration period and again approximately 4 months later. The results revealed that most soldiers reported higher rates of psychological symptoms at 4 months postdeployment than at immediate reintegration. The overall increase was attributed to relatively few soldiers (3%) showing recovery over time combined with a relatively large proportion (15%) of soldiers who were nonsymptomatic at reintegration becoming symptomatic over time.

A larger study of 88,235 Army soldiers returning from Iraq likewise revealed that significant numbers of soldiers experienced posttraumatic distress, with 20% of regular active-duty soldiers and 42% of reserve component soldiers identified across the two assessment sessions as requiring mental health treatment (Milliken, Auchterlonie, & Hoge, 2007). Although the overall trend in the sample indicated that posttraumatic distress increased significantly over time on several mental health measures, a sizable subset of soldiers (49% of activated reservists and 59% of regular active-duty soldiers) reported symptomatic improvement over the 6-month period independently of treatment status.

The findings of Bliese et al. (2007) and Milliken et al. (2007) point to significant fluctuations in reports of posttraumatic distress within a relatively short time frame following return from deployment. There are several potential explanations for the findings, including both actual changes in distress, as well as the influence of contextual factors (e.g., the excitement of being home, concerns that reporting distress may interfere with scheduled leave time) on self-report during the immediate reintegration. Relatedly, the findings suggest that repeated assessments may be necessary to detect difficulties within the first few months following return from deployment.

Prior research on the longer term outcomes of veterans of previous wars allows us to speculate on the potential course of difficulties in the current cohort of returning combat veterans. A retrospective study of longitudinal trajectories among 530 Vietnam veterans suggests that a significant number of veterans will develop chronic distress (Schnurr, Lunney, Sengupta, & Waelde, 2003). In this study, approximately 45% of the sample met criteria for a lifetime diagnosis for either full (31%) or partial (15%) PTSD. Of those with full or partial lifetime PTSD diagnoses, the majority described chronic PTSD symptoms, with 49% describing the early development of chronic symptoms, 24% reporting a chronic course with intermittent symptoms, and 9% reporting delayed onset of symptoms that later became chronic. Only 18% of those experiencing full or partial PTSD at some point in their lives reported full remission. These results underscore two important concepts relative to longitudinal progression: (a) posttraumatic distress is dynamic, often changing over time; and (b) distress trajectories are not uniform across individuals.

Prospective studies of combat veterans have likewise demonstrated varying posttraumatic symptom trajectories. Orcutt, Erickson, and Wolfe (2004) found that veterans of the 1991 Gulf War generally fell into two groups: those who maintained low levels of PTSD symptoms across time (akin to Bonanno's resiliency trajectory), and those who reported higher initial symptoms that increased over time (akin to Bonanno's chronicity trajectory). Examinations of World War II and Korean conflict veterans in later life have provided additional evidence of the potential for chronic PTSD by demonstrating that PTSD symptoms may persist, or even increase, over repeated measurements occurring several decades after trauma exposure (Dirkzwager, Bramsen, & Van Der Ploeg, 2001; Port, Engdahl, & Frazier, 2001). When examined prospectively, veterans with PTSD reported greater psychological and physical symptom increases at retirement, relative to veterans never exposed to trauma or trauma-exposed veterans without PTSD (Schnurr, Lunney, Sengupta, & Spiro, 2005).

As suggested by Schnurr et al.'s (2003) finding of a sizable subset of individuals with an intermittent, yet chronic, course of PTSD, symptoms do not necessarily follow a linear trajectory. A study rare in its inclusion of multiple spaced assessments over a long (20-year) time period likewise demonstrated a fluctuating course of PTSD in Israeli veterans of the 1982 Lebanon War (Solomon & Mikulincer, 2006). Rates of PTSD decreased from immediately postwar to 3 years postwar but rose again 17 years later. Schnurr et al. (2003)'s findings also highlighted that the onset of PTSD may be delayed. A review of studies examining PTSD course indicated that delayed-onset PTSD was prevalent (38%) in military populations (Andrews, Brewin, Philpott, & Stewart, 2007), one study indicating that, among men, combat trauma was more likely to result in delayed onset than other trauma types (Prigerson, Maciejewski, & Rosenheck, 2001). Nonetheless, delayed-onset PTSD with no prior symptoms appears to be rare, with most cases representing an exacerbation of prior symptoms (Andrews et al., 2007). Of concern in regard to multiple deployments, reactivation of symptoms may be especially likely to occur in response to subsequent stress exposure or reexposure (Toren, Wolmer, Weizman, Magal-Vardi, & Laor, 2002).

Associated Difficulties

Although many of the research studies reported in this chapter focus on posttraumatic stress symptoms, we would be remiss not to mention that other psychosocial problems may likewise arise and fluctuate over time. Drawing from cross-sectional studies, we know, for example, that the majority of individuals in the general U.S. population with lifetime diagnoses of PTSD also meet criteria for at least one other psychiatric diagnosis (Kessler et al., 1995). The prevalence of depressive symptoms and substance use in Operation Enduring Freedom (OEF) and Operation Iraqi Freedom (OIF) veterans is likewise elevated (see Chapter 1, this volume). However, relatively little is known about the course of depressive symptoms and substance use problems following traumatic exposure and how their courses may intersect with the course of PTSD. Chilcoat and Breslau (1998) found that longitudinal relationships between substance use disorders could be best explained by a self-medication framework in which individuals with PTSD use alcohol and drugs as a way to "treat" their symptoms. A prospective investigation of 1991 Gulf War veterans also supported a self-medication framework to explain the relationship between PTSD and drug abuse but not alcohol abuse (Shipherd, Stafford, & Tanner, 2005).

Longitudinal studies of PTSD and physical health in military veterans suggest that PTSD leads to negative health outcomes (e.g., Boscarino, 2008; Kubzansky, Koenan, Spiro, Vokonas, & Sparrow, 2007; Spiro et al., 2006). In a 20-year study of Israeli veterans of the 1982 Lebanon War, veterans with acute combat stress reactions reported poorer health across all time points relative to those with similar combat exposure but no acute reaction; furthermore, posttraumatic stress symptoms in the first few years after the war were associated with a slower trajectory of improvement in reported physical health (Benyamini, Ein-Dor, Ginzburg, & Solomon, 2009). Most work examining PTSD and health outcomes in OEF–OIF samples has been cross-sectional; however, Vasterling et al. (2008) reported that more severe postdeployment posttraumatic stress symptoms were associated with pre- to postdeployment declines in health-related functioning via their impact on health complaints.

Interpersonal and Social Context

Over time, the returning veteran's psychological functioning and the integrity of his or her social support network may exert bidirectional impact. In a meta-analytic study of risk factors for PTSD, Brewin, Andrews, and Valentine (2000) found that social support was associated with protective effects against development of PTSD, regardless of whether the findings were derived from cross-sectional or longitudinal designs. However, longitudinal studies have also suggested that psychological distress, including posttraumatic stress symptoms, leads to loss of social support over time (e.g., King, Taft, King, Hammond, & Stone, 2006; Solomon & Mikulincer, 1990). A longitudinal study of disaster survivors (Kaniasty & Norris, 2008) indicated that in the 6 to 12 months after the disaster impact, high levels of social support led to decreased distress; however, in the 12- to 18-month postimpact period, social support was protective, but distress also began to degrade social support. From 18 to 24 months postdisaster, the relationship between social support and distress was almost entirely in the direction of distress eroding social support, suggesting that social support exerts strong protective effects early on but becomes less sustainable as trauma-related symptoms become more chronic. This may be because the symptoms of PTSD, depression, and substance misuse tend to drive would-be supporters away.

The veteran's distress may negatively affect his or her family or partner (Renshaw, Rodrigues, & Jones, 2008), who may then experience their own psychological difficulties that impede their ability to provide needed support for their returning service member (Goff & Smith, 2005). Renshaw et al. (2008) suggested that spouses report greatest symptom severity when they perceive their veteran spouse to be experiencing high levels of distress, but the veteran reports minimal symptoms. Emotional numbing has also been found to be the primary predictor of parent–child relationship quality in Vietnam veterans with PTSD (Ruscio, Weathers, King, & King, 2002). Finally, postdeployment interpersonal conflict appears to increase greatly over time following return home, with one study documenting a fourfold increase over the course of 6 months (Milliken et al., 2007).

Case Illustrations: Long-Term Adjustment

Chris completes his active-duty commitment a year after his return from Iraq. He had always planned to be a firefighter and takes the civil service examination immediately after discharge. While waiting to be hired, he lives with his brother, Joe, and works in Joe's landscaping business. Despite his initial jumpiness, Chris's discomfort gradually decreases. He now enjoys going to baseball games, clubs, and restaurants. He finds that by keeping himself on a regular daily routine of going to sleep and getting up at the same time, he sleeps better. Chris no longer experiences nightmares, although he does think about the IED attack on occasion. Chris has kept in regular contact with Jim, the soldier who survived the explosion, and they talk in detail about what happened that day.

Carla's active-duty commitment ends within a few months after her return from Iraq. Because she feels disconnected from her boyfriend, she ends the relationship and moves to a new location where she can start over. However, after she moves, Carla starts to feel worse. Without the benefit of being around other soldiers and friends, she becomes lonely and disconnected, feeling that no one can possibly understand what she has been through. Chris keeps in touch and encourages Carla to go back to school. After 2 years of bouncing from one job to the next, Carla takes his advice. While in school, she connects with a few other veterans. Gradually, she finds that she enjoys going to school; she begins to date and has started to share with others what she has experienced. Carla also has fewer intrusive images. Although she still feels sad about John's death, she no longer finds it overwhelming.

Sam continues to feel overwhelmed with guilt, shame, and anger. Jane, his wife, was initially supportive but is now frustrated and angry. Jane warns Sam that she will move out if he continues to drink. Sam tries to quit drinking but finds that when he is not drinking, he thinks more about his deployment and the friends that he lost; he quickly relapses. After Jane and the children leave, Sam becomes more depressed and hopeless. He no longer goes to bed in his room. When he does sleep, he often wakes up from a nightmare. Sam distances himself further from his few remaining friends. As Sam becomes more isolated and distressed, Jane has become concerned about how this will affect the children and reduces their visits with him. Sam's boss, a veteran, has been supportive, but because Sam has been coming in late and missing work so often, he fires Sam.

These cases demonstrate how, over time, both the nature and course of posttraumatic reactions differ across individuals. Although Chris and Carla both ultimately function well, even their courses differ. Chris showed a stress response that persisted into homecoming but was fairly mild. His course, with the support of family and friends, is largely one of resilience. Carla initially had more difficulties than Chris but eventually recovers. After some initial interpersonal difficulties, her subsequent focus on educational goals and reentry into a social network helps her cope with her war experiences. Although Sam has a family, he does not have the benefit of regular contact with those that shared his experience. In an attempt to cope, he turns to alcohol and isolates himself, which does not serve him well. Sam's course has become chronic.

CONCLUSION

Compared with investigators who have preceded us, we are better positioned to begin to piece together the psychological, behavioral, and social trajectories of service members deployed to Afghanistan and Iraq. For the first time, we are not limited to retrospective assessments obtained 15 to 20 years after demobilization, as with Vietnam veterans (Kulka et al., 1990). Pre- versus postdeployment comparisons permit an unprecedented level of confidence that reported symptoms of distress, maladaptive behavior, or family and social difficulties were not present before the direct experiencing of life threat, killing, witnessing civilian casualties, military sexual trauma, or other stressful war-zone experiences. Similarly, the initiation of postdeployment assessments soon after return from the war-zone allows us to examine the early course of stress reactions.

In this chapter, we described findings regarding the initial stress response within the war-zone theater and traced the psychological state of service members through homecoming and the later stages of reintegration. It is clear that longitudinal adaptation differs across individuals and that Bonanno's (2004) model of trajectories (i.e., resilience, recovery, delayed onset, and chronicity) provides a useful context within which to understand these data. Most of this information has relied on cross-sectional studies, retrospective accounts of individual trajectories, or longitudinal studies reporting aggregated group data at each time point. The richness of the data, however, has enabled us to explicate useful questions and hypotheses about individual trajectories and appreciate how they are moderated by social context, regular active-duty versus reservist status, and other factors.

We have a long way to go to fill in the blanks. Largely missing is research on trajectories that occur within the war zone. Much can happen during a lengthy deployment (and during repeated deployments). Resilient adaptation may be sustained throughout the deployment, resiliency may wax and wane, or adaptation may falter midway through the deployment and progress toward a state of chronicity while the service member still has to cope with another 6 months of combat. The capacity to predict nonresilient trajectories among deployed service members before homecoming might permit us to develop effective interventions that improve the reintegration process for both service members and their families. We also know little about the impact of multiple deployments on the course of posttraumatic reactions or how reintegration can be best facilitated in the face of pending deployments.

The progression of posttraumatic stress reactions presented throughout this chapter should be considered from both clinical and public health perspectives. The clinical context concerns individuals who at some point exceed a clinical threshold on a standardized screening instrument (as administered in military postdeployment assessments and VA treatment settings) or who meet psychiatric diagnostic criteria (using a standardized instrument or during a clinical evaluation). With approximately 15% to 25% of OEF and OIF veterans at risk of mental health problems (see Chapter 1, this volume), the clinical context is more familiar, and such data have constituted the greater part of this chapter.

The emotional, behavioral, and familial problems experienced by the majority of returning veterans are, however, more difficult to document because they rarely exceed a clinical threshold and do not generate a diagnosis. Such stress-related behaviors may include emotional distancing, harboring a weapon, driving at dangerous speeds, social withdrawal, or controlling behavior or overprotective parenting secondary to excessive concerns about safety and security. In the majority of cases, such behaviors will dissipate within a year (although the genuine possibility of redeployment may alter that trajectory). In other cases, such behavior may persist and escalate until it exceeds a clinical threshold such as PTSD, depression, or substance misuse. A public health preventive perspective demands that we monitor the concerns of returning veterans over time whether or not they exhibit clinical diagnoses at the point of demobilization. Current postdeployment military assessments can only give us a superficial glimpse of these trajectories. We need more fine-grained data.

A public health perspective also demands implementation of a proactive, psychoeducational approach to help returning veterans and their families recognize potentially risky behaviors, monitor them appropriately, and know where to seek further information, social support, and counseling or treatment when necessary. In addition to more traditional resources, there is a growing wealth of Internet-based material that is easily accessible and completely confidential so that concerns about stigma do not suppress information or help-seeking behavior that might abort a slide into a chronic trajectory.

Mirroring the empirical literature, most of our focus has centered on returning veterans. However, families, collectively and individually, also exhibit trajectories spanning the spectrum from resilience to chronicity. As with the returning veterans themselves, we need a better understanding of how partner, child, and family reactions are affected during various stages of the emotional cycle of deployment. Support for families is, of course, critical in and of itself. It is also important because resilient families are more likely to provide the social support that will help promote a resilient trajectory among returning veterans. Families of National Guard and other reservists who live in rural areas, and thus may have less access to institutional resources than active-duty members and less access to social support for geographic reasons, may be at greatest risk (see Slone & Friedman, 2008).

In closing, we have come far in monitoring various phases of reactions among service members who have been deployed to Afghanistan or Iraq, but there is room for improvement. Although there are a few longitudinal studies in progress, most of the data we have reported come from cross-sectional assessments. We need more information about the immediate longitudinal course in the war zone, about the trajectories of demobilized service members who never exceed a clinical threshold, and about how families do and do not adjust to the profound disruption caused by deployment of one of their members.

REFERENCES

Adler, A. B., Wright, K. M., Bliese, P. D., Eckford, R., & Hoge, C. W. (2008). A2 diagnostic criterion for combat-related posttraumatic stress disorder (PTSD). *Journal of Traumatic Stress, 21*, 301–308. doi:10.1002/jts.20336

Aldwin, C. M., Levenson, M. R., & Spiro, A. (1994). Vulnerability and resilience to combat exposure: Can stress have lifelong effects? *Psychology and Aging, 9*, 34–44. doi:10.1037/0882-7974.9.1.34

American Psychiatric Association. (1994). *Diagnostic and statistical manual of mental disorders* (4th ed.). Washington, DC: Author.

Andrews, B., Brewin, C. R., Philpott, R., & Stewart, L. (2007). Delayed-onset posttraumatic stress disorder: A systematic review of the evidence. *The American Journal of Psychiatry, 164*, 1319–1326. doi:10.1176/appi.ajp.2007.06091491

Bartone, P. T., Adler, A. B., & Viatkus, M. A. (1998). Dimensions in psychological stress in peacekeeping operations. *Military Medicine, 163*, 587–593.

Benyamini, Y., Ein-Dor, T., Ginzburg, K., & Solomon, Z. (2009). Trajectories of self-reported health among veterans: A latent growth curve analysis of the impact of posttraumatic stress symptoms. *Psychosomatic Medicine, 71*, 345–352. doi:10.1097/PSY.0b013e31819ccd10

Bliese, P. D., Wright, K. M., Adler, A. B., Thomas, J. L., & Hoge, C. W. (2007). Timing of postcombat mental health assessments. *Psychological Services, 4*, 141–148. doi:10.1037/1541-1559.4.3.141

Bonanno, G. A. (2004). Loss, trauma, and human resilience: Have we underestimated the human capacity to thrive after extremely aversive events? *American Psychologist, 59*, 20–28. doi:10.1037/0003-066X.59.1.20

Booth, B., Segal, M. W., & Bell, D. B. (2007). *What we know about families: 2007 update* (Report prepared for the U.S. Army Family and Morale, Welfare and Recreation Command). Fairfax, VA: ICF.

Boscarino, J. A. (2008). A prospective study of PTSD and early-age heart disease mortality among Vietnam veterans: Implications for surveillance and prevention. *Psychosomatic Medicine, 70*, 668–676. doi:10.1097/PSY.0b013e31817bccaf

Brewin, C. R., Andrews, A., & Valentine, J. D. (2000). Meta-analysis of risk factors for posttraumatic stress disorder in trauma-exposed adults. *Journal of Consulting and Clinical Psychology, 68*, 748–766. doi:10.1037/0022-006X.68.5.748

Browne, T., Hull, L., Horn, O., Jones, M., Murphy, D., Fear, N. T., . . . Hotopf, M. (2007). Explanations for the increase in mental health problems in UK reserve forces who have served in Iraq. *British Journal of Psychiatry, 190*, 484–489.

Chilcoat, H. D., & Breslau, N. (1998). Investigations of causal pathways and between PTSD and drug use disorders. *Addictive Behaviors, 23*, 827–840. doi:10.1016/S0306-4603(98)00069-0

Dirkzwager, A. J. E., Bramsen, I., & Van Der Ploeg, H. M. (2001). The longitudinal course of posttraumatic stress disorder symptoms among aging military veterans. *Journal of Nervous and Mental Disease, 189*, 846–853. doi:10.1097/00005053-200112000-00006

Eaton, K. M., Hoge, C. W., Messer, S. C., Whitt, A. A., Cabrera, O. A., McGurk, D., . . . Castro, C. A. (2008). Prevalence of mental health problems, treatment need, and barriers to care among primary care-seeking spouses of military service members involved in Iraq and Afghanistan deployments. *Military Medicine, 173*, 1051–1056.

Fontana, A., & Rosenheck, R. (1994). Posttraumatric stress disorder among Vietnam theater veterans: A causal model of etiology in a community sample. *Journal of Nervous and Mental Disease, 182*, 677–684. doi:10.1097/00005053-199412000-00001

Goff, B. S. N., & Smith, D. (2005). Systemic traumatic stress: The Couple Adaptation to Traumatic Stress Model. *Journal of Marital and Family Therapy, 31*, 145–157. doi:10.1111/j.1752-0606.2005.tb01552.x

Grossman, D. A. (1996). *On killing: The psychological cost of learning to kill in war and society*. New York: Little, Brown.

Grubaugh, A. L., Macgruder, K. M., Waldrop, A. E., Elhai, J. D., Knapp, R. G., & Freuh, B. C. (2005). Subthreshold PTSD in primary care: Prevalence, psychiatric disorders, healthcare use, and functional status. *Journal of Nervous and Mental Disease, 193*, 658–664. doi:10.1097/01.nmd.0000180740.02644.ab

Hathaway, L.M., Boals, A., & Banks, J.B. (2010). PTSD symptoms and dominant emotional response to a traumatic event: An examination of DSM-IV Criterion A2. *Anxiety, Stress, and Coping, 23*, 119–126.

Hendin, H., & Haas, A. P. (1991). Suicide and guilt as manifestations of PTSD in Vietnam combat veterans. *The American Journal of Psychiatry, 148*, 586–591.

Hobfoll, S. E., Spielberger, C. D., Breznitz, S., Figley, C., Folkman, S., Lepper-Green, B., . . . van der Kolk, B. (1991). War-related stress: Addressing the stress of war and other traumatic events. *American Psychologist, 46*, 848–855.

Hoge, C. W., Auchterlonie, J. L., & Milliken, C. S. (2006). Mental health problems, use of mental health services, and attrition from military service after returning from deployment in Iraq or Afghanistan. *JAMA, 295*, 1023–1032. doi:10.1001/jama.295.9.1023

Hosek, J., Kavanagh, J., & Miller, L. (2006). *How deployments affect service members*. Santa Monica, CA: RAND.

Iversen, A. C., Fear, N. T., Ehler, A., Hacker Hughes, J., Hull, L., Earnshaw, M., . . . Hotopf, M. (2008). Risk factors for post-traumatic stress disorder among UK Armed Forces personnel. *Psychological Medicine, 38*, 511–522.

Johnson, D. R., Lubin, H., Rosenheck, R., Fontana, A., Southwick, S., & Charney, D. (1997). The impact of homecoming reception on the development of post-traumatic stress disorder: The West Haven Homecoming Stress Scale (WHHSS). *Journal of Traumatic Stress, 10,* 259–277. doi:10.1002/jts.2490100207

Kaniasty, K., & Norris, F. H. (2008). Longitudinal linkages between perceived social support and posttraumatic stress symptoms: Sequential roles of social causation and social selection. *Journal of Traumatic Stress, 21,* 274–281. doi:10.1002/jts.20334

Kessler, R. C., Sonnega, A., Bromet, E. J., Hughes, M., & Nelson, C. B. (1995). Post-traumatic stress disorder in the National Comorbidity Survey. *Archives of General Psychiatry, 52,* 1048–1060.

King, D. W., King, L. A., Gudanowski, D. M., & Vreven, D. L. (1995). Alternative representations of war zone stressors: Relationships to posttraumatic stress disorder in male and female Vietnam veterans. *Journal of Abnormal Psychology, 104,* 184–195. doi:10.1037/0021-843X.104.1.184

King, L. A., King, D. W., Salgado, D. M., & Shalev, A. Y. (2003). Contemporary longitudinal methods for the study of trauma and posttraumatic stress disorder. *CNS Spectrums, 8,* 686–692.

King, D., Taft, C., King, L., Hammond, C., & Stone, E. (2006). Directionality of the association between social support and posttraumatic stress disorder: A comparative longitudinal investigation. *Journal of Applied Social Psychology, 36,* 2980–2992. doi:10.1111/j.0021-9029.2006.00138.x

Kubany, E. S. (1994). A cognitive model of guilt typology in combat-related PTSD. *Journal of Traumatic Stress, 7,* 3–19. doi:10.1002/jts.2490070103

Kubzansky, L. D., Koenan, K. C., Spiro, A., Vokonas, P. S., & Sparrow, D. (2007). Prospective study of posttraumatic stress disorder symptoms and coronary heart disease in the Normative Aging Study. *Archives of General Psychiatry, 64,* 109–116. doi:10.1001/archpsyc.64.1.109

Kulka, R. A., Schlenger, W. E., Fairbank, J. A., Hough, R. L., Jordan, B. K., Marmar, C. R., & Weiss, D. S. (1990). *Trauma and the Vietnam war generation: Report of findings from the National Vietnam Veterans Readjustment Study.* Philadelphia, PA: Brunner/Mazel.

Lapierre, C. B., Schwegler, A. F., & LaBauve, B. J. (2007). Posttraumatic stress and depression symptoms in soldiers returning from combat operations in Iraq and Afghanistan. *Journal of Traumatic Stress, 20,* 933–943. doi:10.1002/jts.20278

McFarlane, A. (2009). Military deployment: The impact on children and family adjustment and the need for care. *Current Opinion in Psychiatry, 22,* 369–373. doi:10.1097/YCO.0b013e32832c9064

Maguen, S., Vogt, D. S., King, L. A., King, D. W., & Litz, B. T. (2006). Posttraumatic growth among Gulf War I veterans: The predictive role of deployment-related experiences and background characteristics. *Journal of Loss and Trauma, 11,* 373–388. doi:10.1080/15325020600672004

McEwen, B. S. (1998). Protective and damaging effects of stress mediators. *The New England Journal of Medicine, 338,* 171–179. doi:10.1056/NEJM199801153380307

Milliken, C. S., Auchterlonie, J. L., & Hoge, C. W. (2007). Longitudinal assessment of mental health problems among active and reserve component soldiers returning from the Iraq war. *JAMA, 298*, 2141–2148. doi:10.1001/jama.298.18.2141

National Military Family Association. (2006). *Report on the cycles of deployment: An analysis of survey responses from April through September, 2005*. Alexandria, VA: Author.

Oliver, L. W., Harman, J., Hoover, E., Hayes, S. M., & Pandhi, N. A. (1999). A quantitative integration of the military cohesion literature. *Military Psychology, 11*, 57–83.

Orcutt, H. K., Erickson, D. J., & Wolfe, J. (2004). The course of PTSD symptoms among Gulf War veterans: A growth mixture modeling approach. *Journal of Traumatic Stress, 17*, 195–202. doi:10.1023/B:JOTS.0000029262.42865.c2

Pivar, I. L., & Field, N. P. (2004). Unresolved grief in combat veterans with PTSD. *Journal of Anxiety Disorders, 18*, 745–755. doi:10.1016/j.janxdis.2003.09.005

Port, C. L., Engdahl, B., & Frazier, P. (2001). A longitudinal and retrospective study of PTSD among older prisoners of war. *The American Journal of Psychiatry, 158*, 1474–1479. doi:10.1176/appi.ajp.158.9.1474

Prigerson, H. G., Maciejewski, P. K., & Rosenheck, R. A. (2001). Combat trauma: Trauma with highest risk of delayed onset and unresolved posttraumatic stress disorder symptoms, unemployment, and abuse among men. *Journal of Nervous and Mental Disease, 189*, 99–108. doi:10.1097/00005053-200102000-00005

Renshaw, K. D., Rodrigues, C. S., & Jones, D. H. (2008). Psychological symptoms and marital satisfaction in spouses of Operation Iraqi Freedom Veterans: Relationships with spouses; perceptions of veterans' experiences and symptoms. *Journal of Family Psychology, 22*, 586–594. doi:10.1037/0893-3200.22.3.586

Rona, R. J., Hooper, R., Jones, M., Iversen, A. C., Hull, L., Murphy, D., et al. (2009). The contribution of prior psychological symptoms and combat exposure to post Iraq deployment mental health in the UK military. *Journal of Traumatic Stress, 22*, 11–19. doi:10.1002/jts.20383

Ruscio, A. M., Weathers, F. W., King, L. A., & King, D. W. (2002). Male war-zone veterans' perceived relationships with their children: The importance of emotional numbing. *Journal of Traumatic Stress, 15*, 351–357. doi:10.1023/A:1020125006371

Schell, T. L., Marshall, G. N., & Jaycox, L. H. (2004). All symptoms are not created equal: The prominent role of hyperarousal in the natural course of posttraumatic psychological distress. *Journal of Abnormal Psychology, 113*, 189–197. doi:10.1037/0021-843X.113.2.189

Schnurr, P. P., Lunney, C. A., Sengupta, A., & Spiro, A., III. (2005). A longitudinal study of retirement in older male veterans. *Journal of Consulting and Clinical Psychology, 73*, 561–566. doi:10.1037/0022-006X.73.3.561

Schnurr, P. P., Lunney, C. A., Sengupta, A., & Waelde, L.C. (2003). A descriptive analysis of PTSD chronicity Vietnam veterans. *Journal of Traumatic Stress, 16*, 445–553.

Schnurr, P. P., Rosenberg, S. D., & Friedman, M. J. (1993). Change in MMPI scores from college to adulthood as a function of military service. *Journal of Abnormal Psychology, 102,* 288–296. doi:10.1037/0021-843X.102.2.288

Shipherd, J. C., Stafford, J., & Tanner, L. R. (2005). Predicting alcohol and drug abuse in Persian Gulf War veterans: What role do PTSD symptoms play? *Addictive Behaviors, 30,* 595–599. doi:10.1016/j.addbeh.2004.07.004

Slone, L. B., & Friedman, M. J. (2008). *After the war zone: A practical guide for returning veterans.* Philadelphia, PA: De Capo Press.

Solomon, Z., Horesh, D., & Ein-Dor, T. (2009). The longitudinal course of posttraumatic stress disorder symptom clusters among war veterans. *The Journal of Clinical Psychiatry, 70,* 837–843. doi:10.4088/JCP.08m04347

Solomon, Z., & Mikulincer, M. (1990). Life events and combat-related post-traumatic stress disorder: The intervening role of locus of control and social support. *Military Psychology, 2,* 241–256. doi:10.1207/s15327876mp0204_4

Solomon, Z., & Mikulincer, M. (2006). Trajectories of PTSD: A 20-year longitudinal study. *The American Journal of Psychiatry, 163,* 659–666. doi:10.1176/appi.ajp.163.4.659

Spiro, A., III, Hankin, C. S., Mansell, D., & Kazis, L. E. (2006). Posttraumatic stress disorder and health status: The Veteran's Health Study. *The Journal of Ambulatory Care Management, 29,* 71–86.

Thompson, K. E., Vasterling, J. J., Benotsch, E. G., Brailey, K., Constans, J., Uddo, M., & Sutker, P. B. (2004). Early symptom predictors of chronic distress in Gulf War veterans. *Journal of Nervous and Mental Disease, 192,* 146–152. doi:10.1097/01.nmd.0000110286.10445.ab

Toomey, R., Kang, H. K., Karlinsky, J., Baker, D. G., Vasterling, J. J., Alpern, R., et al. (2007). Mental health of U. S. Gulf War veterans 10 years after the war. *The British Journal of Psychiatry, 190,* 385–393. doi:10.1192/bjp.bp.105.019539

Toren, B., Wolmer, L., Weizman, R., Magal-Vardi, O., & Laor, N. (2002). Retraumatization of Israeli civilians during a reactivation of the Gulf War threat. *Journal of Nervous and Mental Disorders, 190,* 43–45.

Vasterling, J. J., Proctor, S. P., Friedman, M. J., Hoge, C. W., Heeren, T., King, L. A., . . . Eisen, S. A. (2010). PTSD symptom increases in Iraq-deployed soldiers: Comparison with non-deployed soldiers and associations with baseline symptoms, deployment experiences, and post-deployment stress. *Journal of Traumatic Stress, 23,* 41–51.

Vasterling, J. J., Schumm, J., Proctor, S. P., Gentry, E., King, D. W., & King, L. A. (2008). Posttraumatic stress disorder and health functioning in a non-treatment-seeking sample of Iraq war veterans: A prospective analysis. *Journal of Rehabilitation Research and Development, 45,* 347–358. doi:10.1682/JRRD.2007.05.0077

II
ASSESSMENT

3

ASSESSMENT OF TRAUMA, POSTTRAUMATIC STRESS DISORDER, AND RELATED MENTAL HEALTH OUTCOMES

DAWNE S. VOGT, LISSA DUTRA, ANNEMARIE REARDON,
REBECCA ZISSERSON, AND MARK W. MILLER

There are many complexities inherent in the assessment of veterans who have served in Operation Enduring Freedom (OEF) and Operation Iraqi Freedom (OIF). Not only do many OEF and OIF veterans have histories of exposure to a range of potentially traumatic or highly stressful events, but the consequences of these exposures may manifest themselves in varied mental health problems following deployment. Therefore, the development of a comprehensive clinical case conceptualization requires an in-depth understanding of the deployment-related experiences that increase veterans' risk of mental health problems, as well as the postdeployment mental health sequelae that are most relevant for this population.

Consistent with this goal, we begin this chapter with a discussion of predeployment, deployment, and postdeployment factors that may be associated with postdeployment sequelae to provide a conceptual framework

Preparation of this chapter was supported in part by funding from the Department of Veterans Affairs (Project # DHI 05-130-3, "Further Development and Validation of the DRRI: Phase I," Dawne Vogt, Principal Investigator). Additional support was provided by the VA Merit Award Program (Mark Miller, Principal Investigator), National Center for PTSD and the Massachusetts Veterans Epidemiology Research and Information Center (MAVERIC), VA Boston Healthcare System.

for the assessment process. We then review state-of-the-art methods for the assessment of trauma exposure, posttraumatic stress disorder (PTSD), and functional impairment in OEF and OIF veterans. We conclude with a discussion of the importance of assessing motivation to change, particularly as it applies to the veteran's willingness to initiate and engage in treatment, and the importance of comprehensive assessments. To help facilitate an understanding of the clinical applicability of the information covered in this chapter, we reference the following clinical vignettes throughout our discussion.

CLINICAL VIGNETTES

"Bob" is an unemployed 25-year-old OIF Army veteran who was a medic during his recent 12-month deployment in Iraq. He returned from deployment 8 months ago and is now living with his father, a Vietnam veteran, with whom Bob has always had a tumultuous relationship. During his deployment, Bob witnessed two close friends suffer severe injury as a result of improvised explosive devices (IEDs) planted in abandoned cars, as well as the accidental shooting of a civilian adolescent Iraqi boy. Although he was not injured himself, Bob was constantly on guard when passing cars or other objects in the road, and since returning home, he has avoided driving whenever possible. He also avoids the dark, as many of his missions occurred at night, and he sleeps fitfully most nights because of nightmares related to explosives. He has maintained contact with many of the soldiers who were deployed with him. They became close buddies while deployed and now meet up weekly at a local pub to drink and rehash stories about their experiences in Iraq. Because of his tardiness due to hangovers, Bob has lost two jobs since returning from deployment. Bob's father, who struggled with alcoholism throughout Bob's childhood, is concerned about Bob's recent drinking. Bob, however, has brushed off his father's concerns. Drinking helps him to relax and makes it easier for him to participate in conversations about his deployment experiences. Otherwise, he would avoid such conversations altogether because even thinking about Iraq makes him anxious.

"Jane," a 33-year-old Army reservist and stay-at-home mother of twin toddlers, just returned from her deployment to Iraq 6 month ago. Her husband of 5 years cared for their daughters during the 10-month deployment. Although Jane was comforted knowing that she and her husband had adequately prepared their family for her temporary absence, she still found it difficult to be away from them for so long and was particularly upset about missing her daughters' first steps. She had a lonely experience while in Iraq, because she was not close to her fellow soldiers and constantly felt that she had to "prove" herself as a female soldier. The men she worked with seemed to think she was not capable of successfully carrying out her duties as an explosive ordinance disposal specialist because she was a woman. In several instances, men who had been assigned to work on her team complained about the assignment, and she overheard one man tell his peers, "She'll spend too much time doing her hair and nails to get the job done!" She also overheard a few of the men making lewd jokes about her, which made her feel particularly uncomfortable given that she was raped in her early 20s. She did not report these experiences to her superiors because the soldiers never directly harassed her, and she was concerned that her superiors would not take her seriously if she complained. Although Jane was not injured while deployed, nor did she directly witness soldiers being injured, part of her job was to take detailed reports of American troops' injuries and deaths related to explosives. Yesterday, her husband told her that she has been "different" since returning home. She is constantly irritable, easily loses her temper with the children, and seems distant from her family. When he asked if she would consider seeking professional help, Jane responded, "Only weak soldiers see shrinks—I'm fine!"

"Mike" is a married, 53-year-old National Guard veteran who, after 17 years of service and 3 years before his planned retirement from the military, was activated to serve in Iraq. Although the deployment was a surprise to both his immediate family and his family of origin, with whom he maintains strong positive relationships, they were all supportive of his service. Despite this support, as well as his own pride in serving his country, Mike worried about his ability to keep up with the younger soldiers as an older "weekend warrior." He had a difficult time while deployed. The climate was unbearably hot and dusty, and living conditions were crowded. Day-to-day living was a struggle for him, whereas his fellow troops, many half his age with previous deployment experience, appeared to acclimate much faster to the environment. Mike was sleep deprived and physically exhausted, and he felt he could not keep up with his younger peers. Despite having a good relationship with other unit members, he was preoccupied with what was occurring back home, given that his family had been experiencing financial strain before his deployment. Although he had some difficulty with moderate insomnia and mild irritability upon returning from deployment, within a couple of months, he felt back to "normal." He received a job promotion, providing his family with more financial security, and he felt that his deployment experiences helped him realize how important his family was to him. He made an effort to spend more quality time with them and began to enjoy life more than he had before his deployment. Currently, however, he fears being deployed again and worries about the toll another deployment would take on him and his family.

UNDERSTANDING THE DEPLOYMENT EXPERIENCES OF OEF AND OIF VETERANS

A number of psychosocial factors from the predeployment, deployment, and postdeployment period may contribute to OEF and OIF veterans' post-deployment mental health. The following sections review those factors that have been found to be most salient in prior research.

Predeployment Factors

Service members do not experience traumatic stressors in a vacuum, even though they may perceive and describe traumatic experiences as such. Each service member's unique history of prior life experiences is likely to influence how he or she responds and adapts to deployment stressors. It is important to note that veterans struggling with the deleterious effects of deployment-related traumatic stressors may not be aware of the ways in which their predeployment experiences, such as prior trauma exposure, may affect their reaction to subsequent stressful experiences. Therefore, they may not volunteer information about such experiences during a clinical assessment.

Gathering information about a veteran's history of exposure to stressful or traumatic life events can provide a basis for ascertaining what that veteran's baseline propensity for developing posttraumatic sequelae may have been before deployment. We know, for example, that individuals who experience multiple traumas over their lifetimes are significantly more likely than those without such experiences to develop posttraumatic stress symptoms in response to subsequent trauma exposure (Vogt, King, & King, 2007). A careful assessment of the veteran's history of highly stressful or traumatic life events, including exposure to community or domestic violence, physical assault, sexual abuse, emotional abuse, previous combat duty, loss of loved ones, and other highly stressful life events, is important when assessing the impact of deployment-related trauma on OEF and OIF veterans.

In considering Jane's experience, for example, it appears that her exposure to male soldiers' lewd jokes may have been bothersome, in part, due to her predeployment experience of rape in early adulthood. This is not to say that the jokes would not have bothered her if she did not have a rape history, but it is possible that this type of predeployment stressor may have primed her to perceive lewd jokes in a particularly threatening way. If we were to learn that Jane was not taken seriously by the police when she disclosed the rape, a further parallel could be drawn between her predeployment experience and her decision not to disclose her discomfort to her superiors while deployed, for fear of not being taken seriously. Further, such an experience could also be associated with Jane's avoidance of acknowledging or seeking assistance for her postdeployment symptoms. Jane's vignette demonstrates how an assessment of a veteran's predeployment life stressors, including the manner in which the veteran perceived, interpreted, and reacted to such stressors, may aid a clinician in gaining insight into that veteran's experience of and reaction to deployment stressors.

A second predeployment factor that clinicians should consider assessing is the veteran's childhood family environment, particularly with respect to early experiences of cohesion, accord, and closeness in the family of origin. Research has consistently demonstrated that adverse childhood experiences, including childhood abuse, lack of social support, unstable living conditions, and parental interpersonal violence, are implicated in maladaptive stress responses and the development of PTSD in veteran populations (D. A. King, King, Foy, & Gudanowski, 1996; Schnurr, Lunney, & Sengupta, 2004). Moreover, childhood adversity, defined as the presence of mentally ill or alcoholic family members, exposure to domestic violence, childhood abuse, or a combination of these, has been shown to predict the development of PTSD above and beyond combat exposure alone (Cabrera, Hoge, Bliese, Castro, & Messer, 2007). This suggests that childhood adversity and, in particular, adverse childhood family functioning, may place service members at risk for the development of maladaptive reactions in response to deployment-related trauma. Conversely, the experience of a positive, supportive, and cohesive childhood family environment has been demonstrated to act as a protective factor in the face of such stressors (McNally, Bryant, & Ehlers, 2003). This environment may provide children with the opportunity to internalize adaptive social, communication, and problem-solving skills, as well as to develop a perception of the world as generally safe and predictable. These skills and worldviews may, in turn, set the stage for adaptive functioning in response to stressful life events throughout adulthood.

Mike's vignette provides a good example of the protective role that positive relationships within one's family of origin may play. As noted in this vignette, Mike comes from a close family, and it is likely that positive family experiences during childhood contributed to his successful readjustment after returning from deployment through their impact on his ability to cope with the stress of deployment. Bob's vignette describes his historically tumultuous relationship with a father, who struggled with alcoholism throughout Bob's childhood. This history is representative of the type of childhood environment with the potential to increase one's risk of reacting in maladaptive ways to stress, as evidenced by Bob's tendency to drink when triggered by his friends' conversations about Iraq. His adverse childhood experiences may have also increased his risk of developing PTSD symptoms later in life, particularly in response to deployment stressors. Bob does appear to be struggling with such symptoms, including reexperiencing (i.e., distress at traumatic reminders), avoidance (i.e. avoiding driving), and hyperarousal (i.e., difficulty sleeping), and further clinical assessment could potentially reveal that he meets full criteria for PTSD.

As this discussion illustrates, predeployment factors can make service members vulnerable to maladaptive stress reactions in response to deployment stressors in a variety of ways. Inclusion of these factors in clinical assessments of OEF and OIF veterans may help clinicians understand both how and why individual veterans respond in such unique ways to the various types of stressors they encounter while deployed, as well as assess the varying levels of stress or vulnerability to stress that the veterans "carry" with them into their deployment experiences.

War-Zone Deployment Factors

The type of stressors on which most clinicians are likely to focus when assessing OEF and OIF veterans are those most directly related to deployment, namely, direct combat experiences. Although combat experiences may, indeed, represent some of the most stressful experiences endorsed by veterans, many additional deployment-related stressors warrant clinical attention when assessing OEF and OIF veterans. In an attempt to provide a structure for a thorough assessment of such stressors, we propose that these stressors may be conceptualized as belonging to two distinct categories: mission-related and interpersonal stressors. *Mission-related stressors* reflect stressful or traumatic experiences associated with the specific tasks and activities of deployment, as in the case of combat missions and associated warfare-related stressors. *Interpersonal stressors*, in contrast, refer to stressful or traumatic experiences that are associated with being separated from friends and family, as well as having to work and live in close quarters with other service members. Notably, both of these stressor categories have been demonstrated to be significantly associated with posttraumatic symptoms after deployment (L. A. King, King, Vogt, Knight, & Samper, 2006; Vogt, Samper, King, King, & Martin, 2008).

Mission-related stressors include combat experiences traditionally associated with warfare, as well as exposure to the aftermath of battle. Examples of combat experiences that OEF and OIF veterans are likely to endorse include being attacked or ambushed, shooting or directing fire at the enemy, witnessing injury or death, and participating in special missions, patrols, or invasions that involved these experiences. Exposure to the aftermath, or consequences, of battle may involve events such as observing or handling human remains, as well as observing other consequences of combat, such as devastated communities and homeless refugees.

Both Bob's and Jane's vignettes describe their exposure to combat experiences and the aftermath of battle, with Bob having witnessed his friends'

IED-related injuries and the shooting of a civilian boy and Jane having taken detailed reports of service members' injuries or deaths. Bob's experiences of combat and related aftermath consequences were more direct than Jane's because he personally witnessed the events when they occurred and had a personal relationship with the victims of the IED explosives, whereas Jane was informed about injuries or deaths of services members she did not personally know. Because research has demonstrated that both proximity to traumatic events (American Psychiatric Association, 2000) and having a close relationship with the victim(s) of such events (Ziaaddini, Nakhaee, & Behzadi, 2009) increase an individual's risk of developing PTSD, it is possible that Bob's experience may have placed him at particularly high risk for PTSD. Clinicians should be cautioned, however, not to underestimate the potential deleterious effects of more indirect trauma exposure, as in Jane's vignette. Because of the nature of her job, Jane may have actually experienced a longer duration of such exposure, and research has shown that prolonged exposure to trauma is also associated with posttraumatic sequelae (American Psychiatric Association, 2000).

Combat experiences and exposure to the aftermath of battle represent objective events and circumstances and do not include personal interpretations or subjective judgments of these experiences. However, factors that rely heavily on veterans' emotional or cognitive appraisal of such experiences, regardless of whether these appraisals accurately represent reality, should also be captured in the assessment. In defining the type of traumatic event that qualifies for a diagnosis of PTSD, the *Diagnostic and Statistical Manual of Mental Disorders*, 4th edition—text revision (*DSM–IV–TR*; American Psychiatric Association, 2000) describes such an event as having "threatened death or serious injury, or a threat to the physical integrity of oneself or others" (p. 467), a description that appears to capture the concept of an objective stressor. The *DSM–IV–TR* also describes the individual's response to that objective stressor as having "involved intense fear, helplessness, or horror" (p. 467), which seems to reflect the more subjective aspects of an individual's experience. Notably, a person's appraisal of potentially traumatic events is associated with that person's risk of developing PTSD in response to that event (L. A. King, King, Bolton, Knight, & Vogt, 2008), which points to the importance of addressing subjective factors in clinical assessments of OEF and OIF veterans.

Consistent with this perspective, clinicians are encouraged to attend to a veteran's level of perceived threat during deployment, reflected in the extent to which a veteran feared for his or her safety and well-being while deployed, particularly in response to the types of mission-related stressors previously discussed. Some examples of perceived threat include the fear of being unsafe, attacked, or exposed to either enemy or friendly fire, as well as concerns about encountering IEDs or becoming sick in response to vaccinations, pesticides, or pollution. Bob's fear of encountering IEDs in the road illustrates a perceived threat that is common among deployed OIF veterans. Because he personally witnessed his friends being injured by explosives, his fear of being harmed by an IED was likely rooted in a threat that was realistic while he was in Iraq. He continues to perceive this threat after returning to the United States, however, where he is significantly less likely to encounter explosives, and that perception in turn results in his avoidance of driving. Jane's story provides another example of perceived threat in that she may have perceived the soldiers' lewd jokes as threatening, particularly given her history of sexual assault. Although we do not have evidence that these soldiers intended to assault Jane or that she was otherwise physically unsafe, her mental state of feeling unsafe may have negatively affected her experience of and reaction to the variety other stressors she encountered while deployed.

Clinicians should also be cognizant of veterans' exposure to lower level stressors that may not qualify as traumatic events per se but that may render veterans more vulnerable to maladaptive stress reactions. Veterans' experience of difficult living or working environments may cause significant stress in and of themselves, as well as contribute to difficulty coping with other stressful or traumatic events experiences during deployment (L. A. King et al., 2006). Examples of difficult living and working environments that OEF and OIF veterans may report include uncomfortable climates, loud noises, crowded workspaces, long workdays, exhaustion, and lack of daily living resources (e.g., clean clothes, quality food, showers). The day-to-day stress that some OEF and OIF veterans face as the result of such difficult environments may have deleterious effects, rendering them less likely to respond adaptively to the other deployment-related stressors with which they must contend. It is notable that this particular stressor may be objective or subjective in nature (or both), in that some veterans may be exposed to objectively difficult living or working environments, whereas others may subjectively perceive their environments to be more difficult than their peers would. Mike's story illustrates this type of daily stress in that he regularly struggled with an uncomfortable climate and poor living conditions, in addition to feeling constantly exhausted during his deployment. Although his peers are described as adapting more easily than Mike to their environment, Mike's subjective perception of the environment as difficult may have impeded his ability to do his job successfully while deployed, as well as potentially strained his ability to deal adaptively with other deployment stressors.

Mike's vignette also exemplifies his perception of feeling unprepared for deployment, which is another mission-related stressor worthy of clinical attention. In addition to perceptions of the adequacy of training for the deployment experience, the concept of deployment preparedness refers to the perceived availability of necessary supplies, equipment, and protective gear during deployment. The extent to which service members feel prepared for deployment may also depend on the congruence between what they expected to occur during deployment and their actual experiences while deployed.

In addition to the aforementioned mission-related stressors, veterans may also experience a range of interpersonal stressors during deployment. Such interpersonal stressors include concerns about life and family disruptions related to deployment, general or sexual harassment, and lack of social support from military peers and leaders while deployed. As with mission-related stressors, service members may directly experience some of these interpersonal stressors as traumatic in nature, or the stressors may play a more indirect role in increasing service members' risk of maladaptive reactions to other deployment stressors.

Both Mike's and Jane's vignettes describe their experience of family-related concerns during deployment. Whereas Mike worries about his family's financial stability, Jane is distressed about missing her children's development and other important family events. These are examples of interpersonal stressors that often receive little attention in clinical assessment of OEF and OIF veterans but that may serve to distract service members from their deployment duties and generally disrupt their day-to-day functioning during deployment. Service members may worry about the deleterious effects of deployment on their relationships with significant others, as well as about their inability to be available to loved ones to offer them assistance, support, or care. These concerns may be exacerbated by deployment circumstances that render service members unable to communicate easily with loved ones back home. In addition, some National Guard and Reservist service members may worry about losing out on job advancement opportunities and experience deployment as negatively affecting their career advancement.

Another key interpersonal stressor that may have an impact on OEF and OIF veterans' adjustment during and after deployment is harassment, a term encompassing both general and sexual harassment. *General harassment* refers to harassment that is nonsexual in nature but that may occur on the basis of sex, gender role, race, ethnicity, or other personal characteristics. Examples of such harassment include indirect resistance to one's authority, deliberate sabotage, indirect threats, and constant scrutiny. *Sexual harassment* includes unwanted sexual contact or verbal conduct of a sexual nature by other service members, commanding officers, or civilians in the war zone. Such harassment can range on a continuum from gossiping about the service member's sex life to sexual assault or rape. Both general and sexual harassment can contribute to a hostile working environment and generally make day-to-day life unpleasant. In the extreme, serious forms of harassment, such as sexual assault, are often experienced as traumatic by the service member and, in turn, may lead to posttraumatic sequelae. Although both men and women are at risk of experiencing sexual harassment while deployed, research has consistently demonstrated that women are more likely to report military sexual harassment (e.g., Kimerling, Gima, Smith, Street, & Frayne, 2007). Studies investigating the prevalence of military sexual trauma have reported that approximately one quarter (Hankin, Spiro, Miller, & Kazis, 1999) to one half (Katz, Bloor, Cojucar, & Draper, 2007) of all female veterans endorse having had such experiences.

Jane's vignette depicts a deployment experience encompassing both general harassment, with respect to her male colleagues' complaints about having to work with her because she is a woman, as well as sexual harassment, given the lewd jokes they make about her. As previously discussed, these harassing experiences may cause her to feel threatened by her own unit members (i.e., perceived threat), in the context of her rape history (i.e. a predeployment stressor). Jane's experience provides an example of how the interplay of various predeployment and deployment stressors may increase an individual's vulnerability to poor mental health outcomes in response to deployment stress exposure.

Jane's deployment experiences further illustrate the importance of social support from military peers and leaders, which is another interpersonal factor that clinicians should consider when assessing OEF and OIF veterans. Social support has been demonstrated to act as a protective factor in many studies that have examined the impact of stressors on mental health outcomes, and thus it is no surprise that social support experienced during deployment can buffer the impact of stressful experiences on service members (L. A. King, King, Fairbank, Keane, & Adams, 1998). Conversely, a lack of social support can lead to poor mental health outcomes after deployment and, interestingly, this association has been found to be particularly strong for female veterans (Vogt, Pless, King, & King, 2005). In deployment contexts, *social support* refers to assistance and encouragement in the war zone by the military in general (e.g., feeling valued by the military), unit leaders (e.g., perceiving leaders as trustworthy and dependable), and other unit members (e.g., feeling a sense of camaraderie with peers). If we consider Jane's experience, which entailed her feeling lonely, being harassed by peers, and not perceiving her superiors as sufficiently trustworthy to disclose her concerns about these issues, we can logically conclude that her deployment experience was unsupportive. We can further infer that exposure to such an unsupportive deployment environment may have made it particularly difficult for Jane to deal adaptively with the additional stressors she may have experienced while deployed. In contrast, Mike's vignette illustrates the role of positive experiences of social support. Though Mike experienced his deployment as extremely stressful in many ways, the fact that he had good relationships with his peers may have contributed to an easier adjustment after returning from deployment.

In this section, we have presented a conceptualization of deployment stressors that includes both mission-related and interpersonal stressors, the latter of which may sometimes be overlooked in standard clinical assessments of OEF and OIF veteran populations. We now turn our attention to two postdeployment factors that may also play a role in veterans' adjustment following deployment.

Postdeployment Factors

The transition back home from deployment can be a difficult one for many veterans, and the nature of this transition may have important clinical implications for veterans' postdeployment adjustment. Here, we focus on two key postdeployment factors, namely, postdeployment stressors and social support, both of which have been demonstrated to be associated with postdeployment mental health outcomes (Vogt et al., 2007).

Exposure to additional life stressors in the postdeployment period may interfere with the normative recovery process of a veteran who has experienced deployment stress. When assessing postdeployment stressors, clinicians should consider gathering information about general stressful life events that are unrelated to deployment, such as physical or sexual assaults, serious illness or death of loved ones, and vehicular accidents, in addition to events that may be more directly related to reintegration, such as unemployment, legal or financial problems, divorce, and family conflict. Bob's vignette describes the difficulty he experiences maintaining a job after returning from deployment because of his drinking, which represents one example of the type of postdeployment stressor some OEF and OIF veterans may experience. Mike, in contrast, appears to experience an easier transition. He gets a promotion at work, looks forward to spending more time with his family, and does not face any major stressors when he returns, which bodes well for his postdeployment prognosis.

A second important postdeployment factor likely to be associated with postdeployment adjustment is the extent to which family, friends, coworkers, and employers, as well as the community more generally, provide emotional sustenance and instrumental assistance, or social support, to service members when they return from deployment. *Emotional sustenance* reflects the extent to which these individuals provide compassion, companionship, a sense of belonging and general positive regard, whereas *instrumental assistance* refers to the provision of more tangible assistance in the form of resources, materials needs, and help with accomplishing tasks. The importance of social support with respect to the deployment period was discussed earlier, and its importance applies to the postdeployment adjustment period as well. Mike's story stands out as representing a veteran's experience of returning to a supportive family environment, and therefore it is not surprising that he not only quickly reintegrates into his life back home but even appears to enjoy life more than he had before deployment. Bob's postdeployment experience seems to represent a more mixed experience, in that he moves back home with his father, with whom he has not had a good relationship, suggesting that he may not be a good source of support for Bob. Additionally, whereas Bob may perceive his veteran friends as supportive, the fact that he has to drink to tolerate conversations with them is problematic and suggests that they may not provide Bob with sufficient emotional support.

Both of the stressors presented here overlap with factors presented earlier in this section. Specifically, postdeployment stressors are analogous to predeployment stressors, and postdeployment social support parallels the concept of deployment social support. Such overlap points to the importance of assessing the cumulative effect of stressors on service members over time, beginning with the predeployment timeframe (as early as childhood) and moving throughout the deployment time period into the postdeployment time frame. Assessment of deployment stressors in isolation may not provide clinicians with the depth of understanding they are likely to attain by conducting a more longitudinal assessment.

In the next section, we turn to the assessment of PTSD and associated sequelae of deployment stress and trauma exposure, using the previously presented vignettes to illustrate postdeployment health problems that may be especially salient for OEF and OIF veterans.

TRAUMA AND PTSD ASSESSMENT

Many factors must be considered to ensure an adequate assessment of PTSD and associated comorbidity. These factors are discussed in the following subsections and summarized in Table 3.1.

Initiating the Assessment and Setting the Context

Given the sensitive nature of the experiences that will be disclosed, along with the fact that service members may be wary of mental health professionals, it is critical that clinicians begin a PTSD assessment with a focus on establishing rapport and building trust with the veteran. An important first step in this process is to emphasize the collaborative nature of the assessment. Developing this sense of shared purpose might begin by soliciting information from the veteran about what he or she hopes to accomplish by participating in the assessment and including this perspective when talking about what the assessment is intended to achieve. The clinician should describe what will happen during the assessment and how the assessment fits with the veteran's desire for practical help with problems. An explanation about the role of assessment in determining treatment priorities and setting treatment goals can facilitate

TABLE 3.1
Posttraumatic Stress Disorder Assessment Process

Assessment task	Strategy
Introduction	Establish rapport and build trust
	Introduce purpose of assessment and link to treatment goals
	Assess history of presenting problem and level of risk
Assess Criterion A	Traumatic Events Questionnaire
Structured clinical interviews	Clinician-Administered Scale for PTSD
	Structured Clinical Interview for *DSM-IV* (SCID)
Self-report questionnaires	PTSD Checklist
	Mississippi Scale for Combat-Related PTSD
	Minnesota Multiphasic Personality Inventory–2 (MMPI–2)
Assessment of co-occurring problems	SCID
	SCID–IV Axis II Personality Disorders (SCID–II)
	Symptom Checklist–90 (SCL–90–R)
	State–Trait Anger Expression Inventory
	CAGE Questionnaire
	Deployment Risk and Resilience Inventory
Assessment of stages of change	Use transtheoretical model to assess stages of change
	University of Rhode Island Change Assessment

the veteran's commitment to the assessment process. After establishing this shared vision, the session should shift to a more intense, data-gathering mode, with the focus on the recent history of the presenting problem(s), including any current stressors and crises. A thorough risk assessment should be conducted to evaluate the possible presence of suicidal and homicidal ideation, violent and aggressive behaviors, and substance-related problems. This information can then be used to inform the development of a treatment plan.

Importance of Comprehensive Assessment

Just as service members do not experience traumatic stressors in a vacuum, they also do not undergo assessment and treatment planning in one. Their efforts at reintegration are likely to consume significant psychological, physical, and emotional resources that can interfere with their willingness to engage in an extensive assessment process. From a clinician's perspective, a comprehensive assessment of psychological functioning takes time, and clinicians may have legitimate concerns about delaying the start of treatment or worry that veterans may terminate treatment prematurely if the assessment process is too onerous. One way to address these concerns is to use an abbreviated assessment battery. However, there are important advantages to a more comprehensive assessment.

First and foremost, an abbreviated assessment may not provide clinicians with the depth of understanding they are likely to gain through a more comprehensive assessment. By its very nature, the abbreviated assessment requires clinicians to selectively limit the number and type (structured interview vs. self-report) of instruments used, the breadth of the diagnostic evaluation, and the assessment of other domains of functioning that may materially affect case conceptualization and treatment planning. The resultant treatment plan may not accurately reflect the veteran's individual experience.

Second, a comprehensive assessment that incorporates basic psycho-education about issues of concern to the veteran can enhance veterans' commitment to treatment. Continued engagement provides veterans an opportunity to build rapport with and trust in the assessment clinician and to garner much-needed empathy and compassion. Emotional support plays an important role in postdeployment adjustment, and, to the extent that veterans are unable to access sufficient social support in their daily lives, the therapeutic relationship can provide much-needed support.

Finally, a comprehensive assessment can serve to demystify the psycho-therapy process as well as reduce the anxiety that often accompanies early work in psychotherapy. These experiences can be the building blocks of a strong working alliance and may serve the veteran well throughout both the assessment and treatment process.

Risk and Resilience Factors

As previously discussed, clinicians should be encouraged to conduct assessments of OEF and OIF veterans' history in a manner that will capture the complexity of the various risk and resilience factors veterans may have experienced before, during, and after deployment. In turn, thorough assessments of these factors can provide a more integrated clinical picture of veterans' deployment experiences and related sequelae. The Deployment Risk and Resilience Inventory (DRRI; L. A. King et al., 2006; the DRRI is available at http://www.ncptsd.va.gov/ncmain/assessment/drri_intro.jsp) is one tool that may be especially useful in this regard, given that these scales were constructed to explicitly assess each of the factors presented in the model described earlier in this chapter. The scales are designed so that they may be administered as a set or individually, giving clinicians the option to select the scales that are most relevant for their particular assessment goals. The full inventory takes approximately 40 min to complete, and individual scales can be completed in 2 to 3 min. Although there are currently no clinical cutoff scores for the DRRI, these scales may be administered as part of the intake process and can provide a useful starting point for a more in-depth discussion of factors that contribute to current symptomatology.

Identifying the Criterion—A Event

The first step in assessing PTSD is to establish that the traumatic event described by the veteran qualifies as a Criterion A event, as defined by the *DSM–IV–TR* (American Psychiatric Association, p. 467). A qualifying event must meet the following two criteria: "(1) the person experienced, witnessed, or was confronted with an event or events that involved actual or threatened death or serious injury, or a threat to the physical integrity of self or others" (p. 467); and "(2) the person's response involved intense fear, helplessness, or horror" (p. 467). The Traumatic Events Questionnaire (TEQ; Vrana & Lauterbach, 1994), which has demonstrated good test–retest reliability (Vrana & Lauterbach, 1994), is one measure that can assist clinicians in determining whether the event described by the veteran qualifies as a Criterion A event. For each of 11 specific traumatic events, the TEQ inquires about frequency and age at occurrence, as well as to what extent the respondent experienced the event as traumatic. Individuals often endorse more than one qualifying event, thereby creating uncertainty as to which traumatic event should be the focus of the PTSD assessment. Bob, for example, witnessed his friends being injured by IEDs and the shooting of an Iraqi civilian boy. Either or both of these experiences may be related to his PTSD symptoms. For situations in which multiple qualifying events are endorsed, clinicians should ask the veteran to identify the event that continues to cause her or him the most distress, and that event should be used as the index trauma for assessment purposes. This will facilitate the transition to subsequent treatment in which contemporary cognitive–behavioral therapies for PTSD, such as cognitive processing therapy and prolonged exposure, focus on one event at a time. In cases of patients with histories of multiple traumas, it is important for the psychotherapist to remain cognizant of the legacy of these other events and address them in treatment as the focus shifts over time.

Structured Clinical Interviews

After the clinician has identified the index trauma, a structured clinical interview can be administered. Structured interviews are preferred because they yield more accurate diagnoses than unstructured psychiatric interviews (Miller, Dasher, Collins, Griffiths, & Brown, 2001), can be helpful in tracking client progress during treatment, and may lead to improvements in treatment outcome (Lambert et al., 2003). Two well-validated clinical interviews for the assessment of PTSD include the Clinician Administered PTSD Scale

(CAPS; Blake et al., 1995) and the Structured Clinical Interview for *DSM–IV* (SCID; First, Spitzer, Gibbon, & Williams, 1996). These interviews are especially well suited to the assessment needs of veterans because both measures have demonstrated adequate to excellent reliability and validity for veteran populations (Keane et al., 1998; McFall, Smith, Roszell, Tarver, & Malas, 1990; Weathers, Keane, & Davidson, 2001). The CAPS is a particularly useful tool for conducting an in-depth assessment of the three primary PTSD symptom clusters (i.e., reexperiencing, avoidance and numbing, and hyperarousal symptoms) described in the *DSM–IV–TR*. Using a Likert-type response format to rate both the frequency and intensity of each of 17 PTSD symptoms, the CAPS allows for the assessment of both current and lifetime PTSD status, which may be helpful in assessing chronic PTSD. It is important to note that the CAPS also addresses other symptoms often associated with PTSD, including trauma-related guilt and dissociation. In addition, it allows for ratings of subjective distress, as well as social and occupational impairment, which contribute to an understanding about the functional impact of the traumatic sequelae.

Although the CAPS allows for an in-depth assessment of PTSD, the SCID-PTSD module may be a more practical assessment tool for clinicians with time constraints. The PTSD module can be administered in 15 to 45 min depending on the complexity of the veteran's clinical presentation, whereas the CAPS usually requires an hour to administer. The SCID (First et al., 1996) is a widely used structured clinical interview organized into separate modules for each *DSM–IV* Axis I disorder. The PTSD module is a 21-item structured interview corresponding to *DSM–IV* criteria for PTSD, in which symptoms are rated to reflect their absence or presence at a subclinical or clinical level. Given high rates of comorbidity between PTSD and other Axis I disorders (Breslau, Davis, Andreski, & Peterson, 1991; Breslau, Davis, Peterson, & Schultz, 2000; Kessler, Sonnega, Bromet, Hughes, & Nelson, 1995; Kulka et al., 1990), another advantage of the SCID is the availability of modules that assess for mood, anxiety, and alcohol use disorders. Unlike the CAPS, however, the SCID does assess symptom frequency or severity.

The specific assessment goals and the unique clinical presentation of each veteran help determine which clinical interview to employ. Given Bob's symptoms of hypervigilance, nightmares, and avoidance, for example, the CAPS might be preferable because it can provide a thorough assessment of the frequency and intensity of his symptoms, as well as of the impact of these symptoms on his daily functioning. Because Jane has a history of rape in her early 20s and was then exposed to deployment-related stressors a decade later, the CAPS could be a useful tool with which to assess PTSD symptoms over different periods in her life. In Mike's case, the SCID might be a more efficient use of time and resources because it is not immediately apparent whether Mike experienced a Criterion A event or whether he is currently experiencing PTSD symptoms.

Self-Report Measures

Many reliable and valid self-report measures are available for the assessment of PTSD symptomatology. Self-report measures, as adjuncts to structured clinical interviews, can provide useful information about domains of interest. The PTSD Checklist (PCL; Weathers, Litz, Huska, & Keane, 1991) is a 17-item self-report measure with items that correspond directly to *DSM–IV* diagnostic criteria for PTSD. The PCL, which takes approximately 5 to 10 min to administer, can be used as both a screening tool for PTSD and as a measure of symptom severity. The veteran rates how bothered he or she has been by each symptom over the past month using a Likert-type response format. A cutoff score is then employed to identify the probable presence of PTSD. Because it takes a fairly short period of time to administer, the PCL lends itself to tracking treatment progress over time and can be administered at the outset of each treatment session to monitor changes in symptom severity. The PCL has been validated with populations of veterans, car accident survivors, and sexual assault survivors (Smith, Redd, DuHamel, Vickberg, & Ricketts, 1999; Weathers, Litz, Herman, Huska, & Keane, 1993). It has demonstrated adequate test–rest reliability (Ruggiero, Del Ben, Scotti, & Rabalais, 2003) and has been shown to have good sensitivity and specificity in identifying PTSD in soldiers returning from combat (Bliese et al., 2008).

The Mississippi Scale for Combat-Related PTSD (Keane, Caddell, & Taylor, 1988) is a 35-item self-report measure for combat veterans that assesses most of the *DSM–IV* PTSD criteria, as well as other symptoms frequently associated with PTSD, including substance abuse, suicidality, and depression. The measure, which has demonstrated excellent test–retest reliability, sensitivity, and specificity (Keane et al., 1988), takes approximately 10 to 15 min to administer. Respondents are asked to report on the severity of symptoms "since the event," and, as with the PCL, a cutoff score can be used to indicate the probable presence of PTSD. A noncombat version of the measure, the Civilian Mississippi Scale for PTSD (Norris & Perilla, 1996), which has been validated in community samples, may be useful for assessing noncombat-related PTSD symptoms.

When possible, collateral information from family or friends can provide valuable information about veterans' symptoms. Their observations and perceptions can shed additional light on the functional impact of these symptoms. Of course, acquisition of collateral information requires the consent of the veteran, which may be facilitated through a discussion of the perceived benefits of such information. Ideally, this information would be obtained through in-person interviews, but collateral self-report measures can also be used. The Collateral Mississippi Scale for PTSD (Kulka et al., 1990), which is the spouse–partner–family member version of the Mississippi Scale, is one of the few collateral measures that have demonstrated adequate reliability, specificity, and sensitivity.

If time and resources permit, the Minnesota Multiphasic Personality Inventory (MMPI–2; Butcher, Dahlstrom, Graham, Tellegen, & Kaemmer, 1989) may be indicated for veterans with more complicated clinical presentations. The MMPI–2 includes a 46-item, empirically derived PTSD scale (Keane, Malloy, & Fairbank, 1984; Lyons & Keane, 1992), which has demonstrated good test–retest reliability (Herman, Weathers, Litz, & Keane, 1996). This scale is unique in that it is less face-valid than other measures of PTSD, such that veteran's responses are less likely to be influenced by social desirability or other response biases. The PTSD scale, which is highly correlated with other self-report measures of PTSD (Herman et al., 1996), can be administered in conjunction with other scales from the MMPI or as a stand-alone instrument. In addition, the MMPI–2's validity scales can provide useful information about potential over- or underreporting of symptoms. Clinicians should interpret the MMPI–2's validity scales with caution, however, given that combat veterans with severe symptoms may respond in a manner that is consistent with a "fake-bad" response, raising questions about whether these scores reflect elevated psychopathology or overreporting (Frueh, Hammer, Cahill, Gold, & Hamlin, 2000). These extreme symptom elevations may genuinely reflect the sequelae of being exposed to traumatic events. As with the use of other self-report measures, it is important that these data are interpreted within the context of other sources of information.

Assessment of Comorbidity

In populations of veterans who have been diagnosed with PTSD, studies report rates of comorbidity with other Axis I disorders ranging from 50% to 92% (Brown, Campbell, Lehman, Grisham, & Mancill, 2001; Kulka et al., 1990; Orsillo et al., 1996). PTSD also frequently co-occurs with Axis II disorders, as demonstrated by studies that have assessed the full range of range of comorbid personality disorders in samples of individuals with PTSD. For example, among a group of veteran inpatients with PTSD, Bollinger and colleagues (2000) found that 79% of their sample met criteria for an Axis II disorder, including avoidant (47%), paranoid (46%), obsessive–compulsive (28%), and antisocial (15%) personality disorders. PTSD comorbidity can complicate assessment and treatment because individuals with comorbid Axis I or Axis II disorders (or both) tend to have more severe PTSD symptoms (Back, Sonne, Killeen, Dansky, & Brady, 2003; Brady & Clary, 2003; Zayfert, Becker, Unger,

& Shearer, 2002) and may be less likely to respond well to treatment (Cloitre & Koenen, 2001; Zlotnick et al., 1999). Thus, an assessment of comorbid psychiatric disorders is an important component of any comprehensive assessment.

As a practical and time-effective way to assess for potential comorbid disorders, use of a screening measure is recommended. The SCID (First et al., 1996) offers a semistructured screening and history section that can provide information about possible comorbid conditions and the context in which the veteran's presenting complaint occurs. This screen includes probe questions that explore etiological factors, as well as previous coping and treatment efforts. If there is reason to suspect the presence of personality pathology, clinicians may also consider administering the self-report screening questionnaire (SCID–Q) included in the Structured Clinical Interview for *DSM–IV* Axis II Personality Disorders (SCID–II; Spitzer, Williams, Gibbon, & First, 1990). As a follow-up to the SCID–Q, clinicians may selectively administer relevant modules of the SCID–II to assess for specific personality disorders. The Symptom Checklist—90—Revised (SCL–90–R; Derogatis, 1983) is a time-saving measure that allows for the assessment of a broad range of psychiatric symptoms. This self-report inventory, which takes approximately 12 to 15 min to administer, requires respondents to rate how much they are bothered by 90 psychiatric symptoms using a 5-point Likert-type response format, ranging from *not at all* to *extremely*.

Beyond diagnostic symptoms and syndromes, individuals with PTSD often present with other problems that cause functional impairment and require clinical attention. Three factors that warrant special consideration when assessing veterans are an avoidant coping style, anger management problems, and substance abuse. Information about these factors can be obtained through both formal and informal means, including the use of structured and unstructured interviews and self-report measures. If the assessment takes place over multiple sessions, patients can be assigned self-monitoring tasks, similar to cognitive–behavioral homework assignments, which can provide more salient information than retrospective reporting about these factors.

Knowledge about a veteran's coping style can provide relevant information about how the individual manages stress. Veterans may employ a wide variety of coping strategies, including suppression, avoidance, active problem solving, or accessing social support. Because research shows that nonavoidant coping styles are associated with better psychological functioning for Vietnam veterans with PTSD (Wolfe, Keane, Kaloupek, Mora, & Wine, 1993), an avoidant coping style may serve as early target for clinical intervention.

Veterans with PTSD are likely to present with significant anger regulation difficulties (Taft & Niles, 2004). Anger dysregulation may have deleterious effects on many domains of a veteran's life, including his or her social and occupational functioning, and at extreme levels may be associated with violent behavior and related legal consequences. Therefore, a detailed understanding of the manner in which a veteran experiences, expresses, and copes with anger may be critical for effective treatment planning. One widely used self-report measure, the State–Trait Anger Expression Inventory (STAXI; Spielberger, 1988), contains subscales that distinguish between state and trait anger, as well as between the experience and expression of anger. This measure can be used to identify whether individuals are likely to express anger overtly versus contain it, as well as assess their ability to manage feelings of anger effectively.

Alcohol or drug abuse may be a preexisting problem for some veterans or may arise as a result of the significant stressors experienced during the deployment or postdeployment period. Veterans may begin drinking as a means to cope with uncomfortable emotions. In fact, the Millennium Cohort Study (Jacobson et al., 2008) found that Reserve and National Guard service members who endorsed combat exposure were at higher risk for new-onset heavy drinking, binge drinking, and alcohol-related problems compared with non-deployed service members. Notably, the youngest members of this cohort were at highest risk for all alcohol-related problems. The assessment of substance use problems can generally begin with informal questions about the veteran's use of drugs and alcohol. If the veteran's responses suggest significant substance use, a more formal screening measure can be employed. The CAGE questionnaire (Ewing, 1984), which was designed to screen for alcohol use but can be adapted for drug use, can elicit information regarding the quantity and frequency of a veteran's alcohol or drug use, as well as assess the functional impact of such use. For the purposes of diagnosing substance abuse and dependence disorder, the Substance Use Disorder Module of the SCID (First, Spitzer, Gibbon, & Williams, 1996) can be employed.

Other Factors to Consider

Two factors that might have a significant impact on treatment outcome are resistance to change and motivation to change. Among military veterans, there may be unique factors that promote resistance to mental health treatment. Their military training and experiences may promote self-reliance and facilitate the belief that seeking help is a sign of weakness. This issue was raised in Jane's vignette when she expressed concern that going to a "shrink" would mean that she was weak and unable to deal with her own problems. Consistent with this perspective, in a study by Hoge et al. (2004), OEF and OIF veterans reported concern that they would be stigmatized by peers and leaders if they sought help for mental health problems. Particularly emblematic is the finding that OEF and OIF soldiers who screened positive for psychiatric disorders were twice as likely to report concerns about being seen as weak or harming their career compared with those without psychiatric disorders. Furthermore, among those who screened positive for a psychiatric disorder, 38% reported that they did not trust mental health professionals. Being aware of these concerns, clinicians can offer reinforcement for veterans' efforts to seek support. From a practical standpoint, OEF and OIF veterans often have to juggle full-time jobs and family responsibilities that interfere with their ability to attend sessions regularly or to attend sessions that are only available during a 9-to-5 workweek. Scheduling flexibility may facilitate the assessment process and increase the likelihood that the veteran will follow through with treatment recommendations. In addition, motivation to change may be enhanced by building on the existing strengths of patients. For example, to the extent that a patient has supportive family members, enlisting their involvement in treatment may be particularly beneficial. Cognitive–behavioral conjoint therapy for PTSD (Monson, Fredman, & Adair, 2008; Monson, Schnurr, Stevens, & Guthrie, 2004) is an example of a treatment that involves family members in the treatment of PTSD.

The transtheoretical model (Prochaska, DiClemente, & Norcross, 1992) provides a mechanism for assessing motivation to change, particularly as it applies to one's willingness to initiate and engage in treatment. The model explicates five stages of change: precontemplation (i.e., being unaware of or denying the problem), contemplation (i.e., considering change), preparation (i.e., taking initial steps), action (i.e., changing behavior), and maintenance (i.e., sustaining changes over time). An assessment of the veteran's stage of change may be carried out in an unstructured manner by asking her or him which of the symptoms or problems identified during the assessment she or he considers to be problematic. Veterans might also be asked which symptoms or problems their friends, loved ones, or supervisors have told them they need to work on. Once the veteran identifies the key problem(s), follow-up questions can be asked to determine what steps, if any, have been taken to address these problems. Alternatively, a questionnaire may be employed to assess the veteran's motivation to change. The University of Rhode Island Change Assessment (McConnaughy, Prochaska, & Velicer, 1983), for example, is an instrument that assesses general motivation for psychotherapy, as well as an individual's motivation to change specific problems, such as problematic substance use behaviors. Notably, evidence suggests that veterans' motivation to work on symptoms in treatment may be problem-specific (Rosen et al., 2001). Using our clinical vignettes as an illustration of this phenomenon, Bob might be in the precontemplative stage of change with respect to his drinking behavior but in the preparation stage with respect to his PTSD symptoms. Clinicians should consider the level of motivation for change on treatment planning. For example, Bob may be willing to engage in combat-related exposure-based therapy to address his PTSD symptoms, but he may not be willing to talk about the negative consequences of his alcohol use or acknowledge the link between his alcohol use and PTSD symptoms. An assessment of the veteran's motivation for change can provide a clinician with useful information regarding the appropriateness of employing specific motivational enhancement techniques, such as motivation interviewing, as a component of the veteran's treatment plan.

In conclusion, a comprehensive assessment of PTSD facilitates the development of a clinical case conceptualization and salient treatment plan. Conducting such an assessment requires an in-depth understanding of not only the deployment-related experiences that increase a veteran's risk for mental health problems but also the predeployment factors that affect veterans' reactions to trauma experiences. A thorough assessment of related factors, including veterans' coping skills and motivational factors, allows for a treatment plan that is tailored to the unique characteristics and life experiences of the individual veteran. Further, it provides essential information about veteran's motivation to change, particularly as it applies to her or his willingness to initiate and engage in treatment. Assessment and treatment planning should be considered an ongoing process rather than a one-time event. Treatment priorities are likely to change over time, given that factors such as symptom severity, functional impairment, and stage of change rarely remain static. Ongoing assessment of these factors across time is an essential part of providing treatment and evaluating the effectiveness of treatment.

REFERENCES

American Psychiatric Association. (2000). *Diagnostic and statistical manual of mental disorders* (DSM–IV–TR; 4th ed., text revision). Washington, DC: Author.

Back, S. E., Sonne, S. C., Killeen, T., Dansky, B. S., & Brady, K. T. (2003). Comparative profiles of women with PTSD and comorbid cocaine or alcohol dependence. *The American Journal of Drug and Alcohol Abuse, 29,* 169–189. doi:10.1081/ADA-120018845

Blake, D. D., Weathers, F. W., Nagy, L. M., Kaloupek, D. G., Gusman, F. D., Charney, D. S., & Keane, T. M. (1995). The development of a clinician-administered PTSD scale. *Journal of Traumatic Stress, 8,* 75–90. doi:10.1002/jts.2490080106

Bliese, P. D., Wright, K. M., Adler, A. B., Cabrera, O., Castro, C. A., & Hoge, C. W. (2008). Validating the Primary Care Posttraumatic Stress Disorder Screen and the Posttraumatic Stress Disorder Checklist with soldiers returning from combat. *Journal of Consulting and Clinical Psychology, 76,* 272–281. doi:10.1037/0022-006X.76.2.272

Bollinger, A. R., Riggs, D., Blake, D., & Ruzek, J. (2000). Prevalence of personality disorders among combat veterans with posttraumatic stress disorder. *Journal of Traumatic Stress, 13,* 255–270. doi:10.1023/A:1007706727869

Brady, K. T., & Clary, C. M. (2003). Affective and anxiety comorbidity in posttraumatic stress disorder treatment trials of sertraline. *Comprehensive Psychiatry, 44*, 360–369. doi:10.1016/S0010-440X(03)00111-1

Breslau, N., Davis, G. C., Andreski, P., & Peterson, E. (1991). Traumatic events and posttraumatic stress disorder in an urban population of young adults. *Archives of General Psychiatry, 48*, 216–222.

Breslau, N., Davis, G. C., Peterson, E. L., & Schultz, L. R. (2000). A second look at comorbidity in victims of trauma: The posttraumatic stress disorder-major depression connection. *Biological Psychiatry, 48*, 902–909. doi:10.1016/S0006-3223 (00)00933-1

Brown, T. A., Campbell, L. A., Lehman, C. L., Grisham, J. R., & Mancill, R. B. (2001). Current and lifetime comorbidity of the DSM–IV anxiety and mood disorders in a large clinical sample. *Journal of Abnormal Psychology, 110*, 585–599. doi:10.1037/0021-843X.110.4.585

Butcher, J. N., Dahlstrom, W. G., Graham, J. R., Tellegen, A., & Kaemmer, B. (1989). *Minnesota Multiphasic Personality Inventory (MMPI–2): Manual for administration and scoring*. Minneapolis: University of Minnesota Press.

Cabrera, O. A., Hoge, C. W., Bliese, P. D., Castro, C. A., & Messer, S. C. (2007). Childhood adversity and combat as predictors of depression and posttraumatic stress in deployed troops. *American Journal of Preventive Medicine, 33*, 77–82. doi:10.1016/j.amepre.2007.03.019

Cloitre, M., & Koenen, K. C. (2001). The impact of borderline personality disorder on process group outcome among women with posttraumatic stress disorder related to childhood abuse. *International Journal of Group Psychotherapy, 51*, 379–398. doi:10.1521/ijgp.51.3.379.49886

Derogatis, L. R. (1983). *SCL-90-R: Symptom Checklist–90–R: Administration, scoring and procedures manual*. Minneapolis, MN: National Computer Systems.

Ewing, J. A. (1984). Detecting alcoholism: The CAGE Questionnaire. *JAMA, 252*, 1905–1907. doi:10.1001/jama.252.14.1905

First, M. B., Spitzer, R. L., Gibbon, M., & Williams, J. B. W. (1996). *Structured Clinical Interview for Axis I and II DSM–IV Disorders—Patient Edition (SCID–IV/P)*. New York: Biometrics Research Department, New York State Psychiatric Institute.

Frueh, B. C., Hammer, M. B., Cahill, S. P., Gold, P. B., & Hamlin, K. L. (2000). Apparent symptom overreporting in combat veterans evaluated for PTSD. *Clinical Psychology Review, 20*, 853–885. doi:10.1016/S0272-7358(99)00015-X

Hankin, C. S., Spiro, A., III, Miller, D. R., & Kazis, L. (1999). Mental disorders and mental health treatment among U.S. Department of Veterans Affairs outpatients: The veterans health study. *The American Journal of Psychiatry, 156*, 1924–1930.

Herman, D. S., Weathers, F. W., Litz, B. T., & Keane, T. M. (1996). Psychometric properties of the embedded and stand-alone versions of the MMPI–2 Keane PTSD Scale. *Assessment, 3*, 437–442.

Hoge, C. W., Castro, C. A., Messer, S. C., McGurk, D., Cotting, D. I., & Koffman, R. L. (2004). Combat duty in Iraq and Afghanistan, mental health problems, and barriers to care. *The New England Journal of Medicine, 351,* 13–22. doi:10.1056/NEJMoa040603

Jacobson, I. G., Ryan, M. A. K., Hooper, T. I., Smith, T. C., Amoroso, P. J., Boyko, E. J., . . . Bell, N. S. (2008). Alcohol use and alcohol-related problems before and after military combat deployment. *JAMA, 300,* 663–675. doi:10.1001/jama.300.6.663

Katz, L. S., Bloor, L. E., Cojucar, G., & Draper, T. (2007). Women who served in Iraq seeking mental health services: Relationships between military sexual trauma, symptoms, and readjustment. *Psychological Services, 4,* 239–249. doi:10.1037/1541-1559.4.4.239

Keane, T. M., Caddell, J. M., & Taylor, K. L. (1988). Mississippi Scale for Combat-Related Posttraumatic Stress Disorder: Three studies in reliability and validity. *Journal of Consulting and Clinical Psychology, 56,* 85–90. doi:10.1037/0022-006X.56.1.85

Keane, T. M., Kolb, L. C., Kaloupek, D. G., Orr, S. P., Blanchard, E. B., Thomas, R. G., . . . Lavori, P. W. (1998). Utility of psychophysiology measurement in the diagnosis of posttraumatic stress disorder: Results from a Department of Veteran's Affairs cooperative study. *Journal of Consulting and Clinical Psychology, 66,* 914–923. doi:10.1037/0022-006X.66.6.914

Keane, T. M., Malloy, P. F., & Fairbank, J. A. (1984). Empirical development of an MMPI subscale for the assessment of combat-related posttraumatic stress disorder: A comprehensive analysis. *Journal of Consulting and Clinical Psychology, 52,* 888–891. doi:10.1037/0022-006X.52.5.888

Kessler, R. C., Sonnega, A., Bromet, E., Hughes, M., & Nelson, C. B. (1995). Posttraumatic stress disorder in the National Comorbidity Study. *Archives of General Psychiatry, 52,* 1048–1060.

Kimerling, R., Gima, K., Smith, M. W., Street, A., & Frayne, S. (2007). The Veterans Health Administration and military sexual trauma. *American Journal of Public Health, 97,* 2160–2166. doi:10.2105/AJPH.2006.092999

King, D. W., King, L. A., Foy, D. W., & Gudanowski, D. M. (1996). Prewar factors in combat-related posttraumatic stress disorder: Structural equation modeling with a national sample of female and male Vietnam veterans. *Journal of Consulting and Clinical Psychology, 64,* 520–531. doi:10.1037/0022-006X.64.3.520

King, L. A., King, D. W., Bolton, E. E., Knight, J. A., & Vogt, D. S. (2008). Risk factors for mental, physical, and functional health in Gulf War veterans. *Journal of Rehabilitation Research and Development, 45,* 395–407. doi:10.1682/JRRD.2007.06.0081

King, L. A., King, D. W., Fairbank, J. A., Keane, T. M., & Adams, G. (1998). Resilience-recovery factors in posttraumatic stress disorder among female and male Vietnam veterans: Hardiness, postwar social support, and additional stressful life events.

Journal of Personality and Social Psychology, 74, 420–434. doi:10.1037/0022-3514.74.2.420

King, L. A., King, D. W., Vogt, D. S., Knight, J., & Samper, R. E. (2006). Deployment Risk and Resilience Inventory: A collection of measures for studying deployment related experiences of military personnel and veterans. *Military Psychology, 18*, 89–120. doi:10.1207/s15327876mp1802_1

Kulka, R. A., Schlenger, W. E., Fairbank, J. A., Hough, R. L., Jordan, B. K., Marmar, C. R., . . . Grady, D. A. (1990). *Trauma and the Vietnam War generation: Report on the findings from the National Vietnam Veterans Readjustment Study.* New York, NY: Brunner/Mazel.

Lambert, M. J., Whipple, J. L., Hawkins, E. J., Vermeersch, D., Nielsen, S. L., & Smart, D. W. (2003). Is it time for clinicians to routinely track patient outcome? A meta-analysis. *Clinical Psychology: Science and Practice, 10*, 288–301. doi:10.1093/clipsy/bpg025

Lyons, J. A., & Keane, T. M. (1992). Keane PTSD Scale: MMPT and MMPI–2 update. *Journal of Traumatic Stress, 5*, 111–117. doi:10.1002/jts.2490050112

McConnaughy, E. A., Prochaska, J. O., & Velicer, W. F. (1983). Stages of change in psychotherapy: Measurement and sample profiles. *Psychotherapy, 20*, 368–375. doi:10.1037/h0090198

McFall, M. E., Smith, D., Roszell, D. K., Tarver, D. J., & Malas, K. L. (1990). Convergent validity of measures of PTSD in Vietnam combat veterans. *The American Journal of Psychiatry, 147*, 645–648.

McNally, R. J., Bryant, R. A., & Ehlers, A. (2003). Does early psychological intervention promote recovery from posttraumatic stress? *Psychological Science in the Public Interest, 4*(2), 45–79.

Miller, P. R., Dasher, R., Collins, R., Griffiths, P., & Brown, F. (2001). Inpatient diagnostic assessments: 1. Accuracy of structured vs. unstructured interviews. *Psychiatry Research, 105*, 255–264. doi:10.1016/S0165-1781(01)00317-1

Monson, C. M., Fredman, S. J., & Adair, K. C. (2008). Cognitive-behavioral conjoint therapy for PTSD: Application to Operation Enduring and Iraqi Freedom service members and veterans. *Journal of Clinical Psychology, 64*, 958–971. doi:10.1002/jclp.20511

Monson, C. M., Schnurr, P. P., Stevens, S. P., & Guthrie, K. A. (2004). Cognitive-behavioral couple's treatment for posttraumatic stress disorder: Initial findings. *Journal of Traumatic Stress, 17*, 341–344. doi:10.1023/B:JOTS.0000038483.69570.5b

Norris, F. H., & Perilla, J. L. (1996). The Revised Civilian Mississippi Scale for PTSD: Reliability, validity, and cross-language stability. *Journal of Traumatic Stress, 9*, 285–298. doi:10.1002/jts.2490090210

Orsillo, S. M., Weathers, F. W., Litz, B. T., Steinberg, H. R., Huska, J. A., & Keane, T. M. (1996). Current and lifetime psychiatric disorders among veterans with war-zone related posttraumatic stress disorder. *Journal of Nervous and Mental Disease, 184,* 307–313. doi:10.1097/00005053-199605000-00007

Prochaska, J. O., DiClemente, C. C., & Norcross, J. C. (1992). In search of how people change: Applications to addictive behaviors. *American Psychologist, 47,* 1102–1114. doi:10.1037/0003-066X.47.9.1102

Rosen, C. S., Murphy, R. T., Chow, H. C., Drescher, K. D., Ramirez, G., Ruddy, R., & Gusman, F. (2001). Posttraumatic stress disorder patients' readiness to change alcohol and anger problems. *Psychotherapy, 38,* 233–244. doi:10.1037/0033-3204. 38.2.233

Ruggiero, K. J., Del Ben, K., Scotti, J. R., & Rabalais, A. E. (2003). Psychometric properties of the PTSD Checklist—Civilian Version. *Journal of Traumatic Stress, 16,* 495–502. doi:10.1023/A:1025714729117

Schnurr, P. P., Lunney, C. A., & Sengupta, A. (2004). Risk factors for development versus maintenance of posttraumatic stress disorder. *Journal of Traumatic Stress, 17,* 85–95. doi:10.1023/B:JOTS.0000022614.21794.f4

Smith, M. Y., Redd, W., DuHamel, K., Vickberg, S. J., & Ricketts, P. (1999). Validation of the PTSD Checklist—Civilian Version in survivors of bone marrow transplantation. *Journal of Traumatic Stress, 12,* 485–499. doi:10.1023/ A:1024719104351

Spielberger, C. D. (1988). *Manual for the State–Trait Anger Expression Inventory.* Odessa, FL: Psychological Assessment Resources.

Spitzer, R. L., Williams, J. B. W., Gibbon, M., & First, M. B. (1990). *Structured Clinical Interview for DSM–III–R—Patient edition* (with psychotic screen; SCID-P). Washington, DC: American Psychiatric Press.

Taft, C. T., & Niles, B. L. (2004). *Assessment and treatment of anger in combat-related PTSD. Iraq War Clinician Guide* (2nd ed.). Washington, DC: National Center for Post-Traumatic Stress Disorder and Walter Reed Army Medical Center.

Vrana, S., & Lauterbach, D. (1994). Prevalence of traumatic events and post-traumatic psychological symptoms in a nonclinical sample of college students. *Journal of Traumatic Stress, 7,* 289–302. doi:10.1002/jts.2490070209

Vogt, D. S., King, D. W., & King, L. A. (2007). Risk pathways for PTSD: Making sense of the literature. In M. J. Friedman, T. M. Keane, & P. A. Resick (Eds.), *Handbook of PTSD science and practice* (pp. 99–115). New York, NY: Guilford Press.

Vogt, D. S., Pless, A. P., King, L. A., & King, D. W. (2005). Deployment stressors, gender, and mental health outcomes among Gulf War I veterans. *Journal of Traumatic Stress, 18,* 115–127. doi:10.1002/jts.20018

Vogt, D. S., Samper, R. E., King, D. W., King, L. A., & Martin, J. A. (2008). Deployment stressors and posttraumatic stress symptomatology: Comparing active duty and National Guard/Reserve personnel from Gulf War I. *Journal of Traumatic Stress, 21,* 66–74. doi:10.1002/jts.20306

Weathers, F. W., Keane, T. M., & Davidson, J. R. T. (2001). Clinician-Administered PTSD Scale: A review of the first ten years of research. *Depression and Anxiety, 13,* 132–156. doi:10.1002/da.1029

Weathers, F. W., Litz, B. T., Herman, D., Huska, J. A., & Keane, T. M. (1993, October). *The PTSD Checklist (PCL): Reliability, validity, and diagnostic utility.* Paper presented at the annual conference of the International Society for Traumatic Stress Studies, San Antonio, TX.

Weathers, F. W., Litz, B. T., Huska, J. A., & Keane, T. M. (1991). *The PTSD Checklist (PCL).* Boston, MA: National Center for PTSD/Boston VA Medical Center.

Wolfe, J., Keane, T. M., Kaloupek, D. G., Mora, C. A., & Wine, P. (1993). Patterns of positive readjustment in Vietnam combat veterans. *Journal of Traumatic Stress, 6,* 179–193. doi:10.1002/jts.2490060203

Zayfert, C., Becker, C. B., Unger, D. L., & Shearer, D. K. (2002). Comorbid anxiety disorders in civilians seeking treatment for posttraumatic stress disorder. *Journal of Traumatic Stress, 15,* 31–38. doi:10.1023/A:1014379127240

Ziaaddini, H., Nakhaee, N., & Behzadi, K. (2009). Prevalence and correlates of PTSD among high school students after the earthquake disaster in the city of Bam, Iran. *American Journal of Applied Sciences, 6*(1), 132–135. doi:10.3844/ajas.2009.132.135

Zlotnick, C., Warshaw, M., Shea, T. M., Allsworth, J., Pearlstein, T., & Keller, M. B. (1999). Chronicity in posttraumatic stress disorder (PTSD) and predictors of course of comorbid PTSD in patients with anxiety disorders. *Journal of Traumatic Stress, 12,* 89–100. doi:10.1023/A:1024746316245

4

ASSESSMENT AND TREATMENT IN POLYTRAUMA CONTEXTS: TRAUMATIC BRAIN INJURY AND POSTTRAUMATIC STRESS DISORDER

DAVID L. BUTLER, ROBIN A. HURLEY, AND KATHERINE H. TABER

Military personnel deployed to Operation Enduring Freedom (OEF) and Operation Iraqi Freedom (OIF) return from combat with injuries that were fatal in previous wars. This is partially due to more rapid and sophisticated medical responses on the battlefield and partially to improved protective equipment, such as Kevlar vests (Sayer et al., 2008; Warden, 2006). Protective gear and armored vehicles protect soldiers from mortal internal injuries but not from bodily trauma or concussive brain injuries. Recent studies have found that the great majority of injuries were due to explosions, and many involve more than one area of the body (i.e., *polytrauma*; Sayer et al., 2008).

Physical injury during deployment is associated with a higher prevalence of PTSD postdeployment (J. E. Kennedy et al., 2007; Stein & McAllister, 2009). In a recent survey, 9% of soldiers returning from deployment without physical injury screened positive for PTSD (Hoge et al., 2008); however, the rate was almost double (16%) among those reporting bodily injury during

This chapter was coauthored by an employee of the United States government as part of official duty and is considered to be in the public domain. Any views expressed herein do not necessarily represent the views of the United States government, and the author's participation in the work is not meant to serve as an official endorsement.

deployment. This rate is similar to an earlier study assessing the increased risk of PTSD due to combat-related injury (Koren, Norman, Cohen, Berman, & Klein, 2005). Finally, another postdeployment survey of veterans revealed that the incidence of PTSD increased with the number of injury mechanisms: 14% for one, 29% for two, and 51% for three or more (Schneiderman, Braver, & Kang, 2008).

This chapter focuses on how to adapt the assessment and treatment of posttraumatic stress disorder (PTSD) to returning veterans with polytraumatic injuries, especially when the polytrauma involves a traumatic brain injury (TBI). We begin with a review of the empirical literature addressing the prevalence of PTSD in polytrauma populations and the degree to which polytrauma alters PTSD severity and treatment response. Although the evidence base regarding best models of clinical management of PTSD when accompanied by TBI is in its infancy, we present suggestions for assessment of polytrauma and outline techniques and tools useful in optimizing psychosocial and psychopharmacological PTSD treatment interventions in polytrauma contexts.

COMORBID PTSD AND TBI

Although it was once believed that the loss of consciousness and memory deficits that sometimes result from TBI made it unlikely that PTSD would develop (Warden et al., 1997), more recent studies have found that PTSD can develop even when the patient has no conscious memory of the traumatic event (Harvey, Brewin, Jones, & Kopelman, 2003; Klein, Caspi, & Gil, 2003). Studies of military personnel have indicated that higher rates of PTSD are associated with experiencing potentially brain-injuring conditions (J. E. Kennedy et al., 2007; Stein & McAllister, 2009). In a group of returning soldiers who reported experiencing a concussion while deployed (as indicated by altered mental status), 27% screened positive for PTSD (Hoge et al., 2008), whereas 44% of those who reported a loss of consciousness screened positive for PTSD. In a survey study of OEF and OIF veterans, the rate of PTSD was 7% in those without evidence of brain injury, 34% with Level 1 mild TBI (altered mental status), and 47% with Level 2 mild TBI (loss of consciousness, amnesia, or head injury; Schneiderman et al., 2008). Similarly, 32% of active-duty service members (2005–2006) who had experienced both burn and blast injuries and were receiving inpatient care screened positive for PTSD (Gaylord et al., 2008). The rates of PTSD among these burn and blast survivors were 22% among inpatients without mild TBI and 45% among inpatients with mild TBI. A retrospective study of combat veterans found that PTSD diagnosis was associated with history of head injury, and combat-related head injury was associated with increased severity of PTSD (Chemtob et al.,

1998). There is also evidence that military veterans with combat-related PTSD have more severe symptoms than veterans with PTSD due to non-combat-related events (Brinker, Westermeyer, Thuras, & Canive, 2007).

The increased prevalence of PTSD in military personnel experiencing TBI is consistent with findings derived from civilian TBI samples. These studies suggest that psychiatric symptoms develop relatively frequently following TBI (e.g., PTSD in 13%–27%; Kim et al., 2007; Rogers & Read, 2007). History of TBI has also been commonly documented in studies of patients receiving mental health treatment. One study reported that 13% of patients in a treatment facility for serious mental illness had histories of acquired brain injury (Torsney, 2004). Another study found that 33% of patients treated in psychiatric clinics, when asked, reported a history of TBI with loss of consciousness (McGuire, Burright, Williams, & Donovick, 1998). A longer length of inpatient stay and more frequent psychiatric admissions for psychiatric inpatients was found for patients with a history of mild TBI compared with those without such a history (Mateo, Glod, Hennen, Price, & Merrill, 2005). The authors noted that this difference might arise, in part, from impaired recovery when treatment is focused on psychiatric symptoms without regard to the history of mild TBI.

If the TBI involves direct injury to brain regions implicated in PTSD, such as the amygdala, hippocampus, and prefrontal cortex or their connections, it may affect the severity or treatment responsivity of the PTSD. A study of pediatric TBI found that temporal lobe injury was positively correlated with development of PTSD (Vasa et al., 2004). In contrast, there was an inverse correlation between injury to the orbitofrontal cortex and development of PTSD. A study of Vietnam veterans with combat-related penetrating head injuries reported that injuries to ventromedial prefrontal cortex or amygdala (but not other anterior temporal areas) were associated with a lower probability of developing PTSD (Koenigs et al., 2008). Several studies support the idea that presence of TBI can influence the expression of symptoms in PTSD (Bryant, Marosszeky, Crooks, & Gurka, 2000; Feinstein, Hershkop, Ouchterlony, Jardine, & McCullagh, 2002; Turnbull, Campbell, & Swann, 2001; Vasa et al., 2004).

The considerable overlap between symptoms commonly following TBI and those following psychological trauma exposure (J. E. Kennedy et al., 2007; Stein & McAllister, 2009) may contribute to the underrecognition of mild TBI, as has been reported in a study of combat veterans diagnosed with PTSD (Trudeau et al., 1998). The overlap of PTSD symptoms and post-TBI symptoms also suggests the possibility of symptom aggravation due to additive effects, and/or alterations in resilience and coping. At minimum, the presence of TBI might, especially at more severe levels, require alterations of PTSD treatment approaches to adjust for common cognitive and emotional deficits (Corrigan &

Cole, 2008; McAllister, 2008; Nelson, Yoash-Gantz, Pickett, & Campbell, 2009). Cognitive and emotional deficits have the potential to complicate clinical management and can impair recovery and psychosocial outcome.

ASSESSMENT

To date, there is no clearly defined way to distinguish which condition (PTSD or TBI) is responsible for symptoms that are common to the two disorders (e.g., decreased focus and concentration, decreased sleep, agitation, irritability, inability to maintain employment or schooling). Therefore, establishing a clear symptom delineation and prognosis, as well as planning long-term treatment, can be extremely challenging (McAllister, 2008). Diagnosis is further complicated by the severity of the TBI (mild, moderate, severe) and the lack of consensus on both definition of levels of severity and assessment methods for determining severity.

The occurrence and severity of TBI are defined by what happened at the time of injury. A TBI has occurred when an external force has significantly disrupted brain function as indicated by any of the following: a period of loss of or alteration in consciousness, amnesia for events immediately before or after the injury, neurological deficits such as loss of balance or change in vision, intracranial lesion (Management of Concussion/mTBI Working Group, 2009). The presence or absence or duration of each of these defines the severity level (Table 4.1).

The Department of Veterans Affairs (VA) has implemented a two-stage system for identifying OEF and OIF veterans with TBI. Veterans with a previously identified TBI (approximately 3%) are exempt from screening (Carlson et al., 2010; Lew et al., 2009a). The first stage is a four-question brief TBI screen. A positive screen requires answering yes to all questions, indicating a probable historic TBI while deployed and possible persistent postconcussive

TABLE 4.1
Severity Classification for Traumatic Brain Injury (TBI)

Symptom	Mild TBI	Moderate TBI	Severe TBI
Loss of consciousness	0–30 min	> 30 min but < 24 hr	> 24 hr
Alteration of consciousness	Instant up to 24 hr	> 24 hr	> 24 hr
Amnesia	0–1 day	>1 day but < 7 days	> 7 days
Structural imaging	Normal	Normal or abnormal	Normal or abnormal

Note. Adapted from "VA/DoD Clinical Practice Guideline for Management of Concussion/Mild Traumatic Brain Injury", by the Management of Concussion/mTBI Working Group, 2009, *Journal of Rehabilitation Research and Development, 46,* CP16. In the public domain.

symptoms. Preliminary reports indicate that approximately 20% of veterans screen positive (Carlson et al., 2010; Lew et al., 2009b). These veterans are referred for the second stage, a full evaluation by experienced clinicians. Initial reports indicate that the majority (67%–85%) are confirmed to have TBI (Hill et al., 2009; Lew et al., 2009b).

Polytrauma Examination

A thorough assessment of the polytrauma patient ideally involves a multidisciplinary team. At minimum, the evaluation should include a complete physical examination by a clinician (e.g., physician or midlevel practitioner with physician supervision) experienced in the field of brain injury. A psychosocial evaluation (social work) is frequently needed for direct intervention and case management. An audiology evaluation may be needed because 71% of returning service persons have been exposed to loud noises, and 15.6% report tinnitus (Geckle & Lee, 2004; Lew et al., 2009b). Auditory dysfunction (e.g., hearing loss, tinnitus) is more frequently associated with exposure to explosions (Lew, Jerger, Guillory, & Henry, 2007; Lew et al., 2009b). Ophthalmologic or optometric oculomotor evaluation of saccades and antisaccades is an effective screen for TBI and cognitive alterations associated with TBI (Drew et al., 2007; Kraus et al., 2007; Suh, Kolster, Sarkar, McCandliss, & Ghajar, 2006). The evaluation may also be of assistance for eye injuries and changes in visual acuity. Pain assessment often plays a particularly important role in assessing polytrauma patients because pain management may be necessary for patients with chronic pain complaints from embedded shrapnel, burns, musculoskeletal injuries, compression fractures, amputations, or other injuries (DeCarvalho & Whealin, 2006). Because pain and PTSD may maintain and exacerbate each other, coordination between pain management and mental health specialists often facilitates treatment (Sharp & Harvey, 2001). A recent review found a prevalence of 57.8% for headache across 12 studies in individuals with TBI (Nampiaparampil, 2008). Studies from a VA Polytrauma Rehabilitation Center for combat-injured service members receiving inpatient care reported that most (97%) had a TBI, more than half had mental health issues (symptoms of depression—36%, symptoms of PTSD—35%), and all had pain issues (headache—52%, musculoskeletal—48%, neuropathic—14%, other—23%; Sayer et al., 2008, 2009).

Mental Health Evaluation

The first step in managing mental health concerns, whether they stem from psychological stress reactions, brain injury, pain, or other aspects of polytrauma, is to characterize the concerns and available resources to help manage them. Reflecting the range of posttraumatic stress reactions, the mental health professional needs to evaluate for the presence of survivor guilt, anxiety, irritability, substance use, depression, and other psychological and behavioral issues. (See Chapter 3, this volume, for a comprehensive description of PTSD assessment methods.) Determinations should be made regarding the need for psychotherapy, substance abuse interventions, and family therapy, with consultations made to the appropriate professional. Mental health evaluations often neglect the assessment of the potential benefits of pastoral or spiritual counseling, despite the relevance of spirituality for the patient who is conflicted over war-zone actions versus their own religious values.

Evaluation by a rehabilitation psychologist or neuropsychologist (or both) is recommended for any polytrauma patient who complains of cognitive changes or who was exposed to events with the potential to cause brain injury (e.g., explosions, motor vehicle accidents, assault). Neuropsychological testing to discriminate between mild TBI and PTSD (Brenner et al., 2009, 2010) or differentiate the effects of blast-induced brain injury from other causes of brain injury (Belanger, Kretzmer, Yoash-Gantz, Pickett, & Tupler, 2009) has little support. The neuropsychological evaluation in most polytrauma contexts is instead most useful as a tool to identify cognitive strengths and weaknesses that require remediation or that can be capitalized on by the clinician providing PTSD interventions. In fact, consideration of cognitive strengths, weaknesses, and functional deficits has been shown to be more useful even than the severity of the brain injury in designing cognitive interventions (M. R. Kennedy & Turkstra, 2006; Tsaousides & Gordon, 2009). It is important to bear in mind that although some polytrauma patients are open about acknowledging cognitive changes, others may not perceive the alterations as significant or may minimize the impact on their functioning (Lundqvist & Alinder, 2007).

TREATMENT

Chapter 10 of this volume describes current evidenced-based PTSD treatment interventions. Here strategies used in the rehabilitation of TBI are described for potential application to the care of polytrauma patients with PTSD. The focus is on modifications in techniques or programs that can improve the therapeutic outcome for these patients.

Brain Injury Rehabilitation

Modern brain injury rehabilitation programs are comprehensive and complex. Driven by the need to treat a wide and highly variable range of impairments (e.g., physical, social, emotional, communication, cognitive, behavioral, academic–vocational), the programs often encompass components from multiple health care fields, including psychiatry, neurology, nursing, neuropsychology, psychology, behavioral therapy, counseling, social work, occupational therapy, physical therapy, speech therapy, recreational therapy, educators, and vocational rehabilitation. Programs can be outpatient, inpatient, or residential. In hospital settings, polytrauma patients with moderate or severe injuries typically transition directly from the inpatient medical unit to the rehabilitation unit. Because mild brain injuries are not always readily detected, patients with mild TBI may not be enrolled in any inpatient or outpatient rehabilitation.

Cognitive Rehabilitation

Cognitive rehabilitation is an integral component of brain injury rehabilitation. Although not universally accepted, the American Congress of Rehabilitation Medicine definition of cognitive rehabilitation therapy (CRT) has been adopted by the Commission on Accreditation of Rehabilitation Facilities (CARF) and is included in a position paper on cognitive rehabilitation by National Academy of Neuropsychology (Harley et al., 1992). This definition of CRT is

> a systematic, functionally-oriented service of therapeutic cognitive activities, based on an assessment and understanding of the person's brain-behavioral deficits. . . . Services are directed to achieve functional changes by:
> 1. Reinforcing, strengthening or reestablishing previously learned patterns of behavior, or
> 2. Establishing new patterns of cognitive activity or compensatory mechanisms for impaired neurological systems. (Harley et al., 1992, p. 63)

This definition of CRT encompasses a variety of interventions, which can typically be categorized into one of two broad approaches that are not mutually exclusive. The first, *restoration*, involves retraining of the damaged cognitive function. The goal of the intervention is to strengthen the damaged cognitive abilities or underlying neural circuits through application of specific exercises or tasks. The second approach, *compensation*, involves learning or relearning specific skills that are of functional importance. The compensatory approach can be divided into two non–mutually exclusive subcategories, *strategy training* and *adaptive aids*. For example, a semantic memory encoding deficit could be compensated for by learning to use a mnemonic strategy such as visual association or an adaptive aid such as a memory book or personal digital assistant (PDA). Controversy continues regarding the relative benefits of restoration versus compensation for rehabilitation, with greater empirical support for the use of compensatory strategies (Cicerone et al., 2005). A meta-analysis of CRT treatment studies concluded that cognitive rehabilitation is effective when targeted to specific skills but not when delivered as part of a general, nondirected program (Rohling, Faust, Beverly, & Demakis, 2009). CRT interventions are usually provided one-on-one but can sometimes also be delivered in a group setting. A recent pilot study of group-based treatment of OEF and OIF veterans with TBI reported promising results (Huckans et al., 2010). The individual with a TBI can present with myriad cognitive (attention, memory, executive, spatial, others) and emotional alterations (depression, irritability, anxiety, others) depending on the cause and severity of the trauma, the neuroanatomical areas that are disrupted, age, length of time since trauma, and other factors (McCullagh & Feinstein, 2005). Individuals with severe injuries are more likely to have significant residual deficits, whereas many individuals with mild injuries can attain complete recovery (McAllister, 2006; McCullagh & Feinstein, 2005). Individuals vary in their awareness of deficits with limited insight or denial of deficits in severe brain injuries (Flashman, Amador, & McAllister, 2005). Those with mild injuries are typically aware of the presence of a deficit but can be unaware of the parameters of the deficit(s) (Raskin, 2000). The PTSD clinician does not need to provide a cognitive rehabilitation program for the polytrauma patient but rather should augment elements of the PTSD treatment program in a way that will allow the patient to benefit but stay true to the manualized therapy guidelines. The alterations are often small and readily implemented without disruption of service to individuals who do not have a TBI diagnosis. Many of the cognitive impairments of PTSD are similar to those of TBI (Dirkzwager, van der Velden, Grievink, & Yzermans, 2007; Hoge, Terhakopian, Castro, Messer, & Engel, 2007; Hoge et al., 2008).

Adapting Clinical Therapeutic Techniques

The following subsections focus on common clinical situations inherent in both specific contexts and more general settings in which simple modifications in procedures or environment may improve the effectiveness of PTSD interventions for individuals with mild to moderate brain injuries. The techniques are currently in use or have been used by the first author in a clinical setting that serves veterans and active-duty personnel, many of whom have comorbid PTSD and mild TBI. Throughout the assessment and treatment process, it is critical that the clinician continually check for patient understanding of the treatment components. Often, patients with memory deficits will initially acknowledge understanding of a plan or assignment yet not remember it later.

Initial Contact or Appointment

Impairment in attention, concentration, and memory can occur in individuals at all levels of TBI severity but are more commonly persistent at moderate to severe levels (Belanger, Curtiss, Demery, Lebowitz & Vanderploeg, 2005; Iverson, 2005; Schretlen & Shapiro, 2003). Memory impairments can take the form of prospective memory deficits, such as forgetting appointments and difficulty learning new information. A failure of prospective memory causing the patient to forget the initial appointment results in loss of clinician productivity and of potential treatment benefit. There are specific strategies to compensate for prospective memory deficits that the clinician can use to improve attendance at the initial and follow-up appointments. For example, the technique of providing at each session an appointment page printed on colored paper combines the basic cognitive rehabilitation principles of simplicity and organization. The colored paper increases the probability the patient will see the reminder at home and look at it. The patient is asked to look at the page, read aloud the next appointment date, and enter the appointment into a PDA or booklet day organizer. A routine appointment time is preferred over variable appointment times.

Facilitating recall of the appointment removes only one possible barrier to treatment attendance. Patients with all levels of TBI, especially when moderate to severe, may also exhibit a *wayfinding deficit* (i.e., topographical disorientation), which causes them to become lost or unable to determine their location. This may be caused by a failure of memory or impairment in spatial orientation. The initial goal is for the patient to be able to locate the treatment facility for his or her appointments. The effect of a wayfinding deficit can be minimized by sending the patient two maps (area or city and campus) marked with prominent guide points. Other alternatives include use of an online mapping service, a GPS, or a pad of self-adhesive notes with each turn or travel segment written in sequence on a separate note.

Adaptive Aids and Compensatory Strategies

Adaptive aids are generally defined as an item, device, or control that increases the ability to perform activities of daily living; improves perception, control, or communication with the environment; ensures safety, security, and accessibility; or compensates for conditions resulting from disability or loss of function. Adaptive aids can be complex (e.g., motor vehicle controls) or simple (e.g., reading glasses). The cost of adaptive aids that compensate for cognitive impairments may be covered as a cognitive orthotic through workers' compensation, private insurance, or as a veterans' benefit.

For patients with executive or memory deficits, daily organizers often prove to be particularly helpful. The organizer can be a paper-and-pencil (e.g., calendar, daily planner, booklet organizer) or electronic (e.g., PDA, smart phone) device. An organizer, however, provides little benefit unless the patient is taught to use it and understands how it will be useful. PDAs or smart phones can be programmed to provide useful reminders for appointments and medications. The primary drawback of these devices is their complexity. Patients with subtle or mild cognitive deficits will generally learn the procedures with little assistance. However, some will need one-on-one instruction in the use of the device.

Regarding attentional impairment, manualized therapeutic programs, such as Attention Process Training (Sohlberg, Johnson, Paule, Raskin, & Mateer, 2001), exist for improving attention skills. Such programs require therapists who have been trained in the application of the techniques and an investment of time by the patient. Clinicians who are not trained in these techniques, however, can effectively minimize the impact of attentional limitations by reducing environmental distractions as an alternative to improving attention capacity. Simple techniques include closing blinds and doors, using a white noise machine to mask ambient noise, and seating individuals with attention impairments near the front during group interventions.

A memory notebook is a simple and effective tool for compensating for memory impairments (Schmitter-Edgecomb, Fahy, Whelan, & Long, 1995). It is often particularly helpful to integrate a memory notebook into a workbook containing prepared notes or summaries of psychoeducation sessions because semantic encoding deficits may reduce the amount of information retained from the session. Cognitively impaired polytrauma patients may find it difficult to divide their attention between tasks or to shift attention from one task to another. Note taking during a psychoeducation session or class requires the patient to attend to what the presenter is saying and simultaneously write notes on the presentation, or to alternate rapidly between the two tasks. Some cognitively impaired patients who are attempting to write notes find it necessary to interrupt the presenter frequently to ask that the material be repeated. If the clinician provides the patient with a set of notes or summaries before the session, the patient is then able to concentrate on the content of the presentation. The notes can be reviewed multiple times at increasing time periods following the session; this will facilitate encoding and storage in semantic memory. Integrated memory and workbooks can also contain exercises or tasks that the patient is to accomplish between sessions, reducing the need to use prospective memory.

Compensatory strategies that will facilitate the patient with TBI in profiting from PTSD treatment include the establishment of *routines* and *schedules*. The TBI patient generally functions better in a structured environment that incorporates routines and schedules than in a nonstructured setting. The use of routines and schedules is facilitated by having clocks placed in easily and naturally viewed locations. A clock that emits a soft chime on the hour or half hour will increase orientation to the time, thereby reducing failures in prospective memory.

Color can also be used as a simple adaptive and compensatory aid. For example, a patient can be instructed to write notes in different colors depending on the purpose of the note (e.g., green for financial, red for "as-soon-as-possible" or must-do notes, blue for family). Another example of color aids includes using colored file folders and self-adhesive notes, keeping the colors consistent for specific tasks. The use of different ink colors can also be incorporated into therapy. For example, if asked as part of a cognitive–behavioral PTSD intervention to provide a hierarchy of distressing thoughts, events, and stimuli related to their PTSD stressor(s), a patient with cognitive impairment may have difficulty with ranking because of the abstract nature of the task. The task can be made more concrete by asking the patient to write the most stressful events or stimuli in red ink with other ink colors assigned to less disturbing thoughts or stimuli. The association of the ink colors to the stressor should be at the patient's discretion, although the clinician can offer suggestions.

Psychotherapy for Comorbid TBI and PTSD

As summarized in Chapter 10 of this volume, cognitive–behavior therapy is the broad psychotherapy approach most commonly recommended for treatment of PTSD (Mendes et al., 2008; Shalev et al., 2000). Several recent reviews have examined the effects of psychosocial interventions on anxiety, disability, and behavioral disorders in patients with TBI (Snell, Surgenor, Hay-Smith, & Siegert, 2009; Soo & Tate, 2007; Ylvisaker et al., 2007). The Soo and Tate (2007) review found that cognitive–behavioral interventions can be effective in reducing anxiety associated with mild TBI, and Snell et al. (2009) concluded that educational interventions provided shortly after injury might be beneficial in reducing disability in mild to moderate TBI. A thorough review by Ylvisaker et al. (2007) recommended as a practice guideline the use of behavioral interventions classified broadly as contingency management procedures and positive behavior interventions and supports for behavioral problems in patients with TBI.

Although the literature on the treatment of PTSD is extensive, there are few data regarding treatment of PTSD with comorbid TBI. Treatment of the comorbid patient may be complicated by overlapping cognitive symptoms and by the severity of the TBI. It is unknown whether the overlapping cognitive symptoms are independent, additive, or multiplicative (J. E. Kennedy et al., 2007; Stein & McAllister, 2009). A case report of a patient with severe brain injury and PTSD reported success with behavioral exposure therapy (McMillan, 1991); however, King (2002) reported a less encouraging, more protracted course with partial benefit using a PTSD exposure intervention when the TBI was associated with executive impairment.

A study of cognitive behavioral therapy in patients with mild TBI found it to be effective in the treatment of acute stress disorder (Bryant, Moulds, & Nixon, 2003). This study indicates that early treatment may prevent the development of PTSD. There are no substantive data regarding the prioritizing of PTSD or TBI interventions in the comorbid patient. On the basis of the observation that TBI patients function better in structured settings and that the cognitive–behavioral therapies are inherently structured, Manchester and Woods (2001) and Ponsford, Sloan, and Snow (1995) have suggested that cognitive–behavioral–based therapies are particularly appropriate for the TBI population. Modifications to interventions may be necessary depending on individual limitations. An example of a potential modification of exposure therapy in the treatment of a comorbid patient is in the use of imagery. Exposure therapies frequently rely on the patient using visual mental imagery to experience the traumatic event(s). However, individuals vary in their ability to use the "mind's eye." It has been suggested that diffuse disruption of large neural networks could cause loss of visual mental imagery (Bartolomeo, 2008). Loss of visual imagery would adversely affect the patient's ability to benefit from any therapy utilizing mental imagery. A possible adaptation for individuals with comorbid PTSD and TBI who report difficulty with imagery is the use of a prop (e.g., picture, computer graphic).

Family Involvement

Family involvement in PTSD treatment programs can be complicated by the presence of TBI (Cavallo & Kay, 2005). The clinician should not assume that the partner or family has been informed about the emotional and cognitive alterations that can accompany TBI. Mild TBI or injuries that cause minor cognitive deficits may have minimal impact, but other types of injury have the potential to disrupt family functioning because of a perceived disconnect between the severity of injury and the severity of symptoms. Clinical observations suggest that more severe injuries can markedly alter the relationship secondary to issues involving responsibility in decision making, breadwinner status, finances, intimacy, family roles, child rearing, and other concerns. The spouse or family can become depressed and anxious and feel burdened. The family may believe that the patient's undesirable behavior (e.g., laziness, emotional outbursts) is intentional. A session with the family provided by the clinician or rehabilitation specialist may be of benefit. For example, a family member's perception of the patient can alter markedly when provided with information that perceived "laziness" is actually apathy and a neuropsychological symptom of the TBI. The family may also benefit from referral to support organizations.

Adjusting PTSD Medication Management for TBI

At present, no medications for the long-term treatment of psychiatric symptoms due to brain injury have been approved by the Food and Drug Administration (Bernardo, Singh, & Thompson, 2008; Francisco, Walker, Zasler, & Bouffard, 2007; Lombardi, 2008, Warden et al., 2006), and there are no peer-reviewed published studies to guide the clinician in medication treatment for the dual-diagnosis population (PTSD and TBI). Opinions of experts in the field suggest that PTSD clinicians follow the guidelines for other neuropsychiatric populations with "organic" brain injuries (Table 4.2; Silver, Arciniegas, & Yudofsky, 2005).

The VA has now produced clinical practice guidelines to assist practitioners (http://healthquality.va.gov). The authors of this chapter have found the following medication classes or agents to be helpful within the context of good general medical practice. For chronic psychiatric symptoms in mild TBI:

- depression or mild cognitive impairment (or both): selective serotonin reuptake inhibitors (e.g., citalopram, sertraline);
- mood stabilization and seizure prevention and management: anticonvulsants (e.g., sodium valproate, carbamazepine, oxcarbazepine, gabapentin);
- aggression, agitation, or irritability: atypical antipsychotics (e.g., quetiapine, risperidone) or, in severe cases, beta blockers (e.g., propranolol);
- attention, concentration, and focus: methylphenidate, mixed salts of amphetamine, amantadine, or modafinil;
- memory: cholinesterase inhibitors (e.g., galantamine, donepezil);
- mild anxiety or emotional stabilization: buspirone, titrating up toward the maximum tolerated dose within prescribing guidelines; undertreatment with this agent is common;
- insomnia: trazodone, nonbenzodiazepine sedatives (e.g., zolpidem) or quetiapine if other symptoms necessitate an antipsychotic; and
- nightmares: prazosin, quetiapine, and low-dose aripiprazole.

Consult a neuropsychiatric text or review articles for guidance on medication management (Arciniegas et al., 2000; Silver et al., 2005).

SUMMARY

In summary, it is critical to identify patients with comorbid PTSD and TBI. Often, patients do not know to report a history of brain injury spontaneously, especially if the injury was relatively mild; therefore, it is imperative

TABLE 4.2
Medication Management for Patients With Traumatic Brain Injury (TBI)

Guideline	Rationale
Clarify symptoms	Patients may confuse concerns about attention or focus with concerns about memory.
Rule out social factors	Abuse, neglect, caregiver conflict, or environmental issues may be contributing factors to symptoms.
Rule out seizures	Although not common, partial complex seizures without secondary generalization can have a significant impact on treatment choice and recovery.
Limit quantities	The suicide rate in patients with TBI is higher than in the general psychiatric population. Disinhibition and affective lability may contribute (Wasserman et al., 2008).
Start low and go slow	Patients with TBI will need a slower medication titration. They are more sensitive to side effects as titration progresses. Watch closely for toxicity and drug–drug interactions, particularly for additive anticholinergic or sedative effects. Frequent reassessment is important early in the medication management for fine dosage adjustment or augmentation as necessary.
Do not give up early	Undertreatment is common. Titrate slowly but continue toward a clinically appropriate dose.
Medications to minimize: Benzodiazepines Anticholinergics Antidopaminerics Seizure-inducing	These agents can impair cognition, increase sedation, increase disinhibition, or impede neuronal recovery.
Medications to avoid Tricyclics	May be lethal in overdose. Other complications include seizures, heart block, arrhythmias, and anticholinergic effects.
Lithium	Higher risk of delirium, seizures, and encephalopathy in this population.
Monoamine oxidase inhibitors	Increased risk of hypertensive crisis or requires diet restrictions that are too risky in this population.
Bupropion	May increase the risk of seizures.
Other agents to avoid: caffeine herbal products diet products energy products	These all can lead to drug–drug interactions, including a hypertensive crisis, increased aggression, or mania (Hu et al., 2005; Reissig, Strain, & Griffiths, 2009; Spinella, 2002; Wong, Smith, & Boon, 1998).

that all clinicians obtain a thorough history of exposure to potentially brain-injuring situations (e.g., falls, sporting accidents, combat exposure, vehicular accidents). After a history of brain injury is confirmed, a thorough identification of any retained symptoms will assist the clinician in preparing treatment plans and monitoring progress. To date, there are published clinical practice guidelines for the treatment of mild TBI, chronic pain, and PTSD as separate conditions (http://www.healthquality.va.gov). As noted earlier, there are no published guidelines for the treatment of the comorbid patient. Expert opinions from practitioners in the field, however, suggest that all evidenced-based treatments currently in use for PTSD and TBI should be executed as established in the existing guidelines when the two disorders co-occur unless overriding symptoms interfere. For PTSD, if cognitive symptoms do interfere with progression, practitioners can apply strategies described in this chapter to augment or supplement the treatment regime. There are many ongoing research studies in this population. It is anticipated that evidence-based guidance will be available in the near future.

REFERENCES

Arciniegas, D. B., Topkoff, J., & Silver, J. M. (2000). Neuropsychiatric aspects of traumatic brain injury. *Current Treatment Options in Neurology, 2,* 169–186. doi:10.1007/s11940-000-0017-y

Bartolomeo, P. (2008). The neural correlates of visual mental imagery: An ongoing debate. *Cortex, 44,* 107–108. doi:10.1016/j.cortex.2006.07.001

Belanger, H. G., Curtiss, G., Demery, J. A., Lebowitz, B. K., & Vanderploeg, R. D. (2005) Factors moderating neuropsychological outcomes following mild traumatic brain injury: A meta-analysis. *Journal of the International Neuropsychological Society, 11,* 215–227.

Belanger, H. G., Kretzmer, T., Yoash-Gantz, R., Pickett, T., & Tupler, L. A. (2009). Cognitive sequelae of blast-related versus other mechanisms of brain trauma. *Journal of the International Neuropsychological Society, 15,* 1–8. doi:10.1017/S1355617708090036

Bernardo, C. G., Singh, V., & Thompson, P. M. (2008). Safety and efficacy of psychopharmacological agents used to treat the psychiatric sequelae of common neurological disorders. *Expert Opinion on Drug Safety, 7,* 435–445. doi:10.1517/14740338.7.4.435

Brenner, L. A., Homaifar, B. Y., Gutierrez, P. M., Harwood, J. E. F., Adler, L. E., Terrio, H., . . . Warren, D. (2010). Neuropsychological test performance in soldiers with blast-related mild TBI. *Neuropsychology, 24,* 160–167. doi:10.1037/a0017966

Brenner, L. A., Ladley-O'Brien, S. E., Harwood, J. E., Filley, C. M., Kelly, J. P., Homaifar, B. Y., & Adler, L. E. (2009). An exploratory study of neuroimaging, neurologic, and neuropsychological findings in veterans with traumatic brain injury and/or posttraumatic stress disorder. *Military Medicine, 174,* 347–352.

Brinker, M., Westermeyer, J., Thuras, P., & Canive, J. (2007). Severity of combat-related posttraumatic stress disorder versus noncombat-related posttraumatic stress disorder: A community-based study in American Indian and Hispanic veterans.

Journal of Nervous and Mental Disease, 195, 655–661. doi:10.1097/NMD.0b013e
31811f4076

Bryant, R. A., Marosszeky, J. E., Crooks, J., & Gurka, J. A. (2000). Posttraumatic stress
disorder after severe traumatic brain injury. *The American Journal of Psychiatry,
157*, 629–631. doi:10.1176/appi.ajp.157.4.629

Bryant, R. A., Moulds, M. L., & Nixon, R. V. (2003). Cognitive behaviour therapy of
acute stress disorder: A four-year follow-up. *Behaviour Research and Therapy, 41*,
489–494. doi:10.1016/S0005-7967(02)00179-1

Carlson, K. F., Nelson, D., Orazem, R. J., Nugent, S., Cifu, D. X., & Sayer, N. A.
(2010). Psychiatric diagnoses among Iraq and Afghanistan war veterans screened
for deployment-related traumatic brain injury. *Journal of Traumatic Stress, 23*,
17–24.

Cavallo, M. M., & Kay, T. (2005). The family system. In J. M. Silver, T. W.
McAllister, & S. C. Yudofsky (Eds.), *Textbook of traumatic brain injury*
(pp. 533–558). Washington, DC: American Psychiatric Publishing.

Chemtob, C. M., Muraoka, M. Y., Wu-Holt, P., Fairbank, J. A., Hamada, R. S., &
Keane, T. M. (1998). Head injury and combat-related posttraumatic stress disorder. *Journal of Nervous and Mental Disease, 186*, 701–708. doi:10.1097/00005053-
199811000-00007

Cicerone, K. D., Dahlberg, C., Malec, J. F., Langenbaum, D. M., Felicetti, T., Kneipp,
S., . . . Catanese, J. (2005). Evidence-based cognitive rehabilitation: Updated
review of the literature from 1998 through 2002. *Archives of Physical Medicine and
Rehabilitation, 86*, 1681–1692. doi:10.1016/j.apmr.2005.03.024

Corrigan, J. D., & Cole, T. B. (2008). Substance use disorders and clinical management
of traumatic brain injury and posttraumatic stress disorder. *JAMA, 300*, 720–721.
doi:10.1001/jama.300.6.720

DeCarvalho, L. T., & Whealin, J. M. (2006). What pain specialists need to know about
posttraumatic stress disorder in Operation Iraqi Freedom and Operation Enduring Freedom returnees. *Journal of Musculoskeletal Pain, 14*, 37–45. doi:10.1300/
J094v14n03_06

Dirkzwager, A. J., van der Velden, P. G., Grievink, L., & Yzermans, C. J. (2007).
Disaster-related posttraumatic stress disorder and physical health. *Psychosomatic
Medicine, 69*, 435–440. doi:10.1097/PSY.0b013e318052e20a

Drew, A. S., Langan, J., Halterman, C., Osternig, L. R., Chou, L.-S., & van Donkelaar,
P. (2007). Attentional disengagement dysfunction following mTBI assessed with
the gap saccade task. *Neuroscience Letters, 417*, 61–65. doi:10.1016/j.neulet.2007.
02.038

Feinstein, A., Hershkop, S., Ouchterlony, D., Jardine, A., & McCullagh, S. (2002).
Posttraumatic amnesia and recall of a traumatic event following traumatic brain
injury. *The Journal of Neuropsychiatry and Clinical Neurosciences, 14*, 25–30. doi:
10.1176/appi.neuropsych.14.1.25

Flashman, L. A., Amador, X., & McAllister, T. W. (2005). Awareness of deficits.
In J. M. Silver, T. W. McAllister, & S. C. Yudofsky (Eds.), *Textbook of trau-*

matic brain injury (pp. 353–367). Washington, DC: American Psychiatric Publishing.

Francisco, G. E., Walker, W. C., Zasler, N. D., & Bouffard, M. H. (2007). Pharmacological management of neurobehavioural sequelae of traumatic brain injury: A survey of current physiatric practice. *Brain Injury, 21,* 1007–1014. doi:10.1080/02699050701559558

Gaylord, K. M., Cooper, D. B., Mercado, J. M., Kennedy, J. E., Yoder, L. H., & Holcomb, J. B. (2008). Incidence of posttraumatic stress disorder and mild traumatic brain injury in burned service members: Preliminary report. *The Journal of Trauma, 64,* S200–S205. doi:10.1097/TA.0b013e318160ba42

Geckle, L., & Lee, R. (2004, August). Soldier perceptions of deployment environmental exposures. Paper presented at the 7th Annual Force Health Protection Conference, Albuquerque, NM.

Harley, J. P., Allen, C., Braciszewski, T. L., Cicerone, K. D., Dahlberg, C., Evans, S., . . . Smigelski, J. S. (1992). Guidelines for cognitive rehabilitation. *NeuroRehabilitation, 2,* 62–67.

Harvey, A. G., Brewin, C. R., Jones, C., & Kopelman, M. D. (2003). Coexistence of posttraumatic stress disorder and traumatic brain injury: Towards a resolution of the paradox. *Journal of the International Neuropsychological Society, 9,* 663–676. doi:10.1017/S1355617703940069

Hill, J. J., Mobo, B. H. P., Jr., & Cullen, M. R. (2009). Separating deployment-related traumatic brain injury and posttraumatic stress disorder in veterans: Preliminary findings from the Veterans Affairs traumatic brain injury screening program. *American Journal of Physical Medicine & Rehabilitation, 88,* 605–614. doi:10.1097/PHM.0b013e3181ae0f83

Hoge, C. W., McGurk, D., Thomas, J. L., Cox, A. L., Engel, C. C., & Castro, C. A. (2008). Mild traumatic brain injury in U.S. soldiers returning from Iraq. *The New England Journal of Medicine, 358,* 453–463. doi:10.1056/NEMoa072972

Hoge, C. W., Terhakopian, A., Castro, C. A., Messer, S. C., & Engel, C. C. (2007). Association of posttraumatic stress disorder with somatic symptoms, health care visits, and absenteeism among Iraq war veterans. *The American Journal of Psychiatry, 164,* 150–153. doi:10.1176/appi.ajp.164.1.150

Hu, Z., Yang, X., Ho, P. C., Chan, S. Y., Heng, P. W., Chan, E., . . . Zhou, S. (2005). Herb–drug interactions: A literature review. *Drugs, 65,* 1239–1282. doi:10.2165/00003495-200565090-00005

Huckans, M., Pavawalla, S., Demadura, T., Kolessar, M., Seelye, A., Roost, N., . . . Storzbach, D. (2010). A pilot study examining effects of group-based Cognitive Strategy Training treatment on self-reported cognitive problems, psychiatric symptoms, functioning, and compensatory strategy use in OIF/OEF combat veterans with persistent mild cognitive disorder and history of traumatic brain injury. *Journal of Rehabilitation Research and Development, 47,* 43–60. doi:10.1682/JRRD.2009.02.0019

Iverson, G. (2005). Outcome from mild traumatic brain injury. *Current Opinion in Psychiatry, 18,* 301–317.

Kennedy, J. E., Jaffee, M. S., Leskin, G. A., Stokes, J. W., Leal, F. O., & Fitzpatrick, P. J. (2007). Posttraumatic stress disorder and posttraumatic stress disorder-like symptoms and mild traumatic brain injury. *Journal of Rehabilitation Research and Development, 44,* 895–920. doi:10.1682/JRRD.2006.12.0166

Kennedy, M. R., & Turkstra, L. (2006). Group intervention studies in the cognitive rehabilitation of individuals with traumatic brain injury: Challenges faced by researchers. *Neuropsychology Review, 16,* 151–159. doi:10.1007/s11065-006-9012-8

Kim, E., Lauterbach, E. C., Reeve, A., Arciniegas, D. B., Coburn, K. L., Mendez, M. F., . . . ANPA Committee on Research (2007). Neuropsychiatric complications of traumatic brain injury: A critical review of the literature (a report by the ANPA Committee on Research). *The Journal of Neuropsychiatry and Clinical Neurosciences, 19,* 106–127. doi:10.1176/appi.neuropsych.19.2.106

King, N. S. (2002). Perseveration of trauma re-experiencing in PTSD; a cautionary note regarding exposure based psychological treatments for PTSD when head injury and dysexecutive impairment are also present. *Brain Injury, 16,* 65–74. doi:10.1080/02699050110088263

Klein, E., Caspi, Y., & Gil, S. (2003). The relation between memory of the traumatic event and PTSD: Evidence from studies of traumatic brain injury. *Canadian Journal of Psychiatry, 48,* 28–33.

Koenigs, M., Huey, E. D., Raymont, V., Cheon, B., Solomon, J., Wassermann, E. M., & Grafman, J. (2008). Focal brain damage protects against post-traumatic stress disorder in combat veterans. *Nature Neuroscience, 11,* 232–237. doi:10.1038/nn2032

Koren, D., Norman, D., Cohen, A., Berman, J., & Klein, E. M. (2005). Increased PTSD risk with combat-related injury: A matched comparison study of injured and uninjured soldiers experiencing the same combat events. *The American Journal of Psychiatry, 162,* 276–282. doi:10.1176/appi.ajp.162.2.276

Kraus, M. F., Little, D. M., Donnell, A. J., Reilly, J. L., Simonian, N., & Sweeney, J. A. (2007). Oculomotor function in chronic traumatic brain injury. *Cognitive and Behavioral Neurology, 20,* 170–178. doi:10.1097/WNN.0b013e318142badb

Lew, H. L., Garvert, D. W., Pogoda, T. K., Hsu, P.-T., Devine, J. M., White, D. K., . . . Goodrich, G. L. (2009b). Auditory and visual impairments in patients with blast-related traumatic brain injury: Effect of dual sensory impairment on Functional Independence Measure. *Journal of Rehabilitation Research and Development, 46,* 819–826. doi:10.1682/JRRD.2008.09.0129

Lew, H. L., Jerger, J. F., Guillory, S. B., & Henry, J. A. (2007). Auditory dysfunction in traumatic brain injury. *Journal of Rehabilitation Research and Development, 44,* 921–928. doi:10.1682/JRRD.2007.09.0140

Lew, H. L., Otis, J. D., Tun, C., Kerns, R. D., Clark, M. E., & Cifu, D. X. (2009a). Prevalence of chronic pain, posttraumatic stress disorder, and persistent postconcussive symptoms in OIF/OEF veterans: Polytrauma clinical triad. *Journal of*

Rehabilitation Research and Development, 46, 697–702. doi:10.1682/JRRD.2009.01.0006

Lombardi, F. (2008). Pharmacological treatment of neurobehavioural sequelae of traumatic brain injury. *European Journal of Anaesthesiology, 25*, 131–136. doi:10.1017/S0265021507003316

Lundqvist, A., & Alinder, J. (2007). Driving after brain injury: Self-awareness and coping at the tactical level of control. *Brain Injury, 21*, 1109–1117. doi:10.1080/02699050701651660

Management of Concussion/mTBI Working Group (2009). VA/DoD clinical practice guideline for management of concussion/mild traumatic brain injury. *Journal of Rehabilitation Research and Development, 46*, CP1–CP68.

Manchester, D., & Woods, R. (2001). *Applying cognitive therapy in neurobehavioral rehabilitation. Neurobehavioral disability and social handicap following traumatic brain injury*. Hove, England: Psychology Press.

Mateo, M. A., Glod, C. A., Hennen, J., Price, B. H., & Merrill, N. (2005). Mild traumatic brain injury in psychiatric inpatients. *The Journal of Neuroscience Nursing, 37*, 28–33. doi:10.1097/01376517-200502000-00005

McAllister, T. W. (2006). Mild brain injury and the postconcussion syndrome. In J. M. Silver, T. W. McAllister, & S. C. Yudofsky (Eds.), *Textbook of traumatic brain injury* (pp. 279–308). Washington, DC: American Psychiatric Publishing.

McAllister, T. W. (2008). Neurobehavioral sequelae of traumatic brain injury: Evaluation and management. *World Psychiatry; Official Journal of the World Psychiatric Association, 7*, 3–10.

McCullagh, S., & Feinstein, A. (2005). Cognitive changes. In J. M. Silver, T. W. McAllister, & S. C. Yudofsky (Eds.), *Textbook of traumatic brain injury* (pp. 321–335). Washington, DC: American Psychiatric Publishing.

McGuire, L. M., Burright, R. G., Williams, R., & Donovick, P. J. (1998). Prevalence of traumatic brain injury in psychiatric and non-psychiatric subjects. *Brain Injury, 12*, 207–214. doi:10.1080/026990598122683

McMillan, T. M. (1991). Post-traumatic stress disorder and severe head injury. *The British Journal of Psychiatry, 159*, 431–433. doi:10.1192/bjp.159.3.431

Mendes, D. D., Mello, M. F., Ventura, P., De Medeiros Passarela, C., & De Jesus Mari, J. (2008). A systematic review on the effectiveness of cognitive behavioral therapy for posttraumatic stress disorder. *International Journal of Psychiatry in Medicine, 38*, 241–259. doi:10.2190/PM.38.3.b

Nampiaparampil, D. E. (2008). Prevalence of chronic pain after traumatic brain injury: A systematic review. *JAMA, 300*, 711–719. doi:10.1001/jama.300.6.711

Nelson, L. A., Yoash-Gantz, R. E., Pickett, T. C., & Campbell, T. A. (2009). Relationship between processing speed and executive functioning performance among OEF/OIF veterans: Implications for postdeployment rehabilitation. *The Journal of Head Trauma Rehabilitation, 24*, 32–40. doi:10.1097/HTR.0b013e3181957016

Ponsford, J., Sloan, S., & Snow, P. (1995). *Traumatic brain injury: Rehabilitation for everyday adaptive living*. Hove, England: Psychology Press.

Raskin, S. A. (2000). Executive functions. In S. A. Raskin & C. A. Mateer (Eds.), *Neuropsychological management of mild traumatic brain injury* (pp. 113–133). New York, NY: Oxford University Press.

Reissig, C. J., Strain, E. C., & Griffiths, R. R. (2009). Caffeinated energy drinks— A growing problem. *Drug and Alcohol Dependence, 99,* 1–10. doi:10.1016/j.drugalcdep.2008.08.001

Rogers, J. M., & Read, C. A. (2007). Psychiatric comorbidity following traumatic brain injury. *Brain Injury, 21,* 1321–1333. doi:10.1080/02699050701765700

Rohling, M. L., Faust, M. E., Beverly, B., & Demakis, G. (2009). Effectiveness of cognitive rehabilitation following acquired brain injury: A meta-analytic re-examination of Cicerone et al.'s (2000, 2005) systematic reviews. *Neuropsychology, 23,* 20–39. doi:10.1037/a0013659

Sayer, N. A., Chiros, C. E., Sigford, B., Scott, S., Clothier, B., Pickett, T., & Lew, H. L. (2008). Characteristics and rehabilitation outcomes among patients with blast and other injuries sustained during the Global War on Terror. *Archives of Physical Medicine and Rehabilitation, 89,* 163–170. doi:10.1016/j.apmr.2007.05.025

Sayer, N. A., Cifu, D. X., McNamee, S., Chiros, C. E., Sigford, B., Scott, S., & Lew, H. L. (2009). Rehabilitation needs of combat-injured service members admitted to the VA Polytrauma Rehabilitation Centers: The role of PM&R in the care of wounded warriors. *Physical Medicine & Rehabilitation, 1,* 23–28.

Schmitter-Edgecomb, M., Fahy, J. F., Whelan, J., P., & Long, C. J. (1995). Memory remediation after severe closed head injury: Notebook training versus supportive therapy. *Journal of Consulting and Clinical Psychology, 63,* 484–489.

Schneiderman, A. I., Braver, E. R., & Kang, H. K. (2008). Understanding sequelae of injury mechanisms and mild traumatic brain injury incurred during the conflicts in Iraq and Afghanistan: Persistent postconcussive symptoms and posttraumatic stress disorder. *American Journal of Epidemiology, 167,* 1446–1452. doi:10.1093/aje/kwn068

Schretlen, D. J., & Shapiro, A. M. (2003). A quantitative review of the effects of traumatic brain injury on cognitive functioning. *International Review of Psychiatry, 15,* 341–349.

Shalev, A. Y., Friedman, M. J., Foa, E. B., & Keane, T. M. (2000). Integration and summary. In E. B. Foa, T. M. Keane, & M. J. Friedman (Eds.), *Effective treatments for PTSD* (pp. 359–379). New York, NY: Guilford Press.

Sharp, T. J., & Harvey, A. G. (2001). Chronic pain and posttraumatic disorder: Mutual maintenance. *Clinical Psychology Review, 21,* 857–877. doi:10.1016/S0272-7358(00)00071-4

Silver, J. M., Arciniegas, D. B., & Yudofsky, S. C. (2005). Psychopharmacology. In J. M. Silver, T. W. McAllister, & S. C. Yudofsky (Eds.), *Textbook of traumatic brain injury* (pp. 609–639). Washington, DC: American Psychiatric Publishing.

Snell, D. L., Surgenor, L. J., Hay-Smith, E. J. C., & Siegert, R. J. (2009). A systematic review of psychological treatments for mild traumatic brain injury: An update on the evidence. *Journal of Clinical and Experimental Neuropsychology, 31*, 20–38. doi:10.1080/13803390801978849

Sohlberg, M. M., Johnson, L., Paule, L., Raskin, S. A., & Mateer, C. A. (2001). *Attention Process Training* (2nd ed.). Wake Forest, NC: Lash & Associates.

Soo, C., & Tate, R. (2007). Psychological treatment for anxiety in people with traumatic brain injury [review]. *Cochrane Database of Systematic Reviews, 3*, CD005239.

Spinella, M. (2002). Herbal medicines and epilepsy. To the editor. *Epilepsy & Behavior, 3*, 201. doi:10.1006/ebeh.2002.0328

Stein, M. B., & McAllister, T. W. (2009). Exploring the convergence of posttraumatic stress disorder and mild traumatic brain injury. *The American Journal of Psychiatry, 166*, 768–776. doi:10.1176/appi.ajp.2009.08101604

Suh, M., Kolster, R., Sarkar, R., McCandliss, B., & Ghajar, J. (2006). Deficits in predictive smooth pursuit after mild traumatic brain injury. *Neuroscience Letters, 401*, 108–113. doi:10.1016/j.neulet.2006.02.074

Torsney, K. (2004). The need to explore the prevalence and treatment of acquired brain injury among persons with serious and persistent mental illnesses. *Psychiatric Rehabilitation Journal, 28*, 75–77. doi:10.2975/28.2004.75.77

Trudeau, D. L., Anderson, J., Hansen, L. M., Shagalov, D. N., Schmoller, J., Nugent, S., & Barton, S. (1998). Findings of mild traumatic brain injury in combat veterans with PTSD and a history of blast concussion. *The Journal of Neuropsychiatry and Clinical Neurosciences, 10*, 308–313.

Tsaousides, T., & Gordon, W. A. (2009). Cognitive rehabilitation following traumatic brain injury: Assessment to treatment. *The Mount Sinai Journal of Medicine, New York, 76*, 173–181. doi:10.1002/msj.20099

Turnbull, S. J., Campbell, E. A., & Swann, I. J. (2001). Post-traumatic stress disorder symptoms following a head injury: Does amnesia for the event influence development of symptoms? *Brain Injury, 15*, 775–785. doi:10.1080/026990 50110034334

Vasa, R. A., Grados, M., Slomine, B., Herskovits, E. H., Thompson, R. E., Salorio, C., . . . Gerring, J. P. (2004). Neuroimaging correlates of anxiety after pediatric traumatic brain injury. *Biological Psychiatry, 55*, 208–216. doi:10.1016/S0006-3223(03)00708-X

Warden, D. (2006). Military TBI during the Iraq and Afghanistan wars. *The Journal of Head Trauma Rehabilitation, 21*, 398–402. doi:10.1097/00001199-200609000-00004

Warden, D. L., Gordon, B., McAllister, T. W., Silver, J. M., Barth, J. T., Bruns, J., et al. (2006). Guidelines for the pharmacologic treatment of neurobehavioral sequelae of traumatic brain injury. *Journal of Neurotrauma, 23*, 1468–1501. doi:10.1089/neu.2006.23.1468

Warden, D. L., Labbate, L. A., Salazar, A. M., Nelson, R., Sheley, E., Staudenmeier, J., . . . Zitnay, G. (1997). Posttraumatic stress disorder in patients with traumatic brain injury and amnesia for the event? *The Journal of Neuropsychiatry and Clinical Neurosciences, 9,* 18–22.

Wasserman, L., Shaw, T., Vu, M., Ko, C., Bollegala, D., & Bhalerao, S. (2008). An overview of traumatic brain injury and suicide. *Brain Injury, 22,* 811–819. doi:10.1080/02699050802372166

Wong, A. H., Smith, M., & Boon, M. S. (1998). Herbal remedies in psychiatric practice. *Archives of General Psychiatry, 55,* 1033–1044. doi:10.1001/archpsyc.55.11.1033

Ylvisaker, M., Turkstra, L., Coehlo, C., Yorkston, K., Kennedy, M., Sohlberg, M. M., & Avery, J. (2007). Behavioural interventions for children and adults with behaviour disorders after TBI: A systematic review of the evidence. *Brain Injury, 21,* 769–805. doi:10.1080/02699050701482470

5

ASSESSMENT AND MANAGEMENT OF HIGH-RISK SUICIDAL STATES IN POSTDEPLOYMENT OPERATION ENDURING FREEDOM AND OPERATION IRAQI FREEDOM MILITARY PERSONNEL

CYNTHIA A. CLAASSEN AND KERRY L. KNOX

Between 2000 and 2006, 53% of all suicides in the general U.S. population were committed with firearms, and 80% of all suicide decedents were men (Centers for Disease Control and Prevention [CDC], National Center for Injury Prevention and Control, 2009). Although the U.S. military is largely populated by men living under stressful conditions with ready access to guns, military suicide rates have traditionally been lower than corresponding civilian rates (Eaton, Messer, Garvey Wilson, & Hoge, 2006). However, 2008 U.S. Army rates surpassed corresponding civilian rates for the first time ever and were more than double those occurring before initiation of Operation Enduring Freedom (OEF) and Operation Iraqi Freedom (OIF) in 2001 (Suicide Risk Management & Surveillance Office, 2008; see Figure 5.1). Suicide is currently the second leading cause of death in the Marine Corps (U.S. Marine Corps, 2009), second also among young, enlisted Army men (Inspector General, U.S.

This chapter was coauthored by an employee of the United States government as part of official duty and is considered to be in the public domain. Any views expressed herein do not necessarily represent the views of the United States government, and the author's participation in the work is not meant to serve as an official endorsement.

Cynthia A. Claassen, PhD, was formerly affiliated with the Department of Psychiatry, University of Rochester School of Medicine, Rochester, NY.

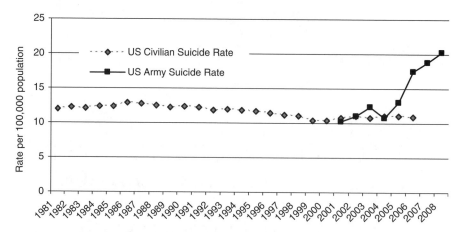

Figure 5.1. Suicide rates for the overall U.S. population, 1981–2005, and the U.S. Army, 2001–2009. Data on U.S. rates are from Centers for Disease Control and Prevention, National Center for Injury Prevention and Control (2005). Data on U.S. Army rates are from Deputy Chief of Staff, Army G-1 (2009).

Department of Defense, 2008), and consistently among the top three causes of death in the Navy (U.S. Navy, 2006).

The mounting concern about military suicide rates has recently given rise to questions about suicide rates among veterans. One well-designed study of veterans receiving care within the Veterans Health Administration (VHA) found that these individuals had a standardized suicide mortality ratio of 1.66 when compared with age-matched, nonmilitary controls (McCarthy et al., 2009). However, the health status of VHA patients is not generally representative of the larger group of all veterans, and results from community-based studies of veteran suicide rates have been mixed (Kaplan, Huguet, McFarland, & Newsom, 2007; M. Miller et al., 2009). Although the findings are not definitive, it is painfully apparent that clinicians working with some military and veteran groups are working with individuals who have unusually high baseline levels of risk for serious and fatal suicidal acts.

This chapter reviews some of the important issues associated with identification and management of suicide risk in OEF and OIF and other military and veteran populations. It provides a brief phenomenological description of suicide risk, as well as risk identification, assessment, and treatment strategies. Real-world application of these strategies is illustrated with two case vignettes involving OEF and OIF veterans. Although the protocols described here are state of the art, the reader is reminded that no risk assessment or suicide management approach is ever infallible and that, ultimately, prediction of human behavior is never entirely possible.

DEFINITIONS

Increased suicide risk levels are frequently dangerous and relatively unpredictable conditions that can progress rapidly into suicidal behavior (Gorman, 2006). Suicidal ideation involves repeated thoughts about intentionally ending one's own life and may or may not include plans by which to do so. Where suicidal behavior seems likely within hours, days, or weeks, *near-term risk* is said to exist (Rudd, 2000). As used in this chapter, *acute* suicide risk status refers to current risk level compared with baseline, taking into account recent circumstance, accessible protective factors, and current mental state. In contrast, *chronic* (heightened) suicide risk involves ongoing, elevated risk that is often maintained by specific, intractable neuropsychological conditions (e.g., certain brain lesions) or the presence of relatively immutable social and demographic factors (Bryan & Rudd, 2006). Triaging and assessing suicide risk is the process of evaluating the relative salience of factors that exacerbate or inhibit an individual's potential for self-destructive behavior in the near term. This assessment process is used to inform both immediate management of suicidal individuals and ongoing treatment (Simon, 2006).

PHENOMENOLOGY OF HIGH-RISK SUICIDAL STATES

In almost all cases, intentionally self-destructive behavior is preceded by at least some measure of suicidal ideation (Kessler, Berglund, & Borges, 2005). This ideation appears to convert to behavior without actual planning of the attempt itself in 9% to 12% of cases, but suicide attempts in the absence of any prior ideation appear to be extremely rare (De Leo, Cerin, Spathonis, & Burgis, 2005; Perez, 2005). The length of time that suicidal ideation is present before an attempt varies considerably, with a striking number of patients (more than 20% in one community-based study) reporting that their self-destructive behavior occurred less than 5 min after onset of ideation (De Leo et al., 2005). Youth and young adults (ages 25–30), Caucasians, and women seem to be most vulnerable to both ideation and nonfatal attempts (Evans, Hawton, Rodham, & Deeks, 2005; Kessler et al., 2005; Welch, 2001), whereas substantially more Caucasian men die by suicide than is the case for any other demographic group (CDC, 2009). In some studies, different life stages have been linked to different risk profiles (Brown, Comtois, & Linehan, 2002; Fairweather, Anstey, Rodgers, & Butterworth, 2006; King et al., 2001). Adolescent cohorts, for instance, sometimes demonstrate routine engagement in other high-risk behaviors when episodes of suicidal behavior are present or impending (T. R. Miller & Taylor, 2005; Perez, 2005). The factors that precede repeated (vs. first) attempts are generally less uniform, regardless of age

(Joiner, Pfaff, & Acres, 2002). The few studies to examine progression across risk levels suggest that large numbers of adverse life experiences occurring in close temporal proximity in a kind of dose–response relationship often, but not always, are associated with self-destructive behaviors (Fairweather et al., 2006).

Suicidal ideation and behavior can occur in the absence of any diagnosable psychopathology, but one of the most salient risk factors for both is the presence of mental illness (Goldstein, Black, Nasrallah, & Winokur, 1991; Jacobs et al., 2003). An estimated 50% to 90% of all suicidal injuries occur in the context of psychiatric problems, and upward of 50% to 60% of all patients experiencing suicidal ideation have either a diagnosable depressive disorder or severe, subjective dysphoria (Jacobs et al., 2003; Witte, Fitzpatrick, Warren, Schatschneider, & Schmidt, 2006). Affective instability, psychoactive substance abuse, hopelessness, and personality disorders are well-known psychological correlates of both ideation and behavior (Jacobs et al., 2003). Severe anxiety, panic attacks, and sleep problems can be proximal correlates of self-harm (Fawcett, 2006), although these conditions are neither prerequisites nor essential triggers for such behavior. Finally, most suicidal crises are time-limited, dynamic processes (Russ, Kashdan, Pollack, & Bajmakovic-Kacila, 1999), suggesting that efforts to ensure survival in the short term often produce lasting results.

OEF- AND OIF-SPECIFIC RISK CONSIDERATIONS

On the basis of data from the Army's Suicide Risk Management and Surveillance Office (2008), active-duty military personnel who present for treatment of suicidal ideation are more likely to die by suicide than are their civilian counterparts. In the civilian U.S. population, there are an estimated 300 cases of suicidal ideation for every suicide, whereas military data include only five reported cases of suicidal ideation per suicide (Suicide Risk Management & Surveillance Office, 2008). In contrast, after adjusting for age and gender, the proportion of suicide attempts resulting in death is similar in Army and civilian populations, with approximately one fatal event for every seven to eight medically treated episode (CDC, 2009; Suicide Risk Management & Surveillance Office, 2008). The extremely high proportion of deaths among soldiers who report suicidal ideation may be related partially to differences in psychological vulnerability among military and civilian populations. Individuals who choose military life may simply be psychologically stronger as a group than matched civilian groups, experiencing fewer episodes of heightened risk overall but more fatal episodes when they do occur. Conversely, the lower rates of suicidal ideation in relationship to suicides may be the result of massive underreporting in a "show no weakness" warrior culture. To the extent that this is the case, a significant number of soldiers may be silently struggling with a condition potentially as lethal as any enemy they could encounter in combat.

For some OEF and OIF personnel, heightened risk levels continue or emerge after discharge. The transition period out of military service is historically a vulnerable period filled with loss of position, shared purpose, and important relationships, and some OEF and OIF veterans experience one or more postdeployment health conditions during this time that further exacerbate risk. For instance, an estimated 14% of returning OEF and OIF service members develop posttraumatic stress disorder (PTSD; Schell & Marshall, 2008). Data from the Collaborative Psychiatric Epidemiology Surveys suggest that up to 40% of individuals with PTSD experience suicidal ideation within the 1st year of onset, and these individuals are also 6 times more likely to attempt suicide within that year, compared with individuals without PTSD (Alegria, Jackson, Kessler, & Takeuchi, 2007). Second, an equal number of returning OEF and OIF service members report significant postdeployment depressive symptoms (Schell & Marshall, 2008), and an estimated 35% of depressed individuals also experience suicidal thoughts and behaviors—again, with onset often occurring early in the course of the depressive illness (Andrews & Lewinsohn, 1992; Garrison, McKeown, Valois, & Vincent, 1993). Third, the striking rates of improvised explosive device (IED)-induced polytrauma in the OEF–OIF population create serious adjustment issues for large numbers of newly disabled soldiers with comorbid traumatic brain injury, many of whom have ready access to multiple classes of potentially lethal prescription medications. In discussing this point, French, Siddharthan, Bass, and Campbell (2008) cautioned that "although it is medically necessary to treat chronic nonmalignant pain, depression, and/or behavioral symptoms associated with polytrauma, prolonged use of these drug regimens may present increased risks to patient safety and further complicate functional recovery" (p. 628).

IDENTIFYING, TRIAGING, AND ASSESSING SUICIDE RISK

Suicidal individuals often initially disclose their high-risk predicament outside of mental health settings. Real-world risk containment, therefore, generally occurs in stages across multiple settings and involves separate risk identification, triage, and assessment processes (O'Connor, Warby, Raphael, & Vassallo, 2004). During all stages of the process, use of well-designed protocols helps balance the need for a scientifically grounded approach with practical considerations such as speed, clarity, and utility.

There are currently no group screening instruments for high-risk suicidal states, and although such an approach would likely be widely used in military, veteran, and civilian settings, it is not currently endorsed because of both a lack of empirically validated tools and the complexity of studying and addressing suicidal phenomena in group settings (Gaynes et al., 2004). Furthermore, there is no single, widely accepted overall standard of care for identifying, triaging, or assessing suicide risk. Therefore, charged with responsibility for the health and well-being of military and veteran populations, the Department of Defense and VHA health care systems increasingly emphasize early identification and triage by laypersons as critical to prevention efforts. A key ingredient in these early identification protocols is awareness of a set of suicide warning signs. Conceptually, a warning sign is understood to be a pathognomic indicator of heightened risk and of urgent need for further assessment. The American Association of Suicidology suggests that the following warning signs designate extremely high risk levels (Rudd et al., 2006): suicidal threats or wishes; preparations for suicidal acts (e.g., evaluating alternative methods, obtaining necessary means); and new-onset discussion about death, dying, or suicide. The American Association of Suicidology also suggests that these behaviors should trigger immediate, emergency help-seeking efforts. In addition, the association identifies nine other behaviors or attributes that signal a need for expedited further evaluation: (a) increased substance (alcohol or drug) use; (b) a sense of purposelessness; (c) anxiety, agitation, changes in sleep patterns; (d) a sense of feeling trapped, as if there is no way out of a miserable situation; (e) hopelessness; (f) withdrawal from friends, family, and society; (g) presence of rage, uncontrolled anger, or a desire for revenge; (h) reckless or high-risk behaviors; and (i) dramatic mood changes.

All four branches of service and the VHA have developed extensive suicide prevention initiatives during the past decade and have disseminated the American Association of Suicidology warning signs widely. In addition, all branches of the military have distributed lists of proximal risk factors for suicidal behavior. In contrast to warning signs, a risk factor is understood to be a variable that has been correlated with suicidal behavior in prior research. Risk factors are not necessarily associated with near-term risk and therefore do not always trigger emergency evaluation. A sampling of military lists of proximal risk factors can be found on the Navy and Marine Corps Public Health Center website (http://www-nehc.med.navy.mil/healthy_living/psychological_health/suicide_prevention/prevsuicide_warningsigns.aspx).

The military's early identification and triage procedures introduce warning signs within the context of standardized, mandated, suicide prevention protocols designed to empower those in a suicidal person's social network to identify and address potential risk. Using slogans such as "Shoulder-to-Shoulder: No Soldier Stands Alone," these protocols include the Army's ACE program (Ask, Care, Escort; U.S. Army, 2009), the Navy's ACT program (Ask, Care, Treat; U.S. Navy, 2006), the U.S. Air Force PRESS protocol (Prepare,

Recognize, Engage, Send, Sustain; U.S. Air Force, 2006), the Marine Corps' AID LIFE protocol (Ask, Intervene, Don't keep it a secret, Locate help, Inform, Find someone to stay with the person; Expedite; U.S. Marine Corp, 2009), and the VHA's Operation S.A.V.E. (Know the Signs, Ask, Validate, and Encourage and Expedite Treatment-seeking; U.S. Department of Veterans Affairs, 2009).

Triaging Suicide Risk—General Guidelines

Regardless of setting or protocol, triage needs to be a straightforward, easily mobilized, responsive process designed to facilitate prompt identification and management of individuals who require further evaluation. At minimum, these protocols should include the following components: (a) immediate, brief evaluation of physical and mental status; (b) determination of current mental capacity and level of consciousness; (c) evaluation of current subjective distress; (d) identification of psychopathology requiring immediate management (e.g., impulsivity, psychosis); (e) need for involuntary treatment; and (f) determination of willingness to consent (Hart, Colley, & Harrison, 2005; National Institute on Clinical Excellence, 2004).

As a means of protecting patients until they are in a safe environment, military protocols often use a "suicide watch." This involves escorts who keep the suicidal soldier in direct eye contact, search immediate belongings and environment for instruments of self-harm, and remain with the soldier until he or she is in a safe environment (U.S. Army Infantry Center, 2008). Such a procedure is necessary because suicidal individuals are sometimes extremely ambivalent about help seeking. For the same reason, triage protocols should provide contingency plans if suicidal individuals refuse to present for further evaluation. If possible, they should be triaged in settings where more than one trained person is available to assist with safety considerations (Clarke, Brown, & Giles-Smith, 2008).

Practice Guidelines for Comprehensive Clinical Assessment of Suicide Risk

Although the primary goal of both triage and formal risk appraisal is to ensure the safety and well-being of suicidal individuals and those around them, triage protocols are never intended to replace a comprehensive evaluation of risk conducted by well-trained mental health clinicians. Within military and VHA settings, no one standard risk assessment protocol is in widespread use, although the VHA is currently piloting a standardized assessment template (Kayman, 2009). In its current form, the template is meant only as a guideline and is not currently available in all facilities. Both the American Psychiatric Association and the (British) Royal College of Psychiatrists (RCP) have published evidence-based practice guidelines that inform this risk evaluation process (Jacobs et al., 2003; National Institute on Clinical Excellence, 2004). The American Psychiatric Association guideline emphasizes the importance of conducting suicide risk assessment within the framework of a comprehensive clinical interview, whereas RCP guidelines address both triage and clinical risk assessment procedures. American Psychiatric Association guidelines suggest that five areas should be investigated during formal risk assessment (Fawcett, 2006): (a) clinical status, with emphasis on modifiable risk factors; (b) diagnoses and comorbidity; (c) history of suicidal states; (d) current psychosocial situation; and (e) patient strengths and vulnerabilities. Both the American Psychiatric Association and RCP guidelines should be considered required reading for mental health clinicians with primary responsibility for suicide risk assessment.

Rapport building is critical to establishing an adequate therapeutic alliance during the risk assessment process. Barry (2008) suggested that a basic familiarity with common military terminology can enhance the therapeutic alliance and recommended that six military-specific questions be asked of new OEF and OIF veterans. The questions include inquiries about traumatic experiences while deployed, military occupational specialty, stop-loss experiences, use of mental health care "downrange" (i.e., while in Iraq or Afghanistan), exact manner of military exit, and Department of Veterans Affairs (VA) enrollment.

Accurately Establishing Level of Risk

As suggested by the warning signs listed earlier, heightened risk status sometimes includes behavioral and emotional changes, including the emergence of difficult-to-control, self-destructive impulses and calculated efforts to access means of self-injury. Such changes often occur partially outside the suicidal individual's critical awareness. The patient may describe, for instance, "suddenly" putting a gun barrel in the mouth, with no identifiable forethought, while dismissing the behavior as inconsequential. This relative lack of regard for the consequences of self-destructive actions can place risk assessment personnel in the position of identifying levels of dangerousness greater than the suicidal individual recognizes. In the military, admitting to suicidal thoughts or behaviors can also be stigmatizing or lead to involuntary treatment—both strong incentives to deny or minimize suicidal states. To the extent that actively suicidal individuals deny or are incapable of understanding their own dangerousness, the validity of interview data is compromised, forcing clinicians to rely heavily on data sources other than explicit self-report during formal risk assessment. In some cases, information from supplemental clinical sources (family, friends) likewise contains bias, rendering much of the available data less than pristine. Unfortunately, empirically based risk assessment instruments do not provide an adequate, stand-alone alternative source of information on which to base clinical decisions about near-term risk. Clinicians can therefore find themselves in a position in which they must render potentially life-and-death decisions using information taken from a variety of sources, none of which have adequate validity or predictive power. This situation necessitates moving between multiple data streams of variable quality in what is essentially a multistep process of weighing the validity of discrete data points to produce a best estimate level of near-term risk status. The nature of this process is illustrated subsequently in fictional case vignettes adapted from actual OEF and OIF case reports.

MANAGEMENT AND TREATMENT OF SUICIDE RISK

Psychological autopsy studies in Europe and America suggest that untreated or undertreated neuropsychological disease processes are present at the time of death in more than 70% of all individuals who complete suicide, whether civilian or military (Henriksson, Boethius, & Isacsson, 2001; Lönnqvist et al., 1995), and therapies designed to treat these conditions should therefore be initiated as soon as safety can be ensured. The primary approaches to treatment of suicidal states currently in use are the biological and psychosocial therapies used to address the underlying neuropsychological processes associated with the emergence of suicidal symptoms. Some of these treatments have demonstrated success in eradicating suicidal states in scientifically rigorous studies (Mann et al., 2005). It should, however, be noted that during the time period when treatment is being initiated, risk remains high. Valenstein et al. (2009) identified the 12 weeks after discharge from inpatient psychiatric settings and the 12 weeks after initiation or change in antidepressant regimens as periods of extremely high suicide risk among VHA-treated veterans. Rates of suicide during these periods run more than 40 times higher than the annual crude rate of suicide in the general U.S. population.

From a risk management perspective, once a high-risk suicidal state has been identified, the patient's immediate and intermediate-term safety needs take priority. In cases of highest risk, the most commonly used protective strategy is closely monitored inpatient care. The use of psychiatric hospitalization to protect at-risk suicidal patients is time-honored but increasingly controversial for some diagnostic groups (Paris, 2004). Linehan (1993) suggested that the increased attention received while on inpatient suicide watch can be both reinforcing and infantilizing for patients with borderline personality disorder. In contrast, within the veteran population, an analysis of VHA patient suicides suggests that easy access to rehospitalization to address persistent suicidality can be associated with reduced rates of completion among VHA psychiatric patients (Desai, Dausey, & Rosenheck, 2005).

When inpatient care is not considered necessary after formal risk assessment, a common strategy used with suicidal patients is the no harm contract (Stanford, Goetz, & Bloom, 1994). In its simplest form, this approach involves creating a contract in which a suicidal individual pledges to contact a specific person(s) or treatment center before engaging in future self-harming behavior. Unfortunately, this technique is often used not to manage risk but to assess it, with refusal to contract interpreted as a sign of high risk. As an assessment shortcut, the no harm contract is extremely poor clinical practice and can be deadly. Agreement to a self-harm contract is not a demonstration that the patient is in no current danger. As Fawcett (2006) asked, "Why should a patient who is deciding that life is too painful to live tell you the truth?" (p. 441). When used as a postassessment intervention strategy as described subsequently, however, the strategy can be both useful and valid.

The VHA recently adopted a safety-planning protocol for use with suicidal outpatients during future episodes of serious suicidal ideation (Henriques, Beck, & Brown, 2003). A safety plan is a prioritized, predetermined list of resources (i.e., coping strategies, sources of support) that patients can access during vulnerable periods. As a therapeutic technique, it provides patients being released into the community with something more than just a referral at the completion of suicide risk assessment (Stanley & Brown, 2008). As used in the VHA, the plan involves the following steps: (a) recognition of signs of escalating risk, (b) use of internal coping strategies to manage episodes of suicidal ideation, (c) use of social contacts that can distract from suicidal ideation and provide support, (d) contact with family members or friends who can assist in resolving an episode of high-risk suicidal ideation, (e) contact with professionals and agencies, and (f) reduction in access to lethal means.

Finally, whether in the context of a safety plan or not, restricting access to firearms may be a particularly critical risk management strategy for suicidal military and veteran groups who are known to have high rates of both gun ownership and suicide by firearm. A recent population-based study of veterans found that they were twice as likely as nonveterans to die by suicide and 58% more likely to use firearms to end their lives (Kaplan, Huguet, McFarland, & Newsom, 2007). Gun safety protocols are therefore regarded as standard of care in some clinical settings that treat large numbers of suicidal veterans.

To summarize this section of the chapter, suicide risk assessment and management techniques are of necessity a meld of clinically derived and scientifically informed strategies adaptable to widely varying presentations and circumstances (Bryan & Rudd, 2006). There is no one empirically validated protocol available that addresses all aspects of this process, including training, screening, assessment, and treatment. Further research is sorely needed to develop scientifically based protocols, and such work will need to incorporate larger numbers and more diverse risk factors and the interactions between them, as well as more sophisticated statistical modeling techniques. Meanwhile, competent risk assessment requires (a) adequate educational background to know what information needs to be gathered, (b) rapport building and interviewing skills, (c) clinical decision-making skills and abilities, and (d) the skills to communicate these decisions and to conduct related interventions (Monahan, 1993). Included is the capacity to synthesize diverse data elements of variable quality into a best estimate of acute risk status.

SUICIDE RISK ASSESSMENT AMONG OEF AND OIF SOLDIERS AND VETERANS

Risk management employs strategies suited to risk level and individual circumstance to ensure safety during suicidal crises. Competency in the therapeutic application of both activities requires clinical skill and experience. Perhaps this is nowhere truer than when assessing suicidality among those recently exposed to military combat. For such individuals, a host of factors conspires to thwart the identification and adequate management of dangerous self-injurious thoughts and impulses, as illustrated in the hypothetical case vignettes that follow.

Case Vignette 1: The Homecoming

"Peter" is a 23-year-old Army reservist who returned from Iraq 4 months earlier. He presented in the hospital emergency department in handcuffs, accompanied by police, after his mother discovered him in the family garage with a noose around his neck. Upon exam, Peter smelled of alcohol, was angry and defensive, reporting that he was only attempting to tie a bicycle to the garage rafters when the noose "accidentally" fell down around his neck. As the interview progressed, however, Peter seemed increasingly agitated and confused, unable to sustain concentration and, at times, even to respond coherently. His blood alcohol level did not seem high enough to explain these factors completely. In Iraq, Peter had been hit by enemy fire, and his flack jacket had taken multiple pieces of shrapnel, yet Peter reported that he had not even been bruised. He had also discussed with his family a disturbing incident in which he witnessed an insurgent execute a pregnant Iraqi woman. He reported having frequent nightmares, often awakening with night sweats.

A few weeks earlier, Peter had called his mother at work tearful and disoriented. He told her that a buddy had just died in Afghanistan. His mother indicated that this friend had actually died over a year before and that she and Peter had discussed his death many times. Peter's family reported that Peter knew he needed help but was worried about being stigmatized. He was still in active duty and expected to be redeployed. Peter's mother also noted that he was having trouble with the homecoming he experienced from some of his high school friends: Instead of saying "Welcome home," they said things like "Hey, Pete! Ya shoot anybody over there?" She noted that Peter would be upset for hours after such an exchange.

Comment: In cases such as Peter's, it is important to note the difference between implicitly and explicitly stated suicidal intent (Beck & Lester, 1976) and to understand the degree to which alcohol can and cannot influence one's behavior. Theoretically, after all clinical information is compiled, risk factors, estimated risk level, subjective distress levels, and collateral information should form a coherent, plausible scenario (Bryan & Rudd, 2006). When this is not the case, the clinician must estimate the probable reliability and validity of each piece of data individually. Peter currently denies suicidality, but his recent behavior, psychological symptoms, and nonverbal presentation are internally consistent with an appraisal of imminent dangerousness. In short, rather than just being under the influence of alcohol, the complete presentation, taken with his recent, intense affective states, suggests that he is currently experiencing an acute and dangerous psychiatric crisis (Hendin, Maltsberger, & Szanto, 2007).

Given Peter's disorientation and fear, his experience of this first-ever encounter in a mental health setting could significantly affect future compliance and willingness to seek mental health assistance (Claassen, Wise, & Krakover, 2006). It is therefore critical that the emergency department clinician establish the best treatment alliance possible. Handcuffs should be removed as soon as possible; the patient's service to his country should be acknowledged and his need for control and respect accommodated. Shea (2007) emphasized the need to delay inquiry about sensitive topics until the patient has begun to feel comfortable with the clinical interview process. Others have suggested that the risk interview is often more successful when it begins with an invitation to the patient to tell his own story in an unstructured, unchallenged manner, rather than with more focused questioning (Bryan & Rudd, 2006; National Institute on Clinical Excellence, 2004). The Collaborative Assessment and Management of Suicidality protocol was developed in military mental health settings and stresses the importance of the working partnership between the clinician and suicidal patient (Jobes & Drozd, 2004; Jobes, Wong, Conrad, Drozd, & Neal-Walden, 2005). Such an approach might help foster the mutual respect and team spirit necessary to diminish resistance to the mandatory inpatient treatment that will be required to evaluate further and adequately treat Peter's current psychiatric state.

Case Vignette 2: Polytrauma

"Joshua" is a 24-year-old triple-amputee veteran who has been treated in an inpatient psychiatric VA service for approximately 3 weeks after ingesting a large quantity of prescription pain and psychotropic medications. His wife discovered his suicide attempt. She reported that he told her at the time that he was "sick of living like this" and that she and the children would be better off without him. She reported that he had refused to attend outpatient medical appointments or wear his prosthetic legs in the weeks before the overdose. "It's like he just finally gave up."

Joshua lost both legs and his left arm in Iraq after an IED detonated under his Humvee. Within a matter of hours after the explosion, what was left of his lower legs was removed in Germany, followed by removal of his arm at Walter Reed. His wife recalled being told by a nurse who flew with him to Germany that Joshua held tightly to a blood-splattered picture of their three children with his one remaining hand throughout the flight, staring at it continuously. After stabilization and 15 months of inpatient rehab, he was finally allowed to return home approximately 9 months earlier. The transition had been difficult for all. Joshua had trouble reconnecting with his children, believing that they were ashamed of a disabled father. In addition, he seemed only minimally adjusted to his disability status, repeatedly expressing amazement that he had gone from being a "whole" man wondering what he was going to eat for lunch to life as a "total cripple" within 72 hr.

On the inpatient unit, he was medication-compliant and minimally cooperative with milieu and group therapies. However, he remained withdrawn, spoke little, and avoided all social activities. He consistently denied suicidal ideation and his mental status was clear, but his sleep was disturbed and appetite remained poor. He reported that the overdose was "a stupid mistake" and something he would never try again. He was anxious to be discharged so that he could return home.

Comment. Joshua's clinical presentation suggests that his depression has not lifted, and his denouncement of recent suicidal ideation is less than reassuring. The high rates of suicide during the 12 weeks after inpatient VA treatment reported in prior research demonstrate that rapid reescalation of risk is a serious concern for some patients even after weeks of inpatient care. Furthermore, although no statistics are available for OEF and OIF cohorts, research on Vietnam-era veterans suggests that the suicide rate among war amputees and soldiers sustaining combat-related disability is at least 37% to 100%

higher than corresponding rates in the civilian population (Bakalim, 1969; Bullman & Kang, 1996). In short, Joshua may be at chronic risk of suicidal behavior for some time. Therefore, risk assessment in this case should include a careful appraisal of both acute and chronic risk levels and the factors that contribute to each (Rudd, 2000). The Chronological Assessment of Suicide Events (CASE) approach to risk assessment (Shea, 1998) is designed to create a "verbal videotape" of the presenting suicidal state in a semistructured, step-by-step manner, with the clinician and patient exploring distant and recent developments collaboratively. The well-executed CASE interview often becomes a therapeutic intervention that helps to identify and transform distorted subjective perceptions, and this approach may be useful in addressing Joshua's struggles with his family. With reference to management of Joshua's chronically elevated risk levels, perhaps one of the most disturbing features of this case is the marked shift in his attitude toward his children. His behavior at the time of injury suggested that this connection was an important protective factor, yet recent actions suggest that he no longer accesses this resource. Given that interpersonal factors were his first coping mechanism, it may be helpful to address the current ambivalence about these relationships during a CASE-type interview format.

In cases such as Joshua's, a well-rehearsed safety plan should be in place and reviewed multiple times before discharge with both the individual and family members. Access to means of self-injury should be restricted within the home, and emergency and crisis line numbers should be readily available. Aggressive treatment of Joshua's depression needs to be continued, and additional rehabilitation may also be in order.

CONCLUSION

Although baseline risk levels for civilians in the same demographic group as the OEF and OIF cohort are significantly lower than levels for older Americans, factors associated with exposure to the Iraqi and Afghan military theaters may engender significantly higher postdeployment risk levels in some active duty military personnel. Risk assessment protocols must consider these specific factors, along with the military culture's strong incentives to deny the presence of suicidal states. Because of the high rates of gun ownership found among those exposed to this culture, restriction of access to firearms may be among the most universal of applicable risk management strategies. The current OEF–OIF cohort is composed entirely of individuals who voluntarily chose to serve and protect. At the very least, they, too, deserve protection— including protection from any potentially suicidogenic factors associated with their service.

REFERENCES

Alegria, M., Jackson, J., Kessler, R., & Takeuchi, D. (2007). Collaborative Psychiatric Epidemiology Surveys, (CPES), 2001–2003 (208 Jun 19 ed.). Ann Arbor, MI: Institute for Social Research, Survey Research Center [producer] and Inter-university Consortium for Political and Social Research [distributor].

Andrews, J., & Lewinsohn, P. (1992). Suicidal attempts among older adolescents: Prevalence and co-occurrence with psychiatric disorders. *Journal of the American Academy of Child and Adolescent Psychiatry, 31,* 655–662. doi:10.1097/00004583-199207000-00012

Bakalim, G. (1969). Causes of death in a series of 4738 Finnish war amputees. *Artificial Limbs, 13,* 27–36.

Barry, M. J. (2008). 6 screening questions for military veterans. *The Journal of Family Practice, 7,* 78–79.

Beck, A., & Lester, D. (1976). Components of suicidal intent in completed and attempted suicides. *Journal of Psychology: Interdisciplinary and Applied, 92,* 35–38.

Brown, M. Z., Comtois, K. A., & Linehan, M. M. (2002). Reasons for suicide attempts and nonsuicidal self-injury in women with borderline personality disorder. *Journal of Abnormal Psychology, 111,* 198–202. doi:10.1037/0021-843X.111.1.198

Bryan, C. J., & Rudd, M. (2006). Advances in the assessment of suicide risk. *Journal of Clinical Psychology, 62,* 185–200. doi:10.1002/jclp.20222

Bullman, T. A., & Kang, H. K. (1996). The risk of suicide among wounded Vietnam veterans. *American Journal of Public Health, 86,* 662–667. doi:10.2105/AJPH.86.5.662

Centers for Disease Control and Prevention, National Center for Injury Prevention and Control. (2009). *Web-based Injury Statistics Query and Reporting System (WISQARS).* Retrieved from http://www.cdc.gov/ncipc/wisqars

Claassen, C. A., Wise, B., & Krakover, B. A. (2006). Involuntary treatment in the ED: At what cost? (*Emergency Medicine & Critical Care Review*). London, England: Touch Briefings.

Clarke, D. E., Brown, A. M., & Giles-Smith, L. (2008). Triaging suicidal patients: Sifting through the evidence. *International Emergency Nursing, 16,* 165–174. doi:10.1016/j.ienj.2008.03.004

Deputy Chief of Staff, Army G-1. (2009). *Suicide Prevention.* Retrieved from http://www.armyg1.army.mil/hR/suicide/default.asp

De Leo, D., Cerin, E., Spathonis, K., & Burgis, S. (2005). Lifetime risk of suicide ideation and attempts in an Australian community: Prevalence, suicidal process, and help-seeking behavior. *Journal of Affective Disorders, 86,* 215–224. doi:10.1016/j.jad.2005.02.001

Desai, R. A., Dausey, D. J., & Rosenheck, R. A. (2005). Mental health service delivery and suicide risk: The role of individual patient and facility factors. *The American Journal of Psychiatry, 162,* 311–318. doi:10.1176/appi.ajp.162.2.311

Eaton, K. M., Messer, S. C., Garvey Wilson, A. L., & Hoge, C. (2006). Strengthening the validity of population-based suicide rate comparisons: An illustration using U.S. military and civilian data. *Suicide & Life-Threatening Behavior, 36*, 182–191. doi:10.1521/suli.2006.36.2.182

Evans, E., Hawton, K., Rodham, K., & Deeks, J. (2005). The prevalence of suicidal phenomena in adolescents: A systematic review of population-based studies. *Suicide & Life-Threatening Behavior, 35*, 239–250. doi:10.1521/suli.2005.35.3.239

Fairweather, A. K., Anstey, K. J., Rodgers, B., & Butterworth, P. (2006). Factors distinguishing suicide attempters from suicide ideators in a community sample: Social issues and physical health problems. *Psychological Medicine, 36*, 1235–1245. doi:10.1017/S0033291706007823

Fawcett, J. (2006). What has clinical research in suicide prevention done for you lately? *CNS Spectrums, 11*, 440–441.

French, D. D., Siddharthan, K., Bass, E., & Campbell, R. R. (2008). Benchmark data on the utilization and acquisition costs of CNS and muscular skeletal drugs among veterans with combat-related injuries. *Military Medicine, 173*, 626–628.

Garrison, C. Z., McKeown, R. E., Valois, R. F., & Vincent, M. L. (1993). Aggression, substance use, and suicidal behaviors in high school students. *American Journal of Public Health, 83*, 179–184. doi:10.2105/AJPH.83.2.179

Gaynes, B. N., West, S. L., Ford, C. A., Frame, P., Klein, J., & Lohr, K. (2004). Screening for suicide risk in adults: A summary of the evidence for the U.S. Preventive Services Task Force. (2004). *Annals of Internal Medicine, 140*, 822–835.

Goldstein, R. B, Black, D. W., Nasrallah, A., & Winokur, G. (1991). The prediction of suicide. *Archives of General Psychiatry, 48*, 418–422.

Gorman, J. M. (2006). Addressing suicide and its risk. *CNS Spectrums, 11*, 415.

Hart, C., Colley, R., & Harrison, A. (2005). Using a risk assessment matrix with mental health patients in emergency departments. *Emergency Nurse, 12*, 21–28.

Hendin, H., Maltsberger, J. T., & Szanto, K. (2007). The role of intense affective states in signaling a suicide crisis. *Journal of Nervous and Mental Disease, 195*, 363–368.

Henriksson, S., Boethius, G., & Isacsson, G. (2001). Suicides are seldom prescribed antidepressants: Findings from a prospective prescription database in Jamtland County, Sweden. *Acta Psychiatrica Scandinavica, 103*, 301–306. doi:10.1034/j.1600-0447.2001.00276.x

Henriques, G., Beck, A., & Brown, G. (2003). Cognitive therapy for adolescent and young adult suicide attempters. *The American Behavioral Scientist, 46*, 1258–1268. doi:10.1177/0002764202250668

Inspector General, U.S. Department of Defense. (2008). Observations and critique of the DoD task force on mental health. Retrieved from http://www.dodig.mil/Inspections/IE/Reports/IE-2008-003.pdf

Jacobs, D. J., Baldessarini, R., Conwell, Y., Fawcett, J., Horton, L., . . . Simon, R., et al. (2003). Practice guideline for the assessment and treatment of patients with suicidal behaviors. *American Journal of Psychiatry, 160*(11, November supplement), 1–60.

Jobes, D. A., & Drozd, J. F. (2004). The CAMS approach to working with suicidal patients. *Journal of Contemporary Psychotherapy, 34*, 73–85. doi:10.1023/B:JOCP. 0000010914.98781.6a

Jobes, D. A., Wong, S. A., Conrad, A. K., Drozd, J. F., & Neal-Walden, T. (2005). The Collaborative Assessment and Management of Suicidality versus treatment as usual. *Suicide & Life-Threatening Behavior, 35*, 483–497. doi:10.1521/suli. 2005.35.5.483

Joiner, T. E., Pfaff, J. J., & Acres, J. G. (2002). Characteristics of suicidal adolescents and young adults presenting to primary care with non-suicidal (indeed non-psychological) complaints. *European Journal of Public Health, 12*, 177–179. doi:10.1093/eurpub/12.3.177

Kang, H. K., & Bullman, T. A. (2008). Risk of suicide among U.S. veterans returning from the Iraq or Afghan war zones. *JAMA, 300*, 652–653. doi:10.1001/jama. 300.6.652

Kaplan, M. S., Huguet, N., McFarland, B. H., & Newsom, J. T. (2007). Suicide among male veterans: A prospective population-based study. *Journal of Epidemiology and Community Health, 61*, 619–624. doi:10.1136/jech.2006.054346

Kayman, D. (2009, July). Monitoring the implementation of the Suicide Assessment and Screening Template. Presented at the 3rd annual VA Mental Health conference, Meeting the Diverse Mental Health Needs of Veterans: Implementing the Uniform Services Handbook, Baltimore, MD.

Kessler, R. C., Berglund, P., Borges, G., Nock, M., & Wang, P. S. (2005). Trends in suicide ideation, plans, gestures, and attempts in the United States, 1990–1992 to 2001–2003. *JAMA, 293*, 2487–2495. doi:10.1001/jama.293.20.2487

King, R. A., Schwab-Stone, M., Flisher, A. J., Greenwald, S., Kramer, R. A., Goodman, S., ... Gould, M. S. (2001). Psychosocial and risk behavior correlates of youth suicide attempts and suicidal ideation. *Journal of the American Academy of Child and Adolescent Psychiatry, 40*, 837–846. doi:10.1097/00004583-200107000-00019

Linehan, M. (1993). *Cognitive behavioral therapy of borderline personality disorder.* New York, NY: Guilford Press.

Lönnqvist, J., Henriksson, M., Sisometsa, E. T., Marttunen, M. J., Heikkinen, M. E., Hillevi, M. A., et al. (1995). Mental disorders and suicide prevention. *Psychiatry and Clinical Neurosciences, 49*(suppl 1), S111–S116. doi:10.1111/j.1440-1819. 1995.tb01912.x

Mann, J., Apter, A., Bertolote, J., Beutrais, A., Currier, C., Haas, A., . . . Hendin, H. (2005). Suicide prevention strategies: A systematic review. *JAMA, 256*, 329–343.

McCarthy, J. F., Valenstein, M., Kim, H. M., Ilgen, M., Zivin, K., & Blow, F. C. (2009). Suicide mortality among patients receiving care in the Veterans Health Administration system. *American Journal of Epidemiology, 169*, 1033–1038. doi:10.1093/aje/kwp010

Miller, M., Barber, C., Azrael, D., Calle, E. E., Lawler, E., & Mukamal, K. J. (2009). Suicide among U.S. veterans: A prospective study of 500,000 middle-aged and elderly men. *American Journal of Epidemiology, 170*, 494–500. doi:10.1093/aje/kwp164

Miller, T. R., & Taylor, D. M. (2005). Adolescent suicidality: Who will ideate, who will act. *Suicide & Life-Threatening Behavior, 35*, 425–435. doi:10.1521/suli.2005.35.4.425

Monahan, J. (1993). Limiting therapist exposure to *Tarasoff* liability: Guidelines for risk containment. *American Psychologist, 48*, 242–250. doi:10.1037/0003-066X.48.3.242

National Institute on Clinical Excellence. (2004). *Clinical Guideline 16: Self-Harm: The short-term physical and psychological management and secondary prevention of self-harm in primary and secondary care.* London, England: National Health Service.

O'Connor, N., Warby, M., Raphael, B., & Vassallo, T. (2004). Changeability, confidence, common sense and corroboration: Comprehensive suicide risk assessment. *Australasian Psychiatry, 12*, 352–360.

Paris, J. (2004). Is hospitalization useful for suicidal patients with borderline personality disorder? *Journal of Personality Disorders, 18*, 240–247. doi:10.1521/pedi.18.3.240.35443

Perez, V. W. (2005). The relationship between seriously considering, planning and attempting suicide in the Youth Risk Behavior Survey. *Suicide & Life-Threatening Behavior, 35*, 35–49. doi:10.1521/suli.35.1.35.59267

Rudd, M. D. (2000). The suicide mode: A cognitive-behavioral model of suicidality. *Suicide & Life-Threatening Behavior, 30*, 18–33.

Rudd, M. D., Berman, A. L., Joiner, T. E., Nock, M. K., Silverman, M. M., Mandrusiak, M., et al. (2006). Warning signs for suicide: Theory, research, and clinical applications. *Suicide & Life-Threatening Behavior, 36*, 255–262. doi:10.1521/suli.2006.36.3.255

Russ, M. J., Kashdan, T., Pollack, S., & Bajmakovic-Kacila, S. (1999). Assessment of suicide risk 24 hours after psychiatric admission. *Psychiatric Services, 50*, 1491–1493.

Schell, T., & Marshall, G. (2008). Survey of individuals previously deployed for OEF/OIF. In T. Tanielian & L. Jaycox (Eds.), *Invisible wounds of war: Psychological and cognitive injuries, their consequences, and services to assist recovery* (pp. 97–115). Santa Monica, CA: RAND Corporation.

Shea, S. C. (1998). The chronological assessment of suicide events: A practical interviewing strategy for the elicitation of suicidal ideation. *The Journal of Clinical Psychiatry, 59*(suppl. 20), 58–72.

Shea, S. C. (2007). My favorite tips from the "Clinical Interviewing Tip of the Month" archive. *The Psychiatric Clinics of North America, 30*, 219–225. doi:10.1016/j.psc.2007.01.006

Simon, R. I. (2006). Assessing the unpredictable. In R. I. Simon & R. E. Hales (Eds.), *Suicide assessment and management* (pp. 1–32). Washington, DC: American Psychiatric Publishing.

Stanford, E. J., Goetz, R. R., & Bloom, J. D. (1994). The No Harm Contract in emergency assessment of suicidal risk. *The Journal of Clinical Psychiatry, 55*, 344–348.

Stanley, B., & Brown, G. K. (2008). Safety plan treatment manual to reduce suicide risk: Veteran version. Retrieved from http://www.sprc.org/library/Veteran_Safety_Plan.pdf

Suicide Risk Management & Surveillance Office. (2008). *Army Suicide Event Report (ASER) Calendar Year 2007*. Tacoma, WA: Office of the Surgeon General of the Army.

U.S. Air Force. (2006). Talking paper on frontline supervisors training. Retrieved from http://airforcemedicine.afms.mil/idc/groups/public/documents/afms/ctb_091856.pdf

U.S. Army. (2009). Army releases June suicide data. Retrieved from http://www.army.mil/-newsreleases/2009/07/09/24113-army-releases-june-suicide-data/?ref=news-releases-title0

U.S. Army Infantry Center. (2008) U.S.AIC suicide prevention planning guide (U.S.IAC Pamphlet Number 600-22). Retrieved from http://www.martin.amedd.army.mil/meddepts/bh/Pam%20600-22.pdf

U.S. Department of Veterans Affairs. (2009). Veterans and suicide. Retrieved from http://www.mentalhealth.va.gov/College/suicide.asp

U.S. Marine Corps. (2009). Suicidal behavior. In *Leader's guide for managing Marines in distress*. Retrieved from http://www.usmc-mccs.org/leadersguide/Emotional/Suicide/generalinfo.cfm

U.S. Navy. (2006). Navy focuses on suicide prevention, awareness. Retrieved from http://www.navy.mil/search/display_word.asp?story_id=26720

Valenstein, M., Kim, H., Ganoczy, D., McCarthy, J., Zivin, K., Austin, K., . . . Olfson, M. (2009). Higher-risk periods for suicide among VA patients receiving depression treatment: Prioritizing prevention efforts. *Journal of Affective Disorders, 112*, 50–58. doi:10.1016/j.jad.2008.08.020

Welch, S. S. (2001). A review of the literature on the epidemiology of parasuicide in the general population. *Psychiatric Services, 52*, 368–375. doi:10.1176/appi.ps.52.3.368

Witte, T. K., Fitzpatrick, K. K., Warren, K. L., Schatschneider, C., & Schmidt, N. B. (2006). Naturalistic evaluation of suicidal ideation: Variability and relation to attempt status. *Behaviour Research and Therapy, 44*, 1029–1040. doi:10.1016/j.brat.2005.08.004

III

NONCOMBAT STRESSORS
AND THEIR RAMIFICATIONS

6

SEXUAL HARASSMENT AND SEXUAL ASSAULT DURING MILITARY SERVICE

AMY E. STREET, RACHEL KIMERLING, MARGRET E. BELL,
AND JOANNE PAVAO

For most people, the stressors that first come to mind when considering military deployments to Iraq and Afghanistan are exposure to combat, difficult environmental living conditions, and extended separations from loved ones. Although these types of deployment stressors do characterize the experiences of many service members deployed in support of the Iraq and Afghanistan wars, they are not the only potentially traumatic events that veterans returning from these conflicts may have experienced. Unfortunately, sexual harassment and sexual assault are all too common stressors for both female and male service members. Given that experiences of sexual trauma during military service can have a significant negative impact on postdeployment mental health and well-being, it is crucial that every clinician working with veterans of the Iraq and Afghanistan wars have knowledge of the assessment and treatment of these experiences and their aftereffects.

Sexual harassment and sexual assault have specific legal definitions that differ across settings, but for the purposes of clinical intervention, definitions

This chapter was coauthored by an employee of the United States government as part of official duty and is considered to be in the public domain. Any views expressed herein do not necessarily represent the views of the United States government, and the author's participation in the work is not meant to serve as an official endorsement.

arising from a mental health perspective are most useful. From a mental health perspective, *sexual harassment,* at the most general level, refers to unwanted sexual experiences that occur in the workplace. Within the military context, the workplace can be broadly defined to include events between military personnel that occur on base or off base, during on-duty or off-duty hours. From a legal perspective, these unwelcome sexual behaviors become sexual harassment when the behaviors create an intimidating, hostile, or offensive working environment or when cooperation with such behaviors is a condition of employment or is used as the basis for employment decisions (Equal Employment Opportunity Commission, 1990). Sexually harassing behaviors of the type frequently referred to as *hostile environment harassment* consist of a relatively large range of experiences including, for example, offensive comments about a person's body or sexual activities (e.g., repeated comments that a coworker has "a nice rack" or that "everyone says she's ready to go whenever you are"), unwanted sexual advances, or the display of pornographic materials or other sexually demeaning objects in the workplace. The other primary form of sexually harassing behaviors are the types of experiences frequently referred to as *quid pro quo* (or "this for that") harassment. These behaviors consist of coerced sexual involvement, either through promises of rewards (e.g., a less hazardous duty assignment) or threats of punishment (e.g., a lowered performance evaluation with implications for promotion).

At the most severe end of the continuum of unwanted sexual experiences in the workplace are experiences of *sexual assault,* or unwanted physical sexual contact involving the use of some type of coercion. Coercion can be the use of physical force, threats of harm, or the abuse of authority (as when a higher ranking service member makes sexual demands of a lower ranking service member) or when the victim cannot or does not consent (e.g., due to intoxication or cognitive impairment). The nature of the physical contact may range from touching or fondling to attempted or completed vaginal, anal, or oral rape.

Within the Department of Veterans Affairs (VA) health care system, the overarching term *military sexual trauma,* often abbreviated as MST, is used to refer to experiences of harassment and assault in the military. Although the specific legal definition of MST is detailed in public law, generally speaking, this term refers to experiences of sexual assault and repeated, threatening experiences of sexual harassment experienced during military service.

CASE EXAMPLES

The following two cases—composites of stories from actual veterans seen in treatment—bring these definitions to life by highlighting some of the sexually traumatic experiences and mental health aftereffects faced by veterans returning from deployments in Iraq and Afghanistan.

Doris

"Doris" is a 38-year-old African American woman who is a single mother of a 9-year-old daughter. Before her military service, she experienced ongoing, nonpenetrative childhood sexual abuse at the hands of a male family friend. Doris believes that she has "dealt with" that experience and states that those memories no longer cause her significant distress. Doris has served as a member of the Army reserves for 20 years to earn extra income for her family. Concurrently in her civilian life, she is a successful legal secretary. It was a surprise to her to learn in 2003 that she would be deployed to Iraq in a combat support role.

In Iraq, Doris served as a truck driver in daily supply convoys, which involved driving through dangerous areas to deliver necessary supplies to away bases. All drivers were trained that if any civilian, even a child, was blocking the road, they must not stop the convoy (which would place everyone at risk of an enemy attack) but must run the civilian over if he or she did not get out of the way. Doris was terrified that she would be confronted with this situation and spent hours ruminating about the possibility, focusing especially on whether she would be able to run over a child to protect herself and others in her unit. She managed nonetheless to function effectively as a convoy driver, but she did mention her apprehensions to several in her unit. Not long after, a higher ranking service member responsible for making job assignments approached her to say that he would change her assignment to staffing the truck depot if she would have sex with him. Although Doris had no romantic or sexual interest in this man, her worry about being in a position to hurt a child was so great that she had sex with him a number of times over a period of several months until her deployment ended. When others in the unit learned of her sexual relationship with the higher ranking service member, she was subjected to frequent offensive comments about being "an easy good time." Another member of her unit approached her repeatedly to say, "Word on the street is that you've got a great body. How about letting me take a look?" As her deployment drew to a close, Doris felt increasingly betrayed by her fellow soldiers, confused about her role in Iraq, and unsure about the overall mission.

After returning from her deployment, Doris had difficulty readjusting to civilian life. She reported feeling "down" and said that she couldn't stop thinking about stories she heard of children being killed or injured by convoys. Currently, she ruminates about whether she made the right choice regarding the change in duty assignment and has begun having some nightmares about her experiences of sexual abuse as a child. She has become distrustful of her male supervisors and is extremely anxious when she must be alone with them. Because of these fears, she has frequently called in sick for work and is considering a career change, reporting that she needs to "keep herself busy" so that she won't "have to think about that time." While Doris was deployed, her mother was the primary caretaker of her daughter, and Doris has been slow to resume primary parenting responsibilities since her return, saying that she doesn't "trust herself" to make the right decisions.

Juan

"Juan" is a 25-year-old Latino man. He has been married for 6 years and is the father of two young children. Juan enlisted in the Marine Corps following the terrorist attacks of September 11, 2001, out of a desire to serve his country. After basic training, Juan was deployed to Afghanistan as a member of a combat infantry unit. During Juan's deployment, he was exposed to significant combat trauma, including being involved in numerous firefights and witnessing other Marines being wounded and killed. During one particularly stressful firefight, Juan became disoriented and was slow to keep up with the other members of his unit as they moved into some of the most dangerous fighting. Afterward, he reported that the other guys were "looking at me funny, like they didn't think they could trust me anymore." The next night, while Juan was on his way to the latrine, he was grabbed by someone and held down while someone else anally raped him. During the assault, the assailants said things like, "This should teach you that you've got to start pulling your weight around here." Juan knew that the two assailants were members of his unit but was not able to identify them specifically.

After this event, Juan returned to his bunk without telling anyone about the experience. He became socially isolated from the others in his unit, preferring to "keep to himself." Despite not having spoken of this incident to anyone, he felt like everyone knew what had happened and continually questioned why he had been singled out to be raped. Juan found combat missions to be progressively more stressful and frightening. He was convinced that the others in his unit could not be depended on to "get his back" and worried about how the slightest misstep on his part might be interpreted.

After returning home from this deployment, Juan reported having frequent nightmares involving themes related to rape and to combat missions. He began using alcohol heavily, stating that it is "the only way that I can sleep at night." He became increasingly aggressive and on several occasions started fights at his neighborhood bar. His relationship with his wife deteriorated significantly. She repeatedly asked him, "What happened to you over there?" and told him, "You have to stop keeping secrets from me." Eventually, she threatened to leave him if he didn't get help for his mental health issues.

PREVALENCE

Unfortunately, Doris and Juan are not alone in their experiences. Although few data exist on rates of sexual harassment and assault among military personnel deployed in support of the wars in Iraq and Afghanistan, data from other samples can provide some context for examining this issue. Although rates differ across studies on the basis of the specifics of the sample and measurement, these data suggest that in peacetime situations, sexual harassment and assault are frequent events during military service. For example, in the 2006 Department of Defense Workplace and Gender Relations Survey of active-duty personnel, 52% of women and 29% of men reported experiencing offensive sexual behavior in the previous year, 31% of women and 7% of men reported receiving unwanted sexual attention in the previous year, 9% of women and 3% of men reported experiencing sexually coercive behavior during the previous year, and 6.8% of women and 1.8% of men reported having been sexually assaulted during the previous year (Lipari, Cook, Rock, & Matos, 2008). Rates of sexual harassment and assault are similarly high in the reserve components of the armed forces. Data from a nationally representative sample of male and female reservists who separated from military service before Operation Enduring Freedom (OEF) or Operation Iraqi Freedom (OIF) (Street, Stafford, Mahan, & Hendricks, 2008) found that 60% of all female reservists and 27.2% of male reservists reported repeated or severe sexual harassment at some point during their military service. In the sample as a whole, 13.1% of women and 1.6% of men reported experiences of sexual assault at some point during their military service.

High rates of sexual trauma during military service are also found among users of VA health care. In a national sample of female veterans who had used VA outpatient care, 55% of women reported experiencing sexual harassment, and 23% reported experiencing sexual assault during military service (Skinner et al., 2000). The VA's universal MST screening program also reveals useful information about experiences of sexual trauma among VA users. Within a national sample of VA health care users, 21.5% of women and 1% of men had disclosed experiences of MST to a health care provider (Kimerling, Gima, Smith, Street, & Frayne, 2007).

Fewer studies have addressed the prevalence of sexual trauma specifically among deployed troops. However, the 2006 Department of Defense Workplace and Gender Relations Survey of active-duty personnel found that 9% of women and 2% of men who had been deployed in the 12 months before taking the survey reported that they had been sexually assaulted in the previous 12 months (Lipari et al., 2008). This was in contrast to rates of 6% of women and 2% of men who were not deployed. Additional relevant data can be drawn from surveys of troops deployed in support of Gulf War I. Rates in one study of deployed women indicate that 66% experienced verbal sexual harassment, 33% experienced physical sexual harassment, and 7% experienced sexual assault during deployment (Wolfe et al., 1998). Data from a second sample of deployed personnel indicate both that 24.0% of women and 0.6% of men reported experiencing sexual harassment and that 3.0% of women and 0.2% of men reported that they had experienced sexual assault during deployment (Kang, Dalager, Mahan, & Ishii, 2005). However, caution should be used when generalizing these Gulf War I data to the current wars in Iraq and Afghanistan context, given the substantial differences between these wars on the nature of the combat operations, the total number of troops deployed, and the length and number of deployments.

MENTAL HEALTH CONSEQUENCES

Although no large-scale studies have specifically examined veterans of the Iraq and Afghanistan wars who experienced sexual trauma (i.e., sexual harassment or sexual assault), associations between experiences of sexual trauma in the military and subsequent mental health problems have been well documented in other samples. Indeed, in both civilian and military populations, there are indications that sexual assault is among the stressors with the highest conditional risk of posttraumatic stress disorder (PTSD), beyond even that of combat exposure (Kang et al., 2005; Kessler, Sonnega, Bromet, Hughes, & Nelson, 1995). Numerous investigations have demonstrated strong associations between experiences of sexual harassment and assault during military service and increased PTSD symptoms or increased likelihood of PTSD diagnosis, including investigations among users of VA health care (Kimerling et al., 2007), members of the reserve forces (Street et al., 2008), Somalian peacekeepers (Fontana, Litz, & Rosenheck, 2000), and deployed Gulf War veterans, even after controlling for combat exposure (Kang et al., 2005).

Although PTSD is the mental health condition most closely associated with experiences of sexual trauma, evidence suggests that sexual assault and harassment in the military increase the risk of a range mental health conditions. For example, a recent study of all veterans using VA health care found that veterans who reported MST as part of the VA's universal screening program were at a threefold increased risk of receiving a mental health diagnosis compared with those who did not report MST (Kimerling et al., 2007). Conditions such as anxiety disorders, depression, dissociative disorders, eating disorders, bipolar disorders, substance use disorders, and personality disorders were among those strongly linked to MST among both men and women. Experiences of sexual harassment and assault during military service also have demonstrated associations with increased symptoms of anxiety and depression among deployed Gulf War veterans (Vogt, Pless, King, & King, 2005).

UNANSWERED RESEARCH QUESTIONS RELATED TO SEXUAL TRAUMA IN THE MILITARY

As should be clear from the preceding review, the most pressing need for research in this area is an examination of the extent to which existing findings generalize to the current wars. Prevalence estimates and mental health consequences will likely be affected by the unique aspects of the wars in Iraq and Afghanistan, including most obviously the interaction between sexual trauma and combat trauma, but also the extended and multiple deployments, difficult war-zone conditions, and heavy reliance on reservist service members. Conducting research focused on the additive affects of exposure to combat and sexual trauma, as well as replicating existing research that suggests combat exposure may increase the risk of experiencing sexual harassment or assault in the military (Fontana et al., 2000) is critical. Furthermore, given the high rates of childhood trauma among individuals entering military service (Rosen & Martin, 1996) and data from active-duty troops suggesting an association between childhood trauma and experiences of sexual trauma in the military (Rosen & Martin, 1998), questions remain about the role that premilitary stressors may play in the complex presentations of some sexually traumatized veterans. Understanding more about the synergistic effects of traumatic experiences before military service, sexual trauma in the military, and combat trauma will shed light on their relative contributions to the multiple mental health comorbidities with which sexually traumatized veterans may present.

Additional research is also necessary to identify unique risk factors associated with experiences of sexual trauma in the military. Preliminary evidence suggests that military environmental risk factors, including, for example, leadership tolerance for inappropriate sexual behavior and mixed-gender sleeping quarters, are powerful predictors of sexual assault in the military, even after controlling for other established risk factors for sexual violence (Sadler, Booth, Cook, & Doebbeling, 2003; Sadler, Booth, Cook, Torner, & Doebbeling, 2001). By the same token, research is needed to identify unique resiliency factors associated with recovery from sexual trauma in the military, including factors such as unit cohesion and leadership support. Identification of unique risk and resiliency factors in military settings may identify important points of intervention when designing prevention and early-intervention programs for military sexual trauma survivors.

Finally, more research is needed to improve understanding of differences and similarities in the experiences of male and female survivors of military sexual trauma. Studies have suggested that the intensity of mental health consequences associated with sexual trauma during military service may vary for men and women, with some investigations demonstrating stronger effects among men (e.g., Street, Gradus, Stafford, & Kelly, 2007; Vogt et al., 2005). It is clear from the existing evidence that sexual victimization is a salient issue to consider in working with all veterans; however, to date, research into men's experiences of victimization has lagged behind that of their female counterparts.

UNIQUE ASPECTS OF SEXUAL TRAUMA OCCURRING IN MILITARY CONTEXTS

Although experiences of sexual harassment and sexual assault that take place in military settings have considerable similarities to such experiences in civilian settings, some unique aspects of the military context have particular relevance to the clinical care of veterans. Few empirical data have directly addressed this issue, but there is some evidence that sexual trauma in military settings is more strongly associated with negative mental health consequences than is sexual trauma that occurs outside of military service (Himmelfarb, Yaeger, & Mintz, 2006). Even though the specific reasons for this association have not been explored empirically, examination of victims' phenomenological experience of sexual trauma in the military suggests some potential explanatory factors.

In the military, lines between "work life" and "home life" are blurred, making it potentially more difficult to experience a sense of relief or escape from experiences of sexual trauma. For example, perpetrators are frequently other military personnel with whom the victim must continue to live and work. This can increase victims' psychological distress and their sense of helplessness and powerlessness. It can also increase their risk of additional victimization, either by increasing their exposure to the perpetrator or, in cases in which perpetrators are in a position to influence performance evaluations, work assignments, or promotion decisions, by increasing opportunities for coercion. Compounding distress, within military settings, the strict chain of command and a perception of a "code of silence" may create environments in which victims fail to report their victimization experiences or decline to seek help for these incidents because they believe that nothing will be done or that they will experience negative repercussions (Pershing, 2003).

Another reason that sexual harassment and sexual assault in the military may be particularly damaging is that being victimized conflicts with core values promoted by the military. For example, military culture prioritizes being strong, tough, and physically powerful, and these attributes may become deeply embedded as part of many military personnel's self-identity. Also, military units are often extremely cohesive groups, functioning as a team with a shared set of goals, something that may feel even more salient during combat deployments when service members are viewed as "soldiers in arms" with an important shared mission. In contrast, being sexually victimized in the military may create a sense of being weak, vulnerable, and unable to defend oneself. Similarly, being victimized by another service member conflicts with a belief in the trustworthiness of and loyalty to members of the unit. Because sexual victimization that occurs during military service is likely to shatter these key worldviews, victims of sexual trauma in the military may find their victimization experiences to be even more incomprehensible and difficult to resolve than do civilian victims.

Veterans who experience sexual trauma during a war-zone deployment also risk the additive effects of multiple types of trauma exposure. Evidence from civilian samples indicating that exposure to multiple types of trauma increases the risk of negative mental health outcomes (Cloitre, Scarvalone, & Difede, 1997; Follette, Polusny, Bechtle, & Naugle, 1996) and evidence among veterans of the Iraq and Afghanistan wars that prior exposure to sexual or physical assault increases the risk of mental health problems following combat exposure (Smith, Wingard, Ryan, Kritz-Silverstein, Slymen, & Sallis, 2008) suggest that veterans who have experienced both combat and sexual trauma during deployment are likely to be at particular risk of readjustment difficulties. Even those veterans not directly exposed to extensive combat trauma during deployment were likely confronted with the generalized decreased sense of safety that accompanies deployment to a war zone. Sexual victimization that occurs within this context of increased danger is likely to be experienced by the victim as even more threatening than similar events that occur within an objectively safer context.

Notably, veterans of the wars in Iraq and Afghanistan who experienced sexual trauma may also struggle with unique issues related to homecoming in that they may believe or be told by others that their traumatic experiences and associated mental health struggles are not as "legitimate" as the experiences of service members who experienced combat trauma. Given the intense shame and attendant secrecy often associated with sexual victimization, veterans may be particularly reluctant to share their experiences with loved ones and thus end up forgoing the support loved ones might be able to provide during the homecoming and recovery process. These veterans may also be disinclined to seek help from treatment programs targeted at returning veterans because of a belief, accurate or inaccurate, that these programs are not designed to meet their specific needs. These fears may be a particular barrier for entry into group-treatment programs when the groups comprise primarily veterans who experienced combat trauma. Sexually traumatized veterans may also be reluctant to seek disability compensation related to their mental health difficulties given the accurate perception that veterans who experienced sexual trauma are less likely to receive compensation than veterans with similar mental health difficulties that are related to combat trauma (Murdoch et al., 2003).

ASSESSMENT AND TREATMENT

As a general rule, veterans who have experienced sexual harassment or sexual assault during their military service should be assessed and treated in a manner consistent with good clinical practice for the assessment and treatment of any type of trauma survivor. However, beyond standard good clinical practice, this population may present with some unique clinical needs that should be considered when planning clinical intervention.

Assessment

In light of the data reviewed earlier on prevalence and associated health consequences, it is important when conducting intake or initial interviews with all veterans of the Iraq and Afghanistan Wars to include questions about sexual assault and sexual harassment in the military. This is particularly crucial because, as is true with sexual trauma in civilian populations, veterans are unlikely to disclose unless asked directly (Fisher, Daigle, Cullen, & Turner, 2003). Conducting even a brief two-item screen, as is universally mandated within the VA health care system, appears to promote access to subsequent mental health treatment (Kimerling, Street, Gima, & Smith, 2008).

Screening can be conducted with self-report questionnaires or oral discussion in session. With either approach, it is often helpful to begin by normalizing the process. This can be done by using introductory language such as, "We ask all of the veterans seen in this clinic about certain types of experiences because we know that they are common and can be hard to talk about" or by including the screening questions in a broader discussion of relationship and abuse experiences more generally. Using behaviorally based language (e.g., "Have you ever been forced or pressured into having sex?" "Has anyone ever touched you in a sexual way or had you touch them in a sexual way that made you uncomfortable?" "Have you ever been touched sexually against your will or without your consent?" "During your deployment did you experience any unwanted sexual attention?" "Did you have any other sexual experience that made you feel uncomfortable?"), rather than *rape, sexual assault,* or *sexual harassment,* will facilitate identifying survivors who have not labeled their experiences using these terms. These types of survivors are important to detect as well, given civilian studies demonstrating similar symptom profiles across individuals with similar behavioral experiences, regardless of whether they identify their experiences as assault or harassment (Harned, 2004; Magley, Hulin, Fitzgerald, & DeNardo, 1999).

Survivors may have encountered negative reactions when disclosing in the past (Campbell, 2008; Campbell & Raja, 2005; Filipas & Ullman, 2001; Ullman, 1999) and will likely be attuned to a clinician's reaction to their "yes" response. Providing immediate validation and appreciation for disclosure (e.g., "I can imagine that was hard to share but am glad you felt able to tell me about it"; "No one deserves to have things like that happen to them"; "Experiences like that can be even more difficult during a deployment or when it was someone you trusted previously") can be tremendously corrective and healing. It is also important to remember that some survivors may initially respond "no" when asked about sexual trauma because of shame or a perceived need for secrecy about their experiences. Responding sensitively, with language such as, "I am glad to hear that. I asked because I know these things can be difficult to talk about and I wanted to make sure to offer some of the resources we have available to help, if that was appropriate," can leave the door open for later disclosure in these situations.

Ideally, positive screens should be followed by more detailed information gathering about issues such as the specifics of the sexual assault or harassment, the veteran's response at the time and afterward, and the impact of the experiences on the veteran's life currently. Information about the context within which the experiences occurred—for example, when during the deployment the sexual victimization occurred, the overlap or intersection between the sexual victimization and other deployment-related stressors, and the general attitude toward sexual assault and harassment in the veteran's unit—are also important to assess. Similarly, asking about any prior or subsequent traumatic experiences can help in understanding how the sexual assault or harassment experiences are situated in the broader context of the veteran's life. Finally, knowing whether the veteran has previously discussed his or her experiences with anyone, and if so, how others responded, may help inform clinician interventions targeting any current struggles with self-blame, trust, or intimacy.

Although gathering this sort of information up front is ideal, as with other types of traumatic experiences, veterans who are sexual trauma survivors may be reluctant or unwilling to discuss these issues until a stronger therapeutic relationship has been established. It is important to respect this decision, as well as to validate any distress the veteran expresses about the prospect of discussing his or her experiences. Simultaneously, clinicians should also be careful not to send the message that they are disinterested, have negative judgments about the veteran as result of the disclosure, or believe that his or her experiences are too difficult, upsetting, or shameful to discuss in therapy.

When it is possible to engage a veteran in a more detailed discussion of his or her experiences, a general guiding principle that may be useful is to strive to make the assessment process concurrently a therapeutic encounter, with a balance between information gathering and respect for what the veteran is ready to disclose at that point in time. Allowing the veteran to control the pacing of disclosure and normalizing statements by the clinician can be helpful. Similarly, spending time during the assessment process helping survivors understand some of the functions their behaviors serve, validating the needs underlying these behaviors, and then considering whether there are alternative ways to meet these needs can be powerfully therapeutic as well.

Treatment

As noted earlier, there are a number of mental health conditions associated with sexual trauma, and survivors may present with multiple comorbidities. Unfortunately, few treatment outcome studies have focused specifically on mental health conditions arising secondary to sexual assault and sexual harassment occurring during military service, and the evidence base is even more limited with regard to treatment of these aftereffects among veterans of the Iraq and Afghanistan wars or male veterans of any era who experienced sexual trauma during military service. That being said, PTSD interventions with the strongest level of empirical support (i.e., exposure-based cognitive–behavioral therapies such as prolonged exposure and cognitive processing therapy) were initially developed for and have been rigorously tested among civilian sexual assault survivors (Foa, Rothbaum, Riggs, & Murdock, 1991; Resick et al., 2008; Resick, Nishith, Weaver, Astin, & Feuer, 2002; Rothbaum, Astin, & Marsteller, 2005). One of these therapies, prolonged exposure, has been tested among a large sample of female veterans and active-duty personnel with PTSD, more than 70% of whom reported experiencing sexual trauma during their military service (Schnurr et al., 2007). The majority of women in this study identified sexual trauma as their worst, or index, event. Consistent with results from civilian sexual assault samples, although both prolonged exposure and present-centered therapy were effective in reducing symptoms of PTSD, depression, and overall mental health, women who received prolonged exposure experienced greater reduction of PTSD symptoms relative to women who received present-centered therapy, effects that were maintained over time.

Given the depth of empirical support for these exposure-based therapies among survivors of sexual assault who develop PTSD, these therapies should be considered as a first-choice treatment, when appropriate. However, coping-skills-based treatments, including cognitive and behavioral coping strategies such as stress management skills, affect regulation skills, and assertiveness skills, also play an important role in the treatment of sexual trauma survivors. Although skills training does not yet have a sufficient evidence base to establish definitively its efficacy in the treatment of PTSD (Institute of Medicine,

2008), it can be a useful precursor for clients whose use of adaptive coping strategies should be strengthened before beginning a course of trauma-processing therapy or in response to residual symptoms following a course of trauma-processing therapy. The literature boasts several examples of skills-based therapy protocols that have been developed for or tested among groups of female veterans who require treatment for the mental health consequences of experiences of sexual trauma experienced during military service (Castillo, 2004; Desai, Harpaz-Rotem, Najavits, & Rosenheck, 2008). Reflecting the civilian literature, these treatment protocols have not yet been subjected to rigorous empirical testing, but preliminary empirical results, coupled with anecdotal evidence from clinical providers, suggest that skills-based protocols, such as Seeking Safety (Najavits, 2002) and dialectical behavior therapy (Linehan, 1993), can make an important contribution to the treatment of veterans who have experienced sexual trauma.

Regardless of the specific treatment strategies adopted, several themes are often prominent in the treatment of sexual trauma survivors. One overarching context to consider is that sexual trauma is fundamentally interpersonal in nature—another human being, often someone trusted, caused the survivor harm—which can lead survivors to struggle with trust, safety, intimacy, and other core features of interpersonal relationships. Identifying and setting appropriate interpersonal boundaries may be difficult, particularly for young victims or those who have experienced multiple instances of sexual trauma, in that they may be confused about what is reasonable behavior in relationships (Hien, Litt, Cohen, Miele, & Campbell, 2009). Given the power differential inherent in sexual harassment and sexual assault experiences, issues of power and control in relationships are often salient to survivors, who may have strong reactions to situations in which one individual has power over another, as in employee–employer or patient–health care provider relationships. These difficulties in interpersonal relationships with others may also be reflected in survivors' views of themselves. Sexual trauma survivors frequently exhibit a great deal of self-blame related to their sexual victimization experiences, at least some of which may derive from questions they have about their decision making during the event. Sexually traumatized veterans may also question their general ability to judge others' intentions or trustworthiness accurately given the occurrence of the trauma.

Like its effect on intimacy in general in relationships, sexual trauma can have a significant impact on survivors' subsequent sexual functioning and gender identity. Rates of sexual dysfunction are high among sexual assault survivors (Hall, 2007; van Berlo & Ensink, 2000), and even those survivors who do not meet formal diagnostic criteria for sexual dysfunction may experience feelings of anxiety, fear, loss of control, or physical pain during sex. In response to these feelings, some survivors may avoid sexual activity entirely. Others may attempt to cope by becoming hypersexual, in an attempt to feel more in control of their sexual activity; others may engage in sexual activity only when heavily intoxicated.

Clinicians working with sexual trauma survivors should always be attuned to the potential for revictimization, particularly for personnel still in units or environments with their perpetrator. Rates of revictimization are high even for personnel not in contact with their original perpetrator (Kilpatrick, Edmunds, & Seymour, 1992; Sadler et al., 2001). Many of the behaviors survivors might engage in to avoid memories and feelings associated with the trauma may unfortunately leave them more susceptible to subsequent victimization, including excessive substance use, inattention to internal sensations and emotions, and dissociation.

Although many practitioners think of sexual trauma survivors as primarily female, clinicians working with military personnel who experienced sexual harassment and assault will almost certainly encounter male survivors. Although a smaller proportion of male than female veterans report experiencing sexual trauma during military service, given the larger numbers of men than women in the military, the absolute numbers of men and women who report these experiences are similar, at least within the VA health care system (Kimerling et al., 2007). However, because the empirical and theoretical literatures relevant to working with male sexual trauma survivors have lagged behind those relevant to female sexual trauma survivors, the needs of male veterans who have experienced sexual trauma have often been overlooked. Men have a higher probability than women of developing PTSD following sexual assault (Kang et al., 2005; Kessler et al., 1995), and evidence is emerging that male military personnel are more susceptible to the negative mental health effects associated with sexual harassment than are their female counterparts (Street et al., 2007; Vogt et al., 2005). Although the treatment issues faced by male survivors are often similar to those faced by female survivors, men who have experienced sexual trauma may also confront some unique issues. Male survivors may be less likely than their female counterparts to disclose their experiences of sexual trauma, maintaining secrecy for years because of beliefs that they will be disbelieved or stereotyped by others if their victimization status is known, and thereby limiting their access to appropriate mental health services. Male survivors may also struggle with greater feelings of shame and self-blame than their female counterparts. This may be due, at least in part, to the widely held discrepancy in our society between "being a victim" and stereotypical notions of the male gender role, particularly in military settings, as being physically strong, emotionally impervious, and in control of themselves and their surroundings. Concerns about gender identity (e.g., "Am I a 'real man'?") and concerns about sexual orientation (e.g., "Does this mean I'm gay?") may be particularly salient for men who were sexually harassed or assaulted by other men (Rentoul & Appleboom, 1997; Walker, Archer, & Davies, 2005), especially among survivors who became involuntarily sexually aroused or experienced physical pleasure in response to sexual stimulation during a sexual assault, causing them to question if they secretly wanted or enjoyed the experience.

Some sexual trauma survivors, male or female, may express a strong preference for a clinician of a given gender. This may reflect a fear of being in close proximity to an individual of the same gender as their perpetrator or may reflect concerns about feeling inhibited or unable to disclose details of sexual trauma due to gender roles. Although no empirical studies address this issue directly, it is widely considered best practice to allow sexual trauma survivors some control in the choice of gender of their therapist. Before meeting survivors' requests for a clinician of a particular gender, however, it may be useful to have a conversation with them about the potential benefits of stepping outside their comfort zone in this area. For example, being able to work successfully with a clinician of the same gender as the perpetrator may help survivors gain a sense of mastery over their trauma-related emotional reactions. It may be similarly corrective for survivors to have an opportunity to examine and challenge assumptions about individuals of a particular gender. This same rationale can be presented to survivors who express reluctance to participate in mixed-gender therapy groups. Even survivors who do not choose to challenge themselves in the therapeutic setting in this way may find issues related to gender affecting their interpersonal interactions outside of therapy. As such, gender-related discussions are likely to be a prominent component of treatment with many sexual trauma survivors.

Finally, although mixed trauma groups are used in many treatment settings, it can be tremendously beneficial to make available at least some groups composed of only sexual trauma survivors if staffing, veteran level of interest, and other resources permit. One reason for this is that the shame and desire for privacy commonly associated with sexual trauma may make sexual trauma survivors reluctant to participate in groups with veterans who have not experienced sexual trauma. Also, as outlined earlier, sexual trauma survivors often struggle with issues such as sexuality and boundaries that may be less of an issue for survivors of other types of trauma and that, consequently, may not be addressed in mixed-trauma groups. Similarly, although survivors of all types of trauma frequently struggle with issues related to trust and safety, the interpersonal nature of sexual trauma can greatly shape the way these issues manifest themselves in the lives of sexual trauma survivors. Of course, there are potential benefits to sexual trauma survivor participation in mixed-trauma groups. For example, some survivors may find it extremely validating to see the similarities between their experiences and those of survivors of other forms of trauma, essentially learning that their experiences were "real traumas" like combat or other experiences more closely associated with military service in public conception. As such, as with the issue of gender composition of groups, clinicians should engage in thoughtful discussions with veterans about the pros and cons of participation in mixed trauma groups. If a sexual trauma survivor does decide to participate in a mixed trauma group, these discussions should also include consideration of whether the survivor wishes to disclose the nature of his or her trauma to the other group members. Although receiving a supportive reaction from other veterans has the potential to be tremendously healing, the choice about disclosure should always ultimately remain with the veteran.

CONCLUSION

Sadly, generations of veterans have been subjected to experiences of sexual harassment and sexual assault while in service to their country, and historically, many of these veterans have suffered in silence. With the newest cohort of veterans now returning from deployments in Iraq and Afghanistan, clinicians have the opportunity to identify those who were sexually traumatized during their military service and provide them with effective treatment before the mental health consequences of these experiences can become chronic. Although programs through the Department of Defense and the Department of Veterans Affairs are targeting the prevention of sexual harassment and assault as well as early identification of and effective intervention with sexual trauma survivors, the treatment needs of this population have not yet been fully met. Clinicians working with veterans of the wars in Iraq and Afghanistan must realize that combat trauma is not the only deployment-related stressor these veterans may be exposed to; military sexual trauma is another form of deployment trauma that affects both male and female veterans. Effective strategies for detection and treatment of are available, and these resources can help clinicians address the full range of mental health service required by newest generation of veterans.

REFERENCES

Campbell, R. (2008). The psychological impact of rape victims' experiences with the legal, medical, and mental health systems. *American Psychologist, 68*, 702–717.

Campbell, R., & Raja, S. (2005). The sexual assault and secondary victimization of female Veterans: Help-seeking experiences with military and civilian social systems. *Psychology of Women Quarterly, 29*, 97–106. doi:10.1111/j.1471-6402.2005.00171.x

Castillo, D. T. (2004). Systematic outpatient treatment of sexual trauma in women: Application of cognitive and behavioral protocols. *Cognitive and Behavioral Practice, 11*, 352–365. doi:10.1016/S1077-7229(04)80052-X

Cloitre, M., Scarvalone, P., & Difede, J. A. (1997). Posttraumatic stress disorder, self- and interpersonal dysfunction among sexually retraumatized women. *Journal of Traumatic Stress, 10,* 437–452. doi:10.1002/jts.2490100309

Desai, R. A., Harpaz-Rotem, I., Najavits, L. M., & Rosenheck, R. A. (2008). Impact of the seeking safety program on clinical outcomes among homeless female veterans with psychiatric disorders. *Psychiatric Services, 59,* 996–1003. doi:10.1176/appi.ps.59.9.996

Equal Employment Opportunity Commission. (1990). Policy guidance on current issues of sexual harassment [updated 1999]. Retrieved from http://www.eeoc.gov

Filipas, H. H., & Ullman, S. E. (2001). Social reactions to sexual assault victims from various support sources. *Violence and Victims, 16,* 673–692.

Fisher, B. S., Daigle, L. E., Cullen, F. T., & Turner, M. G. (2003). Reporting sexual victimization to the police and others: Results from a national-level study of college women. *Criminal Justice and Behavior, 30,* 6–38. doi:10.1177/0093854802239161

Foa, E. B., Rothbaum, B. O., Riggs, D. S., & Murdock, T. B. (1991). Treatment of post-traumatic stress disorder in rape victims: A comparison between cognitive-behavioral procedures and counseling. *Journal of Consulting and Clinical Psychology, 59,* 715–723. doi:10.1037/0022-006X.59.5.715

Follette, V. M., Polusny, M. A., Bechtle, A. E., & Naugle, A. E. (1996). Cumulative trauma: The impact of child sexual abuse, adult sexual assault, and spouse abuse. *Journal of Traumatic Stress, 9,* 25–35. doi:10.1002/jts.2490090104

Fontana, A., Litz, B., & Rosenheck, R. (2000). Impact of combat and sexual harassment on the severity of posttraumatic stress disorder among men and women peacekeepers in Somalia. *Journal of Nervous and Mental Disease, 188,* 163–169. doi:10.1097/00005053-200003000-00006

Hall, K. (2007). Sexual dysfunction and childhood sexual abuse: Gender differences and treatment implications. In S. R. Leiblum (Ed.), *Principles and practice of sex therapy* (4th ed., pp. 350–378). New York, NY: Guilford Press.

Harned, M. S. (2004). Does it matter what you call it? The relationship between labeling unwanted sexual experiences and distress. *Journal of Consulting and Clinical Psychology, 72,* 1090–1099. doi:10.1037/0022-006X.72.6.1090

Hien, D., Litt, L. C., Cohen, L. R., Miele, G. M., & Campbell, A. (2009). Interpersonal functioning. In D. Hien, L. C. Litt, L. R. Cohen, G. M. Miele, & A. Campbell (Eds.), *Trauma services for women in substance abuse treatment: An integrated approach* (pp. 75–98). Washington, DC: American Psychological Association. doi:10.1037/11864-005

Himmelfarb, N., Yaeger, D., & Mintz, J. (2006). Posttraumatic stress disorder in female veterans with military and civilian sexual trauma. *Journal of Traumatic Stress, 19,* 837–846. doi:10.1002/jts.20163

Institute of Medicine. (2008). *Treatment of posttraumatic stress disorder: An assessment of the evidence.* Washington, DC: The National Academies Press.

Kang, H., Dalager, N., Mahan, C., & Ishii, E. (2005). The role of sexual assault on the risk of PTSD among Gulf War veterans. *Annals of Epidemiology, 15,* 191–195. doi:10.1016/j.annepidem.2004.05.009

Kessler, R. C., Sonnega, A., Bromet, E., Hughes, M., & Nelson, C. B. (1995). Posttraumatic stress disorder in the National Comorbidity Survey. *Archives of General Psychiatry, 52,* 1048–1060.

Kilpatrick, D. G., Edmunds, C. N., & Seymour, A. K. (1992). *Rape in America: A report to the nation.* Arlington, VA: National Victim Center and Medical University of South Carolina.

Kimerling, R., Gima, K., Smith, M. W., Street, A., & Frayne, S. (2007). The Veterans Health Administration and military sexual trauma. *American Journal of Public Health, 97,* 2160–2166. doi:10.2105/AJPH.2006.092999

Kimerling, R., Street, A. E., Gima, K., & Smith, M. W. (2008). Evaluation of universal screening for military-related sexual trauma. *Psychiatric Services, 59,* 635–640. doi:10.1176/appi.ps.59.6.635

Linehan, M. M. (1993). *Skills training manual for treating borderline personality disorder.* New York, NY: Guilford Press.

Lipari, R. N., Cook, P. J., Rock, L. M., & Matos, K. (2008). *2006 gender relations survey of active duty members.* Arlington, VA: Department of Defense Manpower Data Center.

Magley, V. J., Hulin, C. L., Fitzgerald, L. F., & DeNardo, M. (1999). Outcomes of self-labeling sexual harassment. *Journal of Applied Psychology, 84,* 390–402. doi:10.1037/0021-9010.84.3.390

Murdoch, M., Hodges, J., Hunt, C., Cowper, D., Kressin, N., & O'Brien, N. (2003). Gender differences in service connection for PTSD. *Medical Care, 41,* 950–961. doi:10.1097/00005650-200308000-00008

Najavits, L. M. (2002). *Seeking safety: A treatment manual for PTSD and substance abuse.* New York, NY: Guilford Press.

Pershing, J. L. (2003). Why women don't report sexual harassment: A case study of an elite military institution. *Gender Issues, 21,* 3–30. doi:10.1007/s12147-003-0008-x

Rentoul, L., & Appleboom, N. (1997). Understanding the psychological impact of rape and serious sexual assault of men: A literature review. *Journal of Psychiatric and Mental Health Nursing, 4,* 267–274. doi:10.1046/j.1365-2850.1997.00064.x

Resick, P. A., Galovski, T. E., O'Brien Uhlmansiek, M., Scher, C. D., Clum, G. A., & Young-Xu, Y. (2008). A randomized clinical trial to dismantle components of cognitive processing therapy for posttraumatic stress disorder in female victims of interpersonal violence. *Journal of Consulting and Clinical Psychology, 76,* 243–258. doi:10.1037/0022-006X.76.2.243

Resick, P. A., Nishith, P., Weaver, T. L., Astin, M. C., & Feuer, C. A. (2002). A comparison of cognitive-processing therapy with prolonged exposure and a waiting condition for the treatment of chronic posttraumatic stress disorder in female rape victims. *Journal of Consulting and Clinical Psychology, 70*, 867–879. doi:10.1037/0022-006X.70.4.867

Rosen, L. N., & Martin, L. (1996). The measurement of childhood trauma among male and female soldiers in the U.S. Army. *Military Medicine, 161*, 342–345.

Rosen, L. N., & Martin, L. (1998). Childhood maltreatment history as a risk factor for sexual harassment among U.S. Army soldiers. *Violence and Victims, 13*, 269–286.

Rothbaum, B. O., Astin, M. C., & Marsteller, F. (2005). Prolonged exposure versus eye movement desensitization and reprocessing (EMDR) for PTSD rape victims. *Journal of Traumatic Stress, 18*, 607–616. doi:10.1002/jts.20069

Sadler, A. G., Booth, B. M., Cook, B. L., & Doebbeling, B. N. (2003). Factors associated with women's risk of rape in the military environment. *American Journal of Industrial Medicine, 43*, 262–273. doi:10.1002/ajim.10202

Sadler, A. G., Booth, B. M., Cook, B. L., Torner, J. C., & Doebbeling, B. N. (2001). The military environment: Risk factors for women's non-fatal assaults. *Journal of Occupational and Environmental Medicine, 43*, 325–334. doi:10.1097/00043764-200104000-00007

Schnurr, P. P., Friedman, M. J., Engel, C. C., Foa, E. B., Shea, M. T., Chow, B. K., . . . Bernardy, N. (2007). Cognitive behavioral therapy for posttraumatic stress disorder in women: A randomized controlled trial. *JAMA, 297*, 820–830. doi:10.1001/jama.297.8.820

Skinner, K. M., Kressin, N., Frayne, S., Tripp, T. J., Hankin, C. S., Miller, D. R., & Sullivan, L. M. (2000). The prevalence of military sexual assault among female Veterans' Administration outpatients. *Journal of Interpersonal Violence, 15*, 291–310. doi:10.1177/088626000015003005

Smith, T. C., Wingard, D. L., Ryan, M. A., Kritz-Silverstein, D., Slymen, D. J., & Sallis, J. F. (2008). Prior assault and posttraumatic stress disorder after combat deployment. *Epidemiology, 19*, 505–512. doi:10.1097/EDE.0b013e31816a9dff

Street, A. E., Gradus, J. L., Stafford, J., & Kelly, K. (2007). Gender differences in experiences of sexual harassment: Data from a male-dominated environment. *Journal of Consulting and Clinical Psychology, 75*, 464–474. doi:10.1037/0022-006X.75.3.464

Street, A. E., Stafford, J., Mahan, C., & Hendricks, A. M. (2008). Sexual harassment and assault experienced by reservists during military service: Prevalence and health correlates. *Journal of Rehabilitation Research and Development, 45*, 409–419. doi:10.1682/JRRD.2007.06.0088

Ullman, S. E. (1999). Social support and recovery from sexual assault: A review. *Aggression and Violent Behavior, 4*, 343–358. doi:10.1016/S1359-1789(98)00006-8

van Berlo, W., & Ensink, B. (2000). Problems with sexuality after sexual assault. *Annual Review of Sex Research, 11*, 235–257.

Vogt, D., Pless, A. P., King, L. A., & King, D. W. (2005). Deployment stressors, gender, and mental health outcomes among Gulf War I veterans. *Journal of Traumatic Stress, 18,* 115–127. doi:10.1002/jts.20018

Walker, J., Archer, J., & Davies, M. (2005). Effects of rape on men: A descriptive analysis. *Archives of Sexual Behavior, 34,* 69–80. doi:10.1007/s10508-005-1001-0

Wolfe, J., Sharkansky, E. J., Read, J. P., Dawson, R., Martin, J. A., & Ouimette, P. C. (1998). Sexual harassment and assault as predictors of PTSD symptomatology among U.S. female Persian Gulf War military personnel. *Journal of Interpersonal Violence, 13,* 40–57. doi:10.1177/088626098013001003

7

COUPLE AND FAMILY ISSUES AND INTERVENTIONS FOR VETERANS OF THE IRAQ AND AFGHANISTAN WARS

CANDICE M. MONSON, STEFFANY J. FREDMAN, AND CASEY T. TAFT

The wars in Iraq and Afghanistan have brought to the fore the stress that deployment and redeployment can have on the families of service members. Deployment of a service member is stressful to the family members who are left behind, but when he or she returns from deployment with trauma-related mental health problems, the family's readjustment can be remarkably complicated. Families can play a role in the course of the veteran's post-deployment mental health problems and can also be affected by those problems.

In this chapter, we review research on family adjustment and deployment and the association between military veterans' trauma-related mental health problems and relationship problems in their families. We then provide an overview of the current evidence-based therapies for military veterans and their families and highlight clinical considerations in the assessment and treatment of this population.

Military families report both positive and negative aspects of deployment (e.g., Newby et al., 2005; Pincus, House, Christenson, & Adler, 2001). A study commissioned by the Department of Defense found that rates of divorce among service members were no higher during the period of time involving deployment to Iraq and Afghanistan when compared with deployments before the beginning of these conflicts (Karney & Crown, 2007). The study authors suggested that other risk factors for dissolution, such as younger age when married, lower education, marriage for improved military-related benefits, and combat exposure, might better explain divorce in these service members. In fact, the extant research suggests that the most negative effects of military deployment on family functioning are associated with veterans' mental health problems arising from their military service and not the effects of deployment itself (Cook, Riggs, Thompson, Coyne, & Sheikh, 2004; Jordan et al., 1992).

Although a range of mental health problems may arise in the wake of military trauma exposure, posttraumatic stress disorder (PTSD) is the mental health condition most commonly associated with traumatic stress exposure and is documented to have a range of severe effects on relational functioning. Therefore, we focus the balance of this chapter on what is known about the relationship between veterans' PTSD symptoms and family functioning and how to integrate veterans' family members into the assessment and treatment of veterans' PTSD and frequently cooccurring conditions such as depression, substance abuse, and intimate aggression.

VETERANS' MENTAL HEALTH PROBLEMS AND FAMILY FUNCTIONING

Epidemiological research reviewed earlier in this book indicates that a significant proportion of veterans of the Iraq and Afghanistan wars are experiencing postdeployment mental health problems. In addition to documenting the rising proportion of veterans who endorse mental health problems, an important point to highlight from this research is the even greater rise in reported interpersonal problems. In a longitudinal study of more than 88,000 soldiers who served in Iraq, Milliken, Auchterlonie, and Hoge (2007) found a fourfold increase in reported interpersonal problems from the first to second waves of assessment (a median of 6 months). Sayers, Farrow, Ross, and Oslin (2009) found similarly high rates of family difficulties among recently returned veterans who screened positive for mental health problems in an outpatient treatment clinic. They found that more than three quarters of married and partnered service members reported difficulties with partners or children. PTSD and major depression were associated with difficulties in family adjustment.

Other recent studies of returning veterans from the Iraq and Afghanistan wars have also found that PTSD symptoms are associated with intimate relationship discord. Goff, Crow, Reisbig, and Hamilton (2007) found that veterans' self-reported PTSD symptom severity was inversely associated with their marital dissatisfaction. In addition, a range of other posttraumatic sequelae were associated with each partners' dyadic adjustment, including veterans' sleep problems, dissociation, and sexual problems. Another study of male National Guard members deployed to Iraq examined the role of their wives' perceptions of soldiers' combat exposure in the association between PTSD and relationship problems (Renshaw, Rodrigues, & Jones, 2008). When wives perceived that their husbands had experienced low levels of combat exposure and their husbands reported high levels of PTSD symptoms, the wives reported lower levels of marital satisfaction. However, when wives perceived their husbands to have experienced high levels of combat, husbands' self-reported PTSD symptoms had no association with their wives' relationship satisfaction. These findings suggest that wives' perceptions of their husbands' combat exposure may be a proxy for how they make sense of their husbands' behaviors. That is, they appear to be less distressed if their husbands' PTSD symptoms can be understood as the result of combat exposure or other consequences of war.

Research with combat veterans from different countries and from prior eras provides a window into the chronic, likely reciprocal effects of PTSD and family relationship problems. These studies show that veterans diagnosed with PTSD and their romantic partners report more numerous and severe relationship problems, more parenting problems, generally poorer family adjustment, and divorce at higher rates relative to trauma-exposed veterans without PTSD (for reviews, see Galovski & Lyons, 2004; Monson, Taft, & Fredman, 2009). Of the PTSD symptom clusters, avoidance–numbing symptoms are most strongly associated with intimate relationship dissatisfaction, impaired intimacy, and lower parenting satisfaction (Cook & Snyder, 2005; Solomon, Dekel, & Mikulincer, 2008). The behavioral avoidance symptoms can interfere with families engaging in pleasurable activities together, and the emotional numbing symptoms can contribute to alexithymia (i.e., difficulty identifying and sharing emotions), as well as a lack of interest in, or even aversion to, physical closeness with another person. When family members feel physically or emotionally distanced from one another, satisfaction and intimacy are compromised. In addition to this phenomenon, Solomon, Dekel, and Mikulincer (2008) recently reported data from a sample of Israeli ex–prisoners of war (POWs) and non-POW combat veteran controls, suggesting that diminished self-disclosure is another potential mechanism accounting for this connection. It is also noteworthy that veterans' emotional numbing symptoms may be less responsive to existing evidence-based individual psychotherapies for PTSD.

Male veterans diagnosed with PTSD, compared with those without PTSD, are more likely to perpetrate verbal and physical aggression against their partners and children (Carroll, Rueger, Foy, & Donahoe, 1985; Glenn et al., 2002; Jordan et al., 1992). Relative to other PTSD symptom clusters, hyperarousal symptoms are most strongly related to intimate partner aggression

(Savarese, Suvak, King, & King, 2001) and general aggression (Taft, Kaloupek, et al., 2007). Problems managing anger may represent an especially salient aspect of hyperarousal that confers risk of perpetrating partner aggression (Taft, Street, Marshall, Dowdall, & Riggs, 2007).

Research on Vietnam and Gulf War I veterans suggests that PTSD symptoms largely account for the effects of stress exposure on family functioning (Gimbel & Booth, 1994; Orcutt, King, & King, 2003). Orcutt et al. (2003) found a negative association between combat exposure and intimate partner physical aggression when a range of factors known to be associated with perpetration and PTSD symptoms were taken into account. These findings suggest a possible "empathy effect" of having experienced trauma that is distinct from the psychopathological processes involved in PTSD that increase the likelihood of perpetrating aggression.

However, problems that commonly cooccur with PTSD play an important role in the association between PTSD and the perpetration of intimate aggression. Savarese et al. (2001) found that alcohol consumption in Vietnam veterans moderated the association between PTSD hyperarousal symptoms and partner aggression such that more frequent, but smaller, quantities of alcohol use diminished the association between hyperarousal and PTSD symptoms. Larger quantities of alcohol interacted with more frequent use such that it strengthened the association between hyperarousal symptoms and PTSD symptoms. In a more recent analysis of data from the same sample, Taft et al. (2005) found that male veterans with PTSD who engaged in partner aggression reported more exposure to war-zone atrocities, had lower marital adjustment, and had more symptoms of depression and drug abuse or dependence compared with nonaggressive veterans with PTSD.

COUPLE AND FAMILY THERAPY FOR VETERANS

Early therapies described in the literature on couple and family therapy for PTSD generally focused on improving the relationship or family environment of the PTSD-identified patient by using general or generic couple or family therapy. More recently developed treatments simultaneously focus on improving conjoint or family functioning and ameliorating the identified client's symptoms. It is important to note at the outset that most of the therapy efforts described in the literature have been aimed at intimate adult couples. There is little research on the inclusion of minor children or nonintimate partners in these interventions.

There has been only one published randomized controlled trial of couple or family therapy for PTSD, and it tested the addition of behavioral family therapy (BFT) to individual evidence-based PTSD therapy. Glynn and colleagues (1999) compared exposure therapy alone with exposure therapy followed by BFT. Participants in both treatment conditions improved more than those assigned to a waiting list on what the authors referred to as "positive" PTSD symptoms (i.e., reexperiencing, hyperarousal) but not the "negative" symptoms of PTSD (i.e., avoidance, numbing) or social adjustment. Improvements in the positive symptoms were roughly twice as large in the group that received BFT compared with the exposure therapy alone group. Participants who completed BFT also showed more improvements in interpersonal problem-solving than did participants who did not receive BFT.

There have been two published uncontrolled trials of behavioral couple therapy for veterans with PTSD; both are disorder-specific treatments designed to treat the avoidance–numbing symptoms of PTSD or all PTSD symptoms and concurrent relationship problems. Sautter and colleagues (2009) developed strategic approach therapy, a 10-session manualized treatment specifically designed to target the avoidance–numbing symptoms of PTSD. Findings from six veteran couples who completed the intervention indicate significant improvements in these symptoms according to patient, partner, and clinician ratings. There were also significant improvements in the veterans' total PTSD symptoms but not reexperiencing or hyperarousal symptoms. The authors did not assess relationship adjustment in this pilot study, and consequently the potential effects of the intervention on dyadic functioning or the utility of the intervention for couples with different levels of distress are not yet known.

Cognitive–behavioral conjoint therapy (CBCT) for PTSD (Monson & Fredman, in press) is designed to ameliorate all symptoms of PTSD and enhance relationship functioning. In a sample of seven couples, including a Vietnam veteran with PTSD, Monson and colleagues (2004) found statistically significant and large improvements in clinicians' and partners' ratings of veterans' PTSD symptoms from pre- to posttreatment. The veterans reported moderate improvements in PTSD and statistically significant and large improvements in depression, anxiety, and social functioning. Wives reported large effect-size improvements in relationship satisfaction, general anxiety, and social functioning (Monson, Stevens, & Schnurr, 2005). More recent application of the therapy to veterans and community members with PTSD reveals clinically significant improvements in clinicians', patients', and partners' ratings of patients' PTSD symptoms, as well as significant improvements in partner-reported relationship satisfaction (Monson et al., 2010).

A few publications have presented program evaluation data related to the inclusion of veterans' family members in psychoeducation and symptom management efforts as part of larger treatment programs for veterans. Devilly (2002) described the results of an uncontrolled study of Australian combat veterans and their partners who participated in an intensive week-long residential group intervention that included psychoeducation about PTSD and symptom management techniques. At follow-up, both veterans and their partners reported significant, but small, reductions in anxiety, depression, and stress; veterans reported a significant reduction in PTSD symptoms. Small improvements were also observed for anger and quality of life but not for relationship satisfaction. Another program for veterans with PTSD and their partners was the Israeli K'oach program (Rabin & Nardi, 1991). This program included psychoeducation about PTSD and communication and problem-solving skills training. Minimal outcome data were reported on this intervention; however, 68% of the men and their wives reported relationship improvements. No decrease in veterans' PTSD symptoms was observed.

Other types of couple and family therapies have been described in the literature; however, no outcome data have yet been published to support their efficacy. These include emotionally focused couple therapy for trauma survivors (Johnson, 2002), systemic family therapy with trauma survivors (Figley, 1989), family consultation adapted for the needs of traumatized families (Erickson, 1989), and family crisis intervention (Harris, 1991).

FAMILY FACTORS IN PTSD TREATMENT ENGAGEMENT AND OUTCOMES

One study has examined factors associated with significant others' engagement in veterans' PTSD treatment. Sautter et al. (2006) telephone-surveyed a sample of cohabitating female partners of male Vietnam combat veterans with PTSD. They found that lower income, greater involvement in the veterans' lives more generally, and higher levels of experienced caregiver burden all predicted more involvement in veterans' treatment.

Even if a couple or family intervention is not included in the treatment plan for a veteran of the Iraq or Afghanistan wars, it is worth considering the role of family variables in the success of individually delivered evidence-based therapy. In their study of individual imaginal exposure and cognitive therapy for PTSD, Tarrier, Sommerfield, and Pilgrim (1999) found that patients whose relatives displayed high levels of criticism, hostility, or both exhibited less improvement in PTSD symptoms, depressive symptoms, and general anxiety following treatment than did patients with relatives who expressed low levels of these behaviors.

Similarly, Monson, Rodriguez, and Warner (2005) studied the role of interpersonal relationship variables in two forms of group cognitive–behavior therapy (CBT) for veterans with PTSD (trauma- vs. skills-focused). Although there were no differences in the PTSD outcomes of the two forms of treatment, intimate relationship functioning variables were more strongly associated with treatment outcomes in the trauma- versus skills-focused treatment.

There was a stronger relationship between pretreatment intimate relationship functioning and violence perpetration outcomes in the trauma- versus skills-focused group. Greater intimate relationship adjustment at pretreatment was associated with lower levels of violence perpetration at follow-up for veterans who received trauma-focused versus skills-focused treatment.

Clinical Considerations in the Assessment and Treatment of Veterans of the Iraq and Afghanistan Wars and Their Families

We limit discussion of clinical considerations for assessing and treating veterans of the Iraq and Afghanistan wars largely to working with intimate couples because the evidence about the integration of veterans' families is most developed in this area. In addition, there are important developmental considerations that must be attended to when including children in any psychoeducation effort or treatment intervention that are beyond the scope of this chapter.

Assessment Considerations

In what follows, we discuss considerations in the assessment of veterans' PTSD and comorbid conditions, as well as assessment of individual family members. Discussion of assessment of relationship-level functioning follows.

Veteran Assessment

Issues related to the assessment of veterans' PTSD and comorbid conditions are relatively straightforward. Even if a couple or family intervention is not requested or going to be, offered, we strongly recommend obtaining collateral reports of veterans' symptoms and functional impairments from adult family members whenever possible as part of a thorough assessment of the clinical problems. In our research and clinical practice, we have created a partner version of the PTSD Checklist (PCL–P; Monson, 2001) that asks intimate partners to rate their perception of their veteran's PTSD symptoms on the measure. The PCL could be adapted for a range of significant others (e.g., parents, siblings, close friends) to report on their perception of a given veteran's symptoms.

Consistent with recent research (Bliese et al., 2008), it is our experience that recently returning veterans tend to report less severe PTSD symptoms that might be characterized as underreporting when compared with the reports of intimate partners and the results of clinician interviews. Discrepancies in the multimodal assessment of PTSD are important information to the clinician regarding case conceptualization of the patient and possible barriers to fully benefiting from treatment. For example, underreporting might be associated with stigma about presenting with mental health problems or deficits in knowledge and awareness of PTSD symptoms. Regarding the latter, many recently returned veterans with whom we have worked are surprised to learn that, in addition to reexperiencing symptoms of PTSD (e.g., flashbacks, nightmares), anger and irritability, social withdrawal, and emotional numbing are also symptoms of PTSD that affect themselves and their loved ones. Discrepancies across reporters can also be highlighted to motivate the veteran toward engagement in an evidence-based treatment for PTSD. Adult family members can provide important information about other frequently cooccurring mental health difficulties such as depression, dissociation, and panic symptoms, as well as specific functional impairments related to intimate relationships, parenting, broader family relationships, activities of daily life, and work problems. Given the high rates of comorbid substance use disorder in PTSD and the well-documented tendency for underreporting and minimization of substance use problems, we strongly recommend specifically inquiring with adult family members about the frequency and quantity of the veteran's substance use. All of this information can be used to highlight the symptoms of the disorder and related untoward consequences of it that others are noticing. It provides a jumping off point for presenting the rationale for evidence-based treatment of PTSD.

A concrete example of important collateral information that we received from a veteran's wife involves a veteran who served three tours in Iraq as an officer. His self-report of PTSD symptoms placed him in the relatively mild range of symptom severity compared with veterans from prior eras; his clinician interview-rated symptom severity was slightly higher but not as severe as the picture that emerged after speaking with his wife. He denied problematic drinking patterns and other substance use and reported little functional impairment. However, his wife complained that he was quick to anger with her and their children. Believing that if he became even mildly distressed, he would suffer a heart attack, she also attempted to shield him from family matters and told the children to be quiet around him. His wife also revealed that he was experiencing significant dissociation and flashbacks in which he was "hitting the deck" and having notable alterations in consciousness when aircraft flew over their home. She indicated that he rarely drove automobiles after returning from Iraq because one of his traumas involved a near-death experience while driving, and he experienced flashbacks, dissociation, and hyperarousal when he had to drive. His wife or other employees at his place of work drove him wherever he needed to go. She noted that he spent significant time in his "war room," a basement room filled with a lifetime of memorabilia from his service, away from her and their young children, and she often encouraged him to retreat there when he became triggered. She also described his going to great lengths to avoid malls, restaurants, school-related events, or larger family gatherings after his return because of his hyper-vigilance, "bordering on paranoia," and reexperiencing symptoms. Furthermore, she provided important information regarding his alcohol consumption. Although he rarely drank alcohol before his third and last deployment, the veteran was drinking at least several beers each and every day, and more when he was "stressed."

The veteran's extreme shame related to seeking assessment and treatment for trauma-related problems because of his officer status in the military and current ranking position at his place of employment had prevented him from sharing his difficulty driving and periods of dissociation (of which he seemed to have minimal awareness). He also denied problems with alcohol and considered his "war room" time normal. The information that his wife provided was instrumental to understanding the types of problems that the veteran was experiencing, the severity of the problems, the extent of functional impairments, and the stigma that seemed to influence the veteran's report. It was also informative to the treatment planning and engagement process.

Assessment of Individual Family Members

In addition to providing psychoeducation, we recommend some assessment of individual psychopathology in family members if they will be included in treatment. Research indicates that veterans' intimate partners will likely present with their own mental health symptoms, with symptoms of depression, substance abuse, PTSD, and general anxiety as the most likely suspected types of problems (for a review, see Monson, Stevens, et al., 2005). Self-report measurement of these symptoms is an efficient way to acquire this information, and most of these measures can be administered on an ongoing basis across treatment to assess individual outcomes related to treatment.

Relationship-Level Assessment

We strongly recommend objective assessment of relationship-level functioning to determine the severity and type of relationship problems as well as to be able to monitor and assess treatment response to any couple or family intervention. The gold standard method of assessing intimate relationship functioning is the Dyadic Adjustment Scale (DAS; Spanier, 1976). Each member of the couple completes this relatively brief self-report measure. The DAS has cut scores indicative of clinical levels of relationship distress, and review of specific items on the DAS provides information regarding areas of distress (e.g., in-laws, money, sex), degree of commitment to the relationship, and emotional expressiveness in the relationship. Other family-level assessment measures that might be used to assess the broader family's functioning include the Family Environment Scale (Moos, 1990) and the Family Adaptability and Cohesion Evaluation Scales, Third Edition (Olson, 1986).

In addition to assessing relationship satisfaction in intimate relationships, clinicians should routinely assess for the presence, frequency, severity, and consequences of physical aggression. Research indicates that approximately 50% of distressed couples presenting for couple therapy report some history of physical aggression in their relationship (e.g., Sherman, Sautter, Jackson, Lyons, & Xiaotong, 2006). We use the Conflict Tactics Scale—Revised (Straus, Hamby, & Boney-McCoy, 1996) to assess intimate aggression because it is a behaviorally anchored measure of a range of aggressive behaviors and their physical consequences (i.e., emotional, physical, sexual, and injury subscales) and includes an assessment of the frequency of these behaviors. Using a questionnaire-based measure completed separately by each member of the couple, versus inquiring in the conjoint context, also decreases possible acquiescent responding, allows the clinician to assess concordance in partners' responses, and provides the clinician with time to consider a course of action if either member of the couple reports any recent severe aggression.

We also recommend inquiring about any behaviors on the part of the family member that, although well intended, may inadvertently serve to reinforce veterans' PTSD-related avoidance. We refer to this phenomenon as *symptom accommodation*. All evidence-based therapies for PTSD include a focus on decreasing this avoidance, and addressing ways in which loved ones contribute to this avoidance can improve the efficacy of therapy. For instance, in the example reviewed earlier, the veteran's wife frequently ran interference with others and helped him arrange his life so as to minimize confronting anxiety-provoking stimuli (e.g., driving, going to malls and grocery stores, hearing loud noises). As a result, the veteran had fewer opportunities to feel anxious initially but then learn that he was not, in fact, in any true danger. Accommodative behaviors that other partners have engaged in include helping the veteran to arrange seating at restaurants so that the veteran's back was against the wall rather than to the door, driving rather than taking public transportation when they go out as a couple, and not sharing one's own feelings, concerns, and needs due to the veteran's irritability or emotional numbing.

Considerations in Treatment Planning

Integrating significant others in veterans' treatment and addressing veterans' family problems require careful consideration at the outset of the treatment planning process. One method of including family members in a treatment plan is to provide generic evidence-based couple or family therapy, with the parsimonious goal of improving general family functioning. A desired effect of this relationship-level focus is that improved dyadic and family functioning will, in turn, translate into improved individual mental and physical health of the individuals in that relationship milieu. As reviewed earlier, prior research provides some support for this notion, although the treatment effects for individual- and couple-level variables have not been as robust as desired. Aside from the parsimony of this approach, another potential benefit of this method is that the "client" is more clearly the couple or family, avoiding the thornier issue of implicitly or explicitly having an identified patient who is being treated in the couple or family context.

In the balance of this section, we discuss how adult family members can be included in veterans' treatment with the simultaneous goals of improving the veteran's individual symptoms, as well as his or her family relationship functioning. We provide principles to consider in determining the optimal manner in which to involve veterans' loved ones in treatment based on our three-stage treatment of CBCT for PTSD previously described. Although we use our treatment to illustrate the principles, we believe these considerations can be more broadly applied when considering how and when to incorporate significant others in returning veterans' treatment for a range of mental health problems.

We have an obvious bias to incorporate veterans' family members in treatment whenever possible. That said, there are some occasions on which it may be contraindicated, or there may be a need to delay the family therapy to ensure safety and increase the likelihood of treatment success. Following recommendations about the provision of couple therapy (Epstein & Baucom, 2002), this modality may not be appropriate for couples in which there has been recent severe intimate aggression, and especially in couples in which the aggression is largely perpetrated by one member toward the other. Individual or group therapy focused specifically on the intimate aggression might be offered. After a period of time without physical aggression, couple therapy might then be initiated with ongoing monitoring of the potential for intimate aggression in the relationship.

Cognitive–Behavioral Conjoint Therapy for PTSD

CBCT for PTSD is a 15-session manualized treatment consisting of three stages: (a) psychoeducation about the dynamic interplay between PTSD and relationship functioning, exercises to promote positivity, and a techniques to promote a shared sense of safety; (b) behavioral interventions that increase approach behaviors and improve dyadic communication; and (c) cognitive interventions designed to address maladaptive thinking patterns that maintain both PTSD symptoms and relationship distress.

Assuming basic levels of safety and stability in the veteran and his or her adult family member, we believe that the next most important factor to

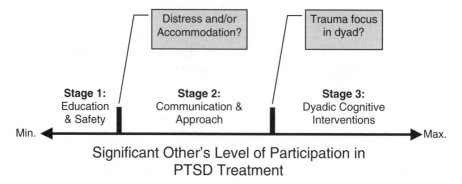

Figure 7.1. Considerations in the use of various stages of cognitive–behavioral conjoint therapy for posttraumatic stress disorder.

consider is the degree to which the veteran and family member(s) are willing to participate in treatment. As shown in Figure 7.1, at the most minimal level of involvement is the provision of psychoeducation about the disorder(s) and the treatment rationale. The interventions involved in Stage 1 of CBCT for PTSD, including a session focused on psychoeducation about PTSD and the reciprocal effects of PTSD and intimate relationship functioning and a session focused on decreasing the most deleterious relationship behaviors (e.g., name-calling) and improving conflict resolution, might be used alone or in conjunction with an evidence-based psychosocial or medication treatment for PTSD to decrease the likelihood of treatment-interfering behavior on the part of loved ones and decrease the most hostile and critical behaviors that have been found to negatively affect individually delivered treatment for PTSD. This primarily psychoeducation-oriented level of intervention might be provided in a family session including the veteran, in an individual session with the family member(s) alone, or to a group of loved ones in settings in which there are sufficient numbers of family members or more scarce resources to provide individual family-level services.

An example of the value of using this stage of intervention comes from a case of a Vietnam veteran with PTSD whom one of us treated. The veteran chose a course of cognitive processing therapy, including the version with a written trauma account (Resick, Monson, & Chard, 2007). The veteran came to the fourth session in which the trauma account is read aloud to the therapist reporting that his wife had poured him a glass of wine before writing the account to "calm his nerves." He indicated that she was concerned about his getting "riled up" from doing the assignment and did not seem to understand the point of "drudging it all back up as raw as possible." He expressed knowledge of the likely role of avoidance in drinking the alcohol but indicated that her concern made him concerned. With the client's permission, the therapist contacted the veteran's wife and invited her to a conjoint session with the client before the next session. The therapist provided psychoeducation to the wife about the course of therapy by encouraging the veteran to explain the rationale of the therapy. The veteran's PTSD symptoms improved with CPT, and at the last session, he requested couple therapy for him and his wife.

With increasing willingness on the part of veterans and family members to participate in treatment, and when there is relationship distress or accommodation to the symptoms of PTSD on the part of family members (one or both are expected to be the prototypical presentation), Stage 2 of CBCT for PTSD can also be provided. This stage includes a focus on improving communication and problem-solving skills, decreasing behavioral and emotional avoidance, and introducing dyadic cognitive restructuring. All of the interventions involved in Stage 2 of CBCT for PTSD are expected to be complementary to, or enhancing of, the current evidence-based psychotherapies for PTSD. For example, all of these therapies include a focus on decreasing avoidance and, to varying degrees, modifying appraisals that have caused or maintain the disorder. Stages 1 and 2 of the therapy could also be used in conjunction with a plan that includes only medication or medication in conjunction with evidence-based psychotherapy.

An example of the use of interventions from Stage 2 of CBCT comes from the Iraq veteran's case described earlier involving the avoidance of malls and driving. Together the couple developed a list of places and things that were avoided because of PTSD and, at the therapist's urging, systematically began approaching those places. They concretely problem-solved how to approach these situations successfully (e.g., when, how, avoiding accommodation). They also identified the wife's cognition that her husband could have a heart attack if placed in distressing situations as a thought that the two could explore together for its rationality and functionality. The couple brainstormed a number of alternative thoughts and agreed that the veteran did not have a history of heart problems or risk factors identified by his physician for a heart attack. They collaboratively came to the thought that his risk for heart problems would likely be greater with chronic PTSD than with time-limited exposure to these situations to recover from it. This greatly facilitated compliance with the in vivo approach assignments out of session.

The provision of Stage 3 of CBCT for PTSD is dependent on the willingness of the veteran and his or her intimate partner to be involved in trauma-focused cognitive restructuring and clinical indication of that involvement. Regarding the latter, we believe that the majority of traumatic material can be discussed within the intimate partner relationship because we focus on the sense- or meaning-making that the veteran and his or her partner engage in about the traumatic experience(s) and the symptoms of PTSD rather than the specific details of trauma events. The therapy is based on a cognitive conceptualization of PTSD that does not necessitate repetitive review of specific details of traumatic events until habituation occurs. We tell clients that we are not interested in the "nitty gritty" details of what happened but rather wish to have enough details to have a shared understanding of the event(s) to evaluate their appraisals about it.

Some veterans may not choose to do trauma-focused treatment, or some partners or veterans may not want to do trauma-focused therapy in a conjoint manner. In those cases, couples could continue to do the interventions in Stage 2 with a continued focus on in vivo approach behavior, improving communication skills and problem solving, and using the dyadic cognitive restructuring skills on here-and-now issues. In fact, earlier versions of CBCT for PTSD had a more present-centered focus and showed significant improvements in veteran, spouse, and relationship outcomes (Monson et al., 2004; Monson, Stevens, et al., 2005).

Other veterans and their partners may prefer to participate in discussions about the appraisals of traumatic events and the implications of those appraisals on intimate and family relations. If Stage 3 of CBCT for PTSD is pursued, we believe that simultaneous pursuit of other trauma-focused PTSD treatment is contraindicated because of the potential for conflicting messages sent by different therapists and the significant "dose" of therapy that would be provided.

We have found processing the meaning of traumatic events in the couple context to be powerful. Significant others can provide alternative explanations for traumatic events, support the veteran in considering such events, and help veterans practice new ways of making sense of these experiences and their consequences in their interpersonal interactions. Consistent with the literature on self-disclosure about traumatic events and relationship functioning (Koenen, Stellman, Stellman, & Sommer, 2003; Solomon, Dekel, & Zerach, 2008), it is our experience that this type of work increases intimacy in the couple beyond that achieved with more traditional behavioral couple therapy techniques and enhances understanding and empathy in the couple's relationship. Across couples, we have found PTSD symptoms to decrease and intimate relationship functioning to increase.

An example of this trauma focus comes from another couple with whom one of us worked involving an Iraq war veteran diagnosed with PTSD secondary to combat-related trauma. The veteran reported that the most disturbing aspect of his service had been seeing the body of a 12-year-old boy who had been tortured and killed by Iraqi insurgents as a way of retaliating against his father for cooperating with the U.S. military. The veteran reported that he had been extremely angry since returning from Iraq as a result of being unable to accept that such an event could have happened when his and other American soldiers' intentions were "good" (i.e., to help the Iraqi people in their quest for freedom from dictatorship). He repeatedly made statements such as, "I can't comprehend how this could have happened" and "I can't make sense of this." The goal of the cognitive portion of the therapy was, therefore, to assist him in being able to make some sense of how this event could have happened without condoning the event itself. It also became apparent that he believed that there should be universally held standards for warfare upheld by all that included not torturing and killing children. His PTSD symptoms stemmed from his difficulty in reconciling this act with these strongly held beliefs. During the cognitive portion of the therapy, his wife proved quite skillful in helping the veteran more fully understand and contextualize the event. For example, as a result of her perspective on the insurgents' potential motivations for harming the child and the existence of cultural differences in the value of life and death, the veteran's thinking began to shift from "All people value life the same and should adhere to universal standards in warfare" to "The insurgents probably thought that they had to do something this extreme to protect themselves and their families from a foreign occupying force; people value life and death differently across cultures; and, there are *not* commonly shared rules in war (whether I want there to be or not). If there were rules, there probably wouldn't be war in the first place." This latter point appeared to be particularly important in helping the veteran reconcile how an act that went so strongly against his own moral code could have happened in the course of a mission that he perceived as noble and just. Shortly thereafter, the veteran's symptoms decreased further, and he reported feeling less distressed.

CONCLUSIONS AND FUTURE DIRECTIONS

Our most recent military engagements are met with greater understanding of the multiple effects of military stressors on the individual and the veteran's larger family unit. With a few exceptions, most research conducted to date on veterans and their families has been done in samples of male veterans who have had chronic PTSD for years and their female intimate partners. We need to better understand the developmental nature of both traumatic stress responses and family roles and functioning, as well as the gender of the traumatized person in these families to more fully appreciate the effects of combat exposure and postdeployment mental health problems on the family and vice versa.

The "family" portion of the "couple–family" label applied to research and treatment in this area is often lost in translation to practice. More research is needed on broader family functioning and the effects of parental postdeployment mental health problems on children to better intervene at the family level. We have had at least one couple who was disappointed that there was not more integration of their minor children in our current trial of CBCT for PTSD. It is also important to consider veterans' different family constellations in research and practice. A significant proportion of veterans are not in a longer term romantic relationship. Parents, siblings, close friends, or fellow veterans may be the veteran's family. Some veterans are in committed same-sex relationships. Current military policy makes inclusion of these partners difficult, if not impossible, in active-duty service members' treatment, and stigma may prevent them from seeking care at a VA medical center.

There has been significant progress in understanding couple and family issues and traumatic stress reactions, but there is substantially more work to be done. The next years will bring a number of important innovations in basic research, prevention, and treatment for veterans and their loved ones. We are hopeful that these efforts will result in improved health and well-being of our veterans of the Iraq and Afghanistan wars and the families that encircle them, a well-deserved outcome for their many sacrifices for our country.

REFERENCES

Bliese, P. D., Wright, K. M., Adler, A. B., Cabrera, O., Castro, C. A., & Hoge, C. W. (2008). Validating the primary care posttraumatic stress disorder screen and the posttraumatic stress disorder checklist with soldiers returning from combat. *Journal of Consulting and Clinical Psychology, 76,* 272–281. doi:10.1037/0022-006X.76.2.272

Carroll, E. M., Rueger, D. B., Foy, D. W., & Donahoe, C. P. (1985). Vietnam combat veterans with posttraumatic stress disorder: Analysis of marital and cohabitating adjustment. *Journal of Abnormal Psychology, 94,* 329–337. doi:10.1037/0021-843X.94.3.329

Cook, J. M., Riggs, D. S., Thompson, R., Coyne, J. C., & Sheikh, J. I. (2004). Posttraumatic stress disorder and current relationship functioning among World War II ex–prisoners of war. *Journal of Family Psychology, 18,* 36–45. doi:10.1037/0893-3200.18.1.36

Cook, W. L., & Snyder, D. K. (2005). Analyzing non-independent outcomes in couple therapy using the actor-partner interdependence model. *Journal of Family Psychology, 19,* 133–141. doi:10.1037/0893-3200.19.1.133

Devilly, G. J. (2002). The psychological effects of a lifestyle management course on war veterans and their spouses. *Journal of Clinical Psychology, 58,* 1119–1134. doi:10.1002/jclp.10041

Epstein, N. B., & Baucom, D. H. (2002). *Enhanced cognitive–behavioral therapy for couples: A contextual approach.* Washington, DC: American Psychological Association. doi:10.1037/10481-000

Erickson, C. A. (1989). Rape and the family. In C. R. Figley (Ed.), *Treating stress in families* (pp. 257–289). New York, NY: Brunner/Mazel.

Figley, C. R. (1989). *Helping traumatized families*. San Francisco, CA: Jossey-Bass.

Galovski, T., & Lyons, J. A. (2004). Psychological sequelae of combat violence: A review of the impact of PTSD on the veteran's family and possible interventions. *Aggression and Violent Behavior, 9,* 477–501. doi:10.1016/S1359-1789(03)00045-4

Gimbel, C., & Booth, A. (1994). Why does military combat experience adversely affect marital relations? *Journal of Marriage and the Family, 56,* 691–703. doi:10.2307/352879

Glenn, D. M., Beckham, J. C., Feldman, M. E., Kirby, A. C., Hertzberg, M. A., & Moore, S. D. (2002). Violence and hostility among families of Vietnam veterans with combat-related posttraumatic stress disorder. *Violence and Victims, 17,* 473–489. doi:10.1891/vivi.17.4.473.33685

Glynn, S. M., Eth, S., Randolph, E. T., Foy, D. W., Urbaitis, M., Boxer, L., . . . Crothers, J. (1999). A test of behavioral family therapy to augment exposure for combat-related posttraumatic stress disorder. *Journal of Consulting and Clinical Psychology, 67,* 243–251. doi:10.1037/0022-006X.67.2.243

Goff, B. S. N., Crow, J. R., Reisbig, A. M. J., & Hamilton, S. (2007). The impact of individual trauma symptoms of deployed soldiers on relationship satisfaction. *Journal of Family Psychology, 21,* 344–353.

Harris, C. J. (1991). A family crisis-intervention model for the treatment of posttraumatic stress reaction. *Journal of Traumatic Stress, 4,* 195–207. doi:10.1002/jts.2490040204

Johnson, S. M. (2002). *Emotionally focused couple therapy with trauma survivors: Strengthening attachment bonds*. New York, NY: Guilford Press.

Jordan, B. K., Marmar, C. R., Fairbank, J. A., Schlenger, W. E., Kulka, R. A., Hough, R. L., . . . Weiss, D. L. (1992). Problems in families of male Vietnam veterans with posttraumatic stress disorder. *Journal of Consulting and Clinical Psychology, 60,* 916–926. doi:10.1037/0022-006X.60.6.916

Karney, B. R., & Crown, J. S. (2007). Families under stress: An assessment of data, theory, and research on marriage and divorce in the military. Center for Mental Health Policy Research. Santa Monica, CA: RAND Corporation.

Koenen, K. C., Stellman, J. M., Stellman, S. D., & Sommer, J. F., Jr. (2003). Risk factors for course of posttraumatic stress disorder among Vietnam veterans: A 14-year follow-up of American Legionnaires. *Journal of Consulting and Clinical Psychology, 71,* 980–986. doi:10.1037/0022-006X.71.6.980

Milliken, C. S., Auchterlonie, J. L., & Hoge, C. W. (2007). Longitudinal assessment of mental health problems among active and reserve component soldiers returning from the Iraq war. *JAMA, 298,* 2141–2148. doi:10.1001/jama.298.18.2141

Monson, C. M. (2001). *PTSD Checklist—Partner Version*. Unpublished measure, Department of Psychology, Ryerson University, Toronto, Ontario.

Monson, C. M., & Fredman, S. J. (under contract). *Cognitive-behavioral conjoint therapy for posttraumatic stress disorder: Therapist's manual*. New York, NY: Guilford Press.

Monson, C. M., Fredman, S. J., Adair, K. C., Stevens, S. P., Resick, P. A., Schnurr, P. P., . . . Macdonald, A. (2010). *Cognitive-behavioral conjoint therapy for PTSD: Pilot results from a community sample*. Manuscript submitted for publication.

Monson, C. M., Rodriguez, B. F., & Warner, R. (2005). Cognitive-behavioral therapy for PTSD in the real world: Do interpersonal relationships make a real difference? *Journal of Clinical Psychology, 61*, 751–761. doi:10.1002/jclp.20096

Monson, C. M., Schnurr, P. P., Stevens, S. P., & Guthrie, K. A. (2004). Cognitive-behavioral couple's treatment for posttraumatic stress disorder: Initial findings. *Journal of Traumatic Stress, 17*, 341–344. doi:10.1023/B:JOTS.0000038483.69570.5b

Monson, C. M., Stevens, S. P., & Schnurr, P. P. (2005). Cognitive-behavioral couple's treatment for posttraumatic stress disorder. In T. A. Corales (Ed.), *Focus on posttraumatic stress disorder research* (pp. 245–274). Hauppague, NY: Nova Science.

Monson, C. M., Taft, C. T., & Fredman, S. J. (2009). Military-related PTSD and intimate relationships: From description to theory-driven research and intervention development. *Clinical Psychology Review, 29*, 707–714. doi:10.1016/j.cpr.2009.09.002

Moos, R. H. (1990). Conceptual and empirical approaches to developing family-based assessment procedures: Resolving the case of the Family Environment Scale. *Family Process, 29*, 199–208. doi:10.1111/j.1545-5300.1990.00199.x

Newby, J. H., McCarroll, J. E., Ursano, R. J., Fan, Z., Shigemura, J., & Tucker-Harris, Y. (2005). Positive and negative consequences of military deployment. *Military Medicine, 170*, 815–819.

Olson, D. H. (1986). Circumplex Model VII: Validation studies and FACES III. *Family Process, 25*, 337–351. doi:10.1111/j.1545-5300.1986.00337.x

Orcutt, H. K., King, L. A., & King, D. W. (2003). Male-perpetrated violence among Vietnam veteran couples: Relationships with veterans' early life characteristics, trauma history, and PTSD symptomatology. *Journal of Traumatic Stress, 16*, 381–390. doi:10.1023/A:1024470103325

Pincus, S. H., House, R., Christenson, J., & Adler, L. E. (2001). The emotional cycle of deployment: A military family perspective. *U.S. Army Medical Department Journal, 2*, 615–625.

Rabin, C., & Nardi, C. (1991). Treating post-traumatic stress disorder couples: A psychoeducational program. *Community Mental Health Journal, 27*, 209–224. doi:10.1007/BF00752422

Renshaw, K. D., Rodrigues, C. S., & Jones, D. H. (2008). Psychological symptoms and marital distress in spouses of Operation Iraqi Freedom veterans: Relationships with spouses' perceptions of veterans' experiences and symptoms. *Journal of Family Psychology, 22*, 586–594. doi:10.1037/0893-3200.22.3.586

Resick, P. A., Monson, C. M., & Chard, K. M. (2007). *Cognitive processing therapy: Veteran/military version*. Washington, DC: Department of Veterans Affairs.

Sautter, F., Glynn, S., Thompson, K. E., Franklin, C. L., & Han, X. (2009). A couple-based approach to the reduction of PTSD avoidance symptoms: Preliminary findings. *Journal of Marital and Family Therapy, 35,* 343–349. doi:10.1111/j.1752-0606.2009.00125.x

Sautter, F. J., Lyons, J. A., Manguno-Mire, G., Perry, D., Han, X., Sherman, M., . . . Sullivan, G. (2006). Predictors of partner engagement in PTSD treatment. *Journal of Psychopathology and Behavioral Assessment, 28,* 123–130. doi:10.1007/s10862-006-7490-x

Savarese, V. W., Suvak, M. K., King, L. A., & King, D. W. (2001). Relationships among alcohol use, hyperarousal, and marital abuse and violence in Vietnam veterans. *Journal of Traumatic Stress, 14,* 717–732. doi:10.1023/A:1013038021175

Sayers, S. L., Farrow, V., Ross, J., & Oslin, D. W. (2009). Family problems among recently returned military veterans. *The Journal of Clinical Psychiatry, 70,* 163–170. doi:10.4088/JCP.07m03863

Sherman, M. D., Sautter, F., Jackson, H. M., Lyons, J. A., & Xiaotong, H. (2006). Domestic violence in veterans with posttraumatic stress disorder who seek couples therapy. *Journal of Marital and Family Therapy, 32,* 479–490. doi:10.1111/j.1752-0606.2006.tb01622.x

Solomon, Z., Dekel, R., & Mikulincer, M. (2008). Complex trauma of war captivity: A prospective study of attachment and post-traumatic stress disorder. *Psychological Medicine, 38,* 1427–1434.

Solomon, Z., Dekel, R., & Zerach, G. (2008). The relationship between posttraumatic stress symptom clusters and marital intimacy among war veterans. *Journal of Family Psychology, 22,* 659–666. doi:10.1037/a0013596

Spanier, G. B. (1976). Measuring dyadic adjustment: New scales for assessing the quality of marriage and similar dyads. *Journal of Marriage and the Family, 38,* 15–28. doi:10.2307/350547

Straus, M. A., Hamby, S. L., & Boney-McCoy, S. (1996). The revised Conflict Tactics Scales (CTS2): Development and preliminary psychometric data. *Journal of Family Issues, 17,* 283–316. doi:10.1177/019251396017003001

Taft, C. T., Kaloupek, D. G., Schumm, J. A., Marshall, A. D., Panuzio, J., King, D. W., & Keane, T. M. (2007). Posttraumatic stress disorder symptoms, physiological reactivity, alcohol problems, and aggression among military veterans. *Journal of Abnormal Psychology, 116,* 498–507. doi:10.1037/0021-843X.116.3.498

Taft, C. T., Pless, A. P., Stalans, L. J., Koenen, K. C., King, L. A., & King, D. W. (2005). Risk factors for partner violence among a national sample of combat veterans. *Journal of Consulting and Clinical Psychology, 73,* 151–159. doi:10.1037/0022-006X.73.1.151

Taft, C. T., Street, A., Marshall, A. D., Dowdall, D. J., & Riggs, D. (2007). Posttraumatic stress disorder, anger, and partner abuse among Vietnam combat veterans. *Journal of Family Psychology, 21,* 270–277. doi:10.1037/0893-3200.21.2.270

Tarrier, N., Sommerfield, C., & Pilgrim, H. (1999). Relatives' expressed emotion (EE) and PTSD treatment outcome. *Psychological Medicine, 29,* 801–811. doi:10.1017/S0033291799008569

8

MEETING THE WARTIME NEEDS OF MILITARY CHILDREN AND ADOLESCENTS

STEPHEN J. COZZA

Although most mental health clinicians receive some training in child and adolescent mental health, few have a clear understanding of the needs of children in the unique circumstances that accompany the combat exposure and deployment experiences of military parents. Children are often the unseen and unheard individuals in the family, and their emotional reactions and needs may go unrecognized or misunderstood by the adult health care community.

The children of military service members constitute a large and integral part of our diverse military communities. Although some literature examines the general health and well-being of military children and families (Castro, Adler, & Britt, 2006), much less research has specifically focused on the impact of parental combat exposure and its consequences. Such exposure directly affects children through parental combat deployment (single, multiple, or extended), parental combat injury, posttraumatic illness, or parental death (Cozza, Chun,

This chapter was coauthored by an employee of the United States government as part of official duty and is considered to be in the public domain. Any views expressed herein do not necessarily represent the views of the United States government, and the author's participation in the work is not meant to serve as an official endorsement.

& Polo, 2005). Because empirical studies of clinical interventions and treatment with military children and families affected by parental combat deployment have not been done, clinical guidance must be sought from the application of approaches with other populations as well as an understanding of developmental principles.

HEALTH AND WELL-BEING OF MILITARY CHILDREN

The size and configuration of the U.S. military force have changed throughout history, reflecting the defense needs of the country. These changes are also reflected in the composition of military families and the population of military children. The concept of a military family is relatively new due to the changing face of the military since the Vietnam War (Schneider & Martin, 1994). Before Vietnam and the establishment of the all-volunteer force in 1973, the vast majority of junior enlisted soldiers were single (Schneider & Martin, 1994). Current statistics reveal a different reality. Today, more than half of the force (active duty and reservists) are married, and many have children (44% of the active force and 38% of the reserves). Two thirds of children of active-duty service members are 11 years old or younger, with 40% being 5 years old or younger (U.S. Department of Defense, 2004).

Most published data reflect the health and well-being of military children, who perform at least as well as their civilian counterparts on measures of psychological health (Jensen et al., 1995; Jensen, Xenakis, Wolf, & Bain, 1991; Ryan-Wenger, 2001). However, military children face unique challenges because of their parents' service.

A literature is developing that describes the impact of current Operation Iraqi Freedom (OIF) and Operation Enduring Freedom (OEF) combat operations and deployments on military children and families during a time of extended or multiple combat deployments. Studies have focused on children of different ages, both preschool (3–5 years) and school-age (6–12 years) children (Chandra, Burns, Tanielian, Jaycox, & Scott, 2008; Chartrand, Frank, White, & Shope, 2008) as well as teenagers (13–18 years; Chandra et al., 2008; Huebner & Mancini, 2005; Huebner, Mancini, Wilcox, Grass, & Grass, 2007). Several findings are consistent. First, the majority of participants identify significant stress that results from parental deployment, regardless of age. Chartrand and colleagues (2008) found that both parents and child-care providers rated the externalizing symptoms of 3- to 5-year-old children of deployed parents as significantly elevated compared with same-age children of nondeployed parents. Children of deployed parents appear typically to experience higher levels of emotional and behavioral difficulties than those in the general population (Chandra et al., 2008). Active-component families have reported greater challenges with child behavior problems than reserve families. Reserve-component children have identified more difficulty with parental readjustment upon return from deployment, as well as greater loneliness and a sense that peers and teachers do not understand the nature of their experiences (Chandra et al., 2008). Huebner and Mancini (2005) reported that most teens in their sample managed the challenge of combat deployment with resilience and maturity. However, these same authors (Huebner et al., 2007) also concluded that changes in routine, redefining of responsibilities, the presence of depression and anxiety, relationship conflict, and challenges related to the reintegration of the returning service member, all within the context of uncertain and potentially frightening outcome, all have the capacity to undermine healthy adolescent development.

Two recent studies reported on the health and well-being of school-age military children (Lester et al., 2010) and adolescents (Chandra et al., 2010) of deployed parents. Both studies identified deployment-related emotional and behavioral challenges in the children who were interviewed. In their younger sample (ages 6–12 years), Lester et al. (2010) reported significantly elevated levels of anxiety in children whose parents were either currently deployed or recently returned, compared with community norms. Chandra et al. (2010) also described greater emotional difficulties in their sample of 11- to 17-year-old children of deployed parents, with older teens and girls of all ages reporting more difficulties at school and with families and friends. Both studies identified poor parental mental health and distress, as well as deployment length, as being positively related to poorer child outcomes.

Several studies have identified increased rates of child maltreatment associated with recent combat deployments. Rentz et al. (2007) examined rates of child maltreatment in military and nonmilitary families in Texas during the period from 2000 to 2003, finding doubled rates of child maltreatment in military families during this high combat deployment period, with no change in child maltreatment in nonmilitary families during the same period. Gibbs, Martin, Kupper, and Johnson (2007) examined the association of child maltreatment and deployment timing in a large sample of substantiated Army enlisted family maltreatment cases, finding that rates of maltreatment were greater during periods of combat deployment than nondeployed periods. In an examination of Army child maltreatment rates in the period from 1991 to 2004, McCarroll, Fan, Newby, and Ursano (2008) found the highest child neglect rates during two periods of large-scale deployment of U.S. forces to the Middle East (1991 and 2002–2004), with the greatest neglect rates being reported in the youngest children.

IMPACT OF PARENTAL DEPLOYMENTS ON CHILDREN: CLINICAL IMPLICATIONS

Military deployments, once considered occasional events with predictable phases (Pincus, House, Christensen, & Adler, 2001), are now likely to be recurrent and continuous, without beginnings and endings or other clear demarcations. It is unclear to what degree this recurring cycle of deployment affects the health and well-being of children in military families. It is also uncertain to what degree recurrent deployments lead to mastery and a capacity to manage future deployments or to a sensitizing to the deployment process and greater ongoing distress. Recent reports suggest that length of parental deployment is associated with emotional and behavioral problems in military children (Chandra et al., 2010; Lester et al. 2010). Further research is needed in this area.

Reports of child distress, behavioral change, and elevated rates of child maltreatment associated with deployment suggest that military children are affected in multiple ways, likely through the direct effect of parental absence and reintegration, as well as through nondeployed parent, family, and community influences. Unlike children who face a sudden traumatic event, such as a natural disaster or an act of terrorism, military children are more likely to be dealing with prolonged moderate levels of distress because of the pervasiveness of deployments that may be punctuated by periods of high anxiety (e.g., impending deployments, awareness of periods of high combat intensity that affect a parent, or news of injury or death in their military communities), a sense of loss (e.g., parental separation during times of emotional need or for special occasions) and the absence of interpersonal connectedness for some children (e.g., lack of availability of the nondeployed parent or misunderstanding of lack of connections with peers for those children living in nonmilitary-attuned settings).

Similar to other children exposed to potentially traumatic stress, military children are likely to demonstrate a range of responses to deployment stress, with most demonstrating health and resilience and a smaller percentage exhibiting symptoms of clinical disorder (Bonanno & Mancini, 2008; Fairbank, 2008). Because neither large-scale nor longitudinal studies of the traumatic impact of deployment on children have been conducted, the range of child responses in this population remains uncertain.

PSYCHOLOGICAL FIRST AID: A DEVELOPMENTAL APPLICATION WITH MILITARY CHILDREN

Psychological First Aid (PFA) is an evidence-informed intervention for early to midlevel mass trauma recovery (for a review, see Hobfoll et al., 2007) that has application in military communities under stress. Five key principles of PFA intervention emphasize (a) establishing a sense of safety, (b) promoting calming through distress reduction, (c) building a sense of self and community efficacy, (d) fostering connectedness, and (e) promoting a sense of hope. These PFA principles can best be implemented to support military children and families on three levels: (a) community-based programs (public service messaging, broadly available and developmentally appropriate recreational activities, child-care and school-based programs, peer mentoring and support groups, family assistance programs, parent guidance, respite programs), (b) family and parentally administered support, and (c) coordinated clinical care for those children considered at higher risk or exhibiting symptoms of a disorder.

Clinicians must remember that any care provided to children must be done within a developmentally sound context. A military child's age directly affects his or her experience of the deployment and frames developmentally specific challenges. For example, infants and toddlers (0–2 years) rely almost entirely on their parents and other child-care providers. Establishing safety and promoting calmness are critical to normal infant development. If deployment severely disrupts the capacity of the nondeployed parent to care for an infant or results in the loss of necessary instrumental support to the family, the young child may evidence problems in sleeping or eating, develop irritability or regulation problems, or develop disturbance of attachment. Ensuring connectedness of young mothers to social networks, peer and senior spouse mentoring, as well as community-based resources may be critical to them, as well as their infant's, health and may reduce the risk of child maltreatment (Brown, Cohen, Johnson, & Salzinger, 1998).

In addition to attending to safety, preschool children (3–5 years old) may have unique requirements for managing distress. Although preschoolers will be keenly aware of the absence of the deployed parent, they also lack the cognitive capacity to understand fully the nature of the deployment or to describe their feelings. Preschoolers are likely to demonstrate distress through regressive behaviors, loss of previously established developmental milestones (as in the development of enuresis or new sleep problems), clinging behavior, and tantrums. Young children gain mastery through play, practice, and repetition. Play, especially as it relates to becoming comfortable with their parents' deployment experience, can be helpful. Playing with uniforms, military gear, or military-related toys can help children become more comfortable with the experiences of their parents. Several deployment-related materials have been developed specifically for children at this age, including the Sesame Workshop's Talk, Listen and Connect series of DVDs and print materials (available at http://www.sesameworkshop.org/initiatives/emotion/tlc).

Clinical Example of PFA Principles: Max and Sarah

"Mary," the 19-year-old wife of a U.S. Army private first class arrived at the pediatrician's office with her 3-year-old son, "Max," and her 10-month-old daughter, "Sarah," for a well-baby check. Their father had deployed 5 months earlier. During the visit, the pediatrician learned that Mary lived in a trailer home 20 miles away from the installation, was new to both the Army and the installation, and had no family members nearby. Although both children appeared healthy, Max was noted to be overly active and demanding of the attention of the male pediatrician, who wore a uniform "just like daddy," suggesting heightened anxiety. Mary shared that she was overwhelmed at home, was sleeping poorly, and was having a difficult time taking care of her two children. The pediatrician referred Mary to the behavioral health clinic, where she received mental health care and case management assistance. Mary's social worker included Max and Sarah in treatment sessions and found that many of Mary's concerns were about Max's behavior. The clinician helped Mary understand that Max's behavior was a reflection of his distress about his father's absence. Mary shared that when her husband deployed, she had stored away as many of his possessions as she could find "to keep them safe." She also rarely spoke about her husband at home because it was too upsetting. The therapist helped Mary see that the sudden disappearance of his father and his father's possessions was likely both confusing and anxiety provoking to Max. By encouraging greater discussion and allowing Max to play with some of his father's uniforms, he seemed to become less distressed and less driven in his behavior. At the therapist's urging, Mary scheduled regular telephone calls with her husband at times when Max could speak with him. Mary learned to help Max think about what he wanted to share with his father when they spoke. Together they created a "countdown" calendar in anticipation of Max's father's return home. The therapist also arranged additional support services for Mary, to include connections with professionals in the New Parent Support Program and other military spouses through her unit's Family Readiness Group, all of which seemed to be helpful. Upon her husband's return, Mary was proud of the accomplishments she had made in his absence. Through this intervention, the therapist used PFA principles effectively to promote calmness, build a sense of efficacy, foster connectedness, and promote hope in all family members.

Safety, distress reduction, self-efficacy, connectedness, and hopefulness are important to older children as well. School-age children (6–12 years old) have a greater understanding of the dangers their deployed parents face and can benefit from ongoing conversations about their worries. Parents can help by clearly stating the reality of what is happening, but they must be careful not to burden the child with either too much information or excessive displays of their own emotional distress. We know that many children respond in ways that are similar to their parents. A parent's ability to talk clearly about the spouse's deployment and to share their emotional responses in a controlled and clear way can be helpful. School-age children participate in many activities outside of the home, and self-efficacy is often achieved through mastery in school and sports or other activities. Children may benefit by being involved in activities that allow them to feel in charge and helpful. Connection to peers and to other helpful adults (teachers, coaches, or religious leaders) and involvement in support groups can be out-of-home opportunities for assistance and success. Although a certain level of worry or sadness is to be expected, when symptoms are severe (social withdrawal, thoughts of death), prolonged, or result in functional impairment (uncharacteristic behaviors, academic failure), clinical referral is indicated.

Teenagers (13–18 years old) possess greater functional capacity but can also face greater challenges during periods when their parents are deployed. Healthy teenage separation and independence brings opportunities for both connectedness and a sense of self-efficacy, as military teenagers join with peers in recreational activities and develop or participate in programs that support military community efforts. In addition to the distress that younger children may experience, teens can also become involved in problematic behaviors (risk-taking sexual encounters, substance use experimentation, truancy, or other conduct-disordered behaviors) that can threaten their health and safety. These problems, along with other prolonged, severe, or functionally impairing conditions require referral for clinical evaluation and treatment.

FAMILY-FOCUSED INTERVENTIONS IN SUPPORT OF CHILD HEALTH

Given changes to the tempo of the military family deployment cycle, models of family sustainment are essential to longer term health and functioning. Several areas of family functioning are likely to support child health. Parental emotional availability, effective and consistent parental discipline, effective family communication, shared family meaning and goal setting, adequate financial health, and connection to services in the community have all been shown to have either direct or indirect influences on the health and well-being of children under stress (Beardslee, Gladstone, Wright, & Cooper, 2003; Brown et al., 1998; Walsh, 2007).

Programs have been developed to specifically address such needs in military communities through strength-based family approaches. Operation FOCUS (Families OverComing Under Stress) is one family-focused resiliency training model that is being used in military communities around the country. Operation FOCUS is designed to assist families in identifying and utilizing inherent strengths to meet the challenge of deployment stress. FOCUS is conducted in a series of family member sessions that promote family communication and mutual understanding, encourage healthy coping strategies, develop and employ effective problem-solving skills, and consolidate a sense of family purpose and identity (program information can be accessed at http://www.focusproject.org). Although the effectiveness of FOCUS has not been systematically studied in the military family population, it is based on successful clinical trials used in populations of at-risk depressed and HIV families (Beardslee et al., 2003; Rotheram-Borus, Lee, Lin, & Lester, 2004) and has been identified by the National Child Traumatic Stress Network as an emerging best practice prevention intervention for at-risk families. Currently, FOCUS should be considered an evidence-informed, promising intervention for military families.

CHILDREN AT RISK AND THOSE IN NEED OF CLINICAL CARE

An understanding of factors associated with poorer clinical outcome in children and families can help clinicians recognize potential at-risk cases that may develop clinical disorders. Early military deployment literature suggests that younger children and boys may be at greater risk of developing symptoms during deployments (Jensen, Martin, & Watanabe, 1996). More recently, girls and older teens have been identified as being at greater risk of deployment-related problems (Chandra et al., 2010). These age and gender discrepancies likely reflect differences in study samples and methods of assessment. Children are likely to variably experience, respond to, and report their reactions depending on gender, age, and developmental needs.

Military children of nondeployed parents who exhibit higher levels of distress and poorer functioning during deployment also appear to do more poorly than children of nondeployed parents without those problems (Chandra et al., 2010; Jensen, Grogan, Xenakis, & Bain, 1989; Lester et al., 2010). The trauma literature identifies those children who are more highly exposed to a traumatic event or have poorer access to a social support network as being at higher risk of the development of posttraumatic psychiatric sequelae (Pine & Cohen, 2002).

Additional risk factors for child traumatic response include the lack of social connectedness (Pine & Cohen, 2002) that may occur when military families are unable to gain access to services, are geographically isolated, live in communities that do not understand or recognize military culture, or when language poses a barrier to connectedness. Preexisting psychiatric illness has also been associated with posttraumatic outcomes in children (Pine & Cohen, 2002). Given the negative impact of child maltreatment on child development and the relationship between deployment and elevated rates of child neglect, risk factors for child maltreatment are likely to put military children and families at risk as well. Demographic risk factors (e.g., low income, low maternal education, maternal youth, or single parent), familial and parenting risk factors (e.g., maternal anger, dissatisfaction, low self-esteem, or illness; low father involvement or warmth), and child risk factors (e.g., difficult temperament) have all been associated with risk of child maltreatment (Brown et al., 1998) and may be relevant in determining military family risk.

Clinical Example of Children at Risk: John

"John," the 16-year-old stepson of a U.S. Marine Corps master sergeant, had been a marginal student for most of his life. Although he had been diagnosed early in elementary school with both attention-deficit/hyperactivity disorder (ADHD) and learning problems, John demonstrated no history of behavioral problems. His relationship with his stepfather was quite good, and they shared many common interests and activities. After his stepfather deployed in the middle of John's junior year of high school, the clinical picture changed. John's mother was contacted by the school principal, who said that he had recently begun skipping school. His grades had slipped, and he was now in danger of failing three of his classes. Over time, John's mother noticed that he became more and more isolated at home, spending all of his time in his room listening to "dark" music. When he left the house, he refused to tell her where he was going and was noted to be hanging out with older teenagers and young adults off-base. One evening, military police brought John home, stating that he had been in the car with other boys who had been caught shoplifting at the local military exchange convenience store. When the car was searched, marijuana was found in John's possession. The following day, when he was seen on intake by a substance abuse counselor, John admitted to ongoing suicidal ideation and two incidents in which he had taken the family car at night (without his mother being aware) and had driven, alone and intoxicated, "because I wanted to die." He was immediately psychiatrically hospitalized. Although John's prior diagnoses of ADHD and learning problems had been previously well managed, these preexisting conditions may have added additional risk as he and his family managed the stress of his stepfather's deployment.

UNIQUE CHALLENGES OF COMPLICATED DEPLOYMENTS TO CHILDREN AND FAMILIES

The effects of complicated deployment experiences, such as deployment-related parental psychiatric illness (e.g., posttraumatic stress disorder [PTSD], depression, substance use disorders), parental injury, or parental death, are undoubtedly more stressful, and potentially traumatic, to military children than uncomplicated deployments. Unfortunately, the scientific community is far less informed on the impact of these events on military children and families. Prospective longitudinal studies are needed to examine these higher risk groups to better understand the immediate and longer term impact on child and family symptoms and function.

Parental Combat-Related Psychiatric Disorders

Postdeployment parental psychiatric illness or combat injuries are likely to make matters worse for military children and families. For example, service member irritability, traumatic reexperiencing, or hypersensitivity can worsen the family environment. Parental withdrawal or emotional numbing can lead to unhelpful changes in discipline styles or difficulties with interpersonal relatedness.

Children of parents with depression evidence significant problems in a wide range of functional areas (Beardslee, Versage, & Gladstone, 1998), as do parents with histories of trauma or PTSD (Banyard, Williams, & Siegel, 2003; Conger, Patterson, & Ge, 1995; Lauterbach et al., 2007). Studies of the impact of parental combat PTSD on children and families largely come from work with American, Australian, and New Zealand Vietnam War veterans and their families. Within these populations, PTSD has been associated with poor intimate partner and marital relationships (Riggs, Byrne, & Weathers, 1998), poorer family functioning, greater family distress, higher levels of family violence, and disrupted parenting and parent–child relationships (Davidson & Mellor, 2001; Jordan et al., 1992; MacDonald, Chamberlain, Long, & Flett, 1999; Roberts et al., 1982; Westerink & Giarratano, 1999). Emotional numbing, avoidance, and anger (Evans, McHugh, Hopwood, & Watt, 2003; Galovski & Lyons, 2004; Ruscio, Weathers, King, & King, 2002) have been identified as contributors to family problems. Children and parent–child relationships were noted to be negatively affected in multiple studies of Vietnam veterans with PTSD (Jordan et al., 1992; Rosenheck & Fontana, 1998; Ruscio et al., 2002). Ruscio et al. (2002) described "the disinterest, detachment, and emotional unavailability that characterize emotional numbing may diminish a father's ability and willingness to seek out, engage in, and enjoy interactions with his children, leading to poorer relationship quality" (p. 355).

Adult clinicians working with military service members or spouses can help not only their patients but also the families and children of patients in simple ways:

1. Become familiar with the members of your patient's family and how he or she relates to spouse and children.
2. Become interested in the impact on patient functioning in all roles. Ask about the impact of the illness on marriages and parenting (e.g., increased irritability, avoidance, decreased

sense of connectedness can lead to problems in engagement and decrease in satisfaction).

3. Listen for signs and symptoms that children are having difficulty and may need intervention of their own, remembering that children of different ages may express these problems differently; assist with referrals when appropriate.

4. Be aware of preexisting psychiatric or developmental problems in children of service members that might place them at risk of greater problems.

5. Remember that the longitudinal course and progression of family relationship difficulties may worsen. Although relationships may initially be fine, they may change over time.

6. With a patient's permission, consider inviting other family members to a clinical session to the discuss nature of family relationships.

Family-based interventions have been used effectively to address parental depression (see Beardslee et al., 2003) and appear readily applicable to intervention in families with other disorders, including PTSD. Experienced clinicians who work with families and children can tailor the intervention to focus on existing family strengths as a method to remain optimistic and to avoid blaming the service member for existing family problems because of his or her illness. Early sessions provide an opportunity for all family members to share concerns that can be shaped into mutually agreed on family goals. Children directly benefit from greater understanding of their parents' illness and its impact on their behaviors. For many, it may be the first opportunity to ask questions, gain greater understanding, and share their own feelings and perspectives. In PTSD, where irritability, substance use, or domestic violence may be more likely, clinicians need to assess for family safety and set safety plans in place. Family skill building (emotional regulation, family problem solving, social activation, goal setting) can all further add stability to family engagement. This combination of outcomes will likely lead to better overall family functioning, reduced child distress, and greater interpersonal connectedness (Beardslee et al., 2003).

Clinical Example of Family-Focused Treatment: Stacy

"Stacy" is a 39-year-old U.S. Army sergeant who returned from a second combat deployment to her family, which included her husband "Bill" and their twin 9-year-old sons. Six months after returning home from deployment and after a heated marital argument, Bill demanded that Stacy seek out mental health treatment for her escalating alcohol use and isolation at home. Although reluctant, Stacy eventually agreed and was seen by a psychiatrist in consultation.

She endorsed a history of recurrent nightmares, flashbacks, and arousal and was given a diagnosis of PTSD and alcohol abuse. At the second session Stacy allowed Bill to attend her mental health appointment. Bill reported that he and Stacy had always had a strong marriage until she returned from her first deployment to Iraq. Because the family was rapidly reassigned after she returned, Stacy was unable to reconnect with any of her prior unit members and was redeployed within 9 months of her return with a new military unit. Since her return from the second deployment, she had become extremely isolated at home and was often verbally angry with Bill and their sons. In turn, the boys were also getting angry and demonstrating behavioral problems. Once an active and loving mom, Stacy no longer attended any of the boys' school or sporting events. Bill also noted that she seemed uncomfortable being physically close to either the twins or him. In discussion with both parents, the psychiatrist made arrangements for a social worker to join them in a future family session that included both boys. In a variety of differently configured parent, child, and family meetings, the two clinicians were able to help the parents explain the nature of their mother's illness to their sons in a way that they could both understand and that clarified their misperceptions that she was angry with them and no longer loved them. Great care was given to set boundaries on the degree of information that was shared. For example, as Stacy talked about her hesitancy to be close to her sons, she shared the traumatic memory of being on the scene of an improvised explosive device explosion that resulted in the deaths of several Iraqi schoolchildren (of which the psychiatrist was previously unaware). Closeness to her sons served as triggers for this memory. Although she eventually felt comfortable sharing this information with Bill, they both agreed that such vivid details were not appropriate for their sons. In family sessions, the social worker skillfully found opportunities to identify and draw on the family's long-standing strengths: their sense of connection and closeness, effective communication skills, and problem-solving capacity. By doing so, family members were able to redevelop a sense of family continuity with predeployment life and develop a sense of future hopefulness. Even though Stacy still evidenced some mild symptoms, the family was no longer defined by these problems.

Parental Combat Injuries

Parental physical injuries can pose similar, but also unique, challenges to children. Case reports have described the anecdotal experience of combat-injured families and children (Cozza et al., 2005; Cozza, Chun, & Miller, in press). From the initial distress to the longer term injury adjustment challenges, children and families face difficult and complex emotional and practical problems. Injuries sustained in combat are likely to cause sudden family distress and a flurry of urgent activity, resulting in disruption of family roles, as well as sources of care and instrumental support. Depending on the severity of injury, the recovery process may be drawn out, requiring effective care management and interventions to be implemented across time and tailored to the specific needs of each family (Zatzick et al., 2001). Continuity of care for combat injury may also be complicated by multiple transitions in care facilities that may be required over time, resulting in changes in family living arrangements and disruptions in community connection (Chesnut et al., 1999). Over time, the consequences of parental injury and required treatment may also include changes in the child's residential community, loss of military careers by the parent, and changes in parenting capacity or personality.

The impact of combat-related injuries on children and families has not been systematically studied using standardized instruments. Of the few studies that have examined the impact of sudden medical events on families, those related to traumatic brain injury (TBI) are most instructive for the combat-injured population (Butera-Prinzi & Perlesz, 2004; Pessar, Coad, Linn, & Willer, 1993; Urbach, 1989; Urbach & Culbert, 1991; Uysal, Hibbard, Robillard, Pappadopulos, & Jaffe, 1998; Verhaeghe, Defloor, & Grypdonck, 2005). TBI often results in profound impact on the child and the family, with greater difficulty in families with young children, those with lesser social or financial support, and in families in which psychiatric problems are prominent (Verhaeghe et al., 2005). Elevated levels of emotional and behavioral difficulties in children of patients with TBI correlate with compromised parenting in both the injured and noninjured parent as well as depression in the non-injured parent, suggesting the importance of family and parental interventions for child mental health protection (Pessar et al., 1993).

Immediately after the initial injury, a cascade of events takes place that can result in distress and interpersonal turmoil for children and adults in the combat-injured family (Cozza et al., 2005). Disruption in parental functioning and family structure is common. Noninjured parents are focused on the medical well-being of the injured service members and may have difficulty recognizing and meeting the needs of their children. Children's developmental and emotional capacities determine their ability to understand and integrate the experience of parental injury. Prior work has established considerable parental interest in making child guidance available early in the hospitalization (Cozza et al., in press). Clinicians can assist parents in helping children accept the injury, manage their distress, prepare for hospital visits, and protect them from unnecessary exposures, reengage the injured parent and effectively communicate their needs.

Clinical Example of Impact of Combat Injury on Children: Nora

"Nora" is a 5-year-old girl who came to a military medical center to visit her father, a U.S. Army National Guard staff sergeant who was injured 1 month previously by a mortar round in Afghanistan that resulted in bilateral above-the-knee lower extremity amputations. Immediately after the injury, Nora's mother, "Karen," was notified and made arrangements to bring Nora's maternal grandmother to the home to stay with her while Karen went to the hospital to be with her husband. Because Karen had made many business trips, leaving Nora with her mother before, she felt that Nora would not be distressed by her absence and did not tell her about the injury. Each evening, Karen would call her own mother and provide news about her husband's medical progress but continued to keep the news from Nora. Eventually, arrangements were made for Nora to visit her father in the hospital, but she was not told what was going to happen until she arrived. While her mother attempted to talk with her about the nature of her father's injuries, Nora was so excited that she would be seeing her father that she seemed not to be paying attention. Upon entering the hospital room, she froze in the doorway when she saw her father, whose stumps were visible from the bedside and who continued to require intravenous tubing, a catheter, and surgical drainage tubes. Over a period of several minutes, Nora was able to come closer to her father, but in the next few days, she became more and more preoccupied with the medical equipment, particularly the drainage bags: "What are they taking out of you?" Over time Nora became increasingly and, at times, ruminatively attentive to her father's health, repeatedly bringing him cups of water to drink. She became cranky and clingy with her mother and would tantrum with any hint of physical separation.

Longer term challenges to children include transitions to new communities, changes in the injured parent's functioning or personality (depending on the nature of the relationship), and future negative impact on parent–child relationships. A recently convened expert Workgroup on Intervention with Combat Injured Families (Cozza, 2009) outlined 10 principles of care for intervention with combat-injured families: (a) principles of PFA are critical to supporting injured families; (b) medical care for the combat injured must be family focused; (c) service providers should anticipate a range of responses to combat injury; (d) injury communication is an essential component of injured family care; (e) injured family programs must be developmentally sensitive and age appropriate; (f) injured family care is longitudinal, extending beyond immediate hospitalization; (g) effective injured family care requires an interconnected community of care; (h) care must be culturally competent; (i) communities of care should address any barriers to service; and (j) communities and service providers must be knowledgeable about injured family recovery.

Parental Combat Death

No identified studies have examined the impact of parental combat death on U.S. children. In general, the scientific literature tends to support vulnerability to psychopathology in children as a result of parental death (Dowdney, 2000). A more recent report supports risk related to bereavement but especially in the presence of comorbid childhood depression when it is associated with parental death (Cerel, Fristad, Verducci, Weller, & Weller, 2006). In addition to depression, bereaved children are more susceptible to the development of PTSD than other populations of traumatized children (Pfefferbaum, Nixon, & Tucker, 1999; Stoppelbein & Greening, 2000).

Children who lose military family members during wartime are similar to other grieving children in many ways. However, there are certain unique aspects to military family loss. For example, military service members may be deployed for long periods of time before a death. Young children may have become adjusted to the physical absence of the deceased parent or family member, making it more difficult to accept the permanence of the loss. Those bereaved families living on military installations will likely be surrounded by community support and interest. Typically families want and appreciate this interest, but they may need to set limits to ensure that interest is not experienced as burdensome. Reserve and National Guard families or those living outside of military communities may find that their grief is less well understood by other well-intentioned civilian families in their neighborhoods. Children who attend schools with few other military children may find themselves isolated in their experiences of loss. Finally, not all military deaths are the same; some children may lose loved ones to combat, but others have loved ones die as a result of accidents, illnesses, suicide, or other causes. Care and concern must be exercised in helping these children and families.

Bereaved military children can benefit from involvement in competent grief counseling programs that have a respect for and appreciation of military family culture. Children may also benefit from engaging mental health clinicians and should be encouraged to do so when symptoms are either more severe or prolonged than would be expected. Childhood traumatic grief (CTG) is an additional and unique consideration that clinicians must consider in situations of unexpected, traumatic death of a loved one. Childhood traumatic grief results in trauma-related symptoms (e.g., hyperarousal, psychological distress, avoidance) that can complicate children's ability to mourn the loss of their loved one (Pynoos, 1992). Although no studies have examined the incidence of CTG in bereaved military children, combat death shares many of the characteristics (unexpected sudden loss) that have been shown to contribute to its development in other vulnerable populations (Cohen, Mannarino, Greenberg, Padlo & Shipley, 2002). Traumatic grief cognitive–behavioral therapy (Cohen, Mannarino, & Deblinger, 2006) and trauma and grief component therapy (Layne, Saltzman, Pynoos, & Steinberg, 2002) are two treatments that have been developed for traumatically bereaved youngsters.

CONCLUSION

Military children face unique challenges as a result of their parents' service. Scientific study of military children is limited, particularly studies examining the impact of combat-related stressors and the effectiveness of clinical interventions in this population. Principles of PFA, to include maintaining safety, reducing distress, developing self and community efficacy, encouraging connectedness, and fostering hope, are helpful in guiding interventions at the community, family, parent, or individual clinical level. Clinicians are likely to provide assistance through expert consultation, parent guidance, or direct clinical care. Mental health providers are encouraged to address the impact of adult patient illnesses on relationships with other family members, including children. Family-focused interventions may be effective methods of clinical engagement in both uncomplicated deployments and in situations when parental psychiatric illness or injury occurs. Adult clinicians should be mindful of the unique developmental needs of military children and the importance of identifying and finding services for those who are at risk or exhibit signs of clinical disorder. Further study of military children is required to develop proposed intervention strategies and understand their benefits.

REFERENCES

Banyard, V. L., Williams, L. M., & Siegel, J. A. (2003). The impact of complex trauma and depression on parenting: An exploration of mediating risk and protective factors. *Child Maltreatment, 8,* 334–349. doi:10.1177/1077559503257106

Beardslee, W. R., Gladstone, T. R., Wright, E. J., & Cooper, A. B. (2003). A family-based approach to the prevention of depressive symptoms in children at risk: Evidence of parental and child change. *Pediatrics, 112,* e119–e131. doi:10.1542/peds.112.2.e119

Beardslee, W. R., Versage, E. M., & Gladstone, T. R. (1998). Children of affectively ill parents: A review of the past 10 years. *Journal of the American Academy of Child and Adolescent Psychiatry, 37,* 1134–1141. doi:10.1097/00004583-199811000-00012

Bonanno, G. A., & Mancini, A. D. (2008). The human capacity to thrive in the face of potential trauma. *Pediatrics, 121,* 369–375. doi:10.1542/peds.2007-1648

Brown, J., Cohen, P., Johnson, J. G., & Salzinger, S. (1998). A longitudinal analysis of risk factors for child maltreatment: Findings of a 17-year prospective study of officially recorded and self-reported child abuse and neglect. *Child Abuse & Neglect, 22,* 1065–1078. doi:10.1016/S0145-2134(98)00087-8

Butera-Prinzi, F., & Perlesz, A. (2004). Through children's eyes: Children's experience of living with a parent with an acquired brain injury. *Brain Injury, 18,* 83–101. doi:10.1080/0269905031000118500

Castro, C. A., Adler, A. B., & Britt, T. W. (Eds.). (2006). *The military family: Vol. 3. Military life: The psychology of serving in peace and combat.* Westport, CT: Praeger Security International.

Cerel, J., Fristad, M. A., Verducci, J., Weller, R. A., & Weller, E. B. (2006). Childhood bereavement: Psychopathology in 2 years postparental death. *Journal of the American Academy of Child and Adolescent Psychiatry, 45,* 681–690. doi:10.1097/01.chi.0000215327.58799.05

Chandra, A., Burns, R. M., Tanielian, T., Jaycox, L. H., & Scott, M. M. (2008). *Understanding the impact of deployment on children and families: findings from a pilot study of Operation Purple Camp participants.* Santa Monica, CA: Center for Military Health Policy Research, Rand Health and the Rand National Security Research Division.

Chandra, A., Lara-Cinisomo, S., Jaycox, L. H., Tanielian, T., Burns, R. M., Ruder, T., & Han, B. (2010). Children on the homefront: The experience of children from military families. *Pediatrics, 125,* 16–25. doi:10.1542/peds.2009-1180

Chartrand, M. M., Frank, D. A., White, L. F., & Shope, T. R. (2008). Effect of parents' wartime deployment on the behavior of young children in military families. *Archives of Pediatrics & Adolescent Medicine, 162,* 1009–1014. doi:10.1001/archpedi.162.11.1009

Chesnut, R. M., Carney, N., Maynard, H., Patterson, P., Mann, N. C., & Helfand, M. (1999). *Rehabilitation for traumatic brain injury.* Rockville, MD: Agency for Health Care Policy and Research.

Cohen, J. A., Mannarino, A. P., & Deblinger, E. (2006). *Treating trauma and traumatic grief in children and adolescents: A clinician's guide.* New York, NY: Guilford Press.

Cohen, J. A., Mannarino, A. P., Greenberg, T., Padlo, S., & Shipley, C. (2002). Childhood traumatic grief: Concepts and controversies. *Trauma, Violence & Abuse, 3,* 307–327. doi:10.1177/1524838002237332

Conger, R. D., Patterson, G. R., & Ge, X. (1995). It takes two to replicate: A mediational model for the impact of parents' stress on adolescent adjustment. *Child Development, 66,* 80–97. doi:10.2307/1131192

Cozza, S. J. (2009). *Proceedings: Workgroup on intervention with combat injured families.* Bethesda, MD: Center for the Study of Traumatic Stress, Uniformed Services University.

Cozza, S. J., Chun, R. S., & Miller, C. (in press). The children and families of combat injured service members. Chapter in *War psychiatry.* Washington, DC: Borden Institute.

Cozza, S. J., Chun, R. S., & Polo, J. A. (2005). Military families and children during Operation Iraqi Freedom. *Psychiatric Quarterly, 76,* 371–378. doi:10.1007/s11126-005-4973-y

Davidson, A. C., & Mellor, D. J. (2001). The adjustment of children of Australian Vietnam veterans: Is there evidence for the transgenerational transmission of the effects of war-related trauma? *The Australian and New Zealand Journal of Psychiatry, 35,* 345–351. doi:10.1046/j.1440-1614.2001.00897.x

Dowdney, L. (2000). Childhood bereavement following parental death. *Journal of Child Psychology and Psychiatry, and Allied Disciplines, 41*, 819–830. doi:10.1111/1469-7610.00670

Evans, L., McHugh, T., Hopwood, M., & Watt, C. (2003). Chronic posttraumatic stress disorder and family functioning of Vietnam veterans and their partners. *The Australian and New Zealand Journal of Psychiatry, 37*, 765–772.

Fairbank, J. A. (2008). The epidemiology of trauma and trauma related disorders in children and youth. *PTSD Research Quarterly, 19*, 1–7.

Galovski, T., & Lyons, J. A. (2004). Psychological sequelae of combat violence: A review of the impact of PTSD on the veteran's family and possible interventions. *Aggression and Violent Behavior, 9*, 477–501. doi:10.1016/S1359-1789(03)00045-4

Gibbs, D. A., Martin, S. L., Kupper, L. L., & Johnson, R. E. (2007). Child maltreatment in enlisted soldiers' families during combat-related deployments. *JAMA, 298*, 528–535. doi:10.1001/jama.298.5.528

Hobfoll, S. E., Watson, P., Bell, C. C., Bryant, R. A., Brymer, M. J., Friedman, M. J., . . . Ursano, R. J. (2007). Five essential elements of immediate and mid-term mass trauma intervention: Empirical evidence. *Psychiatry, 70*, 283–315.

Huebner, A. J., & Mancini, J. A. (2005). *Adjustments among adolescents in military families when a parent is deployed.* West Lafayette, IN: Military Family Research Institute at Purdue University.

Huebner, A. J., Mancini, J. A., Wilcox, R. M., Grass, S. R., & Grass, G. A. (2007). Parental deployment and youth in military families: Exploring uncertainty and ambiguous loss. *Family Relations, 56*, 112–122.

Jensen, P. S., Grogan, D., Xenakis, S. N., & Bain, M. W. (1989). Father absence: Effects on child and maternal psychopathology. *Journal of the American Academy of Child and Adolescent Psychiatry, 28*, 171–175. doi:10.1097/00004583-198903000-00004

Jensen, P. S., Martin, D., & Watanabe, H. (1996). Children's response to parental separation during operation Desert Storm. *Journal of the American Academy of Child and Adolescent Psychiatry, 35*, 433–441. doi:10.1097/00004583-199604000-00009

Jensen, P. S., Watanabe, H. K., Richters, J. E., Cortes, R., Roper, M., & Liu, S. (1995). Prevalence of mental disorder in military children and adolescents: Findings from a two-stage community survey. *Journal of the American Academy of Child and Adolescent Psychiatry, 34*, 1514–1524. doi:10.1097/00004583-199511000-00019

Jensen, P. S., Xenakis, S. N., Wolf, P., & Bain, M. W. (1991). The "military family" syndrome revisited: By the numbers. *Journal of Nervous and Mental Disease, 179*, 102–107. doi:10.1097/00005053-199102000-00007

Jordan, B. K., Marmar, C. R., Fairbank, J. A., Schlenger, W. E., Kulka, R. A., Hough, R. L., & Weiss, D. S. (1992). Problems in families of male Vietnam veterans with posttraumatic stress disorder. *Journal of Consulting and Clinical Psychology, 60*, 916–926. doi:10.1037/0022-006X.60.6.916

Lauterbach, D., Bak, C., Reiland, S., Mason, S., Lute, M. R., & Earls, L. (2007). Quality of parental relationships among persons with a lifetime history of posttraumatic stress disorder. *Journal of Traumatic Stress, 20*, 161–172. doi:10.1002/jts.20194

Layne, C. M., Saltzman, W. R., Pynoos, R. S., & Steinberg, A. M. (2002). *Trauma and grief component therapy*. New York, NY: New York State Office of Mental Health.

Lester, P., Peterson, K., Reeves, J., Knauss, L., Glover, D., Mogil, C., . . . Beardslee, W. (2010). The long war and parental combat deployment: Effects on military children and at-home spouses. *Journal of the American Academy of Child and Adolescent Psychiatry, 49*, 310–320. doi:10.1097/00004583-201004000-00006

MacDonald, C., Chamberlain, K., Long, N., & Flett, R. (1999). Posttraumatic stress disorder and interpersonal functioning in Vietnam War veterans: A mediational model. *Journal of Traumatic Stress, 12*, 701–707. doi:10.1023/A:1024729520686

McCarroll, J. E., Fan, Z., Newby, J., & Ursano, R. J. (2008). Trends in U.S. Army child maltreatment reports: 1990–2004. *Child Abuse Review, 17*, 108–118. doi:10.1002/car.986

Pessar, L. F., Coad, M. L., Linn, R. T., & Willer, B. S. (1993). The effects of parental traumatic brain injury on the behaviour of parents and children. *Brain Injury, 7*, 231–240. doi:10.3109/02699059309029675

Pfefferbaum, B., Nixon, S. J., & Tucker, P. M. (1999). Posttraumatic stress responses in bereaved children after the Oklahoma City bombing. *Journal of the American Academy of Child and Adolescent Psychiatry, 38*, 1372–1379. doi:10.1097/00004583-199911000-00011

Pincus, S. H., House, R., Christensen, J., & Adler, L. E. (2001). The emotional cycle of deployment: A military family perspective. *Journal of the Army Medical Department*, 615–623.

Pine, D. S., & Cohen, J. A. (2002). Trauma in children and adolescents: Risk and treatment of psychiatric sequelae. *Biological Psychiatry, 51*, 519–531. doi:10.1016/S0006-3223(01)01352-X

Pynoos, R. S. (1992). Grief and trauma in children and adolescents. *Bereavement Care, 11*, 2–10.

Rentz, E. D., Marshall, S. W., Loomis, D., Casteel, C., Martin, S. L., & Gibbs, D. A. (2007). Effect of deployment on the occurrence of child maltreatment in military and nonmilitary families. *American Journal of Epidemiology, 165*, 1199–1206. doi:10.1093/aje/kwm008

Riggs, D. S., Byrne, C. A., & Weathers, F. W. (1998). The quality of the intimate relationships of male Vietnam veterans: Problems associated with posttraumatic stress disorder. *Journal of Traumatic Stress, 11*, 87–101. doi:10.1023/A:1024409200155

Roberts, W. R., Penk, W. E., Gearing, M. L., Robinowitz, R., Dolan, M. P., & Patterson, E. T. (1982). Interpersonal problems of Vietnam combat veterans with symptoms of posttraumatic stress disorder. *Journal of Abnormal Psychology, 91*, 444–450. doi:10.1037/0021-843X.91.6.444

Rosenheck, R., & Fontana, A. (1998). Transgenerational effects of abusive violence on the children of Vietnam combat veterans. *Journal of Traumatic Stress, 11*, 731–742. doi:10.1023/A:1024445416821

Rotheram-Borus, M. J., Lee, M., Lin, Y. Y., & Lester, P. (2004). Six-year intervention outcomes for adolescent children of parents with the human immunodeficiency virus. *Archives of Pediatrics & Adolescent Medicine, 158*, 742–748. doi:10.1001/archpedi.158.8.742

Ruscio, A. M., Weathers, F. W., King, L. A., & King, D. W. (2002). Male war-zone veterans' perceived relationships with their children: The importance of emotional numbing. *Journal of Traumatic Stress, 15*, 351–357. doi:10.1023/A:1020125006371

Ryan-Wenger, N. A. (2001). Impact of the threat of war on children in military families. *American Journal of Orthopsychiatry, 71*, 236–244. doi:10.1037/0002-9432.71.2.236

Schneider, R. J., & Martin, J. A. (1994). Military families and combat readiness. In F. D. Jones, L. R. Sparacino, V. L. Wilcox, & J. M. Rotherberg (Eds.), *Military psychiatry preparing in peace for war* (pp. 19–30). Washington, DC: Borden Institute, U.S. Office of the Surgeon General, Department of the Army.

Stoppelbein, L., & Greening, L. (2000). Posttraumatic stress symptoms in parentally bereaved children and adolescents. *Journal of the American Academy of Child and Adolescent Psychiatry, 39*, 1112–1119. doi:10.1097/00004583-200009000-00010

Urbach, J. R. (1989). The impact of parental head trauma on families with children. *Psychiatric Medicine, 7*, 17–36.

Urbach, J. R., & Culbert, J. P. (1991). Head-injured parents and their children: Psychosocial consequences of a traumatic syndrome. *Psychosomatics, 32*, 24–33.

U.S. Department of Defense. (2004). *Report of the 1st Quadrennial Quality of Life Review.* Washington, DC: Author.

Uysal, S., Hibbard, M. R., Robillard, D., Pappadopulos, E., & Jaffe, M. (1998). The effect of parental traumatic brain injury on parenting and child behavior. *The Journal of Head Trauma Rehabilitation, 13*, 57–71. doi:10.1097/00001199-199812000-00007

Verhaeghe, S., Defloor, T., & Grypdonck, M. (2005). Stress and coping among families of patients with. traumatic brain injury: A review of the literature. *Journal of Clinical Nursing, 14*, 1004–1012. doi:10.1111/j.1365-2702.2005.01126.x

Walsh, F. (2007). Traumatic loss and major disasters: Strengthening family and community resilience. *Family Process, 46*, 207–227. doi:10.1111/j.1545-5300.2007.00205.x

Westerink, J., & Giarratano, L. (1999). The impact of posttraumatic stress disorder on partners and children of Australian Vietnam veterans. *The Australian and New Zealand Journal of Psychiatry, 33*, 841–847. doi:10.1046/j.1440-1614.1999.00638.x

Zatzick, D. F., Kang, S. M., Hinton, L., Kelly, R. H., Hilty, D. M., Franz, C. E., . . . Kravitz, R. L. (2001). Posttraumatic concerns: a patient-centered approach to outcome assessment after traumatic physical injury. *Medical Care, 39*, 327–339. doi:10.1097/00005650-200104000-00004

IV

PREVENTION
AND TREATMENT

9

COMPREHENSIVE SOLDIER FITNESS, BATTLEMIND, AND THE STRESS CONTINUUM MODEL: MILITARY ORGANIZATIONAL APPROACHES TO PREVENTION

WILLIAM P. NASH, LILLIAN KRANTZ, NATHAN STEIN,
RICHARD J. WESTPHAL, AND BRETT LITZ

The ongoing wars in Afghanistan and Iraq have generated a mental health challenge for the Department of Defense (DoD) and the military service branches that provide the manpower to prosecute these conflicts. Although most remain resilient in the face of repeated and prolonged wartime deployments, significant numbers of service members, veterans, and their family members have experienced serious mental or behavioral problems. The rate of posttraumatic stress disorder (PTSD) among service members and veterans who have served in recent combat is in the range of 10% to 18%, and the prevalence does not diminish in combat-exposed populations over time (Litz & Schlenger, 2009). War-zone deployments also correlate with elevated rates of depression (Wells et al., 2010) and alcohol abuse (Bray et al., 2009) among service members and with anxiety and depression among family members left behind (Lester et al., 2010). Suicide rates among service members rose alarmingly over the period 2004 to 2009 (Kuehn,

The opinions and assertions contained herein are the private views of the authors and are not to be construed as reflecting official views of the U.S. Department of Defense or any component of it.

2009), as has the rate of suicide attempts, which rose from 0.8% in 2005 to 2.2% in 2008 across all services, according to DoD's annual anonymous health survey (Bray et al., 2009).

Despite massive efforts since the wars in Afghanistan and Iraq began to screen and rescreen service members for mental or behavioral health problems and to reduce the stigma associated with getting help, barriers to care remain substantial (Tanielien & Jaycox, 2008). Yet even with optimal early treatment, such as trauma-focused cognitive–behavioral therapy, the magnitude of benefits from treatment may not be great (Roberts, Kitchiner, Kenardy, & Bisson, 2010). To significantly reduce the mental and behavioral health costs of military operational deployments to individuals, families, and communities, effective prevention programs are needed.

In recent years, the two U.S. military service branches most directly affected by the stress of combat deployments, the Army and the Marine Corps, have risen to this challenge and developed and fielded novel programs to promote resiliency and psychological health and to prevent mental and behavioral disorders. They have faced several obstacles along the way. Among these have been enduring uncertainties about the nature and causes of stress casualties, the paucity of outcome studies of existing military stress prevention and early intervention practices, the great variety of military missions and cultures, and the burden of stigma that is often greatest for those most in need of help. Perhaps even greater than the challenge posed by stigma has been that of integrating empathic psychological health awareness and compassionate prevention practices into necessarily tough, stoic warrior cultures. After all, changes to military cultures that improve the mental health of its members cannot endure if, as a side effect, they render military forces less capable of performing their missions in war and peace.

In this chapter, we review the historical development of mental disorder prevention programs in the military as the context in which to describe two recent sets of programs in the U.S. DoD: the Army's Comprehensive Soldier Fitness (CSF) and Battlemind programs and the Navy and Marine Corps' Combat and Operational Stress Control (COSC) programs, which are based on the stress continuum model. Although these approaches share common features, they diverge in significant ways. We hope to make these differences understandable as various solutions to the same problem: that of integrating modern mental health science with the traditional warrior ethos. After reviewing the scope, goals, methods, underlying assumptions, and empirical support for these two programmatic approaches, we offer an integrated model for the prevention of mental and behavioral problems in the military that encompasses both approaches.

EVOLUTION OF MILITARY MENTAL DISORDER PREVENTION CONCEPTS AND PROGRAMS

As an organizing framework, we adopt the intervention taxonomy recommended by the Institute of Medicine (IOM) Committee for Prevention of Mental Disorders (Mrazek & Haggerty, 1994), which defined prevention interventions—as opposed to treatment or rehabilitation—as those that target individuals who are either asymptomatic or suffering from no more than subclinical symptoms. We follow their recommendation to divide prevention interventions into the following three categories based on whom they target: (a) *universal* prevention is that which targets whole populations; (b) *selective* prevention is that which targets groups at increased risk relative to the rest of the population, although without identified symptoms; and (c) *indicated* prevention is that which targets individuals with identified but preclinical symptoms. Compared with the more familiar public health prevention categories of primary, secondary, and tertiary, the IOM framework has the advantage of drawing a clearer distinction between interventions taken on behalf of preclinically symptomatic individuals (i.e., indicated prevention) and those offered to individuals with clinical mental disorders (i.e., treatment).

Historical Military Universal Prevention

Military organizations and their leaders have always been charged with preventing potentially disabling health problems, of all kinds, in service members because injuries and illnesses deplete units of their most valuable resource—trained and ready personnel. Historically, military organizations have practiced universal prevention activities not as a means of health promotion per se but rather as a way to preserve the fighting strength of military forces to win wars. More recently, especially since the publication of the report of the U.S. Department of Defense Task Force on Mental Health (2007), psychological health in service members and their families has been pursued for its own sake.

Military organizations employ many of the same strategies for universal prevention today as they did millennia ago. The oldest universal prevention strategy is preinduction and periodic screening to exclude or remove individuals judged to be physically or mentally unfit or unsuitable, and therefore at increased risk of physical or mental harm or disability in a war zone. Three additional strategies for universal prevention are common to all military organizations: training, unit cohesion, and leadership (Shay, 1998). Training that is optimally tough and realistic inoculates service members against the stress they will encounter during operations as it instills in them the necessary competencies and self-confidence. Unit cohesion is the social glue, based on mutual trust and respect, that binds members of a unit into an integrated whole while mitigating their fear, motivates them, and gives meaning to their sacrifices. Engaged and effective leadership protects unit members from the toxic effects of operational stress by continually restoring their depleted physical, mental, and spiritual resources to bolster fortitude and courage.

The traditional military universal prevention strategies of selection, screening, training, cohesion, and leadership require virtually no input from mental health or religious ministry personnel. They are direct functions of military line leadership that are taught in military service schools and cultivated throughout careers. Considerable evidence supports the validity of these universal prevention interventions. In their review of approaches to PTSD prevention from a cognitive–behavioral perspective, Whealin, Ruzek, and Southwick (2008) listed four evidence-informed strategies for risk reduction that are all embedded in traditional military universal interventions: (a) make future potential psychological hazards more predictable so that when they occur, exposed individuals will perceive themselves to be more in control and more self-efficacious; (b) encourage more positive cognitive appraisals of potentially traumatic situations in the future through mastery of them in training to reduce negative affectivity; (c) reduce levels of physiological and emotional arousal during stressful events through prior physical and mental conditioning; and (d) enhance the effectiveness of postevent coping by teaching coping skills before exposure. Since the beginning of the current conflicts in Iraq and Afghanistan, the Army and Marine Corps have invested more heavily in universal prevention by immersing service members before deployment in highly realistic simulations of combat environments, using a combination of multisensory, live enactments and virtual-reality technologies. Although the effectiveness of such combat simulators for mental health prevention has not yet been reported, methodologies for performing such assessments have been developed (Taylor et al., 2007), and outcome studies are underway.

Medical and mental health providers have increasingly assisted line commanders in their universal prevention mission by offering deploying service members psychoeducational classes covering sleep hygiene, nutrition, relaxation, and other techniques for maintaining psychological wellness. Chaplains and other religious ministry personnel contribute to universal prevention by promoting meaning, faith, and religious practice as means to strengthen the spiritual "armor" of service members and to maintain core beliefs in the face of discrepant and potentially disillusioning experiences, postulated to be central to persistent posttraumatic distress (e.g., Janoff-Bulman, 1992). Although psychoeducational classes have yet to be proven of preventive benefit by published randomized outcome trials (Wessely et al., 2008), such classes remain in the training schedules of many deploying units, in part because awareness training seems like the right thing to do, and also because such training has enjoyed success in large-scale public health campaigns to prevent physical illnesses such as coronary artery disease, diabetes, and skin cancer.

Historical Military Selective Prevention

The military's traditional selective prevention intervention is informal and unstructured debriefing of units by their own leaders following exposure to particularly stressful events. It is not known when or where this practice began, but it is easy to imagine the most ancient of warriors sitting around a fire in their camp at night recounting the events of the day, sharing perspectives, learning lessons, and giving and receiving support. The practice of postevent informal debriefing, known as after-action reviews (AARs), continues to be taught to modern military leaders as a practice to disseminate lessons learned after a mission or engagement and as a means to restore individuals' confidence in themselves and each other, to promote social support, and to provide meaning and context for what transpired (e.g., U.S. Marine Corps & U.S. Navy, in press). Because AARs require no participation or input from anyone outside the unit, these informal discussions can be undertaken by military leaders at any level and at any time, and they can be repeated as often as necessary to achieve desired effects. No studies have been published reporting the prevention impact of AARs in any military service.

In contrast to AARs, which are informal, unstructured, and usually involve no participation by anyone outside the unit, psychological debriefing (PD) is a practice that brings outside mental health professionals into a unit to conduct a formal, usually structured group discussion of a stressful event and its aftermath. PD developed out of the community mental health literature and practices of crisis intervention of the 1960s, and became a common selective prevention intervention in military services in the late 1970s and early 1980s, around the same time it became popular in civilian emergency services cultures (see U.S. Marine Corps & U.S. Navy, in press). Although still widely practiced in both military and civilian settings, PD has not been found in multiple trials to prevent mental disorders in the aftermath of events involving trauma or loss (Bisson et al., 2009). Notably, a group randomized trial in Army peacekeepers found that PD did not hasten recovery from posttraumatic stress symptoms relative to control conditions (Adler et al., 2008).

Other selective prevention interventions in the military include policies for the rotation of entire units to rear areas for rest and recuperation after prolonged or intense exposure to combat, ceremonies and rituals that honor the fallen and give meaning to the sacrifices of the living, and postdeployment, unit-level reintegration training. In ancient Greece, theater may have served a selective prevention function for returning warriors (Meagher, 2006), a practice that has been revived by the DoD-sponsored "Theater of War" project that has recently brought dramatic readings of modern translations of classical Greek military tragedies to audiences of service members and veterans around the world (e.g., Robbins, 2010). Although never empirically assessed, many of these time-honored military practices enjoy continued wide practice because of their face validity and anecdotal benefits.

Historical Military Indicated Prevention

In contrast to concepts and methods for optimal early care of physical wounds, which are much the same across diverse military and civilian settings, early care of psychological wounds and illnesses lacks a widely accepted theoretical foundation, broad evidence base, and guidelines for practice. Instead of a single coherent model of how and why certain individuals develop chronic PTSD following exposure to potentially traumatic events while others do not, there are a multitude of such models, each narrowly focused on a single or a few functional psychological, biological, or social domains (e.g., Feldner, Monson, & Friedman, 2007; Litz, Gray, Bryant, & Adler, 2002). Likewise, instead of an organized set of principles for reducing the severity of acute distress and dysfunction in the aftermath of trauma or loss and promoting recovery and healing, there are many fragmentary approaches, each based on its own literature and assumption set (e.g., Feldner, Monson, & Friedman, 2007; Litz & Bryant, 2009). One fundamental question that remains unanswered by empirical research is this: To what extent are psychological wounds truly wounds at all, and to what extent do experiences of distress and dysfunction in the aftermath of stressful experiences represent coping choices that, however maladaptive, can always be avoided or reversed by making better choices? This is not merely an esoteric theoretical point; it is the historical axis on which the wheels of military-indicated prevention programs have turned (Nash, Silva, & Litz, 2009).

Prior to 1916, shell shock among allied troops and *Nervenshock* on the German side of World War I were believed to be caused largely by physical disruptions of neurons in the brain due to either nearby artillery blasts or the damaging effects of overwhelming sensory stimulation. Because no evidence of brain damage could be found in shell-shock victims using the technologies then available and because suggestive therapies such as hypnosis and coercive therapies such as electric shock appeared to restore function, neurologic explanations for shell shock came under increasing pressure. The issue was not decided purely on scientific grounds. Because of the economic and political costs to Germany of providing medical care and disability pensions to its *Nervenshock* veterans under the brain-injury model, official policies changed in September 1916, when a majority vote by a congress of psychiatrists and neurologists in Munich decided that persistent posttraumatic symptoms could *only* occur in individuals with a preexisting personality weakness, then known as hysteria (Lerner, 2003).

The British and U.S. militaries never openly endorsed the 1916 Munich psychiatric congress or its outcome, but barely 2 months after the Munich vote, C. S. Myers set up the first forward psychiatry centers in the British Army designed to quickly return to the front most cases of shell shock, renamed "Not Yet Diagnosed, Nervous," after no more intervention than food, rest, exercise, and marching (Jones & Wessely, 2003). In 1917, Thomas Salmon brought the same principles to the American Expeditionary Force, repackaged as the "PIE" principles of proximity, immediacy, and expectancy. Thereafter, the key "treatment" for combat stress casualties was expectancy, which meant segregating stress casualties from other, "truly injured" troops and preventing them from perceiving themselves as wounded or ill. In their review and history of forward psychiatry, Jones and Wessely (2003) explained that the "principal aim of PIE was to return men to duty rather than to address their mental state. This reality too was perhaps disguised for reasons of morale. Contemporary accounts provide little evidence that the primary motivation was therapeutic" (p. 414).

PIE, or one of its modern incarnations, PIES (which adds *simplicity*) or BICEPS (which adds *brevity* and *centrality*), continues to be fundamental to a number of military and civilian indicated prevention programs. The DoD Directive on Combat Stress Control (CSC) Programs (U.S. DoD, 1999/2003) prescribed the use of the PIE principles for adverse stress outcomes in theater, which it labeled *combat stress reactions* (CSRs). The popularity and endurance of PIE may be attributed to its effectiveness at accomplishing exactly what it originally promised: to return stressed individuals back to duty, sometimes despite continued distress or dysfunction. Certainly, the PIE principles are credited with causing the drastic reduction of evacuations for combat stress during the remainder of World War I, as well as in subsequent wars after these principles were rediscovered (Jones & Wessely, 2003).

There are no outcome studies to support the use of PIE as an indicated prevention intervention in U.S. troops. One reason for this lack of empirical outcome studies of the use of PIE for CSRs is because the principle of expectancy, as traditionally practiced in the U.S. military, precluded doing anything that might give symptomatic individuals the impression that there was anything wrong with them that needed to be treated or that deserved to be followed up over time. A different situation existed in the Israeli Defense Forces, which instituted a forward psychiatry program for the management of CSRs during the 1982 Lebanon War that was based on the PIE principles but that differed from U.S. management of CSRs in that it routinely afforded afflicted soldiers psychotherapy from a mental health professional. Solomon and Benbenishty (1986) reported a positive correlation between mental health outcome and the proximity, immediacy, and expectancy with which treatment was provided for in-theater CSRs, but they did not describe the nature or duration of the actual treatment itself. In the U.S. military, PIE does not officially include treatment beyond support and encouragement. Although not direct empirical support for the efficacy of PIE, encouragement for its continued use has been taken from a recent report (Cohen et al., 2010) of much higher return-to-duty rates of combat stress casualties maintained in their units in Iraq (95%) compared with those evacuated to in-theater support hospitals (70%), Kuwait (50%), or Germany (10%). Clearly, evacuation from forward areas negatively correlates with resumption of operational duties in the war zone. No studies have yet assessed whether evacuation from theater also negatively affects mental health symptom trajectories over time independent of other factors such as initial symptom severity, type and duration of treatment offered, and social support.

There have been few indicated prevention programs in the military that have not been based on the principles of PIE. One notable exception is the Boot Camp Survival Training for Navy Recruits—a Prescription (BOOT STRAP) program of brief cognitive–behavioral interventions for U.S. Navy recruits considered "at risk" of depression or other mental health problems on the basis of scores on screening tests of mood and perceived stress. In both a pilot study (Williams et al., 2004) and a group-randomized trial (Williams et al., 2007), this program was found to significantly reduce rates of attrition and to enhance adaptive coping and behavior.

TWO CURRENT MILITARY APPROACHES TO PSYCHOLOGICAL HEALTH PROMOTION

Since 2006, doctrine and methods for psychological health promotion and mental disorder prevention have diverged in the U.S. Army and U.S. Marine Corps, the two most heavily engaged services in recent ground combat in Iraq and Afghanistan. The Navy has also recently adapted the approach developed in the Marine Corps for use in its seagoing, aviation, and shore commands. In this section, current approaches in the Army and Marine Corps in terms of their constructs and methods for universal, selective, and indicated prevention are described.

U.S. Army Approach: Comprehensive Soldier Fitness and Battlemind

The core of the U.S. Army's current approach to psychological health, resilience, and mental disorder prevention is its Comprehensive Soldier Fitness (CSF) program, established in October 2008. Its goal is to increase the resilience of soldiers and families over time by developing their strengths in five key domains: physical, emotional, social, spiritual, and family (U.S. Department of the Army, 2010). The CSF program was developed by Army Brigadier General Rhonda Cornum in collaboration with the Positive Psychology Center at the University of Pennsylvania (see Montgomery, 2010), based partly on Martin Seligman's conceptions of positive psychology and positive health (e.g., Seligman, 2008).

The CSF program is supported by four pillars: (a) a confidential online self-assessment called the Global Assessment Tool (GAT), (b) self-paced online training modules linked to performance on the GAT, (c) institutional resilience awareness training embedded throughout Army career schools, and (d) "master resilience trainers" deployed in large operational units and installations to mentor other Army leaders in methods to promote resilience (Cornum, 2009; U.S. Department of the Army, 2010). Thus, the CSF program provides tools for service members and their families to confidentially assess and enhance their own physical, emotional, social, spiritual, and family fitness in order to promote a greater ability to bounce back from adversity.

In addition to the four pillars of CSF, the Army continues to deploy its Battlemind stress management training program, another strength-based program developed by the Army medical department. *Battlemind* is simultaneously a term for soldiers' "inner strength to face fear and adversity with courage in combat" (Adler, Bliese, McGurk, Hoge, & Castro, 2009; p. 930) and an acronym developed for training soldiers to meet the challenges of readapting to life and work after returning home from deployment. As shown in Exhibit 9.1, each letter of the word *Battlemind* stands for one of 10 skills that soldiers learn

EXHIBIT 9.1
Soldier Skills Highlighted in Battlemind Training That Are Desirable in Combat but That Can Cause Problems if not Readapted Postdeployment

B	Buddies (cohesion) vs. Withdrawal
A	Accountability vs. Controlling
T	Targeted Aggression vs. Inappropriate Aggression
T	Tactical Awareness vs. Hypervigilance
L	Lethally armed Vs. "locked And loaded" At Home
E	Emotional Control vs. Anger/Detachment
M	Mission Operational Security (OPSEC) vs. Secretiveness
I	Individual Responsibility vs. Guilt
N	Non-Defensive (Combat) Driving vs. Aggressive Driving
D	Discipline and Ordering vs. Conflict

Note. From Castro, Hoge, and Cox (2006).

and master during combat but that can cause problems if not readapted for conditions at home.

The scope of Battlemind training and early interventions has grown since 2005, when it consisted only of a training module to be delivered to soldiers at the end of an operational deployment. Currently, the Battlemind program encompasses prevention training for several target audiences, including soldiers, families, and leaders, at various points in each deployment cycle. It also includes an early intervention procedure for use with at-risk groups, known as *Battlemind Debriefing*.

Current Army Universal Prevention

Universal prevention and performance enhancement are the primary targets of Army psychological health promotion programs. Whether delivered to soldiers or families through online or career-school CSF modules or Battlemind deployment-cycle training, Army resilience training aims to instill and enhance individual skills to overcome adversity and thrive in its aftermath, both during and after deployment (Cornum, 2009). Although the specific content of CSF training is tailored to individual strengths and skill needs as assessed by the GAT, CSF training is explicitly not intended only for selected high-risk groups, and it is not a response to an individual negative psychological, physical, social, or professional outcome (Cornum, 2009). Likewise, although Battlemind training was initially delivered only to units returning from combat deployments, which were at increased risk of mental and behavioral problems relative to the Army as a whole, the scope of Battlemind training has broadened to include predeployment modules with clear universal prevention aims.

Although the theoretical and empirical underpinnings of CSF and Battlemind are not clearly stated in published materials, they appear to draw heavily on PTSD risk and resilience research that has identified a number of individual characteristics that consistently correlate highly with positive outcomes after stress exposure. Among these are beliefs that life is meaningful and that one can influence one's own surroundings and life events, unshakable self-confidence, a tendency toward positive rather than negative emotions, and a coping style that is a mixture of active engagement in challenges that can be met and repressive distancing from those that cannot (e.g., Bonanno, 2004). CSF also incorporates holistic health principles from sports psychology and positive psychology, which have demonstrated positive performance, health, and well-being outcomes in individuals who have received training in such coping skills (e.g., Seligman, 2008). No studies have addressed whether individuals can be effectively taught the same traits that have been found in retrospective research to correlate with resilient responses to potentially traumatic events and whether such newly acquired skills will prevent adverse stress outcomes such as PTSD in combat-exposed service members. We are unaware of any existing outcome studies of training in resilience principles similar to those contained in CSF in any populations subsequently exposed to stress of the intensity and duration of current combat deployments.

There exists one publicly available yet unpublished empirical study of the effectiveness of predeployment Battlemind training as a universal prevention intervention. It is briefly described in the U.S. Army's report of its fifth annual Mental Health Advisory Team survey of soldier well-being in Iraq and Afghanistan (Mental Health Advisory Team, 2008). Of a convenience sample of 2,195 Army soldiers surveyed while deployed to Iraq in 2007, 1,438 reported having received Battlemind training before deploying, 688 denied having received this training, and 69 did not respond to the question. After adjusting for rank, gender, months deployed, and levels of combat exposure, 12.0% of soldiers who had received predeployment Battlemind training screened positive for current mental health problems, and 20.5% of those who had not received Battlemind training were said to screen positive using the same measures of posttraumatic stress, depression, and anxiety. The significance of this finding is limited because, as the authors of the report acknowledged, many uncontrolled differences existed between the intervention (Battlemind trained) and control (untrained) groups. These differences were neither enumerated nor analyzed.

Current Army Selective Prevention

The major selective prevention component of Battlemind is a form of single-session PD called Battlemind Debriefing. Battlemind Debriefing is a structured, multiphase group process, facilitated by a behavioral health professional or chaplain along with an enlisted cofacilitator. It is similar in format and goals to other forms of psychological debriefing, such as CISD, except that the challenges of transitioning from a combat theater to home are always a specific focus of Battlemind Debriefing, and a discussion of the 10 skills and challenges that make up the Battlemind acronym is always included. Like CISD, Battlemind Debriefing is a one-shot intervention intended to normalize, educate, and encourage social support and validation. Also similar to CISD, Battlemind Debriefing does not screen group members for symptom burden either before participation in debriefing to determine appropriateness for this level of intervention or afterward to determine the need for more targeted treatment and follow-up. Battlemind Debriefing can be delivered either in theater or in garrison, within 2 weeks of returning from deployment. In theater, it can be offered to units of platoon size either after specific potentially traumatic events (event driven), or after a certain number of months of deployment have passed (time driven; Adler, Castro, & McGurk, 2009).

Although published materials regarding Battlemind Debriefing do not explicitly state its underlying assumptions or empirical foundations, like other forms of PD, its goals seem to include normalizing stress reactions and promoting an expectation of recovery and return to normalcy, similar to the goals of PIE interventions for individuals (Bisson et al., 2009). Like other forms of PD, Battlemind Debriefing also seems based on an assumption that retelling of traumatic experiences in a group setting may be cathartic and may prevent enduring negative stress outcomes such as PTSD.

One outcome study of Battlemind Debriefing has been published (Adler, Bliese, McGurk, Hoge, & Castro, 2009). In this group-randomized trial, 2,297 soldiers returning from a yearlong deployment to Iraq were randomly assigned by platoons to receive one of four immediate postdeployment interventions: Battlemind Debriefing; large-group Battlemind training; small-group Battlemind training; or the control condition, a stress education class of unspecified content. Outcome measures of posttraumatic stress, depression, and sleep were recorded at baseline and 4 months later. Analysis of data from the 1,060 soldiers who completed the follow-up assessment (46%) showed a modest effect size for improvement in all three outcome measures in the Battlemind Debriefing group relative to the stress education group ($d = 0.21$, 0.26, and 0.25 for posttraumatic stress, depression, and sleep scores, respectively), but only among soldiers whose deployment combat exposure scored in the top third. There was no effect for soldiers who had reported lower levels of combat exposure during deployment. The other two active intervention groups in this study—large- and small-group Battlemind training—also showed modest improvements relative to the stress education group at the 4-month follow-up for depression ($d = 0.30$ for those who received large-group Battlemind training) and sleep ($d = 0.27$ and 0.25 for those who received large- and small-group Battlemind training, respectively). As the authors noted, this unreplicated study was limited by its lack of a true control condition and large lost to follow-up rate. If these findings are replicated, additional research will be needed to identify which components of Battlemind training or Debriefing constitute their active ingredients and to promote the development of coherent models to explain how these interventions affect stress trajectories.

Army Indicated Prevention

Neither CSF nor Battlemind includes formal interventions that could be considered to serve *indicated* prevention because neither contains a mechanism to screen for symptom severity or to tailor intervention strategies based on symptom burden. Published materials for Army resilience programs do not explicitly state why they do not include indicated prevention efforts.

U.S. Navy and Marine Corps Approach: The Stress Continuum Model

The stress continuum model is a heuristic tool developed in the Marine Corps to provide a framework for prevention interventions across their spectrum. It categorizes all possible stress states into one of four color-coded stress zones (see Table 9.1; Nash, in press; U.S. Marine Corps & U.S. Navy, in press).

The two ends of the stress continuum are easily defined and well known. The Green "Ready" Zone, to the left end of the continuum, is the zone of low or absent distress or dysfunction due to stress; it is the zone of wellness and resistance to current stress load. The Red "Ill" Zone, to the far right of the continuum, is the zone of diagnosable stress-related mental disorders such as PTSD, depression, and substance abuse. The two intermediate stress zones, color coded yellow and orange, are stress states conceived to lie between wellness and illness. The distinction between these two intermediate stress zones is fundamental to the stress continuum model because the distinction between Yellow and Orange zones is, by definition, one of relative risk—both for failure of role performance and for future mental illness. The Yellow "Reacting" Zone is defined as the stress zone of normal, common, and transient states of distress or changes in functioning. Yellow Zone stress reactions, by definition, always disappear as soon as the source of stress is removed. Yellow Zone stress reactions are not only normal but necessary, because such states of strain are essential to the development of greater capacity and competence, whether physical, mental, social, or spiritual. Yellow Zone reactions can be caused by almost any challenge, either alone or in combination with others stressors. In contrast, the Orange "Injured" Zone is the zone of more severe and persistent states of distress or alterations in functioning, conceived to be caused by one of four stressor types: (a) life threat, (b) loss, (c) moral injury, or (d) cumulative wear-and-tear from many stressors over a prolonged period of time (Litz et al., 2009; Nash, 2007, in press). Orange Zone stress injuries are conceived to be far less common than Yellow Zone stress reactions but potentially more serious when they occur because Orange Zone stress symptoms are those that, by definition, continue for a period of time after the individual is removed from the source of stress. Furthermore, even after they heal (as they usually do), stress injuries leave behind a mental or emotional scar—a mental area of either increased vulnerability or increased strength.

The stress continuum model was developed by Marine operational leaders working in concert with Navy medical, mental health, and religious ministry professionals. In 2007, the commanding generals of all three Marine Expeditionary Forces, representing all operational combat units in the Marine Corps, endorsed the stress continuum model as the foundation for all future resilience and prevention efforts in the corps. They also accepted full ownership of this prevention and wellness programs to be built on this foundation. Subsequently, the chief of naval operations endorsed the stress

TABLE 9.1
Navy–Marine Corps Combat and Operational Stress Continuum Model

	Stress Zone			
	Ready (Green Zone)	Reacting (Yellow Zone)	Injured (Orange Zone)	III (Red Zone)
Defining features	Low state of stress, or stress that doesn't threaten resources or capacity for resilience	Bent by stress; mild and transient distress or changes in functioning; low risk for failure of role performance or mental disorder; always reversible	Damaged by stress; severe and more persistent distress or loss of functioning; high risk for failure of role performance or mental disorder; leaves a mental "scar"	Clinical mental disorder; diagnosable only by a health professional; due to stress injuries that fail to heal normally
Causes or types	N/A	Caused by any of a multitude of possible stressors, which are often cumulative	Four causes: (1) life threat, (2) loss, (3) moral injury, or (4) cumulative wear-and-tear	Common types: PTSD, depression, anxiety, and substance abuse or dependence
Responsibility	Line leaders	Line leaders, chaplains, front-line medical	Chaplains, front-line medical, embedded mental health, line leaders	Medical, mental health, chaplains, line leaders
Possible interventions	Strengthen	Mitigate stress, identify stress zone	Identify stress zone, combat and operational stress first aid, clinical care	Clinical mental health and medical care; combat and operational stress first aid

PTSD = posttraumatic stress disorder.
Note. From Nash, W. P. (in press) and U.S. Marine Corps and U.S. Navy (in press).

continuum model as the basis for all future resilience and prevention programs in the Navy.

With the stress continuum model as a starting point, the Marine Corps subsequently developed a set of five core leader functions for its leaders to promote psychological health and prevent stress disorders: strengthen, mitigate, identify, treat, and reintegrate. To *strengthen*, in this context, means to inoculate to expected stressors, toughen, and provide individuals with necessary predeployment tools and training. To *mitigate* means to reduce unnecessary stress during training and deployment, to ensure adequate rest and recovery periods, and to replenish depleted resources continually. The *identify* function encompasses ongoing assessment of stressors, stress zones, and the effects of interventions provided. *Treat* in this context does not mean clinical medical or mental health care but, more broadly, any and all interventions taken by peers, family members, leaders, caregivers, or service members themselves, to promote recovery and healing. *Reintegrate* in this context does not refer to returning to home, family, and community after a deployment but rather to the role of leaders in restoring the professional and personal competence and self-confidence of individuals who are recovering from stress injuries or illnesses. These five core leader functions form the skeleton of the Navy and Marine Corps' new Combat and Operational Stress Control (COSC) doctrine (U.S. Marine Corps & U.S. Navy, in press).

Prevention programs built on the stress continuum model and the five core leader functions include a number of career-school and deployment-cycle training modules for Marines, sailors, leaders, and family members. In addition, an early intervention tool set called Combat and Operational Stress First Aid has been developed using the stress continuum model as a foundation. These doctrinal elements also form the foundation for the comprehensive COSC program of the Marine Corps and the Operational Stress Control (OSC) program of the Navy (U.S. Marine Corps & U.S. Navy, in press).

Current Marine Corps Universal Prevention

As implied by the first core leader function, strengthening service members and their families before exposure to the rigors of operational deployment remains a function of line leadership at all levels. The primary tools for universal prevention in the Marine Corps and Navy are line leader–directed training, leadership, and unit cohesion. In addition, awareness training in the stress continuum model and other components of COSC doctrine are included in career schools and at various points in deployment cycles for sailors and Marines. Such awareness training is not intended to prevent future mental disorders directly but to make it more likely that individuals will recognize when they, themselves, or others in their units or families have been injured by stress and may benefit from indicated prevention interventions.

The effectiveness of line leader–directed universal prevention programs in the Navy and Marine Corps has not yet been empirically evaluated. Studies are underway, including a large-scale, longitudinal, controlled study of the efficacy of predeployment COSC training in Marine ground combat units bound for Afghanistan.

Current Marine Corps Selective Prevention

The primary selective prevention tools in use in the Navy and Marine Corps are also not interventions delivered by mental health professionals but procedures followed by line operational leaders who use the stress continuum model to (a) recognize when an individual or group of individuals are at increased risk because of prolonged Yellow Zone stress or recent Orange Zone events and (b) take action to mitigate that risk at the unit level (U.S. Marine Corps & U.S. Navy, in press). The selective prevention tools at the disposal of line leaders in the Navy and Marine Corps are those that already have a long tradition in the military, including small-unit after-action reviews, unit rest or rotation policies, memorial services or physical memorials, and ceremonies and celebrations. What the stress continuum model adds to these traditional military selective prevention interventions is a framework and set of tools for line leaders to better recognize when units may be at increased risk because of experiences of life threat, loss, moral injury, or fatigue. In the U.S. Marine Corps COSC doctrine, the second core leader function, mitigate, roughly equates with selective prevention.

A major empirical foundation for Marine Corps selective prevention is the body of research on the role of resources and resource loss in stress and stress disorders (e.g., Hobfoll, 2002). No studies have yet assessed the effectiveness of leader-directed selective prevention practices in the Navy or Marine Corps.

Current Marine Corps Indicated Prevention

The most significant departure from traditional military practices in the new Marine Corps and Navy approach to psychological health promotion is in the area of indicated prevention, encompassed by the last three of the five core leader functions—identify, treat, and reintegrate. The stress continuum model provides a yardstick for assessing who is in need of targeted prevention, and the Combat and Operational Stress First Aid (COSFA) tool set provides specific procedures to promote recovery. COSFA was developed through a collaboration of the Navy, Marine Corps, and Veterans Affairs (VA) National Center for PTSD (Nash, Westphal, Watson, & Litz, 2008). It was built on the framework of Psychological First Aid (PFA) as developed by the National Center for PTSD and the National Center for Child Traumatic Stress (2006). PFA, in turn, had been distilled from the best evidence-informed procedures for restoring well-being and health following exposure to potentially traumatic events (see Hobfoll et al., 2007). COSFA differs from PFA primarily in its use of the stress continuum to recognize when interventions are required and which level of intervention would be most appropriate, as well as to monitor recovery over time. COSFA is a set of tools crafted specifically for use in military organizations with a preexisting structure that includes leadership, cohesive units, and a network of available support. The seven actions of COSFA are

- Check: assess and reassess;
- Coordinate: inform others and refer for additional care, as needed;
- Cover: get to safety and keep safe;
- Calm: reduce physiological and emotional arousal;
- Connect: ensure or restore social support from peers and family;
- Competence: restore self-efficacy and occupational and social competence; and
- Confidence: restore self-esteem and hope.

As a new and novel organizational approach to indicated prevention, COSFA and related concepts and tools have not yet been subjected to empirical scrutiny, although studies are currently underway. Many important empirical questions remain, including (a) whether the upper and lower boundaries of the Orange Zone of stress injuries can be defined with useful metrics; (b) whether non–mental health professionals can reliably recognize signs of subclinical distress or impairment in other service members or family members; (c) whether COSFA tools can be applied by those for whom they were designed, including small unit leaders, chaplains, corpsmen, unit surgeons, family members, and service members, themselves; and (d) whether appropriately applied COSFA interventions reduce rates of mental disorders, suicide, and other adverse outcomes.

INTEGRATED MODEL FOR MILITARY
PSYCHOLOGICAL HEALTH PROMOTION

Recent innovations in Army and Navy–Marine Corps psychological health promotion programs have much in common, and where they differ, they may be more complementary than conflicting. To conceptualize how these seemingly disparate approaches fit together, we return to the IOM taxonomy for mental disorder prevention, discussed earlier. In its 1994 report, the IOM Committee on Prevention of Mental Disorders made a compelling case for applying prevention efforts across the spectrum of possible interventions, from those that may be protective for entire populations to those that target individuals experiencing symptoms possibly foreshadowing a mental disorder (Mrazek & Haggerty, 1994). Universal, selective, and indicated prevention interventions may be conceived of as moderators of risk. The committee went on to recommend activities that more broadly promote psychological health in a population, irrespective of risk. For maximum benefit, all approaches are necessary.

Within this framework, the Army's CSF and Battlemind programs stand out as exemplars of positive health promotion and universal mental disorder prevention, using evidence-informed strategies. These programmatic efforts supplement rather than replace universal prevention functions traditionally used by line leaders, including training, cohesion, and leadership. The stress continuum model and Stress First Aid may be viewed as innovations for intervening at the other end of the prevention spectrum: for identifying and aiding individuals at high risk because they are already experiencing at least subclinical symptoms of distress or dysfunction. Between these two ends of the prevention spectrum lies selective prevention, an area of both overlap and divergence between the Army and Marine Corps. Both services endorse the use of leader-directed after-action reviews, as well as other leader actions to mitigate stress in units, and both services use postdeployment training modules for returning units. Whether structured debriefing led by mental health professionals adds substantial benefits for at-risk units remains an empirical question, although its use was discouraged by the 2004 VA and DoD Clinical Practice Guidelines for Traumatic Stress (U.S. Department of Veterans Affairs & U.S. Department of Defense, 2004).

A metaphor that springs from the IOM prevention framework summarizes the prevention challenge for the military. In American football, 11 players from each team face each other on either side of the line of scrimmage. On defense, those 11 players occupy three tiers of defense: line, backfield, and two safeties. Anyone familiar with this sport would have a hard time imagining a team fielding a defensive squad with only a single tier of defense—for example, a defense comprising solely linemen. No matter how big and fast they were, linemen could not stop the opposing offense at the line of scrimmage on every play. There would always be ball carriers who would break through the line into the secondary or passes that would be caught over the heads of the defensive line. A defensive squad comprising solely backs or safeties, with no big linemen up front, would also be doomed to fail. Similarly, effective mental disorder prevention in the military must operate on several tiers of defense, from the front lines of universal prevention and positive health promotion, to the defensive backfield of selective prevention, to the last level of defense—that provided by indicated prevention interventions such as stress first aid.

REFERENCES

Adler, A. B., Bliese, P. D., McGurk, D., Hoge, C. W., & Castro, C. A. (2009). Battlemind debriefing and Battlemind training as early interventions with soldiers returning from Iraq: randomization by platoon. *Journal of Consulting and Clinical Psychology, 77,* 928–940. doi:10.1037/a0016877

Adler, A. B., Castro, C. A., & McGurk, D. (2009). Time-driven Battlemind psychological debriefing: A group-level early intervention in combat. *Military Medicine, 174,* 21–28.

Adler, A. B., Litz, B. T., Castro, C. A., Suvak, M., Thomas, J. L., Burrell, L., . . . Bliese, P. D. (2008). A group randomized trial of Critical Incident Stress Debriefing provided to U.S. peacekeepers. *Journal of Traumatic Stress, 21,* 253–263. doi:10.1002/jts.20342

Bisson, J. I., McFarlane, A. C., Rose, S., Ruzek, J. I., & Watson, P. J. (2009). Psychological debriefing for adults. In E. Foa, M. Friedman, T. Keane, & J. Cohen (Eds.), *Effective treatments for PTSD: Practice guidelines from the International Society for Traumatic Stress Studies* (2nd ed., pp. 83–105). New York, NY: Guilford Press.

Bonanno, G. A. (2004). Loss, trauma, and human resilience: Have we underestimated the human capacity to thrive after extremely aversive events? *American Psychologist, 59,* 20–28. doi:10.1037/0003-066X.59.1.20

Bray, R. M., Pemberton, M. R., Hourani, L. L., Witt, M., Olmstead, K. L., . . . Bradshaw, M. (2009). *2008 Department of Defense survey of health related behaviors among active duty military personnel.* September 2009, Research Triangle Institute. Retrieved from: http://www.tricare.mil/2008HealthBehaviors.pdf

Castro, C. A., Hoge, C. W., & Cox, A. L. (2006). Battlemind training: Building soldier resiliency. In *Human dimensions in military operations: Military leaders' strategies for addressing stress and psychological support* (RTO-MP-HFM-134). Brussels, Belgium: NATO Research and Training Organization.

Cohen, S. P., Brown, C., Kurihara, C., Plunkett, A., Nguyen, C., & Strassels, S. A. (2010). Diagnoses and factors associated with medical evacuation and return to duty for service members participating in Operation Iraqi Freedom or Operation Enduring Freedom: a prospective cohort study. *The Lancet, 375,* 301–309. doi:10.1016/S0140-6736(09)61797-9

Cornum, R. (2009, December). Comprehensive Soldier Fitness: Master Resilience Trainer Course. Retrieved from http://www.army.mil/csf/resources.html

Feldner, M. T., Monson, C. M., & Friedman, M. J. (2007). A critical analysis of approaches to targeted PTSD prevention: Current status and theoretically derived future directions. *Behavior Modification, 31,* 80–116. doi:10.1177/0145445506295057

Hobfoll, S. E. (2002). Social and psychological resources and adaptation. *Review of General Psychology, 6,* 307–324. doi:10.1037/1089-2680.6.4.307

Hobfoll, S. E., Watson, P., Bell, C. C., Bryant, R. A., Brymer, M. J., . . . Ursano, R. J. (2007). Five essential elements of immediate and mid-term mass trauma intervention: Empirical evidence. *Psychiatry, 70,* 283–315.

Janoff-Bulman, R. (1992). *Shattered assumptions: Towards a new psychology of trauma.* New York, NY: Free Press.

Jones, E., & Wessely, S. (2003). "Forward psychiatry" in the military: Its origins and effectiveness. *Journal of Traumatic Stress, 16,* 411–419. doi:10.1023/A:1024 426321072

Kuehn, B. M. (2009). Soldier suicide rates continue to rise: Military, scientists work to stem the tide. *JAMA, 301,* 1111–1113. doi:10.1001/jama.2009.342

Lerner, P. (2003). *Hysterical men: War, psychiatry, and the politics of trauma in Germany, 1890–1930.* Ithaca, NY: Cornell University Press.

Lester, P., Peterson, K., Reeves, J., Knauss, L., Glover, D., . . . Beardslee, W. (2010). The long war and parental combat deployment: Effects on military children and at-home spouses. *Journal of the American Academy of Child and Adolescent Psychiatry, 49,* 310–320. doi:10.1097/00004583-201004000-00006

Litz, B. T., & Bryant, R. (2009). Early cognitive-behavioral interventions for adults. In E. Foa, M. Friedman, T. Keane, & J. Cohen (Eds.), *Effective treatments for PTSD: Practice guidelines from the International Society for Traumatic Stress Studies* (2nd ed., pp. 117–135). New York, NY: Guilford Press.

Litz, B. T., Gray, M. J., Bryant, R. A., & Adler, A. B. (2002). Early interventions for trauma: Current status and future directions. *Clinical Psychology: Science and Practice, 9,* 112–134. doi:10.1093/clipsy/9.2.112

Litz, B. T., & Schlenger, W. E. (2009). PTSD in service members and new veterans of the Iraq and Afghanistan wars: A bibliography and critique. *PTSD Research Quarterly, 20,* 1–7.

Litz, B. T., Stein, N., Delaney, E., Lebowitz, L., Nash, W. P., Silva, C., & Maguen, S. (2009). Moral injury and moral repair in war veterans: A preliminary model and intervention strategy. *Clinical Psychology Review.* doi:10.1016/j.cpr.2009.07.003

Meagher, R. E. (2006). *Herakles gone mad: Rethinking heroism in an age of endless war.* Northampton, MA: Olive Branch Press.

Mental Health Advisory Team. (2008). Mental Health Advisory Team (MHAT) V Operation Iraqi Freedom 06-08: Iraq, Operation Enduring Freedom 8: Afghanistan, 14 February 2008. Retrieved from http://www.armymedicine. army.mil/reports/mhat/mhat.html

Montgomery, N. (2010, January 3). Army trains soldiers on how to be mentally, emotionally tough. *Stars and Stripes.* Retrieved from http://www.stripes.com/news/ army-trains-soldiers-on-how-to-be-mentally-emotionally-tough-1.97711

Mrazek, P. J., & Haggerty, R. J. (Eds.). (1994). *Reducing risks for mental disorders: Frontiers of prevention research.* Report of the Committee on Prevention of Mental Disorders, Division of Biobehavioral Sciences and Mental Disorders, Institute of Medicine. Washington, DC: National Academies Press.

Nash, W. P. (2007). Combat/operational stress adaptations and injuries. In C. R. Figley & W. P. Nash (Eds.), *Combat stress injuries: Theory, research, and management* (pp. 33–64). New York, NY: Routledge.

Nash, W. P. (in press). U.S. Marine Corps and Navy combat and operational stress continuum model: A tool for leaders. In E. C. Ritchie (Ed.), *Combat and operational behavioral health* (Textbooks of Military Medicine). Washington, DC: Borden Institute and U.S. Army Medical Department.

Nash, W. P., Silva, C., & Litz, B. T. (2009). The historical origins of military and veteran mental health stigma, and the stress injury model as a means to reduce it. *Psychiatric Annals, 39,* 789–794. doi:10.3928/00485713-20090728-05

Nash, W. P., Westphal, R. J., Watson, P., & Litz, B. T. (2008, November). Combat and operational stress first aid (COSFA): *A toolset for military leaders.* Presented at the Defense Centers of Excellence for Psychological Health and Traumatic Brain Injury Warrior Resilience Conference, Fairfax, VA.

National Child Traumatic Stress Network & National Center for PTSD. (2006) *Psychological First Aid: Field operations guide* (2nd ed.). Retrieved from http://www.nctsn.org and www.ncptsd.va.gov

Roberts, N. P., Kitchiner, N. J., Kenardy, J., & Bisson, J. I. (2010). Early psychological interventions to treat acute traumatic stress symptoms. *Cochrane Database of Systematic Reviews, 3,* CD007944. doi:10.1002/14651858.CD007944.pub2

Robbins, S. (2010, May 15). Project aims to connect with troops through tales of ancient warriors. *Stars and Stripes.* Retrieved from http://www.stripes.com/news/project-aims-to-connect-with-troops-through-tales-of-ancient-warriors-1.102692

Seligman, M. E. P. (2008). Positive health. *Applied Psychology, 57,* 3–18. doi:10.1111/j.1464-0597.2008.00351.x

Shay, J. (1998). Trust: Lubricant for "friction" in military operations. Retrieved from http://www.chetrichards.com/modern_business_strategy/shay/trust_and_friction.htm

Solomon, Z., & Benbenishty, R. (1986). The role of proximity, immediacy, and expectancy in frontline treatment of combat stress reaction among Israelis in the Lebanon War. *The American Journal of Psychiatry, 143,* 613–617.

Tanielien, T., & Jaycox, L. H. (Eds.). (2008). *Invisible wounds of war: Psychological and cognitive injuries, their consequences, and services to assist recovery.* Santa Monica, CA: RAND Corporation.

Taylor, M. K., Sausen, K. P., Mujica-Parodi, L. R., Potterat, E. G., Yanagi, M. A., & Kim, H. (2007). Neurophysiologic methods to measure stress during survival, evasion, resistance, and escape training. *Aviation, Space, and Environmental Medicine, 78,* B224–B230.

U.S. Department of the Army. (2010). *Comprehensive soldier fitness.* Addendum G, 2010 Army Posture Statement, February 19, 2010. Retrieved from https://secureweb2.hqda.pentagon.mil/vdas_armyposturestatement/2010/addenda/Addendum_G-Comp.%20Soldier%20Fitness.asp

U.S. Department of Defense. (1999/2003). Combat Stress Control (CSC) programs (Department of Defense Directive 6490.5, February 23, 1999, certified current as of November 24, 2003). Retrieved from: http://www.dtic.mil/whs/directives/corres/pdf/649005p.pdf

U.S. Department of Defense Task Force on Mental Health. (2007). *An achievable vision: Report of the Department of Defense Task Force on Mental Health*. Falls Church, VA: Defense Health Board.

U.S. Department of Veterans Affairs & Department of Defense. (2004). *VA/DoD Clinical practice guideline for the management of post-traumatic stress*. Retrieved from http://www.healthquality.va.gov/ptsd/ptsd_full.pdf

U.S. Marine Corps & U.S. Navy. (in press). Combat and operational stress control (MCRP 6-11C/NTTP 1-15M). Quantico, VA: Marine Corps Combat Development Command.

Wells, T. S., LeardMann, C. A., Fortuna, S. O., Smith, B., Smith, T. C., . . . Blazer, D., for the Millennium Cohort Study Team. (2010). A prospective study of depression following combat deployment in support of the wars in Iraq and Afghanistan. *American Journal of Public Health, 100*, 90–99. doi:10.2105/AJPH.2008.155432

Wessely, S., Bryant, R. A., Greenberg, N., Earnshaw, M., Sharpley, J., & Hughes, J. H. (2008). Does psychoeducation help prevent post traumatic psychological distress? *Psychiatry, 71*, 287–302.

Whealin, J. M., Ruzek, J. I., & Southwick, S. (2008). Cognitive–behavioral theory and preparation for professionals at risk for trauma exposure. *Trauma, Violence & Abuse, 9*, 100–113. doi:10.1177/1524838008315869

Williams, A., Hagerty, B. M., Yousha, S. M., Horrocks, J., Hoyle, K. S., & Liu, D. (2004). Psychosocial effects of the Boot Strap intervention in Navy recruits. *Military Medicine, 169*, 814–820.

Williams, A., Hagerty, B. M., Andrei, A.-C., Yousha, S. M., Hirth, R. A., & Hoyle, K. S. (2007). STARS: Strategies to Assist Navy Recruits' Success. *Military Medicine, 172*, 942–949.

10

EVIDENCE-BASED TREATMENTS FOR POSTTRAUMATIC STRESS DISORDER IN OPERATION ENDURING FREEDOM AND OPERATION IRAQI FREEDOM MILITARY PERSONNEL

BARBARA O. ROTHBAUM, MARYROSE GERARDI, BEKH BRADLEY,
AND MATTHEW J. FRIEDMAN

"Mr. Jones," a 40-year-old African American male veteran, presented to the posttraumatic stress disorder (PTSD) treatment clinic of a Veterans Affairs (VA) Medical Center. His military career spanned 20 years, including service in the U.S. Army regular active-duty forces and the U.S. Army National Guard. During this time, he was deployed in both the 1991 Gulf War and in Operation Iraqi Freedom (OIF), working as a combat medic. His reported traumatic experiences included threats from incoming missiles, the sounds of mortar and rocket fire, as well as the sight of injured and dead soldiers and civilians. At the time of his intake, he reported traumatic memories related to both of his combat deployments. These memories intruded spontaneously and were also triggered by watching news or war movies. He reported impaired sleep, feeling constantly on alert, and increased irritability. Although he was not actively suicidal, he endorsed thoughts of death and dying. He described becoming distressed and paranoid when in heavy traffic and engaging in "evasive maneuvers" when he believed that other cars might be following him. He reported symptoms of depression, including depressed mood, fatigue, anhedonia, and impaired concentration. He described himself as moody and frequently angry, and he experienced difficulty in his interpersonal interactions with his family and others. He was taking online college courses, but he was not employed. He was diagnosed with both major depressive disorder and PTSD and was referred for individual psychotherapy with a PTSD team psychologist, as well as psychopharmacology treatment with a team psychiatrist. He was referred to the VA-supported employment program.

As part of the PTSD team's program evaluation procedure, he completed self-report instruments before, during, and after his treatment. Before treatment initiation, his score on the PTSD Checklist (PCL; Weathers, Litz, Herman, Huska, & Keane, 1993) was 68, and his score on the PTSD Symptom Scale, Self-Report (PSS-SR; Foa, Riggs, Dancu, & Rothbaum, 1993) was 38, both indicating high levels of PTSD symptoms. His score on the PHQ-9 (the nine-item depression scale of the Patient Health Questionnaire; Kroenke, Spitzer, & Williams, 2001) was 27, indicating moderate to severe levels of depression.

His first three sessions of psychotherapy included gathering information about his exposure to traumatic events while in combat and psychological education about common symptoms of PTSD. The symptoms of PTSD were explained as a fear-learning disorder in which the veteran's fight, flight, or freeze response, while appropriately activated during combat, continued to be activated in nondangerous situations. It was explained that his engagement in avoidance and unnecessary self-protective actions (safety behaviors) were serving to maintain his disorder. At the end of the third session, the patient was presented with a rationale for exposure therapy (a psychological intervention in which the trauma is repeatedly recalled in a therapeutic environment) and an explanation of subjective units of distress (SUDS) ratings. SUDS ratings are patient ratings of anxiety in a specific situation, ranging from 0 (*no anxiety or discomfort*) to 100 (*extreme anxiety or discomfort*). His homework for this session included identifying his most common avoidance and safety behaviors. As reported in his fourth session, these included avoiding sporting events, grocery stores, shopping malls, and driving in heavy traffic. His safety behaviors included repeatedly checking the locks on his windows and doors each time he awoke during the night, constantly scanning his surroundings for danger, and planning escape routes while in public places. He was taught relaxation and breathing skills to reduce anxiety.

In Sessions 5 through 12, he engaged in exposure therapy, including interoceptive (i.e., confronting feared bodily symptoms often associated with PTSD), in vivo (i.e., confronting feared yet safe situations in the natural setting), and imaginal (i.e., reliving the trauma in imagination) elements. His interoceptive exposure exercises included holding his breath, breathing through a straw, and hyperventilating. He reported that he initially found these activities distressing because of their association with memories of wearing a gas mask in combat. He engaged in these activities outside of session, and his associated distress decreased by approximately 50% from this practice. He also engaged in in vivo exposure activities, including going to a local grocery store and remaining there until his distress reduced by 50% and going to a local coffee shop and sitting with his back to the door while reading a book. He engaged in imaginal exposure, including making tape recordings of two traumatic events and then listening to these tapes between therapy sessions, three times each day over a several-week period. He reported that during this process, his SUDS while listening to his exposure tape decreased, on a scale of 1 to 100, from 70 or 80 to 20. At Session 12, his PTSD symptoms were greatly reduced (PSS score = 13), but he continued to report symptoms of depression and problems in interpersonal interactions, including irritable and angry reactions to others. At that time, his therapist gave him a Beck Depression Inventory (BDI-II; Beck, Steer, & Brown, 1996) on which he obtained a score of 26, indicating moderate to severe depression. The therapist then shifted the focus of the treatment toward these symptoms using a cognitive–behavioral approach to treatment, situational analysis (Driscoll, Cukrowizc, Reardon, & Joiner, 2004), which focused on analyzing his interpretations and behaviors in response to problematic or stressful situations and behavioral activation strategies over the course of six sessions. He reported a reduction in symptoms of depression and improved interpersonal interactions. At a subsequent follow-up session, his self-report assessments demonstrated a PCL score of 20 and a PSS score of 9, both indicative of minimal PTSD symptoms. Likewise, his PHQ score of 9 and BDI score of 9 were both indicative of minimal symptoms of depression. He was discharged from the PTSD treatment team for follow-up with his primary care physician.

Mr. Jones was also seen by the PTSD treatment team psychiatrist. At the time of his intake, he was started on a selective serotonin reuptake inhibitor (SSRI) antidepressant (citalopram 20 mg) and trazodone (100 mg) as needed to promote sleep. Over the course of his treatment, his dose of citalopram was increased to 40 mg daily to address his symptoms of depression, and his trazodone dose was increased to 150 mg at bedtime. He was discharged from the program on this stable regimen of medications.

This case represents a fairly typical treatment course for an Iraq veteran with PTSD and depression. In this chapter, we summarize the literature on treatments for PTSD, both psychotherapy and pharmacotherapy, as well as combined treatment. Although the intent is to cover the treatment of Operation Enduring Freedom (OEF) and OIF service members, no randomized controlled trials have been completed on this most recent group of PTSD sufferers. Therefore, we review the treatments for PTSD in general and then discuss some clinical characteristics specific to this population.

The experiences of OEF and OIF veterans with PTSD show both similarities to and differences from those of Vietnam veterans with PTSD. For example, both groups were involved in guerilla warfare in unfamiliar environments with an enemy that was difficult to distinguish from the general population.

Both groups found themselves in situations requiring constant vigilance. Both groups experienced problems at home and in the workplace upon return, often due to anger issues, hyperarousal, avoidance symptoms, and substance abuse.

Service members in the war in Iraq, which involves acts of terrorism by civilians, have been required to sustain an unprecedented level of vigilance, resulting in no safe place (Litz, 2005). Stressful ground warfare, extended deployments, the stop-loss policy, and uncertainty regarding discharge and leave have been additional factors affecting soldiers (Bilmes, 2007). The survival rate following serious injury is higher for OEF and OIF service members because of the protective body gear and the efficient and effective medical evacuation capability of the contemporary armed forces (Bilmes, 2007). Survival of serious wounds, however, often means living with debilitating physical injuries such as burns, amputations, blindness, and major head injuries. These types of injuries are a risk factor for severe and persistent psychiatric problems (Hoge, Auchterlonie, & Milliken, 2006).

Because PTSD had not been recognized as an official psychiatric disorder by the end of the Vietnam War, there were no routine assessments or recommended treatments for this disorder. In contrast, the U.S. Departments of Defense (DoD) and Veterans Affairs (VA) have instituted systematic and comprehensive screening protocols for PTSD, traumatic brain injury (TBI), depression, and substance abuse to provide OEF and OIF veterans evidence-based treatments as soon as possible. There are now several published treatment guidelines for PTSD, including those from the International Society for Traumatic Stress Studies (Foa, Keane, Friedman, & Cohen, 2009), the United Kingdom's National Institute for Clinical Excellence (2005), VA and DoD (2003), American Psychiatric Association (APA, 2004), Australian Centre for Posttraumatic Mental Health (2007), and a literature review, the Institute of Medicine (2008) report.

In the pages that follow, we review the literature on these interventions, including representative studies only if the literature base is large. For a comprehensive review of almost all empirically supported treatments for PTSD, the reader is referred to Foa et al. (2009).

PSYCHOTHERAPY FOR PTSD

Even though the nature of PTSD includes prominent avoidance, most professional and laypeople agree with and understand the need to talk about what happened. Psychotherapy is often a natural and understandable choice in the process of working on PTSD. Psychotherapeutic interventions for PTSD include a number of diverse approaches ranging from the interpersonal and dynamic approaches to cognitive and cognitive–behavioral approaches.

CBT includes exposure therapy

Cognitive–behavior therapy (CBT), a set of techniques that are directive, problem-focused, and delivered short term, is the psychotherapy approach with the most empirical support for its effectiveness. All of the treatment guidelines for PTSD recommend CBT for PTSD. The CBT technique with the most evidence for its efficacy (24 randomized trials and nine nonrandomized studies) is exposure therapy, in which patients are aided in confronting the trauma-related memories and cues in a therapeutic manner (Cahill, Rothbaum, Resick, & Follette, 2009). In addition, cognitive therapy is recommended as a CBT treatment for PTSD; it provides tools for patients to correct the erroneous cognitions that perpetuate distressing PTSD symptoms. Eye movement desensitization and reprocessing (EMDR; Shapiro, 1995) is recommended in most guidelines. In general, CBT results in average symptom improvements ranging from 25% to 75%, with a much smaller percentage of patients in remission and treatment gains generally maintained at follow-ups of 6 and 12 months posttreatment.

Cognitive–Behavior Therapy

Exposure Therapy

As illustrated in the preceding case illustration, a CBT-based treatment typically involves several types of interventions, including psychological education about PTSD (e.g., presentation of a learning model of the development of PTSD symptoms) and stress management skills (e.g., relaxation and breathing skills). In addition to these treatment elements, CBT for veterans with PTSD often incorporates exposure to fear–avoidance, inducing trauma-related cues including trauma-related memories, environments (e.g., crowds, traffic), and internal physical sensations (e.g., heart racing). In imaginal exposure, the memory of the trauma is repeatedly focused on in a therapeutic environment. In vivo exposure entails confronting feared yet safe situations in natural settings. Interoceptive exposure involves confronting feared bodily symptoms often associated with PTSD, such as an increased heart rate and shortness of breath. Although all three of these exposure interventions were used in the case study presented, in the delivery of treatment to veterans with PTSD, the most commonly delivered exposure-based therapy, prolonged exposure (PE), combines imaginal exposure and in vivo exposure.

Well-controlled studies in the literature examining the efficacy of PE have found that 60% to 95% of participants who received PE no longer met criteria for PTSD following treatment (Foa, Rothbaum, & Furr, 2003). Schnurr et al. (2007) conducted a large multisite randomized clinical trial (RCT) of PE versus present-centered therapy in the treatment of female veterans and active-duty personnel with chronic PTSD (68% reported index trauma as military sexual trauma). Those in the PE condition evidenced greater

Boudewyns
& Hyer

reduction in symptoms at posttreatment and at 3-month follow-up and were less likely to meet the diagnostic criteria for PTSD; however, there were no significant differences between conditions at 6-month follow-up. Studies have also found other variants of exposure therapy effective. Bryant, Moulds, Guthrie, Dang, and Nixon (2003) investigated PE, the combination of cognitive restructuring (CR) and PE, and supportive counseling (SC), in the treatment of 58 male and female civilian survivors of trauma with chronic PTSD. Those in the PE and the CR/PE conditions showed greater improvement than those in the SC condition, with evidence of greater symptom reduction in the combined condition.

Rothbaum, Hodges, Ready, Graap, and Alarcon (2001) conducted an open clinical trial using another form of exposure, virtual reality exposure (VRE), to treat a small sample of Vietnam combat veterans with PTSD. Participants wore a head-mounted display to view the virtual environments, which included a Huey helicopter and a clearing surrounded by jungle. PTSD symptoms were significantly reduced from baseline to 6-month follow-up. More recent clinical trials using VRE to treat OIF veterans with PTSD using virtual Iraq Humvee and city environments are ongoing. In a case study (Gerardi et al., 2008), a reservist's PTSD symptoms were reduced by 56%. VRE has been successfully used to treat PTSD in firefighters, disaster relief workers, and civilians following the World Trade Center attacks of September 11, 2001 (Difede et al., 2007).

Cognitive Therapy

Cognitive therapies are based on the theory that the meanings that we impose on events contribute to emotional states, and therefore changing how we think about them is the goal of therapy. The cognitive model of PTSD proposed by Ehlers and Clark (2000) addresses the processing of trauma, including negative appraisals of the event or sequelae that lead to a perception of serious, current threat. Cognitive processing therapy (CPT) is a particular form of cognitive therapy with an exposure component in which individuals are taught to challenge faulty assumptions and self-statements and to modify maladaptive thoughts and overgeneralized beliefs in the areas of safety, trust, power and control, esteem, and intimacy. CPT includes an exposure component consisting of a written narrative of the trauma that is read during sessions and at home. CPT has been found effective in the treatment of PTSD in female sexual assault victims (Resick et. al., 2002) and in male and female veterans with chronic PTSD (Monson et al., 2006).

In a dismantling study of CPT, the full protocol was compared with its components, cognitive therapy and written accounts in 150 adult women with PTSD. Each treatment was delivered for 6 weeks, with 2 hr of therapy per week. Patients in all three conditions improved substantially and equivalently on PTSD and related measures (Resick et al., 2008). Although the authors caution against extrapolating from these initial results, these data raise the possibility that patients may benefit from the cognitive component of CPT as a stand-alone intervention. Consistent with this concept and relevant to the treatment of combat veterans, within the Veterans Health Administration, the current training and treatment materials for CPT therapists include an option for the delivery of CPT-C that omits the written trauma account and includes more practice of cognitive techniques.

Other CBT Approaches

Stress inoculation training (SIT; Kilpatrick, Veronen, & Resick, 1982) focuses on managing anxiety that is conditioned at the time of the trauma and generalizes to other situations. Strategies usually include education, muscle relaxation training, breathing retraining, role playing, covert modeling, guided self-dialogue, thought stopping, and sometimes graduated in vivo exposure. SIT received support in studies of female sexual assault victims with PTSD (e.g., Foa et al., 1999) and for anger management in male veterans with PTSD (Chemtob, Novaco, Hamada, & Gross, 1997). A staged approach to therapy with adult female survivors of childhood physical and sexual abuse was found to be successful compared with a wait-list control condition (Cloitre, Koenen, Cohen, & Han, 2002). The two-phase treatment condition involved eight weekly individual sessions including dialectical behavior therapy–based affect and interpersonal regulation skills, followed by eight twice-weekly sessions of PE. CBT treatment programs for PTSD have been delivered via the Internet (Lange et al., 2001) to increase access to treatment.

Eye Movement Desensitization and Reprocessing

EMDR involves identification of distressing trauma memory images, related negative cognitions, and alternative positive cognitions. The patient is asked to hold the image in mind along with the negative cognition and associated bodily sensations while tracking the therapist's fingers across the field of vision (saccadic eye movements). EMDR is suggested to facilitate incomplete information processing related to the trauma and may function as another form of exposure. Recent comparisons indicate that EMDR and PE are roughly equivalent in effectiveness (Spates, Koch, Cusack, Pagoto, & Waller, 2009). For example, Rothbaum, Astin, and Marsteller (2005) evaluated the efficacy of PE and EMDR compared with wait-list control in adult female rape victims with PTSD. Results indicated that both PE and EMDR led to clinically and statistically significant improvements at posttreatment compared with the control condition. The research on EMDR suggests that the effects of EMDR may be present even without the specific use of eye movements or other forms of alternating stimulation (Spates, Koch, Cusack, Pagoto, & Waller, 2009).

Other Types of Psychotherapy

Other therapies commonly used in the treatment of PTSD include group therapy, psychodynamic therapy, and hypnosis (see Foa et al., 2009). Group therapy is a widely used component of treatment and can be cognitive–behavioral, interpersonal, or insight-oriented in focus. Although the numbers of studies on group treatment of PTSD have increased since the late 1990s, few well-powered studies using randomization and adequate control conditions exist. The most well-powered, randomized study of group interventions for PTSD (Schnurr et al., 2003) found that although there were statistically significant improvements in both the exposure and present-centered therapy groups, these improvements were small. Despite the lack of research, group psychotherapy remains a common intervention for combat veterans (Shea, McDevitt-Murphy, Ready, & Schnurr, 2009). One reason for this may be that groups are assumed to be more efficient than delivering similar treatments in individual therapy, particularly in regard to psychoeducational or skills-based interventions for PTSD. It is often suggested that, compared with individual therapy, group interventions for PTSD serve to decrease isolation and may allow for reestablishment of connection and trust with others (Shea et al., 2009). However, few extant data directly compare the efficiency or effectiveness of group to individual psychotherapy for PTSD, leaving this assumption untested.

Psychodynamic therapy for PTSD focuses on improving ego strength and capacity for interpersonal relatedness. The use of psychodynamic therapy in the treatment of PTSD is lacking empirical evidence of efficacy other than the one small study conducted by Brom, Kleber, and Defares (1989) more than 20 years ago. Similarly, there is limited empirical evidence for the efficacy of hypnosis in the treatment of PTSD, although many case studies exist, along with a long history of use in treating trauma-related conditions.

Summary

The current body of research points to CBT approaches as first-line psychotherapy for PTSD. The case report presented at the beginning of the chapter incorporates a number of the psychotherapeutic approaches consistent with the research reviewed in this chapter. The treatment included the use of psychoeducation about PTSD, instruction in breathing and relaxation, and education on self-monitoring of subjective levels of distress. It also included interceptive, in vivo, and imaginal exposure. Importantly, as in all evidence-based approaches to treatment, Mr. Jones's symptoms were evaluated continuously across the course of psychotherapy. This allowed the therapist to determine that Mr. Jones, despite experiencing reduced PTSD intrusion, avoidance, and hyperarousal symptoms following the treatment with exposure therapy, continued to report symptoms of depression and ongoing interpersonal problems. The therapist was then able to incorporate other evidence-based approaches into treatment that targeted these symptoms. If, before his treatment, Mr. Jones had presented with high levels of current suicidal ideation, ongoing thoughts to harms others, or other significant problems in affective regulation not focally related to core PTSD symptoms, then one approach to treatment might have been to spend more time in the initial phases of treatment focused on affect and interpersonal regulation skills. However, if Mr. Jones's symptoms had included higher levels of trauma-related problematic cognitions (e.g., self-blame, guilt, safety–danger, damaged beliefs about self and others), then inclusion of more cognitively oriented approaches to PTSD treatment (e.g., CPT) might have been indicated.

PHARMACOTHERAPY FOR PTSD

Medication remains a major clinical option to treat PTSD for a number of reasons. First, it is effective. As we indicate in the review that follows, the majority of patients treated with pharmacotherapy achieve a clinically meaningful reduction in symptoms, approximately 30% remit with medication alone, and few studies have assessed patients on medication longer than 6 months. Second, medication is useful for treating the comorbid depression and anxiety disorders that often accompany PTSD. Third, medication is generally acceptable to patients, especially those receiving integrated primary–behavioral care in primary care settings. However, there are some exceptions to this, and recent evidence suggests that female rape victims with PTSD more often prefer psychotherapy to pharmacotherapy (Feeny, Zoellner, Mavissakalian, & Roy-Byrne, 2009). Finally, medications are more easily obtained than CBT because there are so many more prescribing clinicians than qualified CBT psychotherapists. Indeed, one study found that in VA settings, only 10% to 20% of practicing psychotherapists were qualified to provide evidence-based CBT treatment (Rosen et al., 2004); however, this number will be increasing because the VA is making systematic efforts to train therapists in evidence-based CBT for PTSD.

In this review, we consider all the major classes of medication that have been investigated in clinical trials with PTSD patients. The greatest emphasis is placed on results from RCTs.

Antidepressants

Selective Serotonin Reuptake Inhibitors

The only medications to receive a Food and Drug Administration (FDA) indication for PTSD, sertraline and paroxetine, are both SSRIs (Brady et al., 2000; Davidson, Rothbaum, et al., 2001; Marshall, Beebe, Oldham, & Zaninelli, 2001; Tucker et al., 2001). Following 12 weeks of treatment with both sertraline and paroxetine, complete remission was observed in approximately 30% of patients across a number of placebo-controlled acute phase trials. SSRIs reduce PTSD reexperiencing, avoidance and numbing, and hyperarousal symptoms and also appear to promote improvement in quality of life that is sustained during treatment. When treatment was extended for another 24 weeks, 55% of those who were not classified as responders at 12 weeks exhibited complete remission; therefore, approximately two thirds of all participants had a clinically significant response at 36 weeks. This result raised an interesting question about what should be considered an adequate trial of medication for PTSD (Londborg et al., 2001). As with pharmacotherapy for most psychiatric disorders, continued treatment is required for maintenance of treatment effects (Davidson, Pearlstein, et al., 2001; Martenyi, Brown, Zhang, Koke, et al., 2002).

The negative findings of pharmacotherapy with male Vietnam combat veterans in VA Medical Centers and the analyses indicating that SSRIs might not be as effective for men as women have led some to conclude that PTSD due to combat trauma is less responsive to pharmacotherapy than is PTSD in civilians (Friedman et al., 2007; Friedman & Davidson, 2007). However, this no longer appears to be the correct conclusion. In the paroxetine studies (Marshall et al., 2001; Tucker et al., 2001), veterans who had been recruited from the general population (rather than from the VA) benefitted as much from SSRI treatment as did male and female civilians. The RCT with fluoxetine (Martenyi, Brown, Zhang, Prakash, et al., 2002) recruited mostly male veterans of recent (United Nations and NATO) deployments and reported positive results. Exposure to combat trauma actually predicted a successful response to fluoxetine. It may be true that male Vietnam veterans in VA settings with chronic and severe PTSD constitute a particularly challenging clinical cohort that is less likely to benefit from any intervention than other veterans or trauma survivors (Friedman, 1997; Friedman et al., 2007; Schnurr et al., 2003). However, there is no conclusive evidence suggesting that SSRIs are not effective for combat-related PTSD.

Newer Antidepressants

Two large multicenter RCTs of long-acting venlafaxine XR, a selective serotonin-norepinephrine reuptake inhibitor (SNRI), demonstrated efficacy relative to placebo, in both 12-week (Davidson, Rothbaum, et al., 2006) and 6-month trials (Davidson, Baldwin, et al., 2006). Interestingly, patients receiving venlafaxine had significantly more resilience than those receiving placebo (Davidson et al., 2008). A number of patients in the 6-month trial did not achieve remission until they had received several months of treatment, similar to the patients in the sertraline trial mentioned previously (Londborg et al, 2001). Mirtazapine, a tetracyclic antidepressant, was significantly more effective than placebo in one RCT (Davidson et al., 2003), as well as in an open-label 8-week trial in Korea (Bahk et al., 2002). Mirtazapine reduced nightmares among 300 refugees who had previously failed to benefit from other medications (Lewis, 2002). Although nefazodone has been shown to be as effective as sertraline for treating PTSD (Saygin, Sungur, Sabol, & Cetinkaya, 2002) nongeneric nefazodone (Serzone) has been withdrawn from the U.S. market because of liver toxicity. Trazodone, which has similar pharmacological actions as nefazodone, is not an effective treatment for PTSD. It has clinical utility, however, used in conjunction with SSRIs to treat insomnia because of its sedating effects and synergistic serotoninergic action. Finally, a recent RCT reported negative results with bupropion for PTSD (Becker et al., 2007).

Older Antidepressants

Tricyclic antidepressants (TCAs) and monoamine oxidase inhibitors (MAOIs) appear to be as effective as SSRIs in their antidepressant effects, but they have more complicated side effect profiles than SSRIs. There have been no RCTs with TCAs since 1990 despite positive findings with imipramine (Kosten, Frank, Dan, McDougle, & Giller, 1991) and amitriptyline (Davidson et al., 1990) but not desipramine (Reist et al., 1989). The only recent TCA study was an interesting prospective RCT showing that children and adolescents hospitalized with severe burn injuries who were treated with imipramine developed significantly lower rates of acute stress disorder than those treated with chloral hydrate (Robert, Blakeney, Villarreal, Rosenberg, & Meyer, 1999). The MAOI phenelzine was extremely successful (and more effective than imipramine) in reducing reexperiencing and arousal PTSD symptoms in Vietnam combat veterans (Kosten et al., 1991). Results have been mixed in other trials (see Friedman & Davidson, 2007).

Antiadrenergic Agents

Despite an early favorable clinical report on the efficacy of both propranolol and clonidine 25 years ago (Kolb, Burris, & Griffiths, 1984), there are few controlled studies with antiadrenergic agents. The most data exist for the postsynaptic alpha-1 antagonist prazosin for reducing nightmares. Findings on its efficacy in reducing other PTSD symptoms have been inconsistent.

Given prazosin's relatively short half-life, the inconsistency may have occurred because the medication was only prescribed once a day rather than in divided doses, (Raskind et al., 2003, 2007). A large-scale multisite trial using divided doses is currently in progress. There have been two favorable reports regarding the alpha-2 adrenergic agonists, clonidine and guanfacine (Kinzie & Friedman, 2004; Kolb et al., 1984). In recent RCTs with older veterans receiving VA care, however, guanfacine was no better than placebo in reducing PTSD severity (Neylan et al., 2006).

The beta-adrenergic antagonist propranolol was associated with beneficial effects on PTSD symptoms including intrusive recollections and reactivity to traumatic stimuli in two small early clinical trials (Famularo, Kinscherff, & Fenton, 1988; Kolb et al., 1984). With regard to prevention, in small single-site studies, acutely traumatized patients who received a brief 10-day course of propranolol beginning in the emergency room exhibited reduced physiological hyperreactivity at 1 and 3 months posttrauma, although it was not associated with a reduced incidence of PTSD (Pitman et al., 2002; Vaiva et al., 2003).

Other Medications

The current evidence is not strong favoring the use of anticonvulsants and mood stabilizers for PTSD, despite their great theoretical interest. Three recent RCTs with tiagabine, valproate, and topiramate reported negative results (Davidson, Brady, Melman, Stein, & Pollack, 2007; Davis et al., 2008; Tucker et al., 2007). There is no evidence that benzodiazepines ameliorate core PTSD symptoms, and in fact they may be contraindicated. Alprazolam did not reduce reexperiencing or avoidance–numbing symptoms in an RCT, although it did lead to improvement in insomnia and generalized anxiety (Braun, Greenberg, Dasberg, & Lerer, 1990). Treatment of recently traumatized emergency room patients with clonazepam (Gelpin, Bonne, Peri, Brandes, & Shalev, 1996) or the hypnotic benzodiazepine temazepam (Mellman, Bustamante, David, & Fins, 2002) did not prevent the later development of PTSD. Other open-label trials with benzodiazepines have also been unsuccessful. There is a small but growing literature yielding favorable results with the atypical antipsychotic agents risperidone, olanzapine, and quetiapine when added as adjunctive agents to augment SSRI effects, especially with treatment-resistant patient groups such as older, chronic American military veterans receiving treatment at VA Medical Centers (see Friedman, Davidson, & Stein, 2009).

Summary

The strongest evidence favors the use of SSRIs and venlafaxine. There is good evidence for mirtazepine, promising findings with prazosin, and positive results with TCAs and MAOIs. Adjunctive pharmacotherapy with atypical antipsychotic agents (e.g., risperidone, olanzapine, quetiapine) appears to be an effective strategy for SSRI partial and nonresponders. With the notable exception of prazosin, there is little evidence supporting the use of antiadrenergic agents. Findings with anticonvulsive agents have been mostly negative. Despite their widespread use, benzodiazepines may not only be ineffective but contraindicated for PTSD patients receiving CBT treatment (especially PE).

In the case report, pharmacotherapy was rather straightforward and successful. Mr. Jones received an SSRI (citalopram) augmented by trazodone for insomnia. This is an appropriate approach given the evidence reviewed previously. What steps might have been necessary had the outcome been less favorable? Venlafaxine would have been a good second choice, given its proven efficacy and wider pharmacological spectrum of action. If Mr. Jones complained of side effects that threatened compliance with either medication, mirtazapine might have been a good third choice. Because Mr. Jones met diagnostic criteria for both PTSD and depression, it made sense to prescribe an antidepressant that is also effective in PTSD. If, however, Mr. Jones had not responded to any of these antidepressants, or complained about side effects, prazosin would have been a good medication to try. Sleep difficulty marked by vivid nightmares might have suggested a trial of prazosin. Prominent PTSD hyperarousal symptoms might also have been an indication to prescribe prazosin. Finally, if Mr. Jones became "stuck" in his improvement, with a partial reduction of symptoms that had not progressed after months of citalopram treatment, it would have been appropriate to add an atypical antipsychotic agent, such as risperidone, to the SSRI as an adjunctive agent.

COMBINED PSYCHOTHERAPY AND PHARMACOTHERAPY

There are no studies evaluating the combined versus individual effects of pharmacotherapy and psychotherapy for PTSD as there are for other mood and anxiety disorders. The clinical reality is that the majority of active-duty military personnel referred for treatment of PTSD, as well as veterans from conflicts other than OEF and OIF (and civilians) with PTSD, end up being treated with both psychotherapy and pharmacotherapy. The research reality is that most psychotherapy trials include patients on medication, and the effect of medications on response to psychotherapy has been examined in only one psychotherapy trial (Schnurr et al., 2007). As an example, the authors are currently conducting an ongoing study combining medication with virtual-reality exposure therapy for Iraq veterans with PTSD. Of the first 40 patients recruited to date, 30 are currently taking psychoactive medication. Only six of these 40 patients were receiving sertraline or paroxetine, the only medications approved by the FDA for treating PTSD, and five of these six were also receiving additional medications. The other 24 patients were receiving off-label medications for PTSD.

There are several strategies for combining pharmacotherapy and psychotherapy, with challenges and advantages to each (Rothbaum, 2008), but the extant data on this issue are not adequate to determine whether there are additive or interactive effects (or both) of simultaneously administered pharmacotherapy and psychotherapy for PTSD. Given that the current literature does not suggest any advantage to combining medications with CBT for any anxiety disorder (Gerardi, Ressler, & Rothbaum, 2010), if one begins treatment with CBT, it might make sense to wait to begin pharmacotherapy for PTSD. Thus, in cases for which PTSD is the only or primary disorder being treated, it may be more appropriate to combine these approaches sequentially. It should be noted, however, that PTSD in combat veterans often presents with a number of psychiatric comorbidities, including major depression and suicidal ideation, and appropriate treatment is likely to be dependent on the overall clinical presentation and psychiatric comorbidity. For those patients who have not been treated with an adequate and appropriate doses of CBT for PTSD and who express no strong preference, we recommend starting with CBT. If the antidepressant is the first treatment, we recommend having it on board at least 4 weeks before commencing with psychotherapy. Patients who achieve complete remission from medication will need no additional treatment, whereas those with a partial response will probably benefit when CBT is added to pharmacotherapy, as in the Rothbaum et al. (2006) trial, described next, for PTSD.

The first published RCT of combined treatment for PTSD augmented sertraline with PE (Rothbaum et al., 2006). In that trial, 88 male and female outpatients with PTSD were treated with open-label sertraline (up to 200 mg) and then were randomly assigned to receive continuation with sertraline alone or augmentation with PE (10 twice weekly sessions of 90–120 min). PE included psychoeducation about trauma reactions, breathing exercises, in vivo exposure, prolonged imaginal exposure, and homework that involved listening to a tape of the imaginal exposure recorded in session (Foa, Hembree, & Rothbaum, 2007). Five additional weeks of treatment with sertraline alone did not result in further improvement on measures of PTSD severity, depression, or general anxiety. However, augmentation with PE resulted in further reduction of PTSD severity only among partial responders to medication. In a recently published trial with almost a mirror design to the Rothbaum et al. (2006) study (Simon et al., 2008), participants first received eight sessions of PE over 4 to 6 weeks and then were randomly assigned to receive paroxetine CR plus five additional sessions of PE or placebo plus five additional sessions of PE. The largest reductions of PTSD symptoms occurred following PE, with no significant differences between placebo and paroxetine in the augmentation phase.

D-cycloserine (DCS) is an N-methyl-D-aspartate partial agonist that has been found to facilitate the extinction of fear. DCS by itself has no beneficial effect on PTSD. However, several ongoing investigations are evaluating the use of DCS to enhance exposure therapy for PTSD. On the basis of animal research showing that DCS facilitates extinction of conditioned fear, it was hypothesized that DCS would facilitate exposure therapy, thereby reducing the number of sessions required for the same effect compared with exposure therapy alone (Ressler et al., 2004). Furthermore, clinical trials using exposure therapy for acrophobia (fear of heights; Ressler et al., 2004), social phobia (Guastella et al., 2008; Hofmann et al., 2006), and panic disorder (Tolin et al., 2007) have shown that fewer sessions of exposure therapy were needed when DCS was administered 1 hr before each psychotherapy session. Research currently in progress will determine whether DCS will also accelerate PTSD treatment with virtual-reality exposure therapy.

The use of DCS to facilitate CBT represents a paradigm shift in psychiatry and psychology. This is a remarkably new approach to combining psychotherapy and pharmacotherapy in that pharmacotherapy is only prescribed to facilitate the learning that takes place during CBT (specifically, exposure-based therapy) and not because of any direct actions on the symptoms of PTSD (or other anxiety disorders). In contrast, studies that combined "traditional" psychiatric medications (i.e., antidepressants, benzodiazepines) with CBT for anxiety disorders have not shown any benefit from adding medication to CBT (Rothbaum, 2008).

TREATMENT ISSUES TO CONSIDER IN OEF AND OIF SERVICE MEMBERS

There is little published on the treatment of active duty OEF and OIF military personnel. The Virtual Iraq open clinical trial with naval service members is one of the few completed trials, although it is not yet published. In the ongoing Virtual Iraq plus DCS study described earlier, most participants are veterans who have separated from active duty in the military and have been home from Iraq for approximately 2 or more years, although we have also included some reservists and National Guardsmen. Almost all are on medications (usually SSRIs and some atypical antipsychotics). In addition, many meet criteria for past substance use disorders.

Regarding choice of psychotherapy technique, we recommend only the empirically supported CBT techniques. Within these techniques, if a patient presents with a preference and that treatment can be provided, we recommend administering the patient's preferred treatment. Otherwise, we allow for full informed consent and present several efficacious treatment options, including exposure therapy, cognitive therapy, or EMDR. Again, unless there is a strong rationale for one treatment being indicated over another, we allow patient preference to determine the treatment. If the patient presents with extreme fear and avoidance, an exposure technique will likely be recommended. If both are available, the choice between virtual reality exposure and imaginal exposure will be based on patient preference. If imaginal exposure is attempted and the patient is avoidant and difficult to engage, we recommend adding virtual reality because its evocative nature renders it a potent exposure that is hard for patients to avoid. If the patient presents with extreme guilt and trust issues, we recommend cognitive therapy.

Here we offer some anecdotal observations regarding OEF and OIF patients receiving PE using virtual reality exposure, but many of our observations apply to other therapeutic techniques and other PTSD patients. We instruct them during exposure to have a "foot there and a foot here" to be able to "put the whole memory together," including emotions and details. The treatment goal to increase control over traumatic memories, so that they do not intrude at unpredictable times, is usually well received. Following the exposure portion of each therapy session, the patients remove their head-mounted display, and then we process (Foa, Hembree, & Rothbaum, 2007) the material that emerged in the exposure. Some of the common themes we have observed are that veterans say they "didn't fit there; don't fit here," implying they do not fit anywhere now. There is usually a lack of connection between their emotions and the memories, so that these veterans present as emotionally numb. They can describe the most horrific incidents with flat affect. They may be embarrassed, considering it a personal failure or weakness that they are experiencing their current symptoms and difficulties. Sometimes they express anger or disappointment with commanding officers. They may wonder why some service members are held accountable for adverse outcomes and not others.

We aim for acceptance, to help them come to terms with what happened in the war zone, to forgive themselves, and move on with life. Often we will ask them to think in terms of "What would you tell your son, daughter, brother, or sister?" to help them gain a different perspective on their actions during the heat of battle. We do not placate and do not absolve them of their responsibility for their behavior. Instead, we help them to identify and accept what was their responsibility and what was the responsibility of others. Often, we find it is most difficult for them to let go when someone died. Through it all, we try to help them make sense of a senseless situation and to integrate these new perspectives into their traumatic memories in a way that does not cause so much intense pain. These are some of the same themes addressed in CPT, indicating that they are common PTSD issues with just the specifics related to the war in Iraq or Afghanistan.

The goals for therapy, in addition to reducing PTSD and associated depression and substance use, include reducing violence and isolation. We aim to increase meaningful social connections, increase activities, and improve sleep. Finally, we often explicitly work with veterans to have them move their weapons to less accessible locations (e.g., out of their cars and bedside tables and from under their pillows) to decrease the chances of injury during impulsive rage and hypervigilant startle reactions.

SUMMARY

Regarding psychotherapy, the strongest evidence exists for the cognitive–behavioral therapies, and within those, for exposure therapies such as PE and cognitive therapies such as CPT. Regarding pharmacotherapy, SSRIs and newer selective serotonin-norepinephrine reuptake inhibitors have the strongest evidence for the treatment of PTSD, but promising results have been obtained with prazosin, other antidepressants, and augmentation of SSRIs with atypical antipsychotics. Preliminary trials show some promise with propranolol, hydrocortisone, and imipramine for preventing the later development of PTSD. Combined approaches using SSRIs generally do not show any additional benefit of adding medication over the benefits of exposure therapy, although adding exposure therapy to those who have not shown a full response to medication does appear helpful. Novel approaches using rational pharmacotherapy—specifically, the augmentation of exposure therapy with DCS—are promising, although we must wait for the conclusion of current trials.

We hope that we may avoid many of the problems with PTSD chronicity that we see in veterans of prior wars and combat zones by identifying and treating returning military personnel as early as possible. We advocate routine screening when troops return stateside and provision of empirically supported treatments as soon as PTSD is identified. Through these efforts, we hope to treat our wounded warriors effectively and return them to society as healthy productive veterans, to whom we all owe a debt of gratitude.

REFERENCES

American Psychiatric Association. (2004). *Practice guideline for the treatment of patients with acute stress disorder and posttraumatic stress disorder.* Arlington, VA: Author.

Australian Centre for Posttraumatic Mental Health. (2007). *Australian guidelines for the treatment of adults with acute stress disorder and posttraumatic stress disorder.* Melbourne, Australia: Author.

Bahk, W.-M., Pae, C.-U., Tsoh, J., Chae, J.-H., Jun, T.-Y., Lee, C., & Kim, K. S. (2002). Effects of mirtazapine in patients with post-traumatic stress disorder in Korea: A pilot study. *Human Psychopharmacology, 17*, 341–344. doi:10.1002/hup.426

Beck, A., Steer, R., & Brown, G. (1996). *Beck Depression Inventory manual* (2nd ed.). San Antonio, TX: The Psychological Association.

Becker, M. E., Hertzberg, M. A., Moore, S. D., Dennis, M. F., Bukenya, D. S., & Beckham, J. C. (2007). A placebo-controlled trial of bupropion SR in the treatment of chronic posttraumatic stress disorder. *Journal of Clinical Psychopharmacology, 27*, 193–197. doi:10.1097/JCP.0b013e318032eaed

Bilmes, L. (2007, January). *Soldiers returning from Iraq and Afghanistan: The long term costs of providing veterans medical care and disability benefits* (KSG Faculty Research Working Paper Series RWP07-001). Paper presented at the Allied Social Sciences Meetings, Chicago, IL.

Brady, K., Pearlstein, T., Asnis, G. M., Baker, D., Rothbaum, B., Sikes, C. R., & Farfel, G. M. (2000). Efficacy and safety of sertraline treatment of posttraumatic stress disorder. *JAMA, 283*, 1837–1844. doi:10.1001/jama.283.14.1837

Braun, P., Greenberg, D., Dasberg, H., & Lerer, B. (1990). Core symptoms of posttraumatic stress disorder unimproved by alprazolam treatment. *The Journal of Clinical Psychiatry, 51*, 236–238.

Brom, D., Kleber, R. J., & Defares, P. B. (1989). Brief psychotherapy for posttraumatic stress disorders. *Journal of Consulting and Clinical Psychology, 57*, 607–612. doi:10.1037/0022-006X.57.5.607

Bryant, R. A., Moulds, M. L., Guthrie, R. M., Dang, S. T., & Nixon, R. D. V. (2003). Imaginal exposure alone and imaginal exposure with cognitive restructuring in treatment of posttraumatic stress disorder. *Journal of Consulting and Clinical Psychology, 71*, 706–712. doi:10.1037/0022-006X.71.4.706

Butterfield, M. I., Becker, M. E., Connor, K. M., Sutherland, S. M., Churchill, L. E., & Davidson, J. R. T. (2001). Olanzapine in the treatment of post-traumatic stress disorder: A pilot study. *International Clinical Psychopharmacology, 16*, 197–203. doi:10.1097/00004850-200107000-00003

Cahill, S., Rothbaum, B., Resick, P., & Follette, V. (2009). Cognitive-behavioral therapy for adults. In E. B. Foa, T. M. Keane, M. J. Friedman, & J. A. Cohen (Eds.), *Effective treatments for PTSD: Practice guidelines from the International Society for Traumatic Stress Studies* (2nd ed., pp. 139–222). New York, NY: Guilford Press.

Chemtob, C. M., Novaco, R. W., Hamada, R. S., & Gross, D. M. (1997). Cognitive–behavioral treatment of severe anger in posttraumatic stress disorder. *Journal of Consulting and Clinical Psychology, 65*, 184–189. doi:10.1037/0022-006X.65.1.184

Cloitre, M., Koenen, K. C., Cohen, L. R., & Han, H. (2002). Skills training in affective and interpersonal regulation followed by exposure: A phase-based treatment for PTSD related to childhood abuse. *Journal of Consulting and Clinical Psychology, 70*, 1067–1074. doi:10.1037/0022-006X.70.5.1067

Davidson, J., Baldwin, D. S., Stein, D. J., Kuper, E., Benattia, I., Ahmed, S., . . . Musgnung, M. T. (2006). Treatment of posttraumatic stress disorder with venlafaxine extended release: A 6-month randomized, controlled trial. *Archives of General Psychiatry, 63*, 1158–1165. doi:10.1001/archpsyc.63.10.1158

Davidson, J., Brady, K. T., Mellman, T. A., Stein, M. B., & Pollack, M. H. (2007). The efficacy and tolerability of tiagabine in adult patients with posttraumatic stress disorder. *Journal of Clinical Psychopharmacology, 27*, 85–88.

Davidson, J., Kudler, H., Smith, R., Mahorney, S. L., Lipper, S., Hammett, E. B., . . . Cavenar, J. O., Jr. (1990). Treatment of post-traumatic stress disorder with amitriptyline and placebo. *Archives of General Psychiatry, 47*, 259–266.

Davidson, J., Pearlstein, T., Londborg, P., Brady, K. T., Rothbaum, B., Bell, J., . . . Farfel, G. (2001). Efficacy of sertraline in preventing relapse of posttraumatic stress disorder: Results of a 28-week double-blind, placebo-controlled study. *The American Journal of Psychiatry, 158*, 1974–1981. doi:10.1176/appi.ajp. 158.12.1974

Davidson, J., Pedersen, R., Allgulander, C., Musgnung, J., Ahmed, S., & Rothbaum, B. O. (2008). Effects of venlafaxine ER on resilience in PTSD: An item analysis of the Connor–Davidson Resilience Scale (CD–RISC). *International Clinical Psychopharmacology, 23*, 299–303. doi:10.1097/YIC.0b013e32830c202d

Davidson, J., Rothbaum, B. O., Tucker, P., Asnis, G., Benattia, I., & Musgnung, J. (2006). Venlafaxine extended release in posttraumatic stress disorder: A sertraline-and placebo-controlled study. *Journal of Clinical Psychopharmacology, 26*, 259–267; corrected in *Journal of Clinical Psychopharmacology* (2006), *26*, 473 (note: dosage error in article text). doi:10.1097/01.jcp.0000222514.71390.c1

Davidson, J., Rothbaum, B. O., van der Kolk, B. A., Sikes, C. R., & Farfel, G. M. (2001). Multicenter, double-blind comparison of sertraline and placebo in the treatment of posttraumatic stress disorder. *Archives of General Psychiatry, 58*, 485–492. doi:10.1001/archpsyc.58.5.485

Davidson, J., Weisler, R. H., Butterfield, M. I., Casat, C. D., Connor, K. M., Barnett, S., & van Meter, S. (2003). Mirtazapine vs. placebo in posttraumatic stress disorder: A pilot trial. *Biological Psychiatry, 53*, 188–191. doi:10.1016/S0006-3223(02) 01411-7

Davis, L. L., Davidson, J., Ward, L. C. Bartolucci, A. A., Bowden, C., & Petty, F. (2008). Divalproex in the treatment of posttraumatic stress disorder: A randomized double-blind, placebo-controlled trial in a veteran population. *Journal of Clinical Psychopharmacology, 28*, 84–88.

Difede, J., Cukor, J., Jayasinghe, N., Patt, I., Jedel, S., Spielman, L., . . . Hoffman, H. G. (2007). Virtual reality exposure therapy for the treatment of posttraumatic stress disorder following September 11, 2001. *The Journal of Clinical Psychiatry, 68*, 1682–1689. doi:10.4088/JCP.v68n1102

Driscoll, K. A., Cukrowicz, K. C., Lyons Reardon, M., & Joiner, T. E., Jr. (2004). *Simple treatment for complex problems: A flexible treatment approach to psychological difficulties and disorders*. Mahwah, NJ: Erlbaum.

Ehlers, A., & Clark, D. M. (2000). A cognitive model of posttraumatic stress disorder. *Behaviour Research and Therapy, 38*, 319–345. doi:10.1016/S0005-7967(99)00123-0

Famularo, R., Kinscherff, R., & Fenton, T. (1988). Propranolol treatment for childhood posttraumatic stress disorder, acute type. *American Journal of Diseases of Children, 142*, 1244–1247.

Feeny, N. C., Zoellner, L. A., Mavissakalian, M. R., & Roy-Byrne, P. P. (2009). What would you choose? Sertraline or Prolonged Exposure for chronic PTSD. *Depression and Anxiety, 26*, 724–731.

Foa, E. B., Dancu, C., Hembree, E., Jaycox, L., Meadows, E., & Street, G. (1999). The efficacy of exposure therapy, stress inoculation training and their combination in ameliorating PTSD for female victims of assault. *Journal of Consulting and Clinical Psychology, 67*, 194–200. doi:10.1037/0022-006X.67.2.194

Foa, E. B., Hembree, E., & Rothbaum, B. O. (2007). *Prolonged exposure therapy for PTSD: Emotional processing of traumatic experiences, therapist guide.* New York, NY: Oxford University Press.

Foa, E. B., Keane, T. M., Friedman, M. J., & Cohen, J. A. (2009). *Effective treatments for PTSD: Practice Guidelines from the International Society for Traumatic Stress Studies* (2nd ed.). New York, NY: Guilford Press.

Foa, E. B., Riggs, D. S., Dancu, C. V., & Rothbaum, B. O. (1993). Reliability and validity of a brief instrument for assessing post-traumatic stress disorder. *Journal of Traumatic Stress, 6*, 459–473. doi:10.1002/jts.2490060405

Foa, E. B., Rothbaum, B. O., & Furr, J. M. (2003). Is the efficacy of exposure therapy for posttraumatic stress disorder augmented with the addition of other cognitive behavior therapy procedures? *Psychiatric Annals, 33*, 47–53.

Friedman, M. J. (1997). Drug treatment for PTSD: Answers and questions. *Annals of the New York Academy of Sciences, 821*, 359–371. doi:10.1111/j.1749-6632.1997.tb48292.x

Friedman, M. J., & Davidson, J. R. T. (2007). Pharmacotherapy for PTSD. In M. J. Friedman, T. M. Keane, & P. A. Resick (Eds.), *Handbook of PTSD: Science and practice* (pp. 376–405). New York, NY: Guilford Press.

Friedman, M. J., Davidson, J. R. T., & Stein, D. J. (2009). Psychopharmacotherapy for adults. In E. B. Foa, T. M. Keane, M. J. Friedman, & J. A. Cohen (Eds.), *Effective treatments for PTSD: Practice guidelines from the International Society for Traumatic Stress Studies* (2nd ed., pp. 245–268). New York, NY: Guilford Press.

Friedman, M. J., Marmar, C. R., Baker, D. G., Sikes, C. R., & Farfel, G. M. (2007). Randomized, double-blind comparison of sertraline and placebo for posttraumatic stress disorder in a Department of Veterans Affairs setting. *The Journal of Clinical Psychiatry, 68*, 711–720. doi:10.4088/JCP.v68n0508

Gelpin, E., Bonne, O., Peri, T., Brandes, D., & Shalev, A. Y. (1996). Treatment of recent trauma survivors with benzodiazepines: A prospective study. *The Journal of Clinical Psychiatry, 57*, 390–394.

Gerardi, M., Ressler, K., & Rothbaum, B. O. (2010). Combined treatment of anxiety disorders. In D. Stein, E. Hollander, & B. O. Rothbaum (Eds.), *Textbook of anxiety disorders* (2nd ed., pp. 147–156). New York, NY: American Psychiatric Publishing.

Gerardi, M., Rothbaum, B. O., Ressler, K., Heekin, M., & Rizzo, A. (2008). Virtual reality exposure therapy using a virtual Iraq: Case report. *Journal of Traumatic Stress, 21*, 209–213. doi:10.1002/jts.20331

Guastella, A. J., Richardson, R., Lovibond, P. F., Rapee, R. M., Gaston, J. E., Mitchell, P., Dadds, M. R. (2008). A randomized controlled trial of D-cycloserine enhancement of exposure therapy for social anxiety disorder. *Biological Psychiatry, 63*, 544–549. doi:10.1016/j.biopsych.2007.11.011

Hofmann, S. G., Meuret, A. E., & Smits, J. A. (2006). Augmentation of exposure therapy with D-cycloserine for social anxiety disorder. *Archives of General Psychiatry, 63*, 298–304. doi:10.1001/archpsyc.63.3.298

Hoge, C. W., Auchterlonie, J. L., & Milliken, C. S. (2006). Mental health problems, use of mental health services, and attrition from military service after returning from deployment to Iraq or Afghanistan. *JAMA, 295*, 1023–1032. doi:10.1001/jama.295.9.1023

Institute of Medicine. (2008). *Treatment of posttraumatic stress disorder: An assessment of the evidence*. Washington, DC: National Academies Press.

Kilpatrick, D., Veronen, L., & Resick, P. (1982). Psychological sequelae to rape: Assessment and treatment strategies. In D. M. Dolays & R. L. Meredith (Eds.), *Behavioral medicine: Assessment and treatment strategies* (pp. 473–479). New York, NY: Plenum.

Kinzie, J. D., & Friedman, M. J. (2004). Psychopharmacology for refugee and asylum-seeker patients. In J. P. Wilson & B. Drozdek (Eds.), *Broken spirits: The treatment of asylum seekers and refugees with PTSD* (pp. 580–600). New York, NY: Brunner-Routledge Press.

Kolb, L. C., Burris, B. C., & Griffiths, S. (1984). Propranolol and clonidine in the treatment of the chronic post-traumatic stress disorders of war. In B. A. van der Kolk (Ed.), *Post-traumatic stress disorder: Psychological and biological sequelae* (pp. 97–107). Washington, DC: American Psychiatric Press.

Kosten, T. R., Frank, J. B., Dan, E., McDougle, C. J., & Giller, E. L. (1991). Pharmacotherapy for post-traumatic stress disorder using phenelzine or imipramine. *Journal of Nervous and Mental Disease, 179*, 366–370. doi:10.1097/00005053-199106000-00011

Kroenke, K., Spitzer, R. L., & Williams, J. B. (2001). The PHQ-9: Validity of a brief depression severity measure. *Journal of General Internal Medicine, 16*, 606–613. doi:10.1046/j.1525-1497.2001.016009606.x

Lange, A., van de Ven, J., Schrieken, B., & Emmelkamp, P. (2001). Interapy: Treatment of posttraumatic stress through the Internet: A controlled trial. *Journal of Behavior Therapy and Experimental Psychiatry, 32*, 73–90. doi:10.1016/S0005-7916(01)00023-4

Lewis, J. D. (2002). Mirtazpine for PTSD nightmares. *The American Journal of Psychiatry, 159,* 1948–1949. doi:10.1176/appi.ajp.159.11.1948-a

Litz, B. (2005). *A brief primer on the mental health impact of the wars in Afghanistan and Iraq: A National Center for PTSD fact sheet.* Boston, MA: National Center for PTSD.

Londborg, P. D., Hegel, M. T., Goldstein, S., Goldstein, D., Himmelhoch, J. M., Maddock, R., . . . Farfel, G. M. (2001). Sertraline treatment of posttraumatic stress disorder: Results of weeks of open-label continuation treatment. *The Journal of Clinical Psychiatry, 62,* 325–331.

Marshall, R. D., Beebe, K. L., Oldham, M., & Zaninelli, R. (2001). Efficacy and safety of paroxetine treatment for chronic PTSD: A fixed-dose-placebo-controlled study. *The American Journal of Psychiatry, 158,* 1982–1988. doi:10.1176/appi.ajp.158.12.1982

Martenyi, F., Brown, E. B., Zhang, H., Koke, S. C., & Prakash, A. (2002). Fluoxetine v. placebo in prevention of relapse in post-traumatic stress disorder. *The British Journal of Psychiatry, 181,* 315–320. doi:10.1192/bjp.181.4.315

Martenyi, F., Brown, E. B., Zhang, H., Prakash, A., & Koke, S. C. (2002). Fluoxetine versus placebo in posttraumatic stress disorder. *The Journal of Clinical Psychiatry, 63,* 199–206.

Mellman, T. A., Bustamante, V., David, D., & Fins, A. I. (2002). Hypnotic medication in the aftermath of trauma [Letter to the editor]. *The Journal of Clinical Psychiatry, 63,* 1183–1184.

Monson, C. M., Schnurr, P. P., Resick, P. A., Friedman, M. J., Young-Xu, Y., & Stevens, S. P. (2006). Cognitive processing therapy for veterans with military-related posttraumatic stress disorder. *Journal of Consulting and Clinical Psychology, 74,* 898–907. doi:10.1037/0022-006X.74.5.898

National Institute for Health and Clinical Excellence. (2005). Post-traumatic stress disorder. London, England: Royal College of Psychiatrists and The British Psychological Society.

Neylan, T. C., Lenoci, M., Samuelson, K. W., Metzler, T. J., Henn-Haase, C., Hierhoizer, R. W., . . . Marmar, C. R. (2006). No improvement of posttraumatic stress disorder symptoms with guanfacine treatment. *The American Journal of Psychiatry, 163,* 2186–2188. doi:10.1176/appi.ajp.163.12.2186

Pitman, R. K., Sanders, K. M., Zusman, R. M., Healy, F., Cheema, N., Lasko, L., . . . Orr, S. P. (2002). Pilot study of secondary prevention of posttraumatic stress disorder with propranolol. *Biological Psychiatry, 51,* 189–192. doi:10.1016/S0006-3223(01)01279-3

Raskind, M. A., Peskind, E. R., Hoff, D. J., Hart, K. L., Holmes, H. A., Warren, D., . . . McFall, M. E. (2007). A parallel group placebo controlled study of prazosin for trauma nightmares and sleep disturbances in combat veterans with post-traumatic stress disorder. *Biological Psychiatry, 61,* 928–934. doi:10.1016/j.biopsych.2006.06.032

Raskind, M. A., Peskind, E. R., Kanter, E. D., Petrie, E. C., Radont, A., Thompson, C., . . . McFall, M. M. (2003). Reduction of nightmares and other PTSD symptoms in combat veterans by prazosin: A placebo-controlled study. *The American Journal of Psychiatry, 160,* 371–373.

Reist, C., Kauffman, C. D., Haier, R. J., Sangdahl, C., DeMet, E. M., Chicz-DeMet, A., & Nelson, J. N. (1989). A controlled trial of desipramine in 18 men with post-traumatic stress disorder. *The American Journal of Psychiatry, 146,* 513–516.

Resick, P. A., Galovski, T. E., Uhlmansiek, M. O., Scher, C. D., Clum, G. A., & Young-Xu, Y. (2008). A randomized clinical trial to dismantle components of cognitive processing therapy for posttraumatic stress disorder in female victims of interpersonal violence. *Journal of Consulting and Clinical Psychology, 76,* 243–258. doi:10.1037/0022-006X.76.2.243

Resick, P. A., Nishith, P., Weaver, T., Astin, M. C., & Feuer, C. A. (2002). A comparison of cognitive processing therapy, prolonged exposure, and a waiting condition for the treatment of posttraumatic stress disorder in female rape victims. *Journal of Consulting and Clinical Psychology, 70,* 867–879. doi:10.1037/0022-006X.70.4.867

Ressler, K. J., Rothbaum, B. O., Tannenbaum, L., Anderson, P., Graap, K., Zimond, E., . . . Davis, M. (2004). Cognitive enhancers as adjuncts to psychotherapy: Use of D-cycloserine in phobic individuals to facilitate extinction of fear. *Archives of General Psychiatry, 61,* 1136–1144. doi:10.1001/archpsyc.61.11.1136

Robert, R., Blakeney, P. E., Villarreal, C., Rosenberg, L., & Meyer, W. J., III. (1999). Imipramine treatment in pediatric burn patients with symptoms of acute stress disorder: A pilot study. *Journal of the American Academy of Child and Adolescent Psychiatry, 38,* 873–882. doi:10.1097/00004583-199907000-00018

Rosen, C. S., Chow, H. C., Finney, J. F., Greenbaum, M. A., Moos, R. N., Sheikh, J. I., & Yesavage, J. A. (2004). VA practice patterns and practice guidelines for treating posttraumatic stress disorder. *Journal of Traumatic Stress, 17,* 213–222. doi:10.1023/B:JOTS.0000029264.23878.53

Rothbaum, B. O. (2008). Critical parameters for D-cycloserine enhancement of cognitive behavioral therapy for obsessive compulsive disorder. *The American Journal of Psychiatry, 165,* 293–296. doi:10.1176/appi.ajp.2007.07121871

Rothbaum, B. O., Astin, M. C., & Marsteller, F. (2005). Prolonged exposure vs. EMDR for PTSD rape victims. *Journal of Traumatic Stress, 18,* 607–616. doi:10.1002/jts.20069

Rothbaum, B. O., Cahill, S., Foa, E. B., Davidson, J. R. T., Compton, J., Connor, K., . . . Hahn, C.-G. (2006). Augmentation of sertraline with prolonged exposure in the treatment of PTSD. *Journal of Traumatic Stress, 19,* 625–638. doi:10.1002/jts.20170

Rothbaum, B. O., Hodges, L., Ready, D., Graap, K., & Alarcon, R. (2001). Virtual reality exposure therapy for Vietnam veterans with posttraumatic stress disorder. *The Journal of Clinical Psychiatry, 62,* 617–622.

Saygin, M. Z., Sungur, M. Z., Sabol, E. U., & Cetinkaya, P. (2002). Nefazodone versus sertraline in treatment of posttraumatic stress disorder. *Bulletin of Clinical Psychopharmacology, 12*, 1–5.

Schnurr, P. P., Friedman, M. J., Engel, C. C., Foa, E. B., Shea, M. T., Resick, P. A., . . . Bernardy, N. (2007). Cognitive behavioral therapy for posttraumatic stress disorder in women: A randomized controlled trial. *JAMA, 297*, 820–830. doi:10.1001/jama.297.8.820

Schnurr, P. P., Friedman, M. J., Foy, D. W., Shea, M. T., Hsieh, F. Y., Lavori, P. W., . . . Bernardy, N. (2003). Randomized trial of trauma–focused group therapy for posttraumatic stress disorder. *Archives of General Psychiatry, 60*, 481–489. doi:10.1001/archpsyc.60.5.481

Shapiro, F. (1995). *Eye movement desensitization and reprocessing: Basic principles, protocols and procedures.* New York, NY: Guilford Press.

Shea, M. T. McDevitt-Murphy, M., Ready, D. J., & Schnurr, P. (2009). Group therapy. In E. B. Foa, T. M. Keane, M. J. Friedman, & J. Cohen (Eds.), *Effective treatments for PTSD: Practice guidelines from the International Society for Traumatic Stress Studies* (2nd ed., pp. 306–326). New York, NY: Guilford Press.

Simon, N. M., Connor, K. M., Lang, A. J., Rauch, S., Krulewicz, S., LeBeau, R. T., . . . Pollack, M. H. (2008). Paroxetine CR augmentation for PTSD refractory to prolonged exposure therapy. *The Journal of Clinical Psychiatry, 69*, 400–405. doi:10.4088/JCP.v69n0309

Spates, C. R., Koch, E., Cusack, K., Pagoto, S., & Waller, S. (2009). Eye movement desensitization and reprocessing. In E. B. Foa, T. M. Keane, M. J. Friedman, & J. Cohen (Eds.), *Effective treatments for PTSD: Practice guidelines from the International Society for Traumatic Stress Studies* (2nd ed., pp. 279–305). New York, NY: Guilford Press.

Tolin, D. F., Pearlson, G. D., Krystal, J. H., Davis M, Meunier SA, & Brady RS. (2007, July). *A controlled trial of D-cycloserine with brief CBT for panic disorder.* Paper presented at the annual meeting of the World Congress of Behavioral and Cognitive Therapies, Barcelona.

Tucker, P., Trautman, R. P., Wyatt, D. B., Thompson, J., Wu, S. C., Capece, J. A., & Rosenthal, N. R. (2007). Efficacy and safety of topiramate monotherapy in civilian posttraumatic stress disorder: A randomized, double-blind, placebo-controlled study. *The Journal of Clinical Psychiatry, 68*, 201–206. doi:10.4088/JCP.v68n0204

Tucker, P., Zaninelli, R., Yehuda, R., Ruggiero, L., Dillingham, K., & Pitts, C. D. (2001). Paroxetine in the treatment of chronic posttraumatic stress disorder: Results of a placebo-controlled, flexible-dosage trial. *The Journal of Clinical Psychiatry, 62*, 860–868.

Veterans Health Administration, Department of Defense. (2004). *VA/DoD clinical practice guideline for the management of post-traumatic stress. Version 1.0.* Washington, DC: Veterans Health Administration, Department of Defense.

Vaiva, G., Ducrocq, F., Jezequel, K., Averland, B., Lestavel, P., Brunet, A., & Marmar, C. R. (2003). Immediate treatment with propranolol decreases posttraumatic stress disorder two months after trauma. *Biological Psychiatry, 54,* 947–949. doi:10.1016/S0006-3223(03)00412-8

Weathers, F., Litz, B., Herman, D., Huska, J., & Keane, T. (1993, October). *The PTSD Checklist (PCL): Reliability, validity, and diagnostic utility.* Paper presented at the annual meeting of the International Society for Traumatic Stress Studies, San Antonio, TX.

V

A PUBLIC HEALTH
APPROACH

11

BARRIERS TO MENTAL HEALTH TREATMENT ENGAGEMENT AMONG VETERANS

TRACY STECKER AND JOHN FORTNEY

Many service members return from war with significant mental health concerns. Although service members with posttraumatic stress reactions and other psychological concerns often struggle postdeployment, they do not necessarily seek services to treat their symptoms. This chapter attempts to answer the central question, What can be improved in existing practices in terms of outreach and screening and treatment engagement? The chapter also outlines the extent to which returning veterans utilize mental health treatment, identifies barriers to receiving care, and presents possible approaches to removing those barriers.

As summarized in Chapter 1 of this volume, service members return from war with a variety of combat-related mental health conditions, including posttraumatic stress disorder (PTSD), depression, non-PTSD anxiety disorders, and substance use disorders (Hoge et al., 2004; Milliken, Auchterlonie, & Hoge, 2007; Rundell, 2006; Schell & Marshall, 2008; Seal et al., 2009; Stecker, Fortney, Hamilton, & Ajzen, 2007). Emerging data also suggest that Operation Enduring Freedom (OEF) and Operation Iraqi Freedom (OIF)

The authors thank Dawne Vogt for her helpful comments on this chapter.

veterans with mental health problems, particularly PTSD, have poorer general health functioning (Hoge et al., 2007; Jakupcak, Luterek, Hunt, Conybeare, & McFall, 2008; Vasterling et al., 2008). According to reports generated from the Department of Veterans Affairs (VA), almost 50% of veterans presenting to VA health care facilities report pain, with the majority presenting with a combination of pain, depression, and PTSD (Seal et al., 2009; Sherbourne et al., 2009; Stecker, Fortney, McGovern, & Sherbourne, in press).

The likelihood of reporting mental health symptoms is higher among service members who were activated from the National Guard or Reserves as opposed to regular active-duty personnel (Kang & Hyams, 2005; Schell & Marshall, 2008). Symptom complaints are also higher among service members who deployed multiple times to a war zone (Mental Health Advisory Team IV, 2006; Schell & Marshall, 2008). Finally, age and gender are also associated with an increased risk of mental health problems (Seal et al., 2009). Among regular active-duty veterans, those younger than 25 years old have higher rates of PTSD and drug use disorders compared with those older than 40 years. Women have a higher risk of depression than do men (Seal et al., 2009).

TREATMENT UTILIZATION AMONG RETURNING VETERANS

Despite the scope of mental health problems stemming from war-zone participation, only one quarter to one half of U.S. service members who acknowledge mental health symptoms seek treatment (Hoge et al., 2004, 2006; Milliken et al., 2007; Stecker et al., 2007). A recent, large population-based study conducted by the RAND Corporation found that half of returning veterans with probable PTSD or depression sought treatment from a provider (Schell & Marshall, 2008). Only 30% of these individuals received minimally adequate treatment (defined as at least eight sessions averaging 30 min in duration for psychotherapy or at least four visits with a doctor staying on the medication prescribed for psychotropic medication; Schell & Marshall, 2008).

Of relevance to some of the recent screening initiatives within the Department of Defense (DoD) and VA, being screened for a mental health disorder may increase treatment utilization. Results from the Post-Deployment Health Assessment (PDHA), a brief screening instrument administered routinely to returning service members in DoD settings, suggest that 35% of Iraq War Veterans accessed mental health services in the year returning home (Hoge et al., 2006). Although approximately one third of the service members assessed accessed mental health services, only 12% of these individuals received a mental health diagnosis. An additional 23% received services but did not have a mental health diagnosis, suggesting that many referrals for service were based on the screening process. However, given that many of the mental health visits were provided on the day of screening and the study did not document the nature of the services, it is not clear whether these services constituted meaningful treatment or were possibly even part of the screening process.

Seal et al. (2008) assessed whether clinician screenings increased the likelihood of mental health attendance in VA health care settings. Screenings were conducted for PTSD, depression, and high-risk drinking at one VA medical center and five affiliated community-based outpatient clinics. Of the 233 veterans who screened positive during the clinician visits, 170 (73%) completed a follow-up mental health visit. Veterans represented in this study were already established within the VA medical system but were willing to initiate specific mental health services as a result of the screenings. Although these results suggest that returning veterans who are already enrolled in a health care system might benefit from mental health screening, additional work is necessary to engage individuals not already established in the VA system or elsewhere.

BARRIERS TO MENTAL HEALTH TREATMENT AMONG VETERANS: DESCRIPTION OF FINDINGS

Several studies have assessed barriers to mental health treatment among returning OEF and OIF service members, including two with relatively large, diverse samples, as well as others with more geographically restricted or specialized samples. One study assessed soldiers and Marines from brigade and regimental combat teams postdeployment and asked respondents about perceived barriers to mental health treatment. Respondents widely endorsed the perceptions that they would be perceived as weak, would be treated differently by leadership, and that treatment would result in others having less confidence in them (Hoge et al., 2004). Respondents who reported the most need for help also reported the greatest number of barriers.

Investigators from the RAND Corporation assessed barriers to mental health treatment among a large, representative sample of active-duty service members and military veterans who had served in Iraq and Afghanistan and who met screening criteria for mental health problems (Schell & Marshall, 2008). Participants in the RAND study rated a list of commonly endorsed barriers to care as falling into three categories: (a) logistical barriers, such as difficulty scheduling appointments; (b) institutional and cultural barriers, such as harming their career; and (c) beliefs about and preferences for treatment, such as treatment not being perceived as effective. Survey respondents who met screening criteria for mental health problems most frequently endorsed as barriers institutional and cultural factors, especially those concerning confidentiality, harm to their career, and concerns about future security clearances. Respondents screening positive for mental health problems also endorsed barriers relating to the preference to rely on friends and concerns about therapeutic effectiveness.

Pietrzak, Johnson, Goldstein, Malley, and Southwick (2009) asked 1,050 OEF and OIF National Guard members and Reservists from a single New England state to complete a survey by mail that assessed perceived stigma, barriers to care, service use, and screened for PTSD, depression, and alcohol use. Although study findings must be viewed with caution because the response rate was low (27%), results indicated that respondents who screened positive for mental health problems were significantly more likely to report perceived stigma and barriers to care. Post hoc analysis revealed the most significant predictor of perceived stigma and barriers to care was screening positive for PTSD. Therefore, individuals most in need are reporting more barriers to treatment engagement.

Other studies of barriers to mental health care among veterans have focused on special populations, such as individuals with serious mental illness and women. Drapalski, Milford, Goldberg, Brown, and Dixon (2008) assessed barriers to medical and mental health care among veterans with serious mental illness and found that veterans' perceived personal factors, such as preferring to solve the problem by themselves, believing the problem would go away on its own, and viewing treatment as ineffective, were greater barriers to treatment than instrumental factors such as cost and travel distance. Women veterans perceived initiating care at the VA and the lack of women-specific services as the most salient barriers to treatment (Vogt et al., 2006).

Overall, the data suggest that service members have many concerns about mental health treatment that interfere with treatment seeking. Those with the most need for help routinely report more barriers to seeking help. Concerns are persistent and pervasive across studies, and significantly affect treatment seeking. Because those most in need are reporting more stigma and other barriers to seeking care, future work should focus on modifying perceptions of mental health treatment and psychological problems, as well reducing instrumental barriers to seeking mental health care.

BARRIERS TO UTILIZATION: CONCEPTUAL EXPLANATIONS

To explain patterns of service utilization among returning OEF and OIF veterans, several investigators have begun to apply existing conceptual models to understanding help-seeking behavior in this population. Two comprehensive models that may apply to OEF and OIF veterans include Andersen's (1995) behavioral model of health service use and the theory of planned behavior (TBP; Ajzen, 1991). These models are now described, followed by a discussion of two models that have been developed specifically to target the role of beliefs about mental illness and mental health treatment in service use.

Comprehensive Models of Service Use

The following sections review Anderson's (1995) behavioral model of health services use and the theory of planned behavior. Both models provide explanations for why individuals choose to engage in particular health behaviors.

Anderson's Behavioral Model of Health Services Use

According to Andersen's (1995) model, three types of factors explain service utilization: (a) individual factors, (b) health care system factors, and (c) the external environment. Individual factors fall into three types of influences: predisposing factors, enabling factors, and need. Predisposing factors include characteristics such as age, gender, race–ethnicity, education, attitudes about health services, knowledge about disease and disorders, and values. Enabling factors include circumstances that enable or impede service use such as family and community resources and access to these resources. Need involves the individual's general state of health, symptoms, and functional capacity. System factors include health policy and resources and how these resources are organized. The external environment includes physical, political, and economic factors.

Theory of Planned Behavior

Whereas Andersen's model has global applications for explaining service utilization on a macro level because it includes societal and contextual factors external to the individual as well as individual factors, TPB (Ajzen, 1991) addresses service use behavior on the individual level by focusing on cognitive and emotional mechanisms internal to the individual. TPB purports that human action is guided by three kinds of considerations: (a) beliefs about the likely consequences of the behavior (behavioral beliefs), (b) beliefs about the normative expectations of others (normative beliefs), and (c) beliefs about the presence of factors that may facilitate or prevent performance of the behavior (control beliefs; Ajzen, 1991). In their respective aggregates, behavioral beliefs produce a favorable or unfavorable *attitude toward the behavior*; normative beliefs result in perceived social pressure or *subjective norm*; and control beliefs give rise to *perceived behavioral control,* the perceived capability of performing the behavior. In combination, attitude toward the behavior, subjective norms, and the perception of behavioral control lead to the formation of a behavioral *intention*. The more favorable the attitude and subjective norm and the greater the perceived control, the stronger should be the person's intention to perform the behavior in question. Finally, given a sufficient degree of actual control over the behavior, people are expected to carry out their intentions. Intention is thus assumed to be the immediate antecedent of behavior and also to guide behavior in a controlled and deliberate fashion. In the health domain, TPB has successfully explained and predicted behaviors such as exercising, donating blood, adhering to a low-fat diet, using condoms for the prevention of HIV–AIDS, and using illegal drugs (Brubaker & Wickersham, 1990; Hardeman et al., 2002; Jemmott, Jemmott, & Fong, 1998; Murphy & Brubaker, 1990). TPB, however, has not previously been invoked to try to understand or influence treatment-seeking behaviors.

According to TPB, the decision to engage in any behavior can ultimately be traced to the person's beliefs about the behavior in question. In two separate studies, we used TPB as a framework to examine barriers to health care among National Guard soldiers who deployed to the wars in Iraq, Afghanistan, or both and who screened positive for one of the following mental health disorders: panic disorder, PTSD, generalized anxiety disorder, major depressive disorder, and alcohol abuse (Stecker et al., 2007; Stecker et al., in press). In the first study, we identified barriers to mental health treatment among returning National Guard soldiers who screened positive for a mental health disorder. In the second study, we examined whether the identified barriers predicted mental health treatment seeking.

The first study identified several barriers to treatment, mostly involving stigma and the respondent's own expectation of wellness postdeployment. Soldiers were asked to answer the following questions: (a) "What are the advantages and disadvantages to seeking mental health treatment?" (b) "Who would support and/or not support your decision to seek mental health treatment?" and (c) "What facilitators and/or barriers are in place for you to seek mental health treatment?" Many soldiers reported that they did not expect to struggle with mental health symptoms postdeployment (Stecker et al., 2007). The majority of returning soldiers indicated that they were prepared for the duties of war and expected to be able to cope with the consequences, including the emotional consequences. One returning soldier indicated:

> To me that is a major hurdle to actually realize that you have mental health problems. Especially coming back from war. You went over there normal and you came back with problems. It is hard to actually sit down and face that.

Another stated:

> The first thing you have to do is admit, yes, I have a problem. You have to admit it to yourself. Once you admit it to yourself you are going to go and find help. But you know that is the biggest step that anybody is going to have to take is to say "I am the problem."

Respondents also reported that they generally preferred self-care to seeking treatment from a professional. Many U.S. service members stated that they recognized their symptoms but believed they should handle their problems and symptoms on their own or did not believe that professional treatment would work for them. For example, one soldier reported: "I think it is mostly self-induced obstacles. Guys not wanting to go to help because they feel like they ought to be able to handle it on their own." Alternatively, they did not believe that treatment would be helpful to them:

> There's not a whole lot of advantages to coming home from war except that you are alive. You can talk to people all day long and I don't think they can ever really tell you how to deal with any of it.

Some even reported looking for excuses not to seek treatment in an attempt to avoid the pain: "They are already looking for a reason not to go [to mental health treatment] because they don't want to talk about the things that hurt them."

As a final but important note about the psychological barriers to mental health treatment, many soldiers in response to our survey described concerns about stigma. Soldiers conveyed having great difficulty admitting that they were the ones struggling (self-stigma). When soldiers were asked whether they believed important others would or would not support their decision to seek mental health treatment, the overwhelming majority (75%) reported that they believed everyone would support their decision to get help. The only stigma from others that they specified in the interviews dealt directly with chain of command within the military. Higher ranking officers reported that they would not want soldiers of lower ranking to know they were seeking treatment. One officer stated, "And there is the stigma. I wouldn't want anyone ranked below me knowing. They would think that I am not capable of making decisions for them." When pressed whether he might also be perceived as a role model for good self-care, this officer admitted that it was possible. He, however, was not willing to risk someone doubting his leadership ability given that lack of confidence in leadership during the head of battle could lead to someone getting killed.

This qualitative, theory-based analysis allowed us to assess barriers to mental health treatment among returning service members who screened positive for a mental health disorder in an extensive and individualized format so that we can develop appropriate models to intervene. Much of the existing literature presented respondents with a finite set of predetermined barriers to rate in terms of their personal relevance. In contrast, our exploratory qualitative work described earlier allowed respondents to generate barriers to treatment from their own perspective.

Qualitative data from this first study informed the development of a quantitative measure (the Perceptions About Services Scale) to differentiate beliefs about mental health treatment between individuals who sought treatment and those who did not. Consistent with TPB, results from the quantitative analysis suggested that beliefs do, in fact, predict mental health treatment seeking. Using multivariate regression analyses, we found that two beliefs (i.e., that symptoms would improve and that work would be hurt by treatment seeking) were significantly predictive of treatment seeking (Stecker et al., in press). Overall, results from these studies indicate that service members may be willing to seek treatment despite expected negative consequences to their work and the difficulty discussing certain symptoms and experiences.

Models Focused on Stigma

Other models have been posed to address specifically how beliefs about mental health—and in particular, mental illness stigma—may affect service use. Greene-Shortridge et al. (2007) proposed a model of barriers to mental health care in military settings. In this model, service members who experience mental health problems may encounter societal stigma inherent to the military culture, which they may then internalize, leading to a "self-stigma." According to this model, such self-stigmatization has high potential to lead to poor self-esteem, which in turn may inhibit behaviors directed toward seeking mental health care. The model further suggests that if the service member perceives additional, non-stigma-related instrumental barriers, such as insufficient time and financial resources or difficulties with transportation, care seeking behavior becomes even less likely. Subsequent factor-analytic work conducted by this group (Britt et al., 2008) revealed that stigma and other perceived barriers to care (e.g., finances, transportation) represented distinct constructs. Further, in their sample of more than 3,500 service members, Britt et al. (2008) found that depression symptoms were more strongly linked to work overload when service members identified more extensive barriers to care. These findings collectively indicate that interventions may need to address multiple barriers to care, including both stigma (societal and self) and instrumental barriers.

Vogt (2010) also recently articulated a model focusing on beliefs related to mental illness and mental health treatment. On the basis of a review of studies conducted on active-duty service members and military veterans that examined mental health–related beliefs as barriers to service use, Vogt (2010) suggested that service use may be influenced by both concerns about public stigma, as reflected in the extent to which an individual believes that he or she will be stigmatized by others for having a mental health problem, as well as personal beliefs about mental illness and mental health treatment, which may to some extent reflect the internalization of public stigma. Vogt's (2010) conceptualization also draws from the work of Corrigan and his colleagues (Corrigan, 2004; Corrigan & Rusch, 2002), who have focused in civilian populations on both public stigma, defined as the general society's reaction to people with mental illness, and self-stigma, reflected in the internalization of negative beliefs about mental illness. Integrating findings from the military and civilian literatures, Vogt (2010) suggested three potential domains of personal beliefs about mental illness and mental health treatment that may be especially relevant: (a) beliefs about people with mental health problems (e.g., Brown, 2008; Corrigan, Lickey, Campion, & Rashid, 2000; Day, Edgren, & Eshleman, 2007; Link, Phelan, Bresnahan, Stueve, & Pescosolido, 1999), (b) beliefs about mental health treatment (e.g., Leaf, Bruce, & Tischler, 1986; Pirkis, Blood, Francis, & McCallum, 2006), and (c) beliefs about treatment seeking (e.g., Mansfield, Addis, & Courtenay, 2005; Ojeda, & Bergstresser, 2008; Perlick & Manning, 2006; Waldron, 1997).

OVERCOMING BARRIERS TO MENTAL HEALTH TREATMENT

The following section describes interventions designed to overcome barriers to mental health treatment. Interventions are both systemic in nature (e.g., Battlemind) and geared to the individual (e.g., the cognitive–behavioral intervention).

Interventions

Although a number of interventions have been proposed to overcome barriers to mental health treatment among service members and military veterans, fewer have been assessed empirically, especially in the context of veterans returning from OEF and OIF deployment. For example, Greene-Shortridge et al. (2007) highlighted three classes of potential interventions to reduce stigma: (a) "protesting," which informs society that veterans should not view mental illness in negative, stereotypical ways; (b) public education that centers on presentation of factual information regarding mental illness; and (c) promoting contact with individuals who have mental illness. In their review, Greene-Shortridge et al. concluded that protesting has rarely been successful and may even be counterproductive, that education has had partial success in the general population, and that promotion of one-on-one contact between supportive others and those suffering psychological symptoms, although proven to be the most successful in nonmilitary contexts, has not been adequately explored within the military.

Within military and military veteran contexts, however, VA and DoD have allocated significant resources toward increasing access to mental health services for returning veterans. Along with the National Institutes of Health, VA and DoD have likewise increased the amount of funding available to study new treatments and delivery models for PTSD and TBI in returning veterans (Burnam, Meredith, Tanielian, & Jaycox, 2009). Individual states have also increased their capacity to address the mental health needs of returning service members. For example, Vermont organized a peer program to make contact with each returning service member in the National Guard or Reserves to assess for need and provide referral information. New Hampshire collaborates with the Department of Human Services and Easter Seals to provide initial counseling for all returning soldiers. The extent to which these programs are effective in reducing barriers to treatment among returning veterans has yet to be determined. These states implemented programs oriented to work within their communities. The fact remains that an unmet need for treatment persists, and those who reach treatment are unlikely to receive adequate treatment (Schell & Marshall, 2008) or to stay in treatment (Rosenheck & Fontana, 2007).

An especially intriguing effort underway within DoD targets perceptions of mental health treatment seeking for psychological problems associated with war. Warrior Resiliency Training (formerly called Battlemind) emphasizes the idea that the skills needed for wartime to stay alert and alive may interfere with functioning and cause problems on the home front. As an example, Warrior Resiliency Training helps service members recognize when it is or is not adaptive to control their emotions. Controlled emotions are critical for mission success. At home, in contrast, the failure to communicate or display emotions can hurt relationships, particularly intimate relationships. One trial of Battlemind training has been conducted and demonstrated some initial success for this training to improve adjustment postdeployment (Adler, Bliese, McGurk, Hoge, & Castro, 2009).

There are also several new clinical and service delivery initiatives in the VA. An example of a service delivery initiative is the use of OEF–OIF outreach coordinators at VHA facilities. VA outreach coordinators might be helpful for veterans in that outreach provides a contact person to call who can help veterans identify useful pathways into care. An example of a clinical initiative involves the VA's efforts to hire returnees as outreach counselors to increase perceived legitimacy and ease of connection.

Finally, Internet-based cognitive–behavior therapy (CBT) may be a useful tool for self-managing PTSD among returning veterans who are unlikely to come in for treatment (i.e., transportation issues). Litz, Engel, Bryant, and Papa (2007) found that in a small study of veterans ($N = 45$), participants who received CBT-based Internet therapy achieved greater gains in PTSD symptom reduction than participants who received supportive counseling, which was also delivered through the Internet. Results of this study should be interpreted with caution, however, because this was a small proof-of-concept trial, and many of the participants did not complete 6-month follow-up interviews (likely because of redeployments).

Case Example

Clearly, it would be insufficient to focus solely on the retention of veterans in treatment if the barriers to accessing treatment prevent a large proportion of veterans from beginning treatment in the first place. We are currently conducting research that focuses more on engaging resistant returning veterans with mental health concerns through the use of motivational interviewing and cognitive–behavioral strategies. We believe that cognitive techniques can help individuals who are struggling with the decision to engage in treatment and have found that such techniques may be particularly useful considering the extent to which cognitive barriers influence engagement in treatment (Stecker, 2010; Stecker, Fortney, Hamilton, Sherbourne, & Ajzen, 2010). This section describes a case from our ongoing study using a cognitive intervention to influence the decision to enter mental health treatment.

"Jill" is a 25-year-old woman who served with the U.S. Army National Guard in two separate deployments. She had been deployed for 1 year when an improvised explosive device exploded near her, killing two other U.S. service members. She was physically injured in the explosion but remained on active duty. She receives disability for this spinal injury from the VA. She served a second 6-month deployment to Iraq after being home for 1 year. Jill screened positive for PTSD and alcohol abuse but does not want treatment at this time because she does not believe that therapy is a useful tool for managing her symptoms. When asked what would be a useful tool for her, she has difficulty clarifying, although she admits that time spent at bars helps her feel more relaxed. She admits to drinking more than 12 drinks at a time several nights a week and admits that she avoids talking or thinking about her deployment. Jill has little social support, although she lives near her mother. She describes her relationship with her mother as "not good" and could not identify anyone whom she would call a friend. She is currently taking classes at a local college but reports conflict with the administration and teachers.

Although she has been attending this college on and off for the past 6 years, she is unable to identify her career path or major.

Jill reported three beliefs about seeking treatment for her PTSD. These included that (a) the decision should be something that she makes on her own, (b) she does not want to talk about her experiences in Iraq, and (c) she is opposed to the human service field. After a lengthy discussion regarding her sense of isolation, lack of social support, and suicidality, we were able to produce three alternative ways of expressing these thoughts. For her first statement, she reframed her belief as she is able to come to the decision regarding her treatment by herself but is only somewhat open to exploring the decision with others. Her second belief was reframed to consider the possibility that talking about what happened could make her feel better. Her third belief was reframed so that she was able to identify issues and problems in which the human service field would be helpful, including helping her with issues such as PTSD (which she admitted to having) but wanted to keep her belief that it would be difficult for her to connect with and trust a therapist. Therefore, treatment might be helpful but difficult for her.

As can be seen, cognitive techniques such as those used in the case example could be useful for engaging veterans in a discussion of treatment seeking. The focus of the discussion would be on modifying stigmatizing beliefs about treatment so that returning service members are better positioned to make a decision about their own treatment needs. Our preliminary results suggest that returning veterans with mental health concerns reported being significantly more likely to seek mental health treatment postintervention.

CONCLUSION

Veterans return from the war zone with a variety of mental health concerns and an array of perceptions and beliefs that potentially interfere with seeking mental health treatment. The decision to seek mental health treatment among returning service members is not casually determined. U.S. service members, especially those in greatest need, report extensive barriers and stigma against treatment. Although the emotional and mental consequences of surviving war continue for many beyond the deployment, admitting the struggle may be the greatest obstacle.

The case example in this chapter illustrates a cognitive technique for overcoming barriers to mental health treatment commonly reported among returning veterans. It is likely that any veteran who makes it to a mental health treatment session experienced some difficulty making the decision to seek help. It may be useful for the treating clinician to acknowledge this decision. This discussion, in and of itself, would help acknowledge the individual's specific belief system about mental health treatment and may increase retention in treatment. This type of individual intervention would be aimed at improving the self-stigma associated with seeking treatment. Interventions to improve cultural beliefs around help seeking are also needed (Greene-Shortridge et al., 2007).

In addition to efforts such as Warrior Resiliency Training (Adler et al., 2009), other sociocultural efforts are underway within the military to improve perceptions of help seeking. For example, military leaders recognize the importance of speaking out to combat the stigma associated with mental health problems. Some leaders have actively recognized their own battles with PTSD, and others have emphasized help seeking as critical for wound care (i.e., the expectation being that one would seek treatment for a gunshot wound the same as someone would seek treatment for a psychological wound).

Other important areas to address to reduce barriers to mental health treatment among service members and military veterans include the involvement of family members in treatment and treatment decisions, reducing the impact of the lack of confidentiality within the military culture, and reducing logistical barriers surrounding mental health care. The VA has developed some avenues to improve logistical barriers, such as offering telepsychiatry at some sites and bundling mental health care within primary care clinics, but more empirical work to evaluate whether reduction of logistical barriers increases initial engagement and meaningful participation in mental health services is needed.

In summary, service members and military veterans report significant barriers to mental health treatment seeking that interfere with their ability to engage and participate in appropriate services. These barriers include societal stigma, self-stigma, perceptions that care may not effect meaningful change, and logistical barriers, such as time constraints, transportation problems, and insufficient financial resources. Several investigations are underway that may help identify ways in which providers (e.g., through use of cognitive strategies that target the perceptions of those seeking services) and communities (e.g., increasing outreach and contact with returning veterans with psychological concerns) can overcome these barriers for successful outcomes postdeployment. We believe that ultimate success in engaging returning veterans in mental health care services will require a multifaceted approach in which multiple levels of barriers (individual, system level, and societal) are addressed.

REFERENCES

Adler, A. B., Bliese, P. D., McGurk, D., Hoge, C. W., & Castro, C. A. (2009). Battlemind debriefing and Battlemind training as early interventions with soldiers returning from Iraq: Randomization by platoon. *Journal of Consulting and Clinical Psychology, 77*, 928–940. doi:10.1037/a0016877

Ajzen, I. (1991). The theory of planned behavior. *Organizational Behavior and Human Decision Processes, 50,* 179–211. doi:10.1016/0749-5978(91)90020-T

Andersen, R. M. (1995). Revisiting the behavioral model and access to medical care: Does it matter? *Journal of Health and Social Behavior, 36,* 1–10. doi:10.2307/2137284

Britt, T. W., Greene-Shortridge, T. M., Brink, S., Nguyen, Q. B., Rath, J., Cox, A. L., . . . Castro, C. A. (2008). Perceived stigma and barriers to care for psychological treatment: Implications for reactions to stressors in different contexts. *Journal of Social and Clinical Psychology, 27,* 317–335. doi:10.1521/jscp.2008.27.4.317

Brown, S. A. (2008). Factors and measurement of mental illness stigma: A psychometric examination of the Attribution Questionnaire. *Psychiatric Rehabilitation Journal, 32,* 89–94. doi:10.2975/32.2.2008.89.94

Brubaker, R. G., & Wickersham, D. (1990). Encouraging college males to perform testicular self-examination: A field application of the theory of reasoned action. *Health Psychology, 9,* 154–163. doi:10.1037/0278-6133.9.2.154

Burnam, M. A., Meredith, L. S., Tanielian, T., & Jaycox, L. H. (2009). Mental health care for Iraq and Afghanistan war veterans. *Health Affairs, 28,* 771–782. doi:10.1377/hlthaff.28.3.771

Corrigan, P. (2004). How stigma interferes with mental health care. *American Psychologist, 59,* 614–625. doi:10.1037/0003-066X.59.7.614

Corrigan, P. W., Lickey, S. E., Campion, J., & Rashid, F. (2000). Mental health team leadership and consumer's satisfaction and quality of life. *Psychiatric Services, 51,* 781–785. doi:10.1176/appi.ps.51.6.781

Corrigan, P. W., & Rusch, L. C. (2002). Mental illness stereotypes and clinical care: Do people avoid treatment because of stigma? *American Journal of Psychiatric Rehabilitation, 6,* 312–334.

Day, E. N., Edgren, K., & Eshleman, A. (2007). Measuring stigma toward mental illness: Development and application of the mental illness stigma scale. *Journal of Applied Social Psychology, 37,* 2191–2219. doi:10.1111/j.1559-1816.2007.00255.x

Drapalski, A. L., Milford, J., Goldberg, R. W., Brown, C. H., & Dixon, L. B. (2008). Perceived barriers to medical care and mental health care among veterans with serious mental illness. *Psychiatric Services, 59,* 921–924. doi:10.1176/appi.ps.59.8.921

Greene-Shortridge, T. M., Britt, T. W., & Castro, C. A. (2007). The stigma of mental health problems in the military. *Military Medicine, 172,* 157–161.

Hardeman, W., Johnston, M., Johnston, D., Bonetti, D., Wareham, N., & Kinmonth, A. L. (2002). Application of the theory of planned behaviour in behaviour change interventions: A systematic review. *Psychology & Health, 17,* 123–158.

Hoge, C. W., Auchterlonie, J. L., & Milliken, C. S. (2006). Mental health problems, use of mental health services, and attrition from military service after returning from deployment to Iraq or Afghanistan. *JAMA, 295,* 1023–1032. doi:10.1001/jama.295.9.1023

Hoge, C. W., Castro, C. A., Messer, S. C., McGurk, D., Cotting, D. I., & Koffman, R. L. (2004). Combat duty in Iraq and Afghanistan, mental health problems, and barriers to care. *The New England Journal of Medicine, 351*, 13–22. doi:10.1056/ NEJMoa040603

Hoge, C. W., Terhakopian, A., Castro, C. A., Messer, S. C., & Engel, C. C. (2007). Association of posttraumatic stress disorder and somatic symptoms, health care visits, and absenteeism among Iraq war veterans. *The American Journal of Psychiatry, 164*, 150–153. doi:10.1176/appi.ajp.164.1.150

Jakupcak, M., Luterek, J., Hunt, S., Conybeare, D., & McFall, M. (2008). Posttraumatic stress and its relationship to physical health functioning in a sample of Iraq and Afghanistan war Veterans seeking postdeploymnet VA health care. *Journal of Nervous and Mental Disease, 196*, 425–428. doi:10.1097/NMD.0b013e31817108ed

Jemmott, J. B., Jemmott, L. S., & Fong, G. T. (1998). Abstinence and safer sex HIV risk-reduction interventions for African American adolescents: A randomized controlled trial. *JAMA, 279*, 1529–1536. doi:10.1001/jama.279.19.1529

Kang, H. K., & Hyams, K. C. (2005). Mental health care needs among recent war veterans. *The New England Journal of Medicine, 352*, 1289. doi:10.1056/NEJMp058024

Leaf, P. J., Bruce, M. L., & Tischler, G. L. (1986). The differential effect of attitudes on the use of mental health services. *Social Psychiatry and Psychiatric Epidemiology, 21*, 187–192. doi:10.1007/BF00583999

Link, B. G., Phelan, J. C., Bresnahan, M., Stueve, A., & Pescosolido, B. A. (1999). Public conceptions of mental illness: Labels, causes, dangerousness, and social distance. *American Journal of Public Health, 89*, 1328–1333. doi:10.2105/ AJPH.89.9.1328

Litz, B. T., Engel, C. C., Bryant, R. A., & Papa, A. (2007). A randomized, controlled proof-of-concept trial of an Internet-based, therapist-assisted self-management treatment for posttraumatic stress disorder. *The American Journal of Psychiatry, 164*, 1676–1684. doi:10.1176/appi.ajp.2007.06122057

Mansfield, A. K., Addis, M. E., & Courtenay, W. (2005). Measurement of men's help seeking: Development and evaluation of the barriers to help seeking scale. *Psychology of Men & Masculinity, 6*, 95–108. doi:10.1037/1524-9220.6.2.95

Mental Health Advisory Team IV. (2006). *Operation Iraqi Freedom 05-07 final report.* U.S. Office of the Surgeon Multinational Force-Iraq and Office of the Surgeon General United States Army Medical Command. Retrieved from http://www. armymedicine.army.mil/reports/mhat/mhat_iv/mhat-iv.cfm

Milliken, C. S., Auchterlonie, M. S., & Hoge, C. W. (2007). Longitudinal assessment of mental health problems among active and reserve component U.S. service members returning from the Iraq war. *JAMA, 298*, 2141–2148. doi:10.1001/ jama.298.18.2141

Murphy, W. G., & Brubaker, R. G. (1990). Effects of a brief theory-based intervention on the practice of testicular self-examination by high school males. *The Journal of School Health, 60*, 459–462. doi:10.1111/j.1746-1561.1990.tb05977.x

Ojeda, V. D., & Bergstresser, S. M. (2008). Gender, race–ethnicity, and psychosocial barriers to mental health care: An examination of perceptions and attitudes among adults reporting unmet need. *Journal of Health and Social Behavior, 49,* 317–334. doi:10.1177/002214650804900306

Perlick, D. A., & Manning, M. R. (2006). Overcoming stigma and barriers to mental health treatment. In J. E. Grant & M. N. Potenza (Eds.), *The textbook of men's mental health* (pp. 389–417). Arlington, VA: American Psychiatric Publishing.

Pietrzak, R. H., Johnson, D. C., Goldstein, M. B., Malley, J. C., & Southwick, S. M. (2009). Perceived stigma and barriers to mental health care utilization among OEF–OIF Veterans. *Psychiatric Services, 60,* 1118–1122. doi:10.1176/appi.ps. 60.8.1118

Pirkis, J., Blood, R. W., Francis, C., & McCallum, K. (2006). On-screen portrayals of mental illness: Extent, nature, and impacts. *Journal of Health Communication, 11,* 523–541. doi:10.1080/10810730600755889

Rosenheck, R. A., & Fontana, A. F. (2007). Recent trends in VA treatment of post-traumatic stress disorder and other mental disorders. *Health Affairs, 26,* 1720–1727. doi:10.1377/hlthaff.26.6.1720

Rundell, J. R. (2006). Demographics of and diagnoses in Operation Enduring Freedom and Operation Iraqi Freedom personnel who were psychiatrically evacuated from the theater of operations. *General Hospital Psychiatry, 28,* 352–356. doi:10.1016/j.genhosppsych.2006.04.006

Schell, T. L., & Marshall, G. N. (2008). Survey of individuals previously deployed for OEF/OIF. In T. Tanielian & L. H. Jaycox (Eds.), *Invisible wounds of war: Psychological and cognitive injuries, their consequences, and services to assist recovery.* Santa Monica, CA: RAND Corporation.

Seal, K. H., Bertenthal, D., Maguen, S., Gima, K., Chu, A., & Marmar, C. R. (2008). Getting beyond "Don't Ask, Don't Tell": An evaluation of US Veterans Administration postdeployment mental health screening of Veterans returning from Iraq and Afghanistan. *American Journal of Public Health, 98,* 714–720. doi:10.2105/AJPH.2007.115519

Seal, K. H., Metzler, T. J., Gima, K. S., Bertenthal, D., Maguen, S., & Marmar, C. R. (2009). Trends and risk factors for mental health diagnoses among Iraq and Afghanistan Veterans using Department of Veterans Affairs health care, 2002–2008. *American Journal of Public Health, 99,* 1651–1658.

Sherbourne, C. D., Asch, S. M., Shugarman, L. R., Goebel, J. R., Lanto, A. B., Rubenstein, L. V., . . . Lorenz, K. A. (2009). Early identification of co-occurring pain, depression and anxiety. *Journal of General Internal Medicine, 24,* 620–625. doi:10.1007/s11606-009-0956-2

Stecker, T. (2010). *Guiding decision making among clients: A brief intervention for mental health and addiction professionals.* Minneapolis, MN: Hazelden.

Stecker, T., Fortney, J. C., Hamilton, F., & Ajzen, I. (2007). An assessment of beliefs about mental health care among veterans who served in Iraq. *Psychiatric Services, 58,* 1358–1361. doi:10.1176/appi.ps.58.10.1358

Stecker, T., Fortney, J. C., Hamilton, F., Sherbourne, C. D., & Ajzen, I. (2010). Engagement in mental health treatment among veterans returning from Iraq. *Patient Preferences and Adherence, 4*, 45–49.

Stecker, T., Fortney, J. C., McGovern, M. P., & Sherbourne, C. D. (in press). Co-occurring medical, psychiatric and alcohol-related disorders among veterans returning from Iraq and Afghanistan. *Psychosomatics*.

Vasterling, J. J., Schumm, J., Proctor, S. P., Gentry, E., King, D. W., & King, L. A. (2008). Posttraumatic stress disorder and health functioning in a non-treatment-seeking sample of Iraq war veterans: A prospective analysis. *Journal of Rehabilitation Research and Development, 45*, 347–358. doi:10.1682/JRRD.2007.05.0077

Vogt, D. (2010). *Mental health-related beliefs as a barrier to service use for military personnel and veterans: Findings and recommendations for future research*. Manuscript submitted for publication.

Vogt, D., Bergeron, A., Salgado, D., Daley, J., Ouimette, P., & Wolfe, J. (2006). Barriers to veterans health administration care in a nationally representative sample of women veterans. *Journal of General Internal Medicine, 21*, S19–S25. doi:10.1111/j.1525-1497.2006.00370.x

Waldron, I. (1997). Changes in gender roles and gender differences in health behavior. In D. Gochman (Ed.), *Handbook of health behavior research* (Vol. 1, pp. 303–328). New York, NY: Plenum.

12

ENHANCING SYSTEMS OF CARE FOR POSTTRAUMATIC STRESS DISORDER: FROM PRIVATE PRACTICE TO LARGE HEALTH CARE SYSTEMS

JOSEF I. RUZEK AND SONJA V. BATTEN

Active-duty personnel and veterans with posttraumatic stress disorder (PTSD) or other deployment-related mental health concerns seldom interact with a single practitioner. Rather, they work with multiple providers over the course of time, interact with various helping resources, and move among sectors of a large and complex treatment system that includes Department of Defense (DoD) facilities and TRICARE, the Veterans Health Administration (VHA) of the Department of Veterans Affairs (VA), and other public and private health care systems. It is therefore useful to conceptualize services for those returning from war zones as a system of care embodying different service sectors, and within each sector, a range of helping services and care environments. Individual practitioners operate as a part of this larger continuum of care, and patients sequentially interact with multiple points of contact along this dimension.

This chapter focuses on the efficient and effective functioning of the system in providing the highest quality mental health care, from the perspectives

This chapter was coauthored by an employee of the United States government as part of official duty and is considered to be in the public domain. Any views expressed herein do not necessarily represent the views of the United States government, and the author's participation in the work is not meant to serve as an official endorsement.

of both the individual practitioner and managers responsible for design and operation of segments of the larger system. We identify cross-system challenges in service improvement and outline implications for action on the part of clinicians and managers of mental health care delivery systems.

IMPORTANCE OF A SYSTEMS PERSPECTIVE

The actual treatment experience of military personnel often takes them sequentially through various elements of a system of care. Combat and Operational Stress Control services may be delivered to service men and women on the field of battle (Ritchie, in press). DoD has also implemented a comprehensive screening process for mental and physical health concerns, both after a deployment and throughout an individual's military career. The process mandates a face-to-face health assessment with a trained health care provider for each individual returning from a deployment. The assessment includes a discussion of mental health or psychosocial issues commonly associated with deployments. This assessment occurs again 3 to 6 months after the deployment, at which time a trained health care provider discusses identified health concerns and determines whether referrals are required. The provider educates individuals on postdeployment health readjustment issues and provides information on available resources. Finally, mandatory annual periodic health assessments address psychological functioning and overall readiness for service members and provide ongoing opportunities for early identification and intervention. As they transition to civilian status, these new veterans may access VA for physical health care or mental health treatment. Their families, and some veterans, will use physical and mental health services offered by organizations and private practitioners in their local communities.

Key elements of the system of direct service provision for those seeking help for PTSD and other postdeployment mental and behavioral health difficulties include physical and mental health treatment programs within DoD and VA systems, purchased care through TRICARE and private insurance, state Departments of Veterans Affairs, and an extended network of community organizations and service providers. Other sources of information and resources available to military service personnel and veterans include various Centers of Excellence that conduct research and educational services related to PTSD and postdeployment mental health, Veterans and military service organizations, and self-help organizations in which individuals sharing similar difficulties offer one another mutual support.

Historically, treatment of PTSD and other postdeployment problems has been relatively fragmented. Among U.S. adults, many of those with PTSD have sought care not in specialized PTSD or general mental health settings but may have received treatment either in primary care or not at all (Wang et al., 2005). Comorbid mental health conditions and multiple co-occurring problems are a significant concern for those with PTSD, presenting challenges to the integrated treatment of the whole person. In the case of substance abuse, for example, the lack of truly integrated care may mean that those who first encounter the substance abuse treatment system may not receive appropriate and timely education and treatment for their PTSD symptoms or may be told that they need to cease substance abuse before they can receive specialized care for PTSD. When moving between sectors or from one treatment setting to another, there may be a loss of continuity of care, resulting in inadequately informed treatment providers, unnecessary assessment procedures, or confusion and lowered satisfaction for patients. Effective care and efficient use of limited helping resources call for increased integration of care within and between sectors (Batten & Pollack, 2008).

Integrated care is important in part because comprehensive care for returnees often requires that they have access to a range of kinds of services. Care for co-occurring problems presents the challenge of mobilizing professionals of different disciplines across treatment settings. A given individual may need treatment for PTSD and substance abuse, help with smoking cessation, management of diabetes or other health problems, job finding or educational counseling, and assistance in managing the sequelae of traumatic brain injury. The individual's family may require help with finances, marital conflict, and parenting. If service members are expected to navigate this system alone, with no guidance, care may end up shuffled between different providers who are able to provide only pieces of an incomplete treatment plan.

In the context of such a system of care, a practitioner's ability to deliver best practices in treating PTSD and to develop a complete treatment plan that can effectively address other needs of the whole person will depend on the practitioner's ability to access several key types of resources for himself or herself—information, training, interpersonal support and consultation, and interconnection with other elements in the system of care—and on the ability of the larger system to support that access. We first explore these resource domains from the vantage point of the individual clinical health care professional or paraprofessional and then revisit the same issues in terms of a larger health care system perspective.

NEEDS AT THE LEVEL OF THE INDIVIDUAL PRACTITIONER

In treating PTSD and other postdeployment mental health problems, the practitioner is critical to effectiveness of care, efficiency of care, and customer satisfaction. Without a caring, competent professional, the best resources will be insufficiently mobilized. In fact, overall quality of care depends on the millions of individual interactions that occur between practitioners and patients, most of which require energy and improvisation on the part of the practitioner:

> To the extent that professional tasks are nonroutine, their effective performance requires committed performance rather than perfunctory conformance. Extrinsic controls . . . are not only difficult to implement—because the tasks are difficult to meter and monitor—but also ineffectual as a means of eliciting appropriate levels of commitment. (Adler, Kwon, & Signer, 2005, p. 45)

To produce the kind of commitment and expertise needed to ensure that provider–patient interactions are managed in the best ways possible and that providers are capable of implementing the most effective, evidence-based practices (EBPs) available, practitioners need to be knowledgeable about recent developments in research and clinical care, informed about resources available to returning service members, trained in effective assessment and treatment methods, supported by supervisors and administrators, and involved in collaborative discussions and decisions about optimal care.

Information

A basic resource needed by all practitioners, wherever they are embedded in a care system, is information. In addition to the knowledge and skills related to their professional training, clinicians working with returning service members will need to know, or be able to find quickly, up-to-date information about a diverse set of issues, including

- military culture, the deployment experience, and postdeployment challenges;
- evidence-based treatments and clinical practice guidelines;
- sources of training for practitioners and information on training quality;
- military and veteran benefits;
- services available in various sectors of care and referral information;
- organizational policies and procedures; and
- resource materials for returning service members and their families (e.g., self-help materials, online patient education resources).

Although there is as yet no single, easily accessible source of the kinds of comprehensive information that providers need, a variety of online sources of useful and authoritative information are available and are listed in the appendix to this chapter. In particular, websites created by VA and DoD Centers of Excellence (e.g., National Center for PTSD, http://www.ptsd.va.gov; Defense Centers of Excellence for Psychological Health and Traumatic Brain Injury, http://www.dcoe.health.mil) contain useful information links related to clinical resources, current research, and available educational and training opportunities.

Training

Whereas access to good quality information may allow clinicians to be aware of best practices in assessment and treatment, training will usually be needed to convert that information into new skills and habits. Importantly, most mental health practitioners are generalists, not specialists in trauma and PTSD. Often, patients with PTSD may be treated in general mental health clinics, rather than in specialty clinics devoted to the treatment of traumatic stress. Community providers and those who are new to VA may lack a familiarity with military culture, and most providers, wherever they are located, are not currently delivering EBPs that are consistent with clinical practice guidelines.

Although best practices for PTSD treatment have been clearly described in several sets of clinical practice guidelines, including one jointly created and endorsed by the VA and DoD (VA/DoD Clinical Practice Guideline Working Group, 2004), such descriptions too seldom influence the behavior of practitioners. In recognition that published practice guidelines can be unwieldy to digest, many guidelines include summaries or decision trees that help practitioners identify practices that careful review of empirical research and expert clinical consensus have determined should be learned (VA/DoD Clinical Practice Guideline Working Group, 2004).

In addition to deciding what to learn, practitioners must be aware of the characteristics of evidence-based training; that is, they must recognize what kinds of training procedures are likely to be effective in giving them the skills that they require. Research suggests that most continuing education activities are not effective in changing clinician behavior (e.g., Jensen-Doss, Cusack, & de Arellano, 2008), perhaps because these activities do not allow sufficient opportunity for participants to practice new skills. Workshop effectiveness is increased when presentation of information is accompanied by demonstration of skills, opportunities for behavioral rehearsal (Fixsen et al., 2005), and interactive participation via discussion, peer performance feedback, and group planning (Grol & Grimshaw, 2003). Most important, training effectiveness increases when initial instruction is supplemented by ongoing coaching and supervision. Newly learned skills are consolidated and sustained through consultation and coaching on the job.

Within DoD and VA health care systems, systematic training in designated evidence-based interventions for PTSD, such as prolonged exposure (PE) and cognitive processing therapy (CPT), is increasingly available. This training includes participation in multiday interactive skills workshops, ideally followed by ongoing telephone consultation as initial cases are seen. However, opportunities to participate in interactive workshops to learn the best-validated treatments for PTSD are limited for many providers across the sectors of care, and opportunities to receive ongoing supervision are more limited still.

Several factors can make it even more difficult for private practitioners to access the highest quality training for the treatment of PTSD. First, there is no centralized repository of training opportunities at this time, which may lead practitioners to choose trainings on the basis of word of mouth or convenience of location. In addition, those who have not specialized in PTSD may not have awareness of the latest research findings that suggest one mode of treatment over another. Further, private practitioners may be limited by the realities of the costs of training and the loss of individual income that comes when they must take days off from work to attend an outside training. Until structured learning opportunities for evidence-based treatments become more accessible, practitioners must be creative in finding effective ways to learn and practice by forming mutual support relationships and peer consultation groups with colleagues who are trained in the treatments or who are also seeking to add to their skills repertoires.

Interpersonal Support and Sharing

Practitioners treating postdeployment PTSD and other mental health challenges benefit from interaction with those providing similar services. PTSD patients often have multiple problems that are difficult to treat. Some may be angry, demanding, at risk for violence, or suicidal; they may present with intense emotional distress and complex, sometimes intractable, problems that are better managed by an interdisciplinary team than a lone practitioner. Despite the individuality of each person seeking help, practitioners throughout the systems of care face many similar challenges. Therefore, it is important that they not be forced to "reinvent the wheel" but instead are able to learn from the experiences of one another. In ideal circumstances, a community of practitioners cooperates to share information, provide mutual emotional and instrumental support, and share promising practices and experiences with evidence-based interventions. This connection is especially important for the community-based private practitioner who may not be connected to the larger community of providers serving returning veterans. Thus, clinical consultation or supervision may be especially valuable as a means to enhance learning, problem solve difficult cases, and prevent burnout. Unfortunately, in many service delivery settings, workload and other organizational priorities have combined to reduce routine access to supervision and consultation on the job after individuals have achieved their professional license. This means that busy practitioners must create opportunities for this kind of activity—for instance, by pulling together colleagues for regular peer consultation activities.

Such consultation is especially necessary in the context of working with those with PTSD, not simply for the acquisition and reinforcement of new skills. It is widely recognized that hearing the trauma stories of returning service members may be stressful for therapists. These stories may also remind military mental health practitioners who may have been deployed themselves of personal traumas, losses, or other stressors. Supervision and consultation activities and mutual support in teams provide important ways to prevent the vicarious traumatization, compassion fatigue, and secondary traumatic stress reactions that can be associated with trauma counseling (Bride, 2004; Follette, Polusny, & Milbeck, 1994).

Interconnection With Other Elements in the System of Care

Many returning service men and women experience a variety of co-occurring problems, both physical and psychological. Practitioners may find themselves faced with clients presenting with PTSD together with a variety of coexisting comorbidities (e.g., depression, pain, substance abuse, relationship problems), such that the intensity of patient needs and demands may more suitably be addressed by a team approach in an intensive outpatient or residential treatment setting. Particularly for clinicians in the private sector, it may be important to establish connections with colleagues in DoD and VA health care systems to enable their patients to benefit from the full range of services available to them. These practitioners also need to have at least a basic awareness of the benefits in VA or DoD to which returning service members are entitled (such information can be found at http://www.oefoif.va.gov). For example, VA services include an extensive national network of specialized PTSD residential and outpatient PTSD treatment programs that typically offer assessment, trauma-related patient education, pharmacotherapy, coping skills training, group therapy, and evidence-based PTSD treatments. VA has women's trauma programs, military sexual trauma treatment providers, and counselors who specialize in outreach to OEF and OIF returnees. VA also can offer a range of associated services, including vocational training and counseling, inpatient hospitalization, substance abuse treatment services, and mental health care for co-occurring mental health disorders. VA's Readjustment Counseling Service comprises a large national network of community-based Vet Center clinics that also address PTSD and other postdeployment stress issues. Vet Centers are often staffed by individuals who have themselves deployed, and they provide care to family members of veterans who are dealing with challenges of bereavement due to death of a service member or those associated with living with a veteran with PTSD.

In DoD, the military health system provides medical care to active-duty service members, medically eligible National Guard and Reserve personnel, retirees, and dependents and dependent survivors. The mental health services may include counseling, substance abuse prevention and treatment programs, specialty care, and preventive services; the venues for treatment range from in-theater care, to small clinics, to larger teaching hospitals and military treatment facilities, as well as TRICARE services in the community. It is important to note that each of the services determines the specific array of treatment options that it will provide (the U.S. Navy provides mental health services for both its service members and U.S. Marine Corps personnel), and there is some level of variation in implementation between the services. Each service has its own specific PTSD programs that include a foundation of evidence-based care yet are implemented in a manner that is sensitive to service cultures.

Programs are also more readily available for family members in DoD than in VA, and these include the Family Advocacy Program, Family Support Centers, and several online resources. Additional support to individuals and couples is also provided by military chaplains, which may be appealing both for spiritual purposes and because greater confidentiality of chaplains may carry less perceived stigma related to seeking psychological health support. Military One Source is another resource that can be accessed by phone, online, or in person by service members and their families and provides up to six free sessions of counseling per year, per problem. However, it is important to note that Military One Source is not designed to treat clinical problems, so for treatment of PTSD, individuals requiring help are generally given referrals elsewhere in the military health system. Finally, much treatment in the military health system, especially for National Guard and Reserve personnel who may not reside near a military installation or military treatment facility, is delivered through TRICARE providers in the community, rounding out the purchased care component of the military health system.

Providers located in different parts of the care system must make active efforts to learn about one another. Many VA and DoD conferences and training activities bring together providers across systems, and some of these events are also open to civilian providers in the local community. Such activities facilitate mutual understanding and enable providers to make contact with one another. These opportunities strengthen not only the knowledge base about available services but also the relationships between the practitioners representing different components of the broader continuum of care.

Summary

For the individual practitioner, key resource needs include up-to-date information, training in best practices that includes interactive hands-on practice opportunities and continuing supervision and consultation, interpersonal support, and connection with other parts of the system of care. Several websites offer authoritative guidance about assessment and treatment of PTSD and other deployment-related problems. Others describe a range of services available in multiple care sectors. However, in the absence of well-implemented systems that facilitate easy access to the full range of needed resources, practitioners must be creative in building opportunities for mutual supervision, information sharing, and interpersonal support from colleagues.

NEEDS AT THE LEVEL OF BROAD SYSTEMS OF TREATMENT

The busy individual practitioner, if working alone, will find it challenging to locate information, training, and interpersonal support and to find ways to work effectively with other elements of a complex system of care. Managers, and the health care systems in which they work, must develop ways to enable and sustain these activities.

Information

As noted earlier, practitioners require a variety of information to perform effectively. However, finding authoritative information on traumatic stress is a time-consuming procedure (Bremner, Quinn, Quinn, & Veledar, 2006). Health care systems and organizations, as well as Centers of Excellence that focus on aspects of mental health care for service members and veterans, must assist providers and systems administrators in this effort. Organizations can also develop web-based materials for their practitioners. For example, Riley et al. (2007) reported on development of a web application, therapyadvisor.com, that is designed to increase awareness of EBPs and build a commitment to try the interventions. Such sites might be usefully developed by health care organizations (Ruzek, in press) and then made available to practitioners in all the relevant sectors of care.

Creation of health care systems that are constantly improving their treatment capabilities requires that systems be established to communicate useful information proactively to clinicians and enable them to find and easily digest information that they need. PTSD knowledge domains that are important for providers and managers to be able to access readily include information about best practices and organizational policies and procedures related to PTSD care. However, information is also needed about how PTSD programs are performing, what local innovations are being tried, what clinicians need and want, what materials are available, and who has what knowledge and skills. Organizations themselves require a systematic approach to knowledge management (Ruzek, Friedman, & Murray, 2005), defined as a set of practices involving the guidance, creation, codification, dissemination, and evolution of knowledge for strategic ends (Davenport & Prusak, 1998). Many business organizations have developed structured efforts to manage the role of knowledge in the processes of doing work (Denning, 2000) in an effort to ensure competitive advantage and spur innovation. Similar efforts should be undertaken by health care organizations.

Training

Effective training for mental health practitioners requires interactive training opportunities that offer hands-on experience with new skills as well as ongoing supervision and support for practitioners as they implement new assessment and treatment methods. This suggests that organizations and health care systems should invest in supporting training initiatives that include evidence-based training and dissemination approaches, rather than relying on conventional continuing education approaches that are likely ineffective in changing practitioner behavior (e.g., Durlak & DuPre, 2008; Ruzek & Rosen, 2009). Training, and especially supervision and consultation, can be labor intensive and expensive. However, they are necessary to support clinicians in offering the best quality of care, and managers must budget for these activities and regard them not as optional costs but as integral processes.

Despite the existence of a VA–DoD Clinical Practice Guideline for PTSD that spells out recommended practices derived from clinical consensus and research findings (available at http://www.healthquality.va.gov/Post_Traumatic_Stress_Disorder_PTSD.asp), there is wide variation in treatment of deployment-related PTSD across federal and private treatment sectors. Until recently, evidence-based treatments for PTSD were not widely available in most treatment settings, including VA and DoD (e.g., Rosen et al., 2004), despite the importance of evidence-based practices. Delivery of training and supervision in these methods is a clear priority.

Managers must consider ways to support both participation in existing learning opportunities and the ongoing functioning of mental health providers. Gray, Elhai, and Schmidt (2007) surveyed members of the International Society for Traumatic Stress Studies and other trauma professionals to examine attitudes toward EBPs and to identify barriers to learning about EBPs. Although most participants were positive about EBPs, a key barrier to learning about them was related to access to training. Specific barriers included insufficient time to learn (38.7%), difficulty finding time to attend training seminars (37.7%), and expense of training seminars (35%). Systems of care should be engineered to encourage participation in training activities as a means to improve services, disseminate EBPs, improve staff morale, and reduce job-related stress and burnout. Practical steps include offering training workshops with posttraining consultation and allowing time off to attend training activities. One form of training and support, as noted earlier, is case supervision and consultation, and it is important to make this available to mental health providers on a routine basis. Although there may be initial costs to an organization to pay for training and allow staff time away from direct patient care to attend trainings and regular consultation sessions, these are costs that systems wishing to advance clinical care, improve staff morale, and reduce burnout should accept.

Interpersonal Support and Sharing

Managers and organizations can take steps to increase support and sharing among their providers. These steps include supporting participation in training events and conferences, promoting development of mutual supervision groups, and creating opportunities for practitioners to meet and explore common challenges (e.g., creating online forums). These activities will succeed only when such participation is expected of employees and is treated as a mainstream job performance requirement with approved time away from direct care activities, rather than something additional for clinicians to add to their already busy schedules.

VA intranet sites support a number of communities of practice, including those related to military sexual trauma, implementation of PE and CPT, suicide prevention, and management of PTSD services. A National PTSD Mentor Program, focusing on supporting managers of mental health services (rather than clinicians), has established PTSD administrative mentors in each of the 21 VHA regions. These mentors participate in monthly national telephone calls to exchange information and learn about important systemwide initiatives. They in turn hold monthly regional calls with all the managers of PTSD programs in their regions.

Interconnection With Other Elements in the System of Care

Since the beginning of OEF and OIF, much effort has been made to connect the operations of DoD and VA systems more effectively to coordinate treatment and transitions between the two health care systems (e.g., development of the National Resource Directory as a collaboration between VA, DoD and Department of Labor, http://www.nationalresourcedirectory.org). To this end, the Recovery Coordination and Federal Recovery Coordination Programs implement reforms to existing policy, programs, and processes within and across DoD and VA. Such efforts are important because improved interconnection and collaboration among systems is likely to result in improved mental health services for those returning from deployment. Increased awareness of services available in each sector can increase mutual, appropriate referrals and spur development of complementary, rather than duplicative, services.

One of the more promising developments related to interconnection is the establishment of a number of state-based consortia that bring together multiple stakeholders—VA and Vet Center staff, DoD personnel from all branches of service (including reserve components), TRICARE providers, state departments of veterans affairs, community-based organizations, and consumer groups—interested in the welfare of Iraq and Afghanistan war returnees. For example, the Northwest Network Deployment Health Summit Regional Conference (McFall, Hunt, Ruzek, & Klevens, 2005) was convened to familiarize and educate partners involved in health care of soldiers and veterans about the nomenclature, function, and roles of each agency and to inventory, map, and coordinate helping resources.

One simple additional way to facilitate collaboration would be to build capacity for integrated training across systems of those serving returnees. Both VA and DoD conduct trainings that often include practitioners from both health care systems, and both have launched training initiatives that focus on delivery of specific evidence-based treatments for PTSD. Further development of web-based training materials may facilitate the goal of integrated training opportunities.

Summary

To enable their practitioners to provide best quality care and adapt rapidly to new knowledge and changing service delivery priorities, health care organizations must expand and systematize their methods of information delivery, training and supervision, and practitioner support. Practitioners require improved access to effective training opportunities, and systems that promote information sharing among practitioners should be created. Wherever possible, these efforts should cut across the systems of care. Participation in training and information-sharing activities should be viewed as a mainstream performance responsibility that is required of mental health practitioners and supported by management.

EXAMPLES OF CROSS-SYSTEM SERVICE
IMPROVEMENT CHALLENGES

Several issues are especially important to both the delivery of effective treatment and to ongoing efforts to improve treatment. These must be addressed throughout the range of service delivery settings in VHA, DoD, and the community.

Identification of Problems and Engagement in Care

Wherever they are situated in the systems of care, and at whatever post-deployment time period they interact with returnees, practitioners must find ways to identify individuals who may benefit from mental health services. Veterans often are unlikely to disclose postdeployment stress problems. Those experiencing higher levels of symptoms may be especially unlikely to seek help (Maguen & Litz, 2006). Perceptions of stigma around mental health help seeking remain significant and include concern about being seen as weak, feelings of embarrassment, and concern about reactions from leadership (Hoge et al., 2004). Some individuals fear that documentation of PTSD-related problems in their medical record might reduce the likelihood of later employment in some civilian occupations (e.g., police) or advancement in a military career.

Outside of the VA and DoD systems, patients may not automatically self-identify as returning military personnel, and it may not be apparent to civilian health care providers that they are serving a veteran or family member of a veteran. National Guard and Reserve personnel in particular may seek care in the private sector. Thus, to promote screening and identification, we recommend that primary care and mental health practitioners routinely ask patients, "Are you a veteran or a family member of a veteran or service member?"

In VA and DoD health care systems, screening for PTSD and other postdeployment problems occurs at multiple points in time. Screening can increase rates of identification of PTSD and rates of referral. Because many veterans and active-duty personnel will receive care outside of VA and DoD systems, it is important that community-based providers in mental health, and, importantly, primary care medical settings, make efforts to identify both whether their patients are veterans and whether they are experiencing symptoms of PTSD and other postdeployment problems.

Affected individuals are likely to present in primary care rather than psychological treatment settings, where they may not disclose problems related to PTSD but may present instead with a variety of physical health complaints or depression. In the civilian community, as elsewhere, there is a need to initiate care where individuals present for treatment. In DOD and VA systems, this has led to increased efforts to screen for PTSD and other postdeployment problems in primary care medical settings (e.g., Engel et al., 2008). At present, however, civilian physicians are unlikely to routinely screen for veteran status or for PTSD, which would be a useful procedure to make routine in civilian settings. Brief screening tools are available and can be easily incorporated into intake procedures (e.g., Prins et al., 2004).

The issue of integration of PTSD awareness into other care environments may be important in a wide range of settings. For example, veterans' use of mental health services may sometimes be driven by issues such as guilt or the weakening of their religious faith than by the severity of their PTSD symptoms or social problems (Fontana & Rosenheck, 2004). This means that help seeking may often be directed toward chaplains or other spiritual leaders. Other settings in which those experiencing postdeployment stress problems may seek help include substance abuse treatment programs, pain clinics, sleep programs, gambling addiction centers, child and family services, employee assistance programs, educational counseling services, and marital and family counseling settings. Practitioners working in these settings should establish procedures to identify veterans and active-duty personnel who may benefit from increased support or referral for mental health treatment.

Family Support

Partners of those with PTSD are significantly affected by their loved one's symptoms and experience burdens associated with caregiving (see Chapter 7, this volume). PTSD symptoms place veterans at increased risk of perpetrating relationship aggression against their partners (e.g., Byrne & Riggs, 1996). Children of those with PTSD may also be affected (see Chapter 8, this volume). In addition, a recent study of veterans receiving treatment for PTSD indicated that more than three quarters of those surveyed would like to see their family members more involved in their PTSD treatment (Batten et al., 2009). Such findings suggest that more attention should be paid to supporting families of those with PTSD and that improvements in family and relationship functioning are appropriate treatment goals for service members and veterans with PTSD. Steps should be taken to involve spouses and partners more systematically in care (Sautter, Lyons, & Manguno-Mire, 2006) during the assessment process, in the setting of treatment goals, and in treatment itself. Couples interventions for PTSD are in development, and early findings suggest that they can reduce survivors' self-reported levels of anxiety and depression (Monson, Schnurr, Stevens, & Guthrie, 2004).

The family support services developed by DoD are especially well suited to address these issues in active-duty populations. In addition, recent changes in public law may make family treatment more accessible throughout the VA system (Government Accountability Office, 2008). Vet Centers are able to address family issues and are an important helping resource. Expertise in child mental health is not generally available in VA because of the system's focus on the veteran. For this reason, private sector practitioners and family-oriented agencies specializing in child and family treatment can fulfill a key role in working with children and family members of those with PTSD and other postdeployment problems.

Outcomes Monitoring and Evaluation

In mental health, at the level of both the individual practitioner and the treatment program, measurement of outcomes is needed to inform treatment delivery and strengthen accountability of PTSD services. The VA–DoD clinical practice guideline for PTSD indicates that practitioners should administer validated measures of PTSD and associated problems at intake to estimate severity of problems and inform treatment planning (VA/DoD Clinical Practice Guideline Working Group, 2004). It also suggests that these tools be readministered periodically to monitor progress in treatment and permit evaluation of its effectiveness. Well-validated questionnaires for measurement of PTSD symptoms are available (e.g., PTSD Checklist; Weathers, Litz, Herman, Huska, & Keane, 1993; Keane, Brief, Pratt, & Miller, 2007) and can be easily and regularly administered throughout treatment to examine changes in symptoms. In addition to symptoms, it is also important to measure outcomes related to family, work, and social functioning. Those returning from deployments often experience significant difficulties with family relationships (e.g., Riggs, Byrne, Weathers, & Litz, 1998). Evidence also indicates that PTSD impairs work performance and reduces work productivity (Kessler & Frank, 1997) and is associated with a lower likelihood of employment (Savoca & Rosenheck, 2000). Although these problem areas may often show significant improvement if PTSD is treated successfully, they should also be made specific targets for treatment and monitored as significant outcomes in their own right.

At the program level as well, it is important to measure treatment outcomes. In VA, the effectiveness of residential PTSD programs has been systematically evaluated for many years, and results have been used to guide policy development. In the absence of such measurement, program managers cannot judge the effectiveness of services. Furthermore, without such data, it will not be clear when to initiate program changes, and when program changes are implemented, it will be difficult to establish their value to patients. At the level of the health care system, measurement of outcomes can enable comparison of various approaches to treatment delivery, evaluation of policy changes and training and dissemination initiatives, and development of a culture of care and accountability that relies on empirical demonstration of effectiveness.

Currently, many clinicians do not routinely monitor progress in treatment or evaluate outcomes of treatment using questionnaires or other formal measurement approaches. Information about well-validated questionnaires is available, and it is important that these be incorporated into routine practice. Similarly, most clinic managers do not have systematic program evaluation data available on which to guide decision making. The establishment of such processes is an important priority for program development.

Dissemination and Implementation of Best Practices

As noted earlier, the treatments that have received the most research support are not yet widely delivered by PTSD treatment providers. This has led organizations to develop training initiatives and other efforts to influence their clinicians to increase use of the best practices identified in clinical practice guidelines (Karlin et al., in press). However, these efforts at dissemination expose some of the very real differences between the perspectives of the individual practitioner and the manager or policymaker. For example, although quality of care is important to all, frontline staff members are concerned about how new approaches will affect their workloads and the "craft" of their treatment provision, and managers are interested in the business aspects of programs (e.g., reducing waiting lists, achieving cost savings; Parker et al., 2009).

Typically, most organizational dissemination efforts are implemented in a top-down fashion, which means that adequate levels of "buy-in" from treatment staff may be lacking, producing a reluctance to adopt new practices as directed (Rohrbach et al., 2006). The adoption of newly disseminated practices often means displacement of other, more familiar practices. It also means that significant effort must be devoted to mastering new protocols. Some evidence indicates that shared decision making—encouraging local involvement and participation in program dissemination—is associated with better and more sustained implementation (Durlak & DuPre, 2008). Practitioners must make an effort to remain flexible and open to learning and trying new treatment approaches. Those who lead dissemination initiatives must work collaboratively with clinicians, find ways to seek their feedback actively at all stages of dissemination, make efforts to address their needs and concerns, and actively communicate the purposes and ongoing results of dissemination projects. If dissemination is to succeed and services are to be improved, creative approaches to establishing quality-improvement dialogues among practitioners, managers, and administrators will be required (Parker et al., 2009).

CONCLUSION

The variety and complexity of the needs of returning service members means that all providers must increasingly see themselves as part of a collaborating, nationwide system of services and, as appropriate for their location in that system and to the specific resources they provide, work to improve their knowledge, effectiveness, and efficiency. It is likely that health care systems will increasingly define aspects of care that must be delivered on the basis of practice guidelines, evolving research, and program evaluation findings and that practitioners will be asked to master those skills and interventions. As research on PTSD and other postdeployment problems accelerates, the need for practitioners to be responsive in adapting their practices will also increase. Given the "shortening half-life of professional knowledge" (Calhoun, Moras, Pilkonis, & Rehm, 1998), the often-stated need for practitioners to embrace lifelong learning reflects an expectation that they be willing to learn and change throughout their careers. Therefore, the mental health provider of the future will need to be proactive in finding the best information, drawing on work at various Centers of Excellence, and locating excellent training opportunities. He or she will increasingly need to base clinical decision making on evidence (e.g., through monitoring outcomes). Directors of clinics will be expected to review their outcomes evaluation data to improve clinic operations and care for patients. For their part, managers and leaders of mental health care organizations will be challenged to support their clinicians more effectively by implementing policies, human systems, and technologies that ensure ongoing effective training and dissemination (Ruzek & Rosen, 2009), managing organizational knowledge in a systematic fashion, making quality information easily accessible to those that need it, systematizing and simplifying outcomes monitoring for clinicians and programs, and reinforcing innovation.

APPENDIX 12.1: WEB RESOURCES

CENTERS OF EXCELLENCE

National Center for PTSD: http://www.ncptsd.va.gov
Defense Centers of Excellence for Psychological Health and Traumatic Brain Injury: http://www.dcoe.health.mil
VA Mental Illness Research Education and Clinical Centers: http://www.mirecc.va.gov
Center for Deployment Psychology: http://www.deploymentpsych.org
Center for the Study of Traumatic Stress: http://www.centerforthe studyoftraumaticstress.org
Deployment Health Clinical Center: http://www.pdhealth.mil
National Center for Telehealth and Technology: http://www.t2health.org
Defense and Veterans Brain Injury Center: http://www.dvbic.org

PROFESSIONAL ORGANIZATIONS

International Society for Traumatic Stress Studies: http://www.istss.org
AMSUS, The Society of the Federal Health Agencies: http://www.amsus.org/home.shtml
Anxiety Disorders Association of America: http://www.adaa.org/
Association for Behavioral and Cognitive Therapies: http://www.abct.org/

VA/DOD MENTAL HEALTH SERVICES

VA Mental Health: http://www.mentalhealth.va.gov
VA Vet Centers: http://www.vetcenter.va.gov
TRICARE Management Activity: http://www.tricare.mil

ONLINE SERVICES FOR VETERANS, ACTIVE DUTY PERSONNEL, AND FAMILY MEMBERS

Afterdeployment.org: http://www.afterdeployment.org
National Suicide Prevention Lifeline: http://www.nationalsuicide preventionlifeline.org
Real Warriors. Real Battles. Real Strength. National public awareness campaign: http://www.realwarriors.net

Military One Source: http://www.militaryonesource.com
Tragedy Assistance Program for Survivors: http://www.taps.org
Military HomeFront: http://www.militaryhomefront.dod.mil
Military Family Life Consultants: http://www.mhngs.com
Military Child Development Initiatives: http://www.naccrra.org/MilitaryPrograms
Coming Together Around Military Families: http://www.zerotothree.org
Parents as Teachers, Heroes at Home: http://www.parentsasteacher.org

PRACTICE GUIDELINES

VA/DoD Clinical Practice Guideline for the Management of Post-Traumatic Stress: http://www.healthquality.va.gov/Post_Traumatic_Stress_Disorder_PTSD.asp

REFERENCES

Adler, P. S., Kwon, S. W., & Signer, J. M. K. (2005). The "six west" problem: Professional and the intraorganizational diffusion of innovations, with particular reference to the case of hospitals (working paper). Los Angeles, California: University of Southern California.

Batten, S. V., Drapalski, A. L., Decker, M. L., DeViva, J. C., Morris, L. J., Mann, M. A, . . . Dixon, L. B. (2009). Veteran interest in family involvement in PTSD treatment. *Psychological Services, 6*, 184–189. doi:10.1037/a0015392

Batten, S. V., & Pollack, S. J. (2008). Integrative outpatient treatment for returning service members. *Journal of Clinical Psychology, 64*, 928–939.

Bremner, J. D., Quinn, J., Quinn, W., & Veledar, E. (2006). Surfing the Net for medical information about psychological trauma: An empirical study of the quality and accuracy of trauma-related websites. *Medical Informatics and the Internet in Medicine, 31*, 227–236. doi:10.1080/14639230600887866

Bride, B. E. (2004). The impact of providing psychosocial services to traumatized populations. *Stress, Trauma and Crisis, 7*, 29–46. doi:10.1080/15434610490281101

Byrne, C. A., & Riggs, D. S. (1996). The cycle of trauma: Relationship aggression in male Vietnam veterans with symptoms of posttraumatic stress disorder. *Violence and Victims, 11*, 213–225.

Calhoun, K. S., Moras, K., Pilkonis, P. A., & Rehm, L. P. (1998). Empirically supported treatments: Implications for training. *Journal of Consulting and Clinical Psychology, 66*, 151–162.

Davenport, T. H., & Prusak, L. (1998). *Working knowledge: How organizations manage what they know.* Boston, MA: Harvard Business School Press.

Denning, S. (2000). *The springboard: How storytelling ignites action in knowledge-era organizations*. London, England: Butterworth Heinemann. Retrieved from http://www.stevedenning.com/what_is_knowledge_management

Durlak, J. A., & DuPre, E. P. (2008). Implementation matters: A review of research on the influence of implementation on program outcomes and the factors affecting implementation. *American Journal of Community Psychology, 41*, 327–350. doi:10.1007/s10464-008-9165-0

Engel, C. C., Oxman, T., Yamamoto, C., Gould, D., Barry, S., Stewart, P., et al. (2008). RESPECT-Mil: Feasibility of a systems-level collaborative care approach to depression and post-traumatic stress disorder in military primary care. *Military Medicine, 173*, 935–940.

Fixsen, D. L., Naoom, S. F., Blase, K. A., Friedman, R. M., & Wallace, F. (2005). *Implementation research: A synthesis of the literature* (FMHI Publication #231). Tampa: Louis de la Parte Florida Mental Health Institute, The National Implementation Research Network, University of South Florida.

Follette, V. M., Polusny, M. A., & Milbeck, K. (1994). Mental health and law enforcement professionals: Trauma history, psychological symptoms, and impact of providing services to child sexual abuse survivors. *Professional Psychology, Research and Practice, 25*, 275–282. doi:10.1037/0735-7028.25.3.275

Fontana, A., & Rosenheck, R. (2004). Trauma, change in strength of religious faith, and mental health service use among veterans treated for PTSD. *Journal of Nervous and Mental Disorders, 192*, 579–584.

Government Accountability Office. (2008). *VA National initiatives and local programs that address education and support for families of returning veterans*. Washington, DC: Author. Retrieved from http://gao.gov/new.items/d0922r.pdf

Gray, M. J., Elhai, J. D., & Schmidt, L. O. (2007). Trauma professionals' attitudes toward and utilization of evidence-based practices. *Behavior Modification, 31*, 732–748. doi:10.1177/0145445507302877

Grol, R., & Grimshaw, J. (2003). From best evidence to best practice: Effective implementation of change in patients' care. *The Lancet, 362*, 1225–1230. doi:10.1016/S0140-6736(03)14546-1

Hoge, C. W., Castro, C. A., Messer, S. C., McGurk, D., Cotting, D., & Koffman, R. L. (2004). Combat duty in Iraq and Afghanistan, mental health problems, and barriers to care. *The New England Journal of Medicine, 351*, 13–22. doi:10.1056/NEJMoa040603

Jensen-Doss, A., Cusack, K. J., & de Arellano, M. A. (2008). Workshop-based training in trauma-focused CBT: An in-depth analysis of impact on provider practices. *Community Mental Health Journal, 44*, 227–244. doi:10.1007/s10597-007-9121-8

Karlin, B. E., Ruzek, J. I., Chard, K. M., Eftekhari, A., Monson, C. M., Hembree, E. A., et al. (in press). Dissemination of evidence-based psychological treatments for post-traumatic stress disorder in the Veterans Health Administration. *Journal of Traumatic Stress*.

Keane, T. M., Brief, D. J., Pratt, E. M., & Miller, M. W. (2007). Assessment of PTSD and its comorbidities in adults. In M. J. Friedman, T. M. Keane, & P. A. Resick (Eds.), *Handbook of PTSD: Science and practice* (pp. 279–305). New York, NY: Guilford Press.

Kessler, R. C., & Frank, R. G. (1997). The impact of psychiatric disorders on work loss days. *Psychological Medicine, 27,* 861–873. doi:10.1017/S0033291797004807

Maguen, S. & Litz, B. T. (2006). Predictors of barriers to mental health treatment for Kosovo and Bosnia peacekeepers: A preliminary report. *Military Medicine, 171,* 454–458.

McFall, M., Hunt, S., Ruzek, J., & Klevens, M. (2005, November). *Meeting the mental health needs of OIF and OEF veterans.* Pre-meeting institute presented at Annual Conference of the International Society for Traumatic Stress Studies, Toronto, Canada.

Monson, C. M., Schnurr, P. P., Stevens, S. P., & Guthrie, K. A. (2004). Cognitive-behavioral couple's treatment for posttraumatic stress disorder: Initial findings. *Journal of Traumatic Stress, 17,* 341–344. doi:10.1023/B:JOTS.0000038483.69570.5b

Parker, L. E., Kirchner, J. E., Bonner, L. M., Fickel, J. J., Ritchie, M. J., Simons, C. E., . . . Yano, E. M. (2009). Creating a quality-improvement dialogue: Utilizing knowledge from frontline staff, managers, and experts to foster health care quality improvement. *Qualitative Health Research, 19,* 229–242. doi:10.1177/1049732308329481

Prins, A., Ouimette, P., Kimerling, R., Cameron, R. P., Hugeishofer, D. S., Shaw-Hegwer, . . . Sheikh, J. I. (2004). The primary care PTSD screen (PC-PTSD): Development and operating characteristics. *Primary Care Psychiatry, 9,* 9–14.

Riley, W. T., Schumann, M. F., Forman-Hoffman, V. L., Mihm, P., Applegate, B. W., & Asif, O. (2007). Responses of practicing psychologists to a web site developed to promote empirically supported treatments. *Professional Psychology, Research and Practice, 38,* 44–53. doi:10.1037/0735-7028.38.1.44

Riggs, D. S., Byrne, C. A., Weathers, F. W., & Litz, B. T. (1998). The quality of the intimate relationships of male Vietnam veterans: Problems associated with posttraumatic stress disorder. *Journal of Traumatic Stress, 11,* 87–101. doi:10.1023/A:1024409200155

Ritchie, E. C. (in press). *Combat and operational behavioral health.* Washington, DC: Borden Institute Press.

Rohrbach, L. A., Grana, R., Sussman, S., & Valente, T. W. (2006). Type II translation: Transporting prevention interventions from research to real-world settings. *Evaluation and the Health Professions, 29,* 302–333.

Rosen, C. S., Chow, H. C., Finney, J. F., Greenbaum, M. A., Moos, R. H., Sheikh, J. I., . . . Yesavage, J. a. (2004). VA practice patterns and practice guidelines for treating posttraumatic stress disorder. *Journal of Traumatic Stress, 17,* 213–222. doi:10.1023/B:JOTS.0000029264.23878.53

Ruzek, J. I. (in press). Disseminating best practices and information in post-trauma care: online training and support for providers serving trauma survivors. In A. Brunet (Ed.), *Trauma and the Internet*. Montreal, Canada: North Atlantic Treaty Organization Press.

Ruzek, J. I., Friedman, M. J., & Murray, S. (2005). Towards a PTSD knowledge management system in veterans health care. *Psychiatric Annals, 35*, 911–920.

Ruzek, J. I., & Rosen, R. C. (2009). Disseminating evidence-based treatments for PTSD in organizational settings: A high priority focus area. *Behaviour Research and Therapy, 47*, 980–989. doi:10.1016/j.brat.2009.07.008

Sautter, F., Lyons, J. A., & Manguno-Mire, G. (2006). Predictors of partner engagement in PTSD treatment. *Journal of Psychopathology and Behavioral Assessment, 28*, 123–130. doi:10.1007/s10862-006-7490-x

Savoca, E., & Rosenheck, R. (2000). The civilian labor market experiences of Vietnam-era veterans: The influence of psychiatric disorders. *The Journal of Mental Health Policy and Economics, 3*, 199–207. doi:10.1002/mhp.102

VA/DoD Clinical Practice Guideline Working Group. (2004). *Management of Post-Traumatic Stress (Office of Quality and Performance Publication No. 10Q-CPG/PTSD-04)*. Washington, DC: Veterans Health Administration, Department of Veterans Affairs and Health Affairs, Department of Defense.

Wang, P. S., Lane, M., Olfson, M., Pincus, H. A., Wells, K. B., & Kessler, R. C. (2005). Twelve-month use of mental health services in the United States: Results from the National Comorbidity Survey Replication. *Archives of General Psychiatry, 62*, 629–640. doi:10.1001/archpsyc.62.6.629

Weathers, F., Litz, B., Herman, D., Huska, J., & Keane, T. (1993, October). The PTSD Checklist (PCL): Reliability, validity, and diagnostic utility. Paper presented at the Annual Convention of the International Society for Traumatic Stress Studies, San Antonio, Texas.

CONCLUSION: UNDERSTANDING THE EFFECTS OF DEPLOYMENT TO A WAR ZONE

PAULA P. SCHNURR, JOSEF I. RUZEK, JENNIFER J. VASTERLING, AND MATTHEW J. FRIEDMAN

The terrorist attacks on September 11, 2001, led to increased recognition and understanding of the consequences of exposure to traumatic events. The 9/11 attacks also led us on a path to war, with military forces deployed to Afghanistan as part of Operation Enduring Freedom (OEF) in 2001 and then to Iraq as part of Operation Iraqi Freedom (OIF) in 2003. Authors have argued that aspects of these wars, such as the length, number, and rapid pace of deployments with relatively short periods at home between deployments, may promote the development of posttraumatic difficulties (e.g., Friedman, 2004; Schnurr, Lunney, Bovin, & Marx, 2009; Tanelian & Jaycox, 2008). Furthermore, widespread use of improvised explosive devices by insurgents has resulted in a large number of cases of traumatic brain injury (TBI) and multiple serious injuries, or polytrauma. A report by the RAND Corporation (Tanelian & Jaycox, 2008) notes how advances in battlefield medicine and protective gear translate to a greater likelihood of survival than ever before, which also means

This chapter was coauthored by an employee of the United States government as part of official duty and is considered to be in the public domain. Any views expressed herein do not necessarily represent the views of the United States government, and the author's participation in the work is not meant to serve as an official endorsement.

that a large proportion of OEF and OIF service members who might have died on the battlefield in prior conflicts are retuning home to a life with significant physical disability.

Added to the distinctive mixture, the opportunity to study the effects of war-zone exposure in real time—before, during, and after the exposure—is helping us understand war-zone trauma in a new light. For example, almost all previous research on the etiology of war-zone-related posttraumatic stress disorder (PTSD) has been conducted using cross-sectional designs that are subject to potentially serious recall and retrospective biases. Now longitudinal studies such as those by Smith et al. (2006, 2008) and Vasterling et al. (2006, 2010) are allowing us to learn how factors measured before deployment predict posttraumatic consequences. Research has been supported by significant funding from the National Institutes of Health and the Departments of Veterans Affairs (VA) and Defense (DoD). VA and DoD also have committed substantial resources to prevention, screening, and treatment, and in so doing are changing what (we think) we know about the expected course of recovery based on data from prior wars. In what follows, we describe the knowledge gained from this historic mix of factors and identify gaps in understanding that need to be addressed.

WHAT THE WARS IN IRAQ AND AFGHANISTAN ARE TEACHING US ABOUT TRAUMA

Among the things we are learning is that posttraumatic readjustment problems are prevalent despite the enhanced VA and DoD programs (Hoge et al., 2004; Schell & Marshall, 2008, Smith et al., 2008). Disorders such as PTSD, depression, and substance abuse often co-occur with one another and with physical health problems and reduced quality of life (Hoge, Terhakopian, Castro, Messer, & Engel, 2007; Schnurr et al., 2009; Vasterling et al., 2008).

Several chapters in this book detail the type and extent of difficulties. Ramchand, Schell, Jaycox, and Tanelian, in Chapter 1, report that the prevalence of PTSD in OEF and OIF veterans ranges between 10% and 15%; the range of estimates for depression is similar in most studies. Alcohol problems and alcohol abuse are also prevalent. Classen and Knox (Chapter 5) focus on the problem of suicide, which has become an important concern because data show that the prevalence of suicide and suicidal ideation is related to deployment. Monson, Fredman, and Taft (Chapter 7) review the evidence on how deployment leads to family conflict and how returning service members may experience impairment in performing marital and family roles. In addition, Vasterling, Daly, and Friedman (Chapter 2) describe other common problems—such as aggression, reckless driving, difficulty with authority, disaffection in the workplace, and social withdrawal—that do not exceed a diagnostic threshold but can disrupt functioning and reduce quality of life.

This list of problems should be familiar to anyone who knows about the consequences of traumatic exposure. A new emphasis in the OEF and OIF cohort is the added complication presented by TBI. Chapter 4, by Butler, Hurley, and Taber, reviews this issue, showing not only that mild TBI is prevalent but also that it often co-occurs with PTSD. Of course, this makes sense. An explosion or accident severe enough to cause a TBI is also likely to be psychologically traumatic as well. Beyond the specific TBI event, the broader context that leads to risk of war-zone TBI (i.e., combat and other dangerous missions) also increases risk of PTSD.

However, the comorbidity between PTSD and TBI has contributed to controversy in the health care, policy, and research arenas (c.f., Hoge, Goldberg, & Castro, 2009). The controversy centers on the cause of persistent symptoms in cases of mild TBI because of symptom overlap between postconcussive syndromes and psychiatric disorders such as PTSD and depression (Hoge et al., 2008; Schneiderman, Braver, & Kang, 2008). The root causes of postconcussive symptoms in any given individual have important implications for treatment as well as the systems of care in which that treatment is delivered. If symptoms are caused at least in part by a comorbid psychiatric disorder, it seems only sensible to treat that disorder. Likewise, the potential impact of brain injury on psychiatric outcomes (Bryant et al., 2010) should be taken into account as care is planned. Even in cases in which postconcussive symptoms also reflect the unremitted consequences of mild TBI, any comorbid psychiatric problems should be addressed. The chapter by Butler and colleagues provides specific information about promoting recovery in TBI patients.

Risk of mental health problems in OEF and OIF personnel varies as a function of personal and environmental factors in the same way risk varies in other cohorts (Hoge et al., 2004; Schell & Marshall, 2008; Smith et al., 2006, 2008). National Guard and Reserve personnel may be at particular risk (e.g., Milliken, Auchterlonie, & Hoge, 2007). In Chapter 1, Ramchand and colleagues discuss whether risk is also elevated in women. The wars in Iraq and Afghanistan offer a unique opportunity to study this question because women are being exposed to combat in ways like never before (Hoge, Clark, & Castro, 2007). Prior meta-analyses identified a gender difference in risk of PTSD (Brewin et al., 2000; Tolin & Foa, 2006). Compared with men, women had roughly double the risk of developing PTSD, but the difference only occurred in civilian samples. Some early reports have indicated a lack of gender difference in risk of PTSD among OEF and OIF veterans (e.g., Hoge, Clark, & Castro, 2007). In a RAND Corporation study (Schell & Marshall, 2008), women did not differ from men according to unadjusted analyses, but when risk factors including amount of war-zone exposure were taken into account, women had a 70% greater risk than men; women's likelihood of developing PTSD was higher than expected given their risk profile. A similar finding occurred for depression, although women had elevated risk even according to unadjusted analyses. As of now, the question of whether men and women differ in the prevalence of PTSD following war-zone exposure is not settled. However, we are likely to find an answer as investigators continue to study women who have had substantial amounts of the same kind of exposure as men.

If the risk of PTSD turns out to be elevated in women who have comparable war-zone exposure to that of men, it is possible that the difference would be due to the unmeasured effect of prior sexual trauma, which could increase vulnerability to combat stressors. Women are much more likely than men to have been exposed to nonmilitary sexual trauma (e.g., Tolin & Foa, 2006) as well as military sexual harassment and assault (e.g., Street, Stafford, Mahan, & Hendricks, 2008). In Chapter 6 of this volume, Street, Kimerling, Bell, and Pavao discuss key issues in dealing with military sexual trauma, arguing that the unique aspects of the military context may promote negative consequences. These authors suggest that the experience of sexual trauma in a war zone may be especially threatening, increasing the sense of danger that arises from combat events. This chapter includes specific information about the effect of military sexual trauma on men, who may be at increased risk of posttraumatic difficulties because they are less likely than women to disclose their assault and more likely to struggle with issues of shame, self-blame, and gender identity.

The good news is that in comparison with the aftermath of the Vietnam War and other earlier wars, we now have effective treatments to offer patients. Chapter 10, by Rothbaum, Gerardi, Bradley, and Friedman, indicates that several types of cognitive–behavioral psychotherapy are particularly effective, something we did not know with as much certainty even after the Gulf War in 1991. Although there have been no randomized controlled trials of any treatment for OEF and OIF populations, we have every reason to think that existing treatments, many of which have been tested in patients with chronic PTSD, may be even more effective when delivered soon after a person develops problems. Chapter 7, by Monson, Fredman, and Taft, reflects an increasing emphasis on engaging couples and families to promote recovery. Although there is little empirical evidence on the effectiveness of such treatments, these authors describe a promising approach that is currently undergoing evaluation.

Despite the availability of effective treatments, OEF and OIF service members and veterans are reluctant to seek mental health treatment because of perceived stigma as well as logistical barriers (Hoge et al., 2004; Schell & Marshall, 2008). In Chapter 11, Stecker and Fortney suggest a strategy based on the principles of cognitive–behavioral therapy to help engage veterans in care. Such approaches targeted at individuals are complemented by the system changes within DoD and VA to conduct population screening for psychiatric disorders and enhance referral. Recent data suggest that the efforts are paying off. Among OEF and OIF veterans who sought VA care, four out of five patients who were screened had a mental health referral, compared with one in five who were not screened (Seal et al., 2008).

Underlying this rich knowledge base is a good understanding of how to assess exposure and its consequences carefully, described in detail by Vogt, Dutra, Reardon, Zisserson, and Miller (Chapter 3). Like others in this book, the chapter emphasizes the multiplicity of effects of factors occurring before, during, and after war-zone service. This kind of comprehensive approach to assessment has permitted the advance of scientific understanding as well as better diagnosis and delivery of appropriate treatment. Nevertheless, important questions remain.

TOPICS IN NEED OF INVESTIGATION

Despite the knowledge we have acquired from OEF and OIF and prior wars, four interrelated topics deserve our urgent attention: reintegration, screening, prediction, and prevention. Chapter 2, by Vasterling, Daly, and Friedman, illustrates the challenges faced by individuals after returning from deployment to a war-zone. Those of us who have never been to war—including the authors of this book, and probably the majority of readers—can only imagine the difficulties of returning to civilian life after such an extraordinary experience. Anecdotally, many returning service members report a sense of disconnection and unreality at home, feeling that people who have not been to war simply cannot understand. Even service members with few posttraumatic adjustment problems must deal with the stress of life events, such as returning to a family that has had to function without them, resuming work after a time away, or perhaps needing to find a new job. Whereas this book focuses primarily on the needs of OEF and OIF personnel with more substantial readjustment problems, we need to know how to promote adaptation and reintegration successfully across the spectrum of possible outcomes. We also need to know whether the programs developed by VA and DoD to facilitate reintegration are effective and, if not, how to make them more effective and efficient.

To help returning service members reintegrate into society, we must identify who is in need of intervention. Vasterling et al. discuss the public health surveillance programs developed by VA and DoD to do just that. There is no doubt that the current programs are crucial for helping many returning service members receive necessary care; Seal et al.'s (2008) data on VA's program make the case quite convincingly. We believe that the optimal system should help to identify needs and connect individuals to the appropriate level of services across the spectrum of care. In the ideal case, the system would identify not just those in need of services but also individuals who are at risk for future problems. For example, data from the U.S. Army's postdeployment screening program indicate that a large number of soldiers who do not screen positive upon return may screen positive 6 to 9 months later (e.g., Milliken et al., 2007). Whether these findings reflect underreporting at return or a genuine increase in need, we need to develop better models for predicting future risk.

In addition to screening, there is also a need to develop better strategies for predicting who is likely to develop PTSD during and following deployment to a war zone. Despite all of the epidemiological research on PTSD and other posttraumatic reactions and the high consistency of risk factors across studies (e.g., Brewin et al., 2000), no one has been able to predict with sufficient accuracy who will develop problems given exposure to trauma—here we mean "sufficient" for implementation in a screening program. There is no absolute level of accuracy needed for a screening program. A variety of cost–benefit trade-offs of false-negative and false-positive outcomes need to be considered. In the case of screening before war-zone service, these trade-offs would include protecting individuals who are at highest risk of difficulties if deployed to a war zone while not preventing deployment by misclassified individuals who are unlikely to have difficulties. We may never achieve the level of accuracy required to implement such screening in a way that maximizes protection of the truly vulnerable without harming those who are not. However, this is a legitimate scientific question that needs to be evaluated more fully.

There is an additional need to know more about how to prevent PTSD and other problems among individuals who are deployed to a war zone. Chapter 9, by Nash, Krantz, Stein, Westphal, and Litz, describes Battlemind, a large-scale, nonclinical psychoeducational intervention—an example of a universal prevention strategy. These interventions are given to essentially everyone, regardless of need. Although Battlemind has been used routinely to facilitate reintegration of OEF and OIF veterans, only one randomized controlled trial on the intervention's efficacy has been published. Adler, Bliese, McGurk, Hoge, and Castro (2009) recently reported the results of a randomized clinical trial with more than 1,000 Army soldiers who were assigned to receive a single session of either standard postdeployment stress education or to Battlemind in one of three formats: debriefing conducted in groups of 20 to 32 soldiers, small-group Battlemind training conducted in groups of 18 to 45 soldiers, or large-group Battlemind training conducted in groups of 126 to 225 soldiers. Battlemind had no overall benefit relative to stress education at the 4-month follow-up. However, there was a preventive benefit among veterans with the highest levels of combat exposure (who could be expected to have the greatest risk for mental health problems). Also, only some formats were effective for some outcomes. Perhaps the most interesting differential benefit was observed for stigma, which occurred only among veterans with high combat exposure who received large-group Battlemind. This "strength in numbers" effect suggests that it may be most effective to deliver messages designed to reduce stigma in groups that allow members to see large numbers of peers receiving the same message. Across outcomes, the effects of Battlemind were small, but this is not surprising given the nonclinical nature of the sample.

In a public health framework, the first goal is to find ways to increase resilience among all servicemen and women before they are deployed to a war zone. Next, it is essential to develop reliable methods for identifying at-risk individuals to make them the focus of more intensive prevention efforts, as illustrated by the Navy and Marine Corps selective and indicated interventions. This is where our knowledge gap is widest. Although cognitive–behavioral therapy can help individuals with acute stress disorder or early PTSD symptoms after traumatic exposure (e.g., Bryant et al., 2008; Sijbrandij et al., 2007), we have no evidence-based interventions to help prevent the development of posttraumatic disorders in at-risk individuals before exposure. Studying such interventions is hindered by the lack of ability to determine who is at high risk in the first place. Yet despite the difficulty of answering this question, prevention of PTSD and other serious outcomes in at-risk individuals should be a priority.

RECOMMENDATIONS AND CONCLUSIONS

The chapter by Vasterling and colleagues, although focused on the phases of reintegration, provides a useful framework for the creation of strategies to help veterans returning from the current and future wars. Understanding the reactions of service members during each phase can be helpful to clinicians in formulating an appropriate treatment plan. This same understanding can be helpful to administrators and policy makers who need to decide on the services and resources to be provided. At all stages, however, it is important to remember that reactions to war-zone deployment are multidimensional and include both positive and negative outcomes. The reactions change over time, although the trajectories may vary for different outcomes and different individuals. For example, a service member who returns home from Afghanistan may develop PTSD and substance abuse. Following treatment, he may experience remission of the substance abuse only, but over time may experience posttraumatic growth in the form of a commitment to give back to others by volunteering in a peer-support program. Another service member from the same unit may initially experience positive outcomes in the form of career advancement due to computer skills obtained during deployment, but then after breaking up with her fiancée, she may develop delayed PTSD and become suicidal.

Clinicians and the systems of care in which they practice need to be available to meet the needs of military personnel by anticipating the multi-dimensional and dynamic nature of reactions to war-zone deployment. Chapter 12, by Ruzek and Batten, explores this topic more fully by examining the needs of clinicians and systems of care from the perspectives of four kinds of needs: information, training, interpersonal support and consultation, and interconnection with other elements in the system of care. It is difficult to prioritize any of these needs because all are important. However, for a well-trained clinician who is familiar with treating traumatic stress, the most important need may be that for information, particularly about military culture, deployment, and unique aspects of the experiences of military personnel. Learning as much as possible can facilitate therapeutic alliance and provide a source of insight into a patient's posttraumatic difficulties. In contrast, for a system of care, interconnection with other systems is perhaps the most important need to enhance overall care delivery and use resources most efficiently. Attempts by VA and DoD to enhance transition from one system to another exemplify the kind of effort that is needed.

War touches the lives of everyone involved, from the combatants and civilians in the war zone to the families and civilians back home, as well as the governments waging the war. During World War II, a survey by the National Opinion Research Center found that almost 80% of veterans said they had been changed by the war, with the majority of them reporting negative changes. However, 47% of nonveterans said they had been changed as well, with negative changes also reported by the majority. These findings were presented in a remarkable series, titled *The American Soldier* (Stouffer, Lumsdaine, et al., 1949; Stouffer, Suchman, DeVinney, Star, & Williams, 1949), that described studies conducted during and after the war to better understand the experiences and problems encountered by the service members of that era. Reading this book, contemporary scholars are likely to be amazed and humbled by the knowledge that was acquired so long ago, as well as the sophistication of the research methods. One study used archival data obtained early after entry in the military service to examine risk factors for being subsequently diagnosed as a psychoneurotic case following deployment. Many of the issues and even the findings are strikingly similar to those reviewed in this book. Reading through *The American Soldier*, along with other studies of war-zone trauma before and after World War II, it is reasonable to ask what is new and different now. We believe it is the quality of our knowledge. Although the questions and answers are similar, how we pose those questions and the answers themselves are much more refined and in-depth for a scientific standpoint, and our investigation is conducted within a much more advanced theoretical and empirical framework for conceptualizing traumatic stress. Even if there is much to learn, our current knowledge is enabling us to make a real difference in the lives of those who go to war on our behalf.

REFERENCES

Adler, A. B., Bliese, P. D., McGurk, D., Hoge, C. W., & Castro, C. A. (2009). Battlemind debriefing and Battlemind training with soldiers returning from Iraq: Randomization by platoon. *Journal of Consulting and Clinical Psychiatry, 77,* 928–940. doi:10.1037/a0016877

Brewin, C. R., Andrews, B., & Valentine, J. D. (2000). Meta-analysis of risk factors for posttraumatic stress disorder in trauma-exposed adults. *Journal of Consulting and Clinical Psychology, 68,* 748–766. doi:10.1037/0022-006X.68.5.748

Bryant, R. A., Mastrodomenico, J. A., Felmingham, K. L., Hopwood, S., Kenny, L. M., Kandris, E., . . . Creamer, D. (2008). Treatment of acute stress disorder: A randomized controlled trial. *Archives of General Psychiatry, 65,* 659–667. doi:10.1001/archpsyc.65.6.659

Bryant, R. A., O'Donnell, M. L., Creamer, M., McFarlane, A. C., Clark, C. R., & Silove, D. (2010). The psychiatric sequelae of traumatic injury. *The American Journal of Psychiatry, 167,* 312–320. doi:10.1176/appi.ajp.2009.09050617

Friedman, M. J. (2004). Acknowledging the psychiatric cost of war. *The New England Journal of Medicine, 351,* 75–77. doi:10.1056/NEJMe048129

Hoge, C. W., Castro, C. A., Messer, S. C., McGurk, D., Cotting, D. I., & Koffman, R. L. (2004). Combat duty in Iraq and Afghanistan, mental health problems, and barriers to care. *The New England Journal of Medicine, 351,* 13–22. doi:10.1056/NEJMoa040603

Hoge, C. W., Clark, J. C., & Castro, C. A. (2007). Commentary: Women in combat and the risk of post-traumatic stress disorder and depression. *International Journal of Epidemiology, 36,* 327–329. doi:10.1093/ije/dym013

Hoge, C. W., Goldberg, H. M., & Castro, C. A. (2009). Care of war veterans with mild traumatic brain injury—flawed perspectives. *The New England Journal of Medicine, 360,* 1588–1591. doi:10.1056/NEJMp0810606

Hoge, C. W., McGurk, D., Thomas, J. L., Cox, A. L., Engel, C. C., & Castro, C. A. (2008). Mild traumatic brain injury in U.S. soldiers returning from Iraq. *The New England Journal of Medicine, 358,* 453–463. doi:10.1056/NEJMoa072972

Hoge, C. W., Terhakopian, A., Castro, C. A., Messer, S. C., & Engel, C. C. (2007). Association of posttraumatic stress disorder with somatic symptoms, health care visits, and absenteeism among Iraq war veterans. *The American Journal of Psychiatry, 164,* 150–153. doi:10.1176/appi.ajp.164.1.150

Milliken, C. S., Auchterlonie, J. L., & Hoge, C. W. (2007). Longitudinal assessment of mental health problems among active and reserve component soldiers returning from the Iraq War. *JAMA, 298,* 2141–2148. doi:10.1001/jama.298.18.2141

Schell, T. L., & Marshall, G. N. (2008). Survey of individuals previously deployed for OEF/OIF. In T. L. Tanielian, L. Jaycox, & RAND Corporation (Eds.), *Invisible wounds of war: Psychological and cognitive injuries, their consequences, and services to assist recovery* (pp. 87–115). Santa Monica, CA: RAND Corporation.

Schneiderman, A. I., Braver, E. R., & Kang, H. K. (2008). Understanding sequelae of injury mechanisms and mild traumatic brain injury incurred during the conflicts in Iraq and Afghanistan: Persistent postconcussive symptoms and posttraumatic stress disorder. *American Journal of Epidemiology, 167*, 1446–1452. doi:10.1093/aje/kwn068

Schnurr, P. P., Lunney, C. A., Bovin, M. J., & Marx, B. P. (2009). Posttraumatic stress disorder and quality of life: Extension of findings to veterans of the wars in Iraq and Afghanistan. *Clinical Psychology Review, 29*, 727–735. doi:10.1016/j.cpr.2009.08.006

Seal, K. H., Bertenthal, D., Maguen, S., Gima, K., Chu, A., & Marmar, C. R. (2008). Don't ask, don't tell: An evaluation of US Veterans Administration postdeployment screening for veterans returning form Iraq and Afghanistan. *American Journal of Public Health, 98*, 714–720. doi:10.2105/AJPH.2007.115519

Sijbrandij, M., Olff, M., Reitsma, J. B., Carlier, I. V. E., De Vries, M. H., & Gersons, B. P. R. (2007). Treatment of acute posttraumatic stress disorder with brief cognitive behavioral therapy: A randomized controlled trial. *The American Journal of Psychiatry, 164*, 82–90. doi:10.1176/appi.ajp.164.1.82

Smith, T. C., Ryan, M. A., Wingard, D. L., Slymen, D. J., Sallis, J. F., & Kritz-Silverstein, D. (2008). New onset and persistent symptoms of post-traumatic stress disorder self reported after deployment and combat exposures: Prospective population based US military cohort study. *British Medical Journal, 336*, 366–371. doi:10.1136/bmj.39430.638241.AE

Smith, T. C., Wingard, D. L., Ryan, M. A., Kritz-Silverstein, D., Slymen, D. J., Sallis, J. F., & the Millennium Cohort Study Team. (2008). Prior assault and posttraumatic stress disorder after combat deployment. *Epidemiology, 19*, 505–512. doi:10.1097/EDE.0b013e31816a9dff

Stouffer, S. A., Lumsdaine, A. A., Lumsdaine, M. H., Williams, R. M., Smith, M. B., Janis, I. L., . . . Cotrell, L. S., Jr. (1949). *The American soldier: Combat and its aftermath*. Princeton, NJ: Princeton University Press.

Stouffer, S. A., Suchman, E. A., DeVinney, L. C., Star, S. A., & Williams, R. M. (1949). *The American soldier: Adjustment during Army life*. Princeton, NJ: Princeton University Press.

Street, A. E., Stafford, J., Mahan, C. M., & Hendricks, A. M. (2008). Sexual harassment and assault experienced by reservists during military service: Prevalence and health correlates. *Journal of Rehabilitation Research and Development, 45*, 409–419. doi:10.1682/JRRD.2007.06.0088

Tanelian, T., & Jaycox, L. H. (Eds.). (2008). *Invisible wounds of war: Psychological and cognitive injuries, their consequences, and services to assist recovery*. Santa Monica, CA: RAND Corporation.

Tolin, D. F., & Foa, E. B. (2006). Sex differences in trauma and posttraumatic stress disorder: A quantitative review of 25 years of research. *Psychological Bulletin*, *132*, 959–992. doi:10.1037/0033-2909.132.6.959

Vasterling, J. J., Proctor, S. P., Amoroso, P., Kane, R., Heeren, T., & White, R. F. (2006). Neuropsychological outcomes of Army personnel following deployment to the Iraq war. *JAMA*, *296*, 519–529. doi:10.1001/jama.296.5.519

Vasterling, J. J., Proctor, S. P., Friedman, M. J., Hoge, C. W., Heeren, T., King, L. A., & King, D. W. (2010). PTSD symptom increases in Iraq-deployed soldiers: Comparison with nondeployed soldiers and associations with baseline symptoms, deployment experiences, and postdeployment stress. *Journal of Traumatic Stress*, *23*, 41–51.

Vasterling, J. J., Schumm, J., Proctor, S. P., Gentry, E., King, D. W., & King, L. A. (2008). Posttraumatic stress disorder and health functioning in a non-treatment-seeking sample of Iraq war veterans: A prospective analysis. *Journal of Rehabilitation Research and Development*, *45*, 347–358. doi:10.1682/JRRD.2007.05.0077

INDEX

ABOUT THE EDITORS

Josef I. Ruzek, PhD, is the director of the Dissemination and Training Division of the U.S. Department of Veterans Affairs National Center for Posttraumatic Stress Disorder (PTSD). He is coeditor of *Cognitive-Behavioral Therapies for Trauma* (2nd ed.; 2006), and a contributing author for the National Center for PTSD's *Iraq War Clinician Guide*. Dr. Ruzek is cochair of the Early Intervention special interest group of the International Society for Traumatic Stress Studies and was a member of the team that developed the joint Veterans Affairs–Department of Defense Clinical Practice Guidelines for Management of Traumatic Stress.

Paula P. Schnurr, PhD, has served as deputy executive director of the National Center for Posttraumatic Stress Disorder since 1989. She is a research professor of psychiatry at Dartmouth Medical School and is editor-in-chief of the *Journal of Traumatic Stress* and the *Clinician's Trauma Update—Online*. She received her doctorate in experimental psychology at Dartmouth College in 1984 and then completed a postdoctoral fellowship in the Department of Psychiatry at Dartmouth Medical School. Dr. Schnurr is past president of the International Society for Traumatic Stress Studies and is a fellow of the American Psychological Association and of the Association for Psychological Science.

Her research focuses on methodological and statistical issues as well as substantive topics, especially PTSD treatment and risk and resilience factors associated with the long-term physical and mental health outcomes of traumatic exposure. Her current projects include a trial evaluating a PTSD decision aid and another trial evaluating integrated primary care treatment for PTSD.

Jennifer J. Vasterling, PhD, obtained her doctorate in psychology from Vanderbilt University in 1988, subsequently completing pre- and postdoctoral training in clinical neuropsychology at the Boston Veterans Affairs (VA) Medical Center. She currently serves as chief of psychology at VA Boston Healthcare System and as a clinical investigator in the Behavioral Science Division of the National Center for Posttraumatic Stress Disorder. Dr. Vasterling is a professor of psychiatry at Boston University School of Medicine and a lecturer in psychiatry at Harvard Medical School. Prior to her current positions, Dr. Vasterling served as the associate director for research for the VA South Central (VISN 16) Mental Illness, Research, Education, and Clinical Center; as staff psychologist at the New Orleans VA Medical Center; and as a clinical professor of psychiatry and neurology at Tulane University School of Medicine. Dr. Vasterling's research has centered on furthering the understanding of the neurocognitive and emotional changes that accompany war-zone deployment and posttraumatic stress responses. She is the lead editor of a book on the neuropsychological correlates of PTSD and currently serves on the editorial board of the *Journal of the International Neuropsychological Society*. Her recent work includes a longitudinal study examining neuropsychological and emotional outcomes of military deployment to Iraq.

Matthew J. Friedman, MD, PhD, is executive director of the National Center for Posttraumatic Stress Disorder and professor of psychiatry and of pharmacology and toxicology at Dartmouth Medical School. He has worked with PTSD patients as a clinician and researcher for 35 years and has published extensively on stress and PTSD, biological psychiatry, psychopharmacology, and clinical outcome studies on depression, anxiety, schizophrenia, and chemical dependency. He has more than 200 publications, including 19 books and monographs. Listed in the "Best Doctors in America," he is a Distinguished Lifetime Fellow of the American Psychiatric Association, past president of the International Society for Traumatic Stress Studies (ISTSS), past chair of the scientific advisory board of the Anxiety Disorders Association of America, a member of the American Psychiatric Association's *DSM–V* Anxiety Disorders Work Group, and has served on many Veterans Affairs, Department of Defense, and National Institute of Mental Health research, education, and policy committees. He has received many honors, including the ISTSS Lifetime Achievement Award in 1999 and the ISTSS Public Advocacy Award in 2009.